Country Music Originals

Country Music Originals
The Legends and the Lost

TONY RUSSELL

OXFORD
UNIVERSITY PRESS

2 0 0 7

OXFORD
UNIVERSITY PRESS

Oxford University Press, Inc., publishes works that further
Oxford University's objective of excellence
in research, scholarship, and education.

Oxford   New York
Auckland   Cape Town   Dar es Salaam   Hong Kong   Karachi
Kuala Lumpur   Madrid   Melbourne   Mexico City   Nairobi
New Delhi   Shanghai   Taipei   Toronto

With offices in
Argentina   Austria   Brazil   Chile   Czech Republic   France   Greece
Guatemala   Hungary   Italy   Japan   Poland   Portugal   Singapore
South Korea   Switzerland   Thailand   Turkey   Ukraine   Vietnam

Published by Oxford University Press, Inc.
198 Madison Avenue, New York, NY 10016

www.oup.com

Library of Congress Cataloging-in-Publication Data
Russell, Tony.
Country music originals : the legends and the lost / Tony Russell.
p. cm.
Includes bibliographical references (p.) and discographies.
ISBN 978-0-19-532509-6
1. Country musicians—Biography.
2. Country music—History and criticism.   I. Title.
ML394.R87 2007
781.642092'273—dc22
[B] 2007008471

1 3 5 7 9 8 6 4 2

Printed in the United States of America
on acid-free paper

In memoriam
Charles K. Wolfe
Bob Pinson

Contents

Acknowledgments

As the reader will discover, this is not a footnoted book, and that is by design, but I should at least give a general description of my sources. I have been researching old-time music for a good many years and was lucky enough to be in time to meet and talk to more than a score of my subjects. Others, by then dead, I learned about from family members, friends, or fellow musicians. I have also put in many hours reading old fanzines and songbooks, peering at microfilm, investigating record company files and promotional literature, and penetrating internet genealogy sites. But a huge debt remains to my fellow hunters in the thickets of old-time music research: to the many contributors to my own magazine *Old Time Music*, to the long run of the indispensable *JEMF Quarterly*, and to other periodicals; to the authors of numerous excellent books and articles on individual artists, regional music traditions, and other topics, listed in the Bibliography; and to innumerable correspondents who unselfishly shared their findings with me. Much of the information in these essays was derived from those friends and co-workers, and if I do not acknowledge their writings specifically in every place where I have drawn on them, it is only because this is not the kind of minutely sourced book that some of them have themselves written. My gratitude to them is nonetheless warm, admiring, and comprehensive.

That said, I must name some colleagues without whose work this book could not have been written: Kerry Blech, Joe Bussard, Joyce Cauthen, Kevin Coffey, John Cohen, Norm Cohen, Bob Coltman, David Crisp, Wayne Daniel, Ken Davidson, Gene Earle, Kevin Fontenot, David Freeman, Cary Ginell, Archie Green, Martin Hawkins, Fred Hoeptner, Patrick Huber, Mark Humphrey, Rich Kienzle, Paul Kingsbury, Lance and April Ledbetter, Kip Lornell, W. K. McNeil, Bill Malone, Frank Mare, Wayne Martin, Guthrie T. Meade, Toru Mitsui, Donald L. Nelson, Richard Nevins, Robert Nobley, Robert K. Oermann, Jack Palmer, Bob Pinson, Nolan Porterfield, Barry Poss, Ronnie Pugh, Bill Rattray, Margaret Riddle, Kinney Rorrer, Joe Specht, Dick Spottswood, Chris Strachwitz, Nick Tosches, Ivan Tribe, Richard Weize, Gene Wiggins, Joe Wilson, Mark Wilson, and, last only because of the alphabet but most gratefully of all, my friend for more than thirty years, the late Charles K. Wolfe. Readers who are familiar with the world of old-time music appreciation will recognize many of these names as authorities in their fields, while those who are not will find, if they pursue their interest, no better guides to further enlightenment.

I am specially grateful to Paul Kingsbury, Nolan Porterfield, and Michael Gray for their helpful and encouraging comments on draft chapters. Wayne Martin very generously shared his research into David Fletcher and Gwin Foster, which was the foundation of my essay on the Carolina Twins. Thanks also to Dale Wilken of Marion, Iowa, for genealogical data on the Golden Melody Boys, and to Carla Chlouber of the Washington Irving Trail Museum for valuable material on Otto Gray & His Oklahoma Cowboys.

I am indebted to family members of some of my subjects for sharing treasured memories of their forebears, among them Alcyone Bate Beasley, Hazel Foster Bowling, Anita Davis, Mildred, Sonny, and Terresa Dutton, Al and Rubin Everidge, Bill Jones, Dixie Landress, Juanita McMichen Lynch, Margaret Mackin, Ted and Ginger Townsend and Ted's sisters Ada Lee and Virginia, and the Whitehead family. Some of them also kindly allowed me to copy photographs from their family albums, while other photographs were generously supplied by Bear Family Records, Kevin Coffey, Norm Cohen, Frank Dalton, Peter Feldmann, Brian Golbey, H. O. Jenkins, Wayne Martin, Barry Poss, Kinney Rorrer, Mike Seeger, Dave Sichak (www.hillbillymusic.com), Jeremy Stephens, Big Boy Woods, and Marshall Wyatt. I am also grateful to Gail Miller DeLoach and Steven Engerrand at the Georgia Archives, Peter Roberts of Special Collections and Archives at Georgia State University, and Cassie M. Robinson at the Liston R. Ramsey Center for Regional Studies, Mars Hill College, for their prompt and sympathetic responses to requests for material.

My editor at Oxford University Press, Suzanne Ryan, her colleagues Norm Hirschy and Lora Dunn, and my production editor, Joellyn Ausanka, have been models of supportiveness. I wish other authors so pleasant a relationship with their publishers.

Many of these essays have their origin in two series written for English country music magazines over the last dozen or so years, "Hillbilly Heaven" in *Country Music International* and "Beyond the Sunset" in *Maverick*. I am grateful to their editors for giving me the opportunity to compose them. All of them have been extensively revised and expanded, often considerably and sometimes drawing on other writings of mine. Twenty-three essays have been added that were written specifically for this book.

Introduction

Before Americana and alt.country, before Beck and Bob Dylan, before Nashville and Bakersfield, before rock 'n' roll, before Elvis Presley and Hank Williams . . . there was another music. It shaped them all, yet its own outlines are indistinct. It furnished them with models, but many of those primary designers are forgotten. Old-time music, country music in its sunlit morning years, is a chapter in the story of popular music that is too seldom read. Half-lost voices. You might almost call it a secret history.

Not entirely secret, to be sure. From those formative decades, the first half of the twentieth century, a few names come down to us with some of their glory still intact: Jimmie Rodgers and The Carter Family, Gene Autry and Bob Wills, Charlie Poole and Uncle Dave Macon. But behind and alongside those standard-bearers of old-time country music lies a great company. Some of them now are shadowy figures, but they were style-makers in their day, pioneers in their particular genres; men and women who erected signposts along the musical highway that are still followed, left messages we still read and act upon, though we no longer recognize their handwriting and even their names are all but drowned in the hubbub of the electronic present.

In this book I hope to recover some of this vanishing history, to tell again stories that were once familiar to millions of Americans, to map some of the winding, untraveled roads that connect today's music to its ancestors. What has Dylan to do with Frank Hutchison or Chris Bouchillon? Presley with Johnnie Lee Wills? *O Brother, Where Art Thou?* with Dick Burnett, Emry Arthur, or Harry "Mac" McClintock? In making such journeys of exploration, following the lost highways of which Hank Williams and Gram Parsons sang, we may return to our own time with a fresh appreciation of the strength, tenacity, and beauty of the original country music.

*   *   *

This is not a conventional history. Other writers have painstakingly traced the intricate patterns of country music's development from Old World to New, or the growth of today's industry from its less organized beginnings. *Country Music Originals* is not that sort of book. Not a continuous film, but a sequence of snapshots of the personalities who gave this music its color and character. They are arranged more or less chronologically, so that, read consecutively, they do make an unfolding story, but the reader is free to dip in, skip, jump backward and forward in time, make his or her own connections and juxtapositions. Think of it as a jigsaw puzzle that can be assembled in many different configurations, each presenting essentially the same picture, but with suggestive differences of emphasis and perspective.

From time to time, however, in order to ease a tricky transition from subject to subject, or to make a point that finds no appropriate home in an individual essay, I have inserted a bridging passage, filling in the background or describing some pivotal moment.

A theme that particularly fascinates me is how this music got on to record in the 1920s, '30s, and '40s: the collaboration—sometimes enthusiastic, sometimes uneasy, sometimes unconscious—between musician and record company to interpret old-time music for a new medium, to turn songs and tunes that were as familiar and unremarkable as old shoes into performances for which friends and strangers alike would pay a sizable piece of a day's wages. So my emphasis, almost throughout, is on musicians who made records in those days, and on what happened to those records: how they were advertised and distributed, how well or poorly they sold, how elusive they can sometimes still be today. I am aware, of course, that for many lovers of old-time music, especially those who play it, the honor roll of influential or remarkable artists includes some who did not record until much later and in very different circumstances, such as Roscoe Holcomb, Tommy Jarrell, Henry Reed, Hobart Smith, Buddy Thomas, Wade Ward, or Melvin Wine. I share their respect and affection for those artists and others like them, and I pass them over only because they do not exactly fit into the story I am concerned to tell.

Historical narrative lures the writer to re-create the past not as it was but as he would like it to have been. To put at least one obstacle in the way of this temptation, I have tried, wherever it was possible, to balance my own impressions of my subjects with authentic voices of the period: either the words of the musicians themselves, or what was said about them in contemporary media such as local newspapers, radio periodicals, record companies' promotional literature, and the country music fanzines that have been connecting artist and enthusiast since the '30s.

Unlike standard histories, this book offers readers the opportunity to compile their own accompanying soundtrack. Almost every essay is equipped with a Playlist of recordings that can be found on currently available CDs; the diligent searcher will also be able to find many of them on internet music sites. (I say "almost every" because a few artists still await the renewed attention of the record industry.) I urge readers to pursue these leads, because having the music in their ears will bring these performers to life as no mere storyteller can aspire to do.

* * *

Why did I choose these 110 subjects? The answer lies in the wordplay of my title. Many of the artists discussed here are originals inasmuch as they originated some particular strain or style of country music, or at least were the first to give it currency through recordings. Obviously my story could not properly be told without the figures I named above, or others such as Fiddlin' John Carson, the Skillet-Lickers, Jimmie Davis, Bradley Kincaid, and many more. But there is another kind of original, the artist who is gifted with singularity, whether it was recognized as such at the time, or is now: the one-off, the stand-alone, incomparable and unique. Here I have chosen the subjects that interested me most, regardless of how great or small their impact upon the music—though sometimes I have tried to show that the roles they played were a little more significant than historians have allowed. A few important acts have been passed over, not because I dispute their importance but because they have been authoritatively covered by other writers. A few, too, though undeniably interesting, do not happen to interest me. This is explicitly and unapologetically a personal choice. That said, early country music is thronged with originals of the second sort, and I could have added dozens more essays on them. For the present they rest in a file expectantly headed *Country Music Originals 2*, in the hope that readers will like this book well enough to ask for more.

Tony Russell
London, February 2007

I should be very glad to hear from readers who can amplify (or perhaps correct) the information I give here, particularly if they have family or other close connections with the artist. I should be equally pleased to hear from readers with an ancestor, not included here, whose story they feel should be told. Write to me at 22 Cranbourne Road, London N10 2BT, England, or email me: tonyrussell@ bluetone.demon.co.uk.

Notes on Playlists

Recordings under the heading Playlist are arranged thus: first, CDs devoted entirely or chiefly to the subject of the essay (preceded by •); second, compilations of material by various artists (preceded by ••), with all the tracks by the subject listed, in alphabetical order (ignoring "A" and "The"). With artists whose work is well covered by the first kind of CD, I have sometimes omitted tracks on compilations; but not always, since the availability of the former may be uncertain. Some artists, who either made too few recordings to fill a CD or have not found enough favor with record companies to be granted an entire CD, are represented only by compilations to which they contribute.

In each of these categories, CDs are listed in alphabetical order of label, and then numerically by catalog number. Multiple-CD sets are identified as such by 2CD, 3CD, and so on, following the catalog number. Brief comments, in parentheses, have sometimes been added, usually to give the reader some idea of the range or period of the material on a particular CD.

Song and tune titles are quite often reported inaccurately when the recordings are reissued on CD, so for the sake of consistency all cited titles, both in the Playlist sections and in the essays themselves, are given as they appeared on the original 78 rpm recordings, as documented in my *Country Music Records: A Discography, 1921–1942* (Oxford, 2004). The CDs' own titles, however, are reported with fidelity—inconsistencies and all.

I have not attempted to make these listings complete, but have concentrated on CDs which at the time of writing were, with a few exceptions, in print and reasonably accessible. If a track is available on several compilation CDs, I may not list its every appearance. To save space, a few compilations have been omitted or cited only selectively; these are mostly large boxed sets that contain only one or two recordings relevant to any particular essay. But I would not wish to conceal from the reader such indispensable collections as the following:

Anthology of American Folk Music (Smithsonian/Folkways SW CD 40090 6CD) [the almost legendary "Harry Smith Anthology," which was first issued in 1952 and opened the ears of a generation to the riches of Anglo- and African-American vernacular music, among them tracks by Clarence Ashley, Dock Boggs, Dick

Burnett, Carolina Tar Heels, The Carter Family, G. B. Grayson, Kelly Harrell, Frank Hutchison, Buell Kazee, Bascom Lamar Lunsford, Uncle Dave Macon, Hoyt Ming, Charlie Poole, Eck Robertson, and Ernest Stoneman]

Anthology of American Folk Music, Volume Four (Revenant RVN 211 2CD)

Good for What Ails You: Music of the Medicine Shows 1926–1937 (Old Hat CD-1005 2CD)

Goodbye Babylon (Dust-to-Digital DTD-01 5CD) [an exceptional and beautifully presented collection of black and white religious music]

Many recordings of country music from the 1920s to '50s have been issued on CD by the British Archive of Country Music. These issues, which are available from the BACM and a small number of mail-order outlets, are not factory pressings but CD-Rs, and their sound quality can be variable; some tracks appear to be derived from downloads, and often, though not invariably, the original sound of the recording has been somewhat compromised by sonic restoration tools. Consequently BACM CDs are included in the Playlists only when I can vouch for their listenability, or when there is little or nothing else available by the artist. But for the reader who is curious to hear an artist and doesn't mind some shortcomings in sound quality, the BACM web site (www.bacm.users.btopenworld.com) is an extensive and well-organized shopping mall.

Country Music Originals

A. C. "Eck" Robertson

(1887–1975)

In the summer of 1922, two fiddlers from the Southwest made the long journey east to Richmond, Virginia, for a Civil War veterans' reunion. One day they took a train to New York to audition for Victor Records. It was not as whimsical a venture as it sounds. Victor, like other record companies, had already issued a few discs of violinists playing well-loved dance tunes, but most of those musicians were from vaudeville or orchestral backgrounds; at any rate, they didn't play in what we now think of as old-time styles.

These fiddlers from the prairies were different. Alexander Campbell "Eck" Robertson was born in Delaney, Arkansas, but grew up in north Texas, while his traveling companion Henry Gilliland was a retired Justice of the Peace from Oklahoma. (Very retired: he was in his late seventies.) So far as we know, they were the first musicians to record in a southern regional fiddling style, and in doing so they claim the earliest entries in the discography of country music.

The first tune cut on June 30, 1922, was, rather appropriately, that profoundly old-time piece "Arkansaw Traveler," but shorn of its customary comic dialog. Robertson and Gilliland play it as a duet, with no accompaniment. The two fiddles step together in an intricate dance, vigorous but well-mannered. The tune was chosen for the first release from the session, and hearing it today you will probably feel that country music got a good start.

But on the other side of the disc was Robertson's solo performance of "Sallie Gooden," and, listening to *that*, you feel the hair rise on your neck. Even through the mist of a pre-electrical recording more than eighty years old, the speed, the accuracy, the dynamics of the fiddling are astonishing. "Sallie Gooden" is not just good for its time, it is great for all time, a small but perfect masterpiece of American music.

Victor dawdled until April 1923 before issuing this coupling, but they gave it an enthusiastic write-up in their release sheet, describing "Sallie Gooden" as "in the very best style of the travelling cowboy fiddler, with almost continuous double-stopping, one string being used for a kind of bag-pipe drone-bass, and the other to carry the melody." Robertson did indeed dress as a cowboy for his professional appearances, as we know from a piece of silent newsreel footage from the early '20s.

Two more releases from that historic session came out in 1923–24, accompanied by further colorful prose from Victor's promotion department. Describing one of them, a medley of "Sallie Johnson" and "Billy in the Low Ground" coupled with "Done Gone," the copywriter recounted how "when we first saw these two artists, it was at our own Victor door, in the garb of Western plainsmen. . . . Robertson and Gilliland are men who have had rough and interesting lives in the great West. . . . Robertson's first violin was made of a gourd, and the bow was strung with hair from the tail of one of the ranch horses. These . . . are splendid

Eck Robertson, 1964. (Copyright 1976, 2006 by Peter Feldmann, www.BlueGrassWest.com, used by permission)

INSTRUMENTAL RECORDS

Henry C. Gilliland   Eck Robertson   George Hamilton Green

18956 { **Sallie Gooden**   A. C. (Eck) Robertson
10-in. list
price 75c. { **Arkansaw Traveler**   Henry C. Gilliland-A. C. (Eck) Robertson

One day, not so many months ago, two Southwesterners blew into our laboratory and told us they could play the fiddle. Now we know an awful lot of people who can play the fiddle, so we weren't impressed. Here is their first record. Eck made "Sallie Gooden" alone—a medley of jigs and reels, in the very best style of the travelling cowboy fiddler, with almost continuous double-stopping, one string being used for a kind of bag-pipe drone-bass, and the other to carry the melody. In both numbers there is no accompaniment, none being needed. In the Arkansaw Traveler, you will realize there are two of a kind, for Gilliland gets to it in as business-like a style as his partner.

19014 { **Liebesfreud**   George Hamilton Green
10-in. list
price 75c. { **Fair Rosmarin**   George Hamilton Green

Simply to slambang a xylophone for dancers, half-lost among the hootings of a jazz orchestra, is no test for any master of this difficult instrument. So George Hamilton Green, therefore, the famous xylophonist of the All Star Trio and other organizations, is making two records for us, as soloist with an orchestral accompaniment. Furthermore, he is not interpreting low-grade music, but two compositions of Fritz Kreisler's own, based on old Viennese airs. Both numbers are old Vienna waltzes, and although primarily concert numbers, skilful dancers, or "old fashioned" ones, which amounts to the same thing, will be interested to try them out. The long shivery tremolo of the instrument adapts itself very well to sustained passages, and its icy tinkle, its trills and scales, give the compositions brilliancy.

8

The release of the first country record: "New Victor Records For April 1923." (Author's collection)

examples of the American reel with its tricky and tantalizing rhythm."

The third coupling was "Turkey in the Straw," a duet, and "Ragtime Annie," another virtuoso solo by Robertson. All three discs seem to have sold well and remained in catalog for several years; the original 78s are not uncommon, as such things go. Nonetheless, Robertson did not record again until August 1929, when Victor sent a location recording team to Dallas. His wife Nettie accompanied him on guitar, as she had for over twenty years while they followed the dusty trail of the small-town vaudeville circuit or put on lantern-slide shows to go with their music. Their daughter Daphne and son Dueron joined in on tenor guitar and banjo. By that time other Texas fiddlers had made records and Robertson's music had nothing novel about it, but he was still a master player, as he demonstrated in "There's a Brown-Skin Girl Down the Road Somewhere" or, a couple of months later, in the sparkling "Brilliancy Medley."

At that October session he also recorded a pair of fiddle duets with J. B. Cranfill, a Dallas doctor almost thirty years his senior. Cranfill was a journalist as well, and wrote about the occasion. "Big Eck and I stood toeing the mark as we played our fiddles. He stood on one side of the mike toeing the mark—and it's awfully hard to get Eck to toe the mark of any kind."

The October '29 recordings would be his last for years, but he found work in radio. During the summer of 1944 fiddler Buddy Durham reported to *The Mountain Broadcast and Prairie Recorder*: "There is a . . . swell recorded program on the air from KWBU in Corpus Christi, Texas, six days a week at 6:45 A.M. It features three fiddlers, Georgia Slim [Rutland], Eck Robertson, and Irish Cramer. It is a program of straight fiddling."

In the '60s Robertson was visited at his home in Amarillo and taped by John Cohen and other admirers. He was still playing well and appeared at a few folk festivals, sporting a white goatee that made him look uncannily like the old cartoonists' image of Uncle Sam. But the fiddle scholar Earl Spielman, who visited him in 1969, found him in straitened circumstances and indifferent health, and detected "an undercurrent of despair and resentment." As Robertson saw it, "I mostly improved every old hoedown tune that ever was put out. I generally played better than anybody else, a better arrangement of tunes. . . . I don't know if I sound funny, but I should have been a millionaire instead of a pauper. I got beat out of everything I made."

Playlist
• *Old Time Texas Fiddler* (County CO-CD-3515)
•• *Old-Time Texas String Bands Volume One* (County CO-CD-3524): "Arkansaw Traveler," "Great Big Taters," "There's a Brown-Skin Girl Down the Road Somewhere" •• *There Is No Eye: Music for Photographs* (Smithsonian/Folkways SFW CD 40091): "Sally Goodin" [1963 recording] •• *Close to Home: Old Time Music from Mike Seeger's Collection* (Smithsonian/Folkways SF CD 40097): "Leather Breeches" (with the New Lost City Ramblers) •• *Before the Blues Vol. 2* (Yazoo 2016): "There's a Brown-Skin Girl Down the Road Somewhere" •• *Times Ain't Like They Used to Be Vol. 6* (Yazoo 2064): "Sallie Gooden"

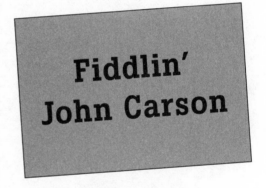

Fiddlin' John Carson

(1874–1949)

They were like Sanford & Daughter, Fiddlin' John and his Moonshine Kate: John cackling and secretive, stealing nips of corn whiskey whenever Kate's severe eye wandered, confiding to his beloved old fiddle, "Look out! Here she comes!" Even on crackly eighty-year-old records John Carson comes across three times bigger than most of his contemporaries, an amiable old rogue with a taste for short skirts and long drinks, new Fords and old-time fiddling.

As old as it gets, in one way. John Carson has an unassailable place in the history of country music, because he was the first musician to make a record in the South. Eck Robertson and Henry Gilliland preceded him with their 1922 discs of fiddle tunes, and the Vaughan Quartet from Lawrenceburg,

(Author's collection)

Carson with his friends Joe Hatfield, a fiddler from Colorado, and B. B. Bennett. (OTM collection)

Tennessee, also around 1922, with gospel songs, but those sessions were held in the North. Almost a year passed before the first recording unit ventured below the Mason-Dixon line, heading for Atlanta, Georgia. Following a tip from a local furniture store owner and record distributor, Polk Brockman, OKeh Records had John Carson on their list of artists to summon to the microphone.

A native of Fannin County in north Georgia, a former jockey, cotton mill worker, and house painter, Carson had been well known for years on the local fiddlers' convention circuit and was generally regarded as the state's champion fiddler. Between 1913 and 1922 he won the Georgia Old-Time Fiddlers' Association's annual contest in Atlanta seven times. Recently he had become a radio personality too, making his first appearance on Atlanta's WSB on September 9, 1922. "Fiddlin' John Carson," said the *Atlanta Journal* next day, "is an institution in himself and his singing of 'The Little Old Log Cabin in the Lane' and the playing of 'Turkey in the Straw,' 'Old Joe Clark,' and 'The Old Hen Cackles' . . . was enough to put any program over with a rush." We can get close to hearing what WSB's listeners heard that day, because

some time around the middle of June 1923 Carson played "Old Hen Cackled" and "Little Old Log Cabin in the Lane" for the men from OKeh Records.

Back in New York at the company's offices, John's debut sides were judged "pluperfect awful," and OKeh initially released them only in the Atlanta area. (The often told story, originating with Peer, that OKeh didn't even give the first pressing a catalog number seems unlikely to be true; at any rate, no unnumbered copy has ever been found.) But as the repeat orders came rolling in from Brockman they had to change their attitude, and soon John was recording two or three times a year—sometimes on his own, sometimes with his Virginia Reelers stringband, but most memorably with his daughter Rosa Lee, a spirited young woman (she was born in 1909) who played guitar and banjo, sang, and in her Moonshine Kate guise partnered the old man in droll, downhome country comedy.

John's fiddling was cut from an old cloth, and its style was very different from that of younger Georgians like Lowe Stokes or Clayton McMichen. Closer in age and outlook to Gid Tanner, he sang and played as and when

The following news item, superb as dry wit, was taken from the New York Times of last Sunday. It appeared under the following head-line, as is

LOCAL BOY MAKES GOOD
Jascha Heifetz, returning from a concert tour afield, has made good, as evidenced from the following letter from a Tennessee impresario:

Kingsport, Tenn.,
Feb. 25, 1929.
Dear Mr. Heifetz:
I notice that you will give a musical program at Knoxville March 6, 1929. Would you be interested in giving a musical program at Kingsport, Tenn.? If you can come I will make a date for you. What part of the net proceeds would you want?
I have been traveling with Fiddling John Carson and giving musical programs. He says that he made more money with me than any man he has traveled with. We made about $1,000 a month. We went fifty-fifty on the net proceeds. I did the advertising and also paid the oil and gas bill. We gave a program about every night.
Would you be interested in traveling with me this Spring and Summer and give musical programs? I feel sure than we can make good money. If you are interested in this, I will bill up a month's playing for you.
Please let me know whether you can come to Kingsport and what date would suit you and also whether you would be interested in traveling with me as above mentioned.

From the *Knoxville Times,* March 27, 1929.
(Author's collection)

he felt like it, and to blazes with the bar lines. Playing with him must have been torment. But his willful oddities only enhance his music, and besides, he was an exceptional singer. As Norm Cohen noted in an appreciative essay, "There is not another commercial hillbilly singer who could match his beautifully ornate, melismatic vocals. . . . [His] melodies sometimes give the listener the feeling that he is singing arhythmically, in the free meter of the oldest ballad singing style; but it is only an illusion (except in a very few cases), fostered by his slow pace and frequent omission of a half-measure at the end of a line." His recordings of Victorian and Edwardian sentimental songs like "The Lightning Express" or "In the Baggage Coach Ahead" are arrestingly individual.

Ada Powers, of the musical Powers family, met Carson at a show in Johnson City, Tennessee, in 1924. Sixty years later she remembered how Carson could play on the feelings of an audience.

He had composed and had recorded this song "You Will Never Miss Your Mother until She Is Gone." He called me out on stage—I was just a little girl, remember, about twelve—and he asked me how long my mother had been gone. I told him that she had died when I was three. He said [to the audience], "Now I am going to play and sing for you an old song. I have the ballets [songsheets] printed out, and I am going to ask this little girl to pass them through the audience, and whatever you want to give for one, you drop it in the hat. It goes to her."
That was a big theater, and I started out, but soon someone asked my other two sisters to help out, and loaned them hats, and each took a hat in hand and a sheaf of ballets, and it seemed everybody there wanted one. When it was over we had three hats full of money.

Carson also had saltier specialities like "Bachelor's Hall" or "It's a Shame to Whip Your Wife on Sunday" ("when you've got Monday, Tuesday . . ."), strange old guys' songs that not even a hardline country chauvinist could get away with today. Yet in working with his daughter he created a country music opportunity not simply for women but for feisty women. John's fingers might be on his fiddle, but when Kate was around he was under her thumb.

"Say, Kate," he might say, "go down to the hogpen and git me a jar of licker."
"Git that ol' gal you's flirtin' with the other day to git you licker," Kate retorts. "When I tell Maw, you'll get licker, but it'll be a lick over the head with a fire poker."

"If you don't tell your maw, I'll git you a new pair o' red stockings," John promises.

"Red stockings won't wash here," Kate replies. "I'll have to have a new dress too!"

After a long career Carson retired to a safe job in local government, operating the elevator in Atlanta's state capitol. He had always been tight with Georgia politicians, playing for their campaigns and even writing songs about them. He died full of years, honor, and, who knows, maybe a shot or two of moonshine. On his gravestone is carved: "Look out! There he goes!" No, not really. Pity.

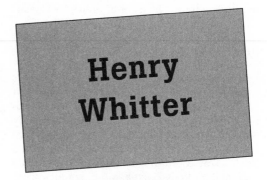

Henry Whitter

(1892–1941)

By his own account, Henry Whitter was the first country singer. He claimed that he made records in March 1923, three and a half months before Fiddlin' John Carson stood before a microphone in Atlanta and cut what is generally accepted to have been the first record of a country song. Record company files provide no evidence for Whitter's assertion, but it's possible that he made undocumented test recordings. Certainly by December 1923 he was on board the hillbilly gravy train, making the first recordings of the

Playlist
• *Fiddlin' John Carson Vol. 1 to Vol. 7* (Document DOCD-8014 to 8020) [Carson complete, with good notes, but sound quality very variable—investigate with caution]
•• *When the Sun Goes Down Vol. 6: Poor Man's Heaven* (Bluebird 50958): "Taxes on the Farmer Feeds Them All" •• *Old Mountain: Stringband Songs & Tunes* (Living Era CD AJA 5577): "Hell Bound for Alabama" •• *Good for What Ails You: Music of the Medicine Shows 1926–1937* (Old Hat CD-1005 2CD): "Gonna Swing on the Golden Gate" •• *Raw Fiddle* (Rounder Select 1160): "Arkansas Traveler," "Don't Let Your Deal Go Down" •• *Times Ain't Like They Used to Be Vol. 2* (Yazoo 2029): "Swanee River" •• *Hard Times Come Again No More Vol. 1* (Yazoo 2036): "Dixie Boll Weevil" •• *Times Ain't Like They Used to Be Vol. 3* (Yazoo 2047): "Christmas Time Will Soon Be Over" •• *Times Ain't Like They Used to Be Vol. 4* (Yazoo 2048): "Bachelor's Hall" •• *Times Ain't Like They Used to Be Vol. 7* (Yazoo 2067): "Little More Sugar in the Coffee"/"Peter Went a Fishin'"

(Author's Collection)

harmonica tunes "Lost John" and "Fox Chase" and of songs like "Lonesome Road Blues."

Through 1924–26 he repeatedly took time off from his job at a textile mill in Fries, Virginia, to supply the OKeh "Old Time Tunes" catalog with repertoire like "The New River Train," "Goin' Down the Road Feelin' Bad," and "Put My Little Shoes Away." He also responded to what his rivals were doing, covering "Keep My Skillet Good and Greasy," which Uncle Dave Macon had cut a few months before, and "I Wish I Was a Single Girl Again," previously recorded by Kelly Harrell, a fellow millworker in Fries. Eighty years later, the junkshopper or fleamarketeer can still find worn copies of Whitter's OKeh discs. They obviously sold.

But it's not immediately obvious why. Even allowing for the distancing effect of pre-electric recording, Whitter's performances are unimpressive, his voice thin, his delivery monotonous, his guitar playing a basic strum. He's rather better on the mouth harp, but there would soon be records by virtuosos of the instrument like DeFord Bailey who could blow him off the stage. So what was the appeal of this gawky performer with a talent any small-town musician could match?

Simply that he was there first. If you wanted a disc of "Little Brown Jug" on the harmonica, or of someone singing "Watermelon Hanging on the Vine," you didn't, in 1924, have a great deal of choice. Whitter profited from being quick off the mark. So, in a sense, did those who came after him, because he set the bar at a comfortably low level.

Early in 1924 another ambitious country musician, the thirty-year-old Ernest Stoneman, dropped into a Bluefield, West Virginia, store and heard Whitter's record of "The Wreck of the Old 97." Whitter, he concluded, "was just merely a very amateurish musician. And he sung through his nose something terrible." Nevertheless, the record became a hit, because people were fascinated by the train wreck narrative, which Whitter was the first to put on disc. And consequently, as Stoneman sourly noted, "Everybody in the country thought all hillbillies had to sing through the nose."

Stoneman went home and told his wife Hattie about it. "I said, 'I know that I can out-sing Henry Whitter any time. If I couldn't, I'd quit.' And my wife said, 'Why don't you go and make one?' " A few months later he did, opening a career in country music that would stretch across four decades.

Perhaps it was the arrival on the recording scene of more talented musicians like Stoneman and Macon in 1924, and Harrell and

Charlie Poole the following year, that brought the curtain slowly down on Whitter's performance. OKeh dropped him from their roster in 1926; he was back in 1927 on Gennett and Victor, but only because he had had the wit to team up with the superb singer and fiddler G. B. Grayson, an association that kept him in the record business for another couple of years and gave him the chance to cut some further discs in his own name, mostly harmonica solos. One of them even came out in the UK, the coupling of "The Lost Girl of West Virginia" and "Poor Lost Boy" on the Zonophone label. It is among the rarest of hillbilly 78s: to date only one copy has ever surfaced. His last recordings were in 1930, playing guitar backup for the banjoists Fisher Hendley and Marshall Small.

Whitter is remembered by family and friends as a jolly fellow, a good-looker and smart dresser, who loved to play music. When he showed up at someone's house, "Lord," said his son Paul, "it would be a sight of people come around. They couldn't all get in the house. He wasn't real good, but he enjoyed it. The world is full of good music now, but back then it wasn't." Another Fries resident remembers that when Whitter performed, "women would scream and holler, sort of like [at] Elvis Presley."

Almost forty years after Whitter's death, his home town acknowledged his role in the history of country music. On Labor Day in 1980, local musicians like fiddler Glenn Neaves and singer Early Upchurch gathered to perform some of his songs, and a historical marker on Fries' Main Street was unveiled to "honor the working men who started country music . . . the unsung heroes who had the perseverance to get country music before the public."

Playlist
•• *The Bristol Sessions* (Country Music Foundation CMF-011-D 2CD): "Henry Whitter's Fox Chase" •• *Old Time Mountain Banjo* (County CO-CD-3533): "Shuffle, Feet, Shuffle" (with Hendley & Small) •• *The North Carolina Banjo Collection* (Rounder CD 0439/40 2CD): "Shuffle, Feet, Shuffle" (with Hendley & Small) •• *The Rose Grew Round the Briar: Early American Rural Love Songs Vol.* 1 (Yazoo 2030): "A Pretty Gal's Love" (with Hendley & Small) •• *The Stuff That Dreams Are Made Of* (Yazoo 2202 2CD): "It's a Rough Road to Georgia" see also G. B. Grayson

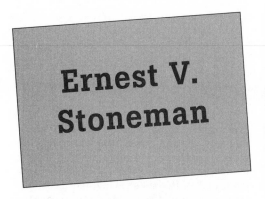

Ernest V. Stoneman

Ernest Stoneman's Blue Ridge Corn Shuckers, Galax, Virginia, 1928. Left to right: Iver Edwards, George Stoneman, Eck Dunford, Ernest Stoneman, Hattie Stoneman, Bolen Frost. (Norm Cohen collection)

(1893–1968)

It is often said of Ernest V. Stoneman that he was the only country musician whose recordings spanned the phonograph cylinder and the stereo LP. This is true, but it doesn't simply mean that he lived a long time: it acknowledges that he saw, more clearly than most of his contemporaries, the potential of country music on record, and made it his business to explore and exploit it. His own entrance into the business having been sparked by scorn for a less talented predecessor, he quickly perceived that professionals like himself could give their music, as he later put it, "its niche in the world." "If it has a chance to be advertised and spread over the country," he said, "it will keep its own. It may go down, but it'll always stay here."

He spent the decade from 1924 to 1934 covering almost every one of country music's bases: songs and ballads of past times, mountain dance music, family-group gospel songs, and what the record business then called "descriptive novelties": enactments or gentle parodies of rural culture, such as "Old Time Corn Shuckin'" or "Possum Trot School Exhibition." Only the blues eluded him. He stacked up more than 150 sides to his own credit, as well as arranging and contributing to sessions by other artists. His repertoire, as laid out on those discs, entitles him to be called one of the leading conservationists in American vernacular music, second only to The Carter Family.

Stoneman was born on a smallholding in Carroll County, Virginia; his ancestors were English on his father's side, German on his mother's. As a young man he worked in carpentry, iron mining, and on the railroad. In 1919 he married Hattie Frost and they moved to Bluefield, West Virginia. At this point he was chiefly playing autoharp and harmonica—together, with the mouth-harp on a rack. In the summer of 1924 he took a train to New York, kept a couple of appointments he had made with record companies, and ended up with Ralph Peer at OKeh. After some tests that satisfied neither himself nor Peer, he began recording productively in January 1925, singing old-time numbers like "Sinful to Flirt" and "The Lightning Express." Before long he replaced the autoharp with a guitar. He also formed a group, so that he could offer Peer band music as well as solos.

Over the next ten years he logged sides for OKeh, Edison, Gennett, Plaza, and ARC, but his best move was to follow Peer to Victor, where he made his finest and most varied recordings. Peer's first commission was for sacred numbers, which Stoneman arranged for a five-piece singing group with Hattie's older sister Irma playing the organ, but subsequent sessions elicited more worldly material like "The Mountaineer's Courtship," sung in delightful dialog with Irma Frost, lilting stringband-accompanied versions of "The Little Old Log Cabin in the Lane" and "The Spanish Merchant's Daughter," and several two-part sketches featuring comic recitations, spelling bees, and generous sprinklings of dance music. Back now in Carroll County, Stoneman led a crew of musicians from the Galax area that included the fiddler Kahle Brewer, his own brother-in-law Bolen Frost on banjo, and the remarkable fiddler, singer, and monologist Uncle Eck Dunford, whose mountain brogue seems to place him in another century, not so much old-time as Old Father Time.

A bounteous consignment of old-timey virtues, then; we are glad and grateful to take delivery of it, and although there is a bill to follow, it is not excessive. Stoneman was a team leader rather than a star player, and seldom more than respectably competent with guitar, harmonica, or voice. Listen to him singing one of the several numbers he shared with Charlie Poole, and then listen to the other man's version. Poole has brio, character, star quality: he is Henry V to Stoneman's Attendant Lord. Possibly Stoneman felt that his songs told their own tales, needed no garnish. A modern audience, perhaps finding too little shift of expression between the regret of "Goodbye Dear Old Stepstone" and the sour humor of "All Go Hungry Hash House," may disagree. He took trouble over finding songs, collecting them from family and friends or copying them from other people's discs, and he prepared them carefully for recording, but he was not always able to bring their stories to life. The words lie on the page and he reads them to us like a conscientious but prosaic schoolteacher.

His original audience may have felt otherwise, for he was very successful. When Peer set up a location recording in Bristol, Tennessee, in July 1927, to attract local talent, he took care to book a reliable act already known to him,

and Stoneman's group led off the session. Later in the week a reporter from the *Bristol News Bulletin* strolled up to the second floor of the Taylor-Christian Hat Company building on State Street and witnessed them in action. He enjoyed Eck Dunford singing "What Will I Do, for My Money's All Gone":

The synchronizing is perfect: Ernest Stoneman playing the guitar, the young matron [Hattie Stoneman] the violin and a young mountaineer [Iver Edwards] the banjo and the mouth harp. Bodies swaying, feet beating a perfect rhythm, it is calculated to go over big when offered to the public. . . . The quartette costs the Victor Company close to $200 per day—Stoneman receiving $100, and each of his assistants $25. . . . [Stoneman] received from the company $3,600 last year as his share of the proceeds on his records.

That was only part of his income, because he had also filled recording engagements in 1926

Frank Jenkins' Pilot Mountaineers, 1929: Oscar Jenkins, Frank Jenkins, Ernest Stoneman. (Courtesy of H. O. Jenkins, photo restoration by Jeremy Stephens)

with several other labels and continued to do so in 1927 and 1928. Peer eventually got him to sign a near-exclusive contract with Victor; he was permitted to carry on with Edison, probably because Edison discs, being playable only on Edison phonographs, were not much of a sales threat to Victor's go-anywhere platters. He did sneak in a 1928 session for Gennett under a pseudonym, and a couple in 1929 for Gennett and Paramount as the uncredited singer and guitarist with Frank Jenkins' Pilot Mountaineers, when his sober account of "The Burial of Wild Bill" was a moving elegy to the old Western hero.

By then his recording career seemed to be all but over. He would show up in New York five years later with his thirteen-year-old son Eddie and rerecord a sheaf of his stock numbers, but most of them were left on the shelf, and he would not return to a recording studio for more than a decade. In the meantime, however, he had had a stint as a radio personality in a lye-soap opera called "Irma and Ezra," on a station in upstate Virginia. The Stonemans had moved to Washington, D.C., and when the radio gig ended Ernest returned to carpentry and to raising his thirteen children. When enough of them were of an age to perform in public, he turned them into a family band for radio and stage work, and when bluegrass was a buzzword in the '50s they became the Bluegrass Champs, featuring the brilliant tearaway fiddling of Scotty Stoneman. Later they moved to Nashville, appeared on the Grand Ole Opry, and had their own TV show. Ernest himself has been gone for almost forty years, but Stoneman Family bands continue to realize his vision by occupying a place on the country music stage.

Playlist

• *Edison Recordings—1928* (County CD-3510)
• *Volume 1* (Old Homestead OH-4172)
• *Volume 2* (Old Homestead OH-4173)
•• *The Bristol Sessions* (Country Music Foundation CMF-011-D 2CD): "Are You Washed in the Blood?", "Midnight on the Stormy Deep," "The Mountaineer's Courtship," "Old Time Corn Shuckin', Parts 1 & 2," "The Resurrection," "Skip to Ma Lou, My Darling," "Tell Mother I Will Meet Her" •• *Old-Time Mountain Ballads* (County CD-3504): "Burial of Wild Bill" (with Frank Jenkins' Pilot Mountaineers) •• *Country Music Pioneers on Edison* (Document DOCD-1102): "Hop Light Ladies," "Sally Goodwin," "West Virginia Highway" •• *Mountain Gospel* (JSP JSP 7755 4CD): "Down to Jordan and Be Saved," "Going Down the Valley," "Hallelujah Side," "He Is Coming after Me," "I Am Resolved," "I Know My Name Is There," "I Remember Calvary," "No More Good-byes," "The Sinless Summerland," "Sweeping through the Gates," "Tell Mother I Will Meet Her," "There's a Light Lit Up in Galilee" •• *Serenade in the Mountains* (JSP JSP 7780 4CD): "Barney McCoy," "Possum Trot School Exhibition, Parts 1 & 2," "Serenade in the Mountains," "Skip to Ma Lou, My Darling," "What Will I Do, for My Money's All Gone" •• *Times Ain't Like They Used to Be Vol. 2* (Yazoo 2029): "Lonesome Road Blues," "Piney Woods Girl" •• *The Rose Grew Round the Briar: Early American Rural Love Songs Vol. 2* (Yazoo 2031): "The Railroad Flagman's Sweetheart" (with Frank Jenkins' Pilot Mountaineers) •• *Hard Times Come Again No More Vol. 1* (Yazoo 2036): "All I Got's Gone" •• *Hard Times Come Again No More Vol. 2* (Yazoo 2037): "Broke Down Section Hand" •• *My Rough and Rowdy Ways Vol. 1* (Yazoo 2039): "John Hardy" (with the Sweet Brothers), "The Fate of Talmadge Osborne"

Uncle Dave Macon

(1870–1952)

On November 6, 1925, Uncle Dave Macon and his sidekick, Fiddlin' Sid Harkreader, played a benefit for the Nashville police force. When he came on stage, Uncle Dave "confessed to some embarrassment," said a newspaper account, that he missed having a fireplace to spit in, as he would if he were at home. Undeterred, he and Sid played a set that "kept the audience in an uproar."

The concert was at the Ryman Auditorium, later the home of the Grand Ole Opry, and was broadcast over WSM, the Nashville station

(Author's collection)

that carries the Opry to this day. This was three weeks before the Opry's official birthdate of November 28, 1925, when Uncle Jimmy Thompson supposedly fiddled the show into being, though it would be a while before it acquired that name.

So Uncle Dave was there at the dawn of the country music industry. He had already made records, soon he would be a regular on the Opry, and he was known in several states for his personal appearances. "Most of his songs were just three-chord numbers," said his musical colleague Kirk McGee, "and keys didn't matter too much to him, but he was a showman. You knew you were going to have a crowd with Uncle Dave, 'cause he'd been in the business so long. His dress and everything was just different from everything else."

Uncle Dave Macon is one of the few artists who can twitch aside the curtain that hangs between early country music and its forerunners like vaudeville and minstrelsy. His father had owned a Nashville hotel where show people stayed, and the boy grew up listening to their songs and jokes and learning to pick the banjo. He might have remained an amateur, playing for neighbors, but he was spotted at a party by a talent scout for a theater chain, and in his mid-fifties he began a professional career.

He brought his stage tricks into the recording studio, cackling at his own rustic jokes, prefacing his songs and banjo breakdowns with outrageous plugs for local businessmen. "Now, good people," he announces at the beginning of "Uncle Dave's Travels—Part 1," "I'm a-singing this song especially for my old schoolmate friend, Joe Morris of Nashville, Tennessee, one of the leading clothing names. He's a man who'll address you at the door and he'll dress you up before you go out." But amid the foolery was a great deal of wonderful music. Accompanied by the superb guitarist Sam McGee, Kirk's brother, he sang lonesome bluesy songs and pungent commentaries on issues of the day like presidential elections and farmers' problems.

He also recorded a sheaf of songs from the era of the blackface minstrel show, such as "Stop That Knocking at My Door" and "Sassy Sam." Like a trove of ancient glass negatives from the dawn of photography, these are priceless documents of a musical past that is almost enveloped in silence. Most of the artists who promulgated such songs in the 1870s and '80s had no opportunity to record them, because the technology did not yet exist. Uncle Dave preserved them in his remarkable memory, and now we have them for all time.

More swiftly than any other country artist of his era, Macon grasped the possibilities of the recording form. Many of his discs are stage shows in miniature: a banjo flourish heralds a comic introduction or a tall story, a banjo tune, a few verses of a song, maybe two or three songs. It's the work of a canny old stager who, presented with a wholly new medium, didn't simply use it to sing a song or play a tune— how prosaic, how *literal* would that be?—but brilliantly condensed his entire act.

"I played with him for about twenty years," said Sam McGee, "and he'd always tell me, 'Now, Sammy, you know what we want to tell 'em?'

"I'd say, 'No, I don't, Uncle Dave. What do you want to tell 'em?'

" 'Tell 'em: We was born in the mountains, raised in the bluff—come here to shake wicked feet and strut our stuff.' "

Unlike many of country music's pioneers, Macon kept going through the '30s and '40s, working with the Delmore Brothers, going out on Opry tours with Bill Monroe. When the shows were well attended he'd remark airily, "The old man's still got what it takes!", but when the crowds were thin he'd turn to Monroe and say, "You're not pulling them in tonight, Bill."

At the age of seventy he had an opportunity to demonstrate his imperishable skills in front of a movie camera. If *The Grand Ole Opry* should ever be billed in an obscure TV slot, it's not to be missed. (Alternatively, Bear Family's boxed set offers it on DVD.) It isn't much of a movie, but there is a priceless sequence of Uncle Dave singing "Take Me Back to My Old Carolina Home" with a parade of banjo acrobatics. He swings it, twirls it, even dances with it.

Uncle Dave had a long and cheerful life, full of music to the end. "It was a pity a man like him had to die," said Kirk McGee. "He was so much pleasure to everybody."

Uncle Dave Macon & Sam McGee. (OTM collection)

Playlist
• *Keep My Skillet Good and Greasy* (Bear Family BCD 15978 9CD+DVD) [all of his nearly 200 commercial recordings, plus Opry airshots from the '30s and '40s, and a 1951 session for a local folklorist]
• *Travelin' Down the Road* (County CCS-CD-115) [Bluebird recordings, 1935–38]
• *Go Long Mule* (County CO-CD-3505)
• *Classic Sides 1924–1938* (JSP JSPCD 7729 4CD)
• *Volume 2: Classic Cuts 1924–1938* (JSP JSPCD 7769 4CD)
• *Keep My Skillet Good and Greasy* (Old Homestead OH-4148)
• *Early Recordings* (Old Homestead OH-4184)
•• *Uncle Dave at Home* (Spring Fed SFR-101) [his last recordings]
•• *Nashville—The Early String Bands Volume One* (County CD-3521): "I'm a-Goin' Away in the Morn," "Oh Baby, You Done Me Wrong," "Railroadin' and Gamblin' " •• *Nashville—The Early String Bands Volume Two* (County CD-3522): "Bake That Chicken Pie," "Over the Road I'm Bound to Go" •• *Hard Times In the Country* (County CO-CD-3527): "Farm Relief," "From Earth to Heaven," "The Wreck of the Tennessee Gravy Train" •• *Old Mountain: Stringband Songs & Tunes* (Living Era CD AJA 5577): "Hold That Wood-pile Down" •• *Times Ain't Like They Used to Be Vol. 2* (Yazoo 2029): "Sail Away Ladies" •• *Hard Times Come Again No More Vol. 1* (Yazoo 2036): "All In Down and Out Blues" •• *My Rough and Rowdy Ways Vol. 1* (Yazoo 2039): "Way Down the Old Plank Road" •• *Times Ain't Like They Used to Be Vol. 3* (Yazoo 2047): "Rock about My Sara Jane" •• *Times Ain't Like They Used to Be Vol. 7* (Yazoo 2067): "Go On, Nora Lee" •• *Times Ain't Like They Used to Be Vol. 8* (Yazoo 2068): "Tennessee Tornado"

Vernon Dalhart

(1883–1948)

Vernon Dalhart, in the judgment of the great talent scout Ralph Peer, "was a professional substitute for a real hillbilly. He had the peculiar ability to adapt hillbilly music to suit the taste of the non-hillbilly population."

Dalhart was an artist of a kind hardly known nowadays, the professional record maker, ready to sing whatever his producer might hand him. He cut his first record in 1916 and by the early '20s was a seasoned New York studio hand with scores of discs to his name, everything from light classical to current vaudeville songs. Then in 1924 he made, for Victor, a record of the hillbilly disaster song "Wreck of the Old 97." It had already been done by Henry Whitter for OKeh, and indeed by Dalhart himself for at least one other label. What was special about this record was its flipside, a piece called "The Prisoner's Song," allegedly written by his cousin Guy Massey and so copyrighted, but actually an older song, possibly passed to Massey by his brother Robert, who had picked it up in his travels, though the accounts of its genesis are numerous and contradictory.

Victor, unconcerned about their provenance, advertised them as "genuine songs of the Southern mountaineers, given with all their original lyric vigor and their quaint melody," but added, with just a touch of embarrassment, that " 'The Prisoner's Song' is from the hair-brooch and weeping-willow period, and it would take a Mark Twain, perhaps, to describe it." For all that, the record sold a million—and that was just for Victor. Over the next nine months Dalhart recorded it for nine other companies, who released it on forty-nine labels, probably at least doubling Victor's sales. By then Dalhart was unstoppable.

His appeal is not easy for the present-day listener to fathom. His harmonica and jew's harp playing has a folksy charm but otherwise his accompaniments, typically by studio violinists and guitarist Carson Robison, are polite, and his southern accent seems artificial. The latter criticism would have surprised him: in a 1918 interview he remarked, à propos his command of dialect, "When you are born and brought up in the South your only trouble is to talk any other way . . . the sure 'nough Southerner talks almost like a Negro, even when he's white. I've broken myself of the habit, more or less, in ordinary conversation, but it still comes pretty easy."

Then again, one could always understand what he was singing, and that was important, because Dalhart loved to tell a story, usually of death and disaster, like "Casey Jones" or "The Cowboy's Lament," or "The Sinking of the Titanic," still a potent subject thirteen years after the great ship went down. Abbe Niles, who reviewed hillbilly and what were then termed "race" (i.e., African-American) recordings in the literary magazine *The Bookman*, called him "the official hired mourner to the nation." The title receives confirmation of a kind in an anecdote retailed by Jim Walsh, a historian of popular music who wrote about recording pioneers for many years in *Hobbies* magazine.

Vernon Dalhart in Columbia's "Old Familiar Tunes" catalog, 1927. (Author's collection)

A record dealer once told me of a visit he received just before Christmas of 1927 from a lanky, somewhat intoxicated, mountaineer. The rustic gentleman bought a dozen Dalhart records, all of them dealing with train wrecks, floods, earthquakes, murders, and similar tragic happenings, and all, of course, ending with a moral admonition. . . . As his records were being wrapped, the mountaineer explained they were a Christmas present "for the old woman and the kids." Said he: "The old woman and the kids will play these here sad pieces and cry their d— fool heads off! With all this here mis'ry music they're sure gonna have one h— of a Merry Christmas!"

Once Dalhart acquired a song (often from Robison) he recorded it for every label in the business. During 1925–26, when the story of the trapped potholer was taking up acres of newsprint, Dalhart had recordings of "The Death of Floyd Collins" on twenty-six labels; the Columbia version alone sold more than 300,000 copies. There were twenty-eight different discs of "The Runaway Train," not counting the jaunty version he recorded on a visit to London in 1931, which became a standby of the BBC's radio request program Children's Favourites and could still be heard regularly into the '50s. Quite a few of Dalhart's earlier recordings had been issued in the UK, as well as in Australia and other overseas territories.

The individual songs in the hillbilly section of Dalhart's discography number several hundred, but the multiple issues run into thousands. Many were under pseudonyms, ranging from the transparent (Vernon Dell) to the mock-hillbilly (Al Craver, Tobe Little) to the enigmatic (Mr X). Dalhart himself claimed that he was unaware of most of these false names, and that the few he did know of were chosen by recording managers, but the Dalhart scholar Walter Haden notes the curious fact that "an impressive number of [them] are still familiar last names in Jefferson, Texas," in Marion County, where Dalhart came from. "Certain of the *noms de plumes* . . . are identical given names and surnames of Marion Countians," Haden continues, adding that Mack Allen, the singer's third most-used pseudonym, sounds just like McAllen, Texas, a town Dalhart would have known well. Actually, Vernon Dalhart was a pseudonym too, since he was born Marion Try Slaughter. He derived his professional name from two Texas cattle towns near where he grew up.

The point of all the pseudonyms was to maximize sales without making buyers tired of the name of Vernon Dalhart, and the strategy appears to have worked. Business papers of most of the companies Dalhart recorded for have not survived, but thanks to a nameless clerk we do have sales figures for his discs in the Columbia "Old Familiar Tunes" series, one of the leading hillbilly catalogs. His sixty-six releases sold, in all, over two million copies, establishing him as the list's best seller. Suggestively, he was less successful in his own name than as Al Craver: the average sale of the pseudonymous issues was almost twice as large, swelled not only by the Floyd Collins obituary but by three other six-figure sellers: "The Wreck of the 1256" (train disaster), "Little Marion Parker" (murder of mountain maid), and "The Letter Edged in Black" (death news comes by mail). What we cannot know is whether Al Craver's patrons saw through the thin disguise of the pseudonym, but since all his records sounded virtually identical, whatever the billing, at least some listeners must surely have done so.

"He goes about his composition and recording work," wrote the anonymous author of the syndicated column "New York Today" in November 1928, "much as another man would go about his stock or bond business. He has combined business with art and by a routine system has been able to compose and record what is believed to be a record for output. His records are played in every town and hamlet in the country."

But with the Depression Dalhart's balloon-flight career came swiftly to earth. By the '40s he was a sad figure, unable to cash in on his vast recording experience, reduced to working as a night watchman or hotel clerk, vainly offering his services as a voice coach. There was no place for him in a country music full of hell-for-leather stringbands and honkytonk steel guitars, and he died forgotten by the business he had helped to create.

Strange, though, that the most prolific recording artist in country music history, as Dalhart unquestionably was for at least a quarter of a century, should have been a graduate of the Dallas Conservatory of Music, a reputable light opera singer, and a hit on the New York stage in Gilbert and Sullivan's *H.M.S. Pinafore.*

Playlist
• *Lindberg the Eagle of the USA* (BACM CD D 017)
•• *The Columbia Label: Classic Old Time Music* (BACM CD D 057): "Frank Dupree," "Kinnie Wagner" •• *When the Sun Goes Down Vol. 6: Poor Man's Heaven* (Bluebird 50958): "The Farm Relief Song" •• *When the Sun Goes Down Vol. 10: East Virginia Blues* (Bluebird 60085): "The Prisoner's Song," "Wreck of the Old 97" •• *Country Music Pioneers on Edison* (Document DOCD-1102): "Just a Melody," "Kinnie Wagner's Surrender," "The Wreck on the Southern Old 97" •• *Serenade in the Mountains* (JSP JSP 7780 4CD): "Ain't Gonna Grieve My Mind," "Get Away Old Man Get Away," "Little Green Valley," "Oh Susannah," "Shine on Harvest Moon" •• *Howdy!: 25 Hillbilly All-Time Greats* (Living Era CD AJA 5140): "The Runaway Train," "Wreck of the Old 97" •• *My Rough and Rowdy Ways Vol. 2* (Yazoo 2040): "Billie the Kid" •• *The Story That the Crow Told Me Vol. 2* (Yazoo 2052): "Jesus Loves Me"

Fiddlin' Powers

(1877–1953)

Folks, we're goin' to have a real old-time square dance. And while the crowd is gathering and everybody getting their partners, we will have a little rehearsal by Fiddlin' Powers and Family. First, Miss Orpha with the mandolin."

Thus the anonymous master of ceremonies on Fiddlin' Powers and Family's record of "Old Virginia Reel." It was a two-part recording, with one side devoted to a display of the family's individual talents. After "Miss Orpha" we hear her sisters Ada and Carrie on ukulele and guitar, respectively, her brother Charles on banjo, and Fiddlin' Powers himself, the paterfamilias, playing "Buck Creek Girl." Then, on the other side, the full band plays a medley of old southern dance tunes. It was 1927, yet this was the family's last release. They had been recording since 1924, which puts them among the earliest pioneers of recorded old-time music.

James Cowan Powers raised his four musical children in Russell County in southwest Virginia. He had one day of schooling in his life—"he learned to write his name," remembers Ada, "and never went back"—but as well as a farmer he was a proficient carpenter and leatherworker. "He had his own special pattern for making leggings," said Ada. "He would order a whole cow-hide at a time . . . and there was other leather business too. At that time every young man in the county had to have an underarm holster, and he had to make a lot of those. Now that tells you something about the times back then."

He began fiddling in his boyhood and as a young man won many local contests, but it was not until 1918 that he entered seriously on the life of a professional musician. His wife had died of tuberculosis, and rather than leave his children while he worked away from home, he decided to form a family band and keep them with him.

"We made our best money in those West Virginia and Kentucky mining towns," Ada remembered. "It was not unusual in there to take in over $200 a night—at twenty-five cents an adult and fifteen cents a child. . . . At first we traveled by train, but then Daddy bought one of the first two Model T Fords in the community, and we went in that. I can still hear those old curtains in the back flapping in the cold wind." Carrie learned to play backup guitar, taught by Byrd Moore, a local musician who would himself become a well-known recording artist. In time each of the children worked up a specialty, as heard on "Old Virginia Reel."

In 1924, after Fiddlin' Powers won a big contest in Johnson City, Tennessee, a local businessman decided that the family had a future in the new trade of making records. An appointment was arranged with Victor, and in August the Powerses rode the train to New York and, over two days, recorded seventeen tunes. Victor would issue eight of these, advertising them in their catalog as "absolutely American music, sprung up in the hollows of

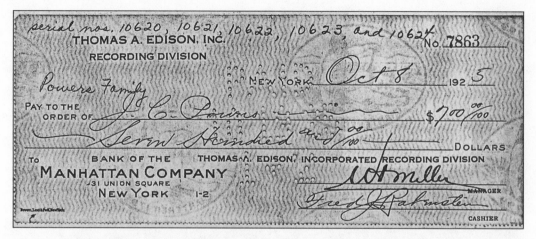

serial nos. 10620, 10621, 10622, 10623, and 10624

THOMAS A. EDISON, INC.
RECORDING DIVISION

No. 7863

NEW YORK Oct 8 192 5

PAY TO THE ORDER OF Powers Family   J. C. Powers $ 700/100

Seven Hundred and 00/100 DOLLARS

To BANK OF THE   THOMAS A. EDISON, INCORPORATED RECORDING DIVISION
MANHATTAN COMPANY
31 UNION SQUARE   W. H. Miller
NEW YORK   1-2   MANAGER
                         Fred J. Palmster
                                             CASHIER

The reward of two days' work. A second check brought Powers' earnings for October 6–7, 1925, to $750. (Author's collection)

the Southern Appalachian ranges . . . strange, remote harmonies, to which you could dance all night. . . . To listen to them will be, for many of us, to bring up the memories of many a happy gathering in some little out-of-the-way place where the lights of the city never penetrate."

This handful of acoustically recorded discs, containing venerable dance tunes such as "Ida Red," "Cripple Creek," and "Old Joe Clark," is a turning-point in the history of old-time music— the first recordings of a working mountain stringband. They sold well, rousing the interest of rival companies: the family went on to record for Edison in 1925 and OKeh in 1927. When Ernest Stoneman signed with Victor in 1926, one of the first tasks the company gave him was to remake the Powers discs, using the new technology of electric recording.

The Powers Family toured with other leading hillbilly artists of the time, including Clarence Ashley and Dock Boggs, and broadcast over WOPI in Bristol, Tennessee. Eventually the girls married and left the performing arena, but Fiddlin' Powers continued to play at contests and with local bands through the '30s and '40s. In the early '50s he formed an unusual link between antique old-time music and the new sound of bluegrass by occasionally teaming up with the Stanley Brothers. It was on stage with the Stanleys that he played his last, succumbing to a heart attack while fiddling "Cluck Old Hen."

Playlist
•• *Rural String Bands of Virginia* (County CD-3502): "Old Virginia Reel—Parts 1 & 2"
•• *Old-Time Music from South-West Virginia* (County CO-CD-3523): "Callahan's Reel," "Old Virginia Reel—Part 2," "Patty on the Turnpike" •• *Country Music Pioneers on Edison* (Document DOCD-1102): "Ida Red" •• *The Cornshucker's Frolic Vol. 1* (Yazoo 2045): "Old Virginia Reel—Parts 1 & 2" •• *The Cornshucker's Frolic Vol. 2* (Yazoo 2046): "Old Molly Hair"

Charlie Poole

(1892–1931)

Consider yourself under arrest!" snapped one of the policemen, as they burst into the bootlegging joint.

"Consider, hell!" said the banjo player. He slammed his instrument down over the officer's head so that the neck hung down in front like a tie.

Another policeman shoved a gun into the banjo player's ear. The musician forced it aside as it went off, chipping his teeth. Infuriated, he seized a walking stick and knocked several cops through the windows before leaping into a car and heading for the mountains.

An everyday story in the life of Charlie Poole, old-time singer, banjoist, and hell-raiser. Eighty years on, people in his neck of the woods still talk about the rowdy young man who rambled the Appalachians during the Depression, dispensing romantic songs and merry dance tunes. In the old cotton mill towns of North Carolina and Virginia, Charlie Poole is a local hero yet.

But why? His kind of music, the flowing blend of banjo, guitar, and fiddle that was the classic stringband sound of early country music, has all but died out, except in its vigorous descendant, bluegrass. His songs, Victorian and Edwardian tear-jerkers like "There'll Come a Time," narratives of forgotten events like "Baltimore Fire," strutting jazz numbers such as "Beale Street Blues," have no kin in the catalogs of Music Row. His manner, clipped and snappy, rough as an old saw, belongs to another time.

Yet for some those facts are recommendations. Charlie Poole was one of a kind. Listen to his stories of the sweet sixteen-year-old who wouldn't stop chewing gum, or the terrible boarding house where the butter had red hair and the baby had its feet in the soup. Or hear him in sentimental vein, on a wistful song of parted lovers like "Budded Rose," or

(Kinney Rorrer collection)

Charlie Poole & the North Carolina Ramblers: Posey Rorer (fiddle), Roy Harvey (guitar). (Kinney Rorer collection)

remembering childhood long ago in "Sweet Sunny South." These are scenes of the fancy rather than of actual rural life, but they belong to the authentic imaginative world of early country music. Poole's voice reaches across the decades, gathering us into that world and its music, still exhilarating, still believable.

He was the grandson of an Irish immigrant, and grew up in the cotton mill village of Haw River, North Carolina. He began playing banjo before he was in his teens, and by his mid-twenties, when he moved to nearby Spray, he was a seasoned picker. Spray and adjoining Leaksville and Draper (now amalgamated as Eden) boasted a remarkable group of musicians, among them fiddler Posey Rorer and guitarist Norman Woodlieff, the first recorded lineup of Poole's North Carolina Ramblers.

Their 1925 debut, "Don't Let Your Deal Go Down Blues" and "Can I Sleep in Your Barn To-night, Mister?", sold over 100,000 copies, making a lot of money for Columbia Records (the trio received only a one-off fee of $75) and assuring Poole of regular sessions for several years. He went on to record over seventy songs, mostly accompanied by the adept guitarist Roy Harvey and a succession of brilliant fiddlers: Rorer, Lonnie Austin, and Odell Smith.

Southern communities were not always eager to make official acknowledgment of their hillbilly artists, but in his part of the country Poole's discs were received with warm and public applause. An ad in the *Burlington Daily Times* of February 3, 1927, headlined "Charlie Poole, Burlington's Native Son, Makes Another Hit for Columbia Records!," declared: "The boy we all know has again made a popular flash . . . to hear his latest records is to recall those childhood days when many of us knew him 'down on the farm.'" The new release was "Leavin' Home" and "There'll Come a Time," and M. B. Smith's store reported that they had just received 100 copies. Eight days later they announced with satisfaction: "Our first shipment of Charlie's Records were sold almost before they were unpacked, but we have just received another 100 of this number and will have plenty on hand from now on." Subsequent store ads trumpet Poole as "Burlington Boy Who Is Now One of Columbia's Greatest Southern Artists."

As well as his rough-cut versions of parlor ballads like "There'll Come a Time," Poole liked to sing comic vaudeville songs such as "Monkey on a String." He was no purist. Like Jimmie Rodgers, he aimed to play his way out of hillbilly music and into something more respectable, and he persuaded Columbia to let him record some ragtime banjo solos. They were studied and lifeless, and the company wanted no more of them. Poole returned to what he did best, translating the peppy spirit of the Jazz Age into animated, swinging string-band music.

For five years he rampaged through Appalachia, playing for mill workers and coal miners, in bootleggers' joints and red-light districts, and at high-school graduation days. But by 1931, with the Depression deepening, he had no recording contract, few bookings, and a moonshine monkey on his back.

One morning in May 1931 a couple of his buddies found him clutching the railings in front of the Spray post office. "We need you to play music," they said. "Old Charlie's sung all night long," he muttered. "But this time old Charlie's gonna kick the bucket." He weaved away to his sister's house. That evening he had a heart attack and died.

Since then, three generations of musicians have remembered him by singing his songs. In the '60s County Records began reissuing his old recordings on LP, and the albums sold in thousands to his old fans and their descendants, as well as to new generations of admirers all over the world. In the CD era, it happened all over again. Three quarters of a century after his death, Charlie Poole's deal shows no sign of going down.

Kelly Harrell

(1889–1942)

Around the midpoint of the state line between Virginia and North Carolina lies what used to be, and arguably still is, the heartland of old-time music. Here are Galax, where the annual fiddlers' convention still pulls in thousands; Danville, where the "old 97" train was heading when she crashed; and Eden, formerly Spray, the home of Charlie Poole. Here too are Hillsville, Fries, Mt. Airy, Independence: to the casual traveler, insignificant mountain hamlets or textile mill towns, but to

Playlist
• *"You Ain't Talkin' to Me": Charlie Poole and the Roots of Country Music* (Columbia/Legacy C3K 92780 3CD) [within the *faux*-cigar-box packaging are not only many of Poole's finest sides, together with work by contemporaries such as Kelly Harrell and the Red Fox Chasers, but examples of Poole's repertoire by popular singers of a generation before, made in the dawn light of the early recording industry]
• *Old Time Songs* (County CO-CD-3501)
• *Volume Two* (County CO-CD-3508)
• *Volume 3* (County CO-CD-3516)
• *Charlie Poole* (JSP JSP 7734 4CD)

(Author's collection)

the music lover, places resonant with history. These are the streets and courthouse squares once haunted by Ernest Stoneman and his friends. Here, Henry Whitter blew the "Fox Chase" on his harmonica. There, eighty years ago, Ben Jarrell and Frank Jenkins conversed on fiddle and banjo.

It was in the mill towns especially that the patterns of this music were woven. Relaxing after their shifts in the choking heat of the weave-room, men turned to their instruments, or to song. One of the most distinctive voices to rise from this melée of music-making belonged to a millhand in Fieldale, Virginia, named Kelly Harrell.

He would stand up and sing the story of the "Rovin' Gambler" or the "Broken Engagement" in the wind-dried voice of an Appalachian working man only two or three generations on from Scots or Irish immigrants. There was nothing sweet or smooth about Harrell. He had none of the polish of Riley Puckett or the warm humor of Jimmie Rodgers. Yet there was a rugged, gloomy grace to his singing, a plainness and reticence that made something terribly touching out of a song of parting like "In the Shadow of the Pine," and something macabre of his satirical tall tale of itinerant farm labor, "My Name Is John Johannah." You *see* the dark forests of pine trees, the starved features of the Arkansas dirt farmer.

As a young man Harrell was acquainted with Henry Whitter, one of country music's recording pioneers, and it may have been Whitter who pointed him toward Victor, the label for which he made most of his forty-odd records in the second half of the '20s, though there was also a 1925 session for OKeh. On that occasion Whitter furnished the accompaniment, a favor Harrell might afterward have regretted, since on "Wild Bill Jones" Whitter played guitar and harmonica in the wrong key throughout.

The early Victor recordings with New York studio musicians are pleasingly sung but, to modern ears, a little stiff. Victor's publicists described the first release, "Butcher's Boy" coupled with "I Wish I Was a Single Girl Again," as "folk-ballads of the kind that exist everywhere in the South, but which musical scholarship seems to have missed for a couple of generations. . . . There is nothing more unsophisticated that we can find anywhere in the balladry of Europe. The tunes, one slow, the other like a steady reel, are repeated over and over." It was not, perhaps, the glowing recommendation that Harrell might have wished, but the record and its successors seem to have sold.

From the standpoint of the lover of old-time stringband music, Harrell's moment came when Victor let him hire his own accompanists, including a pair of fiddlers associated with Charlie Poole—Posey Rorer and Lonnie Austin. From those two wonderful sessions in March and August 1927 come such choice pieces as "My Name Is John Johannah," "In the Shadow of the Pine," "Henry Clay Beattie," about a Virginia murder sixteen years previously, and "Charles Giteau," the story of the assassination of President James Garfield, written in the "come-all-ye" form of the broadsheet ballads that were the street literature of the seventeenth and eighteenth centuries:

> Come all ye tender Christians, wherever you may be,
> And likewise pay attention [to] these few lines from me:
> I was down at the depot to make my getaway,
> And Providence being against me, it proved to be too late. . . .
> My name is Charles Giteau, my name I'll never deny,
> To leave my aged parents to sorrow and to die.
> But little did I think, while in my youthful bloom,
> I'd be carried to the scaffold to meet my fatal doom.

He recorded once more, in 1929. Victor's budget no longer stretched to paying for a full band to accompany the singer to their studios in Camden, New Jersey, so Harrell just brought guitarist Alfred Steagall, who accompanied him alone on a stoic communique from the marital trenches, "The Henpecked Man." For the rest of the session Victor added a couple of studio players, Sam Freed on fiddle and Roy Smeck on harmonica and jew's harp, who gave the recordings something of the flavor of Vernon Dalhart's. They were not Harrell's best work, and Victor delayed releasing two of them until 1932, when they sold next to nothing.

The Depression killed Harrell's recording career, but he still had his mill job, and he sang locally for a while. He also had some income from his composition "Away Out on the Mountain," recorded by Jimmie Rodgers on the reverse side of "Blue Yodel." Harrell's first royalty check for the song was for $985.

Like many millworkers, Harrell suffered from asthma. After a coughing fit at work one day, he was advised by his fellows to go home. To show he was as fit as the next man, he jumped out of the restroom window on to the path a few feet below—and collapsed. He died on the way to the hospital.

Playlist
• *Kelly Harrell Volume 1 (1925–1926)* (Document DOCD-8026)
• *Kelly Harrell Volume 2 (1926–1929)* (Document DOCD-8027)
• *Worried Blues* (JSP JSPCD 7743 4CD) [duplicates the contents of the Document CDs and adds material by Frank Hutchison and others]
•• *Rural String Bands of Virginia* (County CD-3502): "My Name Is John Johannah" •• *Old-Time Mountain Ballads* (County CD-3504): "Charles Giteau" •• *Hard Times in the Country* (County CO-CD-3527): "My Name Is John Johannah" •• *Old Mountain: Stringband Songs & Tunes* (Living Era CD AJA 5577): "Charles Giteau"

Da Costa Woltz's Southern Broadcasters

Ben Jarrell (1880–1946) • Frank Jenkins (1888–c. 1945) • Da Costa Woltz (1892–??) • Price Goodson (1915–48)

What a splendid name it is, and how piquant a bonus that the Southern Broadcasters never actually set foot in a radio studio. It was all pie in the sky, created by the band's leader in the probably sincere belief that his three men from the mountains (to say nothing of the small boy) would become 1927's hottest thing in string music.

Sincere, because the Southern Broadcasters were unquestionably fine musicians, some

Da Costa Woltz's Southern Broadcasters, 1927: Woltz, Price Goodson, Ben Jarrell, Frank Jenkins. (Author's collection)

Ad for Herwin Records, including several by the Southern Broadcasters, in *Southern Agriculturist*, September 1, 1927. (Author's collection)

of the best in the music-rich borderlands of southwestern Virginia and northwestern North Carolina. The recordings they made over three days in May 1927 were brilliant: restless performances rendered even more intense by the absence of the soothing low tones of a guitar. The high-strung concentration of Ben Jarrell's singing and fiddling and the rippling twin banjos of Da Costa Woltz and Frank Jenkins pierce the murk of surface noise like a lighthouse beam on a dark night.

One of the band's most affecting performances is "Take Me Back to the Sweet Sunny South." As originally written, this is the song of an ex-slave, who yearns in his old age to return to the haunts of his youth, "where the flowers from the river's green margins may blow their sweets to the banks where we played." Yet he knows that "the smiles and the forms I have seen now lie in the dark mossy ground." It would be easy to overload this fragile bark, but Jarrell's unsentimental, even brisk delivery keeps it bravely afloat, and the effect is only a little spoiled by his forgetting the words in the last verse. Evidently no one at Gennett Records noticed, or cared, and the record was issued that way. "Yellow Rose of Texas," though better known today in its Western movie version, is another composition for the blackface minstrel stage, and Jarrell preserves its original language in the few verses he can find breath for amid the hectic fiddling and picking.

The Southern Broadcasters recorded eighteen numbers at this, their only session. Some, like the sacred song "Are You Washed in the Blood of the Lamb" and the dance tune "Richmond Cotillion," were quite good sellers, but Jenkins's banjo solo "Baptist Shout" and his fiddle song "Roving Cowboy" became maddeningly hard to find, and it took many years before it was possible to assemble the band's complete recordings in decent condition. Rarity often plays a part in the aesthetics of old-time music, but the Southern Broadcasters excite a fervor among their admirers that goes beyond collectorism.

Jarrell lived in Round Peak, North Carolina, and Jenkins in Dobson, while Woltz was over the state line in Galax, Virginia, a city he eventually served as mayor. Banjos and politics were only two of his interests. An instinctive entrepreneur, attuned to the get-up-and-go spirit of the '20s, he also marketed patent medicines and dabbled in other schemes. He seems to have set up the band as he would a business, with high ideas and headed notepaper.

And what today we would call a USP, a unique selling point, the twelve-year-old Price Goodson strumming his little ukulele and blowing his little harmonica—quite well, too, on his recorded showpieces "Lonesome Road Blues" and "Lost Train Blues." It was a strategy that would become popular in country music: in the '30s there were Asher Sizemore & Little Jimmie, and Cliff Carlisle with his Sonny Boy Tommy. Those youngsters were fairly horrible singers, but Goodson is competent as well as confident on his voice-harmonica-ukulele specialty "Be Kind to a Man When He Is Down." He might have had a career in music but he never pursued it, and he died young.

By then Jarrell and Jenkins, men already in early middle age when they made their recordings, were both dead too, but their singular music was replicated by their sons, and in the '60s and '70s several excellent albums on the County label preserved the legacy inherited by Tommy Jarrell and Oscar Jenkins. Tommy Jarrell became a source of inspiration to another generation, and his fiddle and banjo playing is imprinted upon many who have taken up old-time string music in the last four decades.

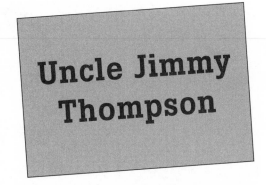

Uncle Jimmy Thompson

(1848–1931)

I've got grown grandchildren and great big great-grandchildren," boasted the man with the long white beard. "I'm runnin' cars and trucks yet, and a-playin' the fiddle yet. And I love to look at a pretty woman just as good as I ever did."

Not bad for eighty-two, but Uncle Jimmy Thompson had always led an active life. Born in Tennessee and raised in Texas, he farmed and fiddled all his days, traveling widely in the South and winning many contests—most famously, an eight-day affair in Dallas in 1907 when he beat eighty-six fiddlers. Eighteen years later he would reminisce about that great victory to George D. Hay, the "Solemn Old Judge" of Nashville's WSM, during a two-hour program of his fiddling. "Telegrams were received from all parts of the United States," reported the Nashville *Tennessean* not long afterward, "encouraging him in his task of furnishing barn dance music for a million homes." Historians now recognize that November evening's broadcast in 1925 as, if not the actual birth of the Grand Ole Opry, at least one of its first contractions.

Uncle Jimmy's Opry broadcasts may have vanished into the ether, but decades later he was still fondly remembered by many old Tennesseans. Leaving their home in Laguardo, in Wilson County, he and his wife Ella would tour the country in a kind of prototype RV, which he constructed by adding a truck bed to a Ford sedan, building a house on the truck bed, and equipping it with all the couple's needs. "He had a cot in there," remembered his daughter-in-law Katherine Womack, "a water bucket, a dipper, washpan, towel, even a little wood stove." They would stop at small towns and unroll a rug for Ella, an accomplished buck-dancer, to make her steps on while Uncle Jimmy played. He called his fiddle "Old Betsy" and every night would "put her to bed" with a

Playlist
• *Da Costa Woltz's Southern Broadcasters & Frank Jenkins' Pilot Mountaineers (1927–1929)* (Document DOCD-8023) [includes six sides by Frank and Oscar Jenkins with Ernest Stoneman]
•• *Old Time Mountain Banjo* (County CO-CD-3533): "Baptist Shout," "Home Sweet Home" (Frank Jenkins solos) •• *Old Mountain: Stringband Songs & Tunes* (Living Era CD AJA 5577): "Yellow Rose of Texas" •• *Before the Blues Vol. 2* (Yazoo 2016): "Roving Cowboy" (Frank Jenkins solo) •• *The Cornshucker's Frolic Vol. 2* (Yazoo 2046): "John Brown's Dream" •• *Times Ain't Like They Used to Be Vol. 7* (Yazoo 2067): "Jack of Diamonds" •• *Times Ain't Like They Used to Be Vol. 8* (Yazoo 2068): "Yellow Rose of Texas"

The music of Tommy Jarrell and Oscar Jenkins is exemplified by their CDs with the fiddler and banjoist Fred Cockerham, *Down to the Cider Mill* (County CO-CD-2734) and *Stay All Night* (County CO-CD-2735).

Uncle Jimmy Thompson & Eva Thompson Jones. (Author's collection)

piece of red flannel lovingly spread over her. He was a keep-fit fanatic, a dedicated chewer of gum and tobacco, a knowledgable stargazer, and a notable drinker.

And he was no stick-in-the-mud. Twentieth-century innovations fascinated him. "He would just sit and daydream all the time after he had heard radio and records," remembered Katherine Womack. "Why, he thought it would be wonderful to make records of his music, or to play

Uncle Jimmy Thompson and his "camper van." (Author's collection)

it on the air. 'I want to throw my music out all over the American,' he used to say. He wouldn't say 'America,' but 'the American.'"

He had a couple of chances to do so. In 1926, accompanied on the piano by his niece and longtime musical assistant Eva Thompson Jones, he recorded a pair of vigorous old-time fiddle tunes, "Karo" and "Billy Wilson." Four years later, when a portable recording unit was set up for a week or two in Knoxville, Tennessee, in the WNOX studio in the St. James Hotel, he and Eva stopped by to play "Lynchburg" and a medley of "Flying Clouds" and "Leather Breeches" which was issued as "Uncle Jimmy's Favorite Fiddling Pieces." Not simply tunes, these were illustrated interviews, as the venerable fiddler, prompted by recording assistant Bill Brown, looked back on his life, remembering cheaper whiskey, comelier girls, and more modest fashions.

"Say, Uncle Jimmy," Brown asks, "were the girls as pretty back in 1866 as they are now?"

"They were prettier! Just healthy. Stout. Fat. Plump."

"What kind of clothes did they wear?"

"They just wore nice, good clothes. Plenty width in the skirts, and long enough to come down to the shoes."

"Did you have many girls?" Brown asks. No, says Uncle Jimmy, not back then. "But I've had some since!" In the background, Eva dissolves into laughter.

These recordings brim with history. Uncle Jimmy Thompson is one of the oldest southern old-time musicians whose playing is preserved on records. We know of only a few fiddlers senior to him. Col. John A. Pattee, from Michigan, was born in 1844, and Henry Gilliland, the recording partner of Eck Robertson, in 1845. There is a 1925 disc by "Uncle" John Wilder from Plymouth, Vermont, born in 1845, the uncle of Calvin Coolidge, and another by Captain M. J. Bonner of Fort Worth, Texas, who is thought to have been born about 1848. Ambrose "Uncle Am" Stuart from Virginia recorded before most of these, in 1924, but was born a year or two after Uncle Jimmy. These men were more than a decade older than venerable fiddlers such as Alabama's Dix Hollis or Galax, Virginia's Emmett Lundy, and a whole generation before Fiddlin' John Carson. Listening to them, we may well be hearing fiddling styles from as far back in history as the Civil War.

Forty-four years after Uncle Jimmy Thompson's death, Opry old-timers like Roy Acuff and Johnny Wright gathered to commemorate this pioneer figure of the Grand Ole Opry with a new gravestone.

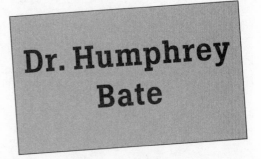

(1875–1936)

A white-haired old gentleman sits in solitary dignity at the WSM microphone, his fiddle tucked beneath his copiously bearded chin. Yes, it is Uncle Jimmy Thompson, and what a splendid image he provides for the birth of country radio. But though his legendary broadcast of November 28, 1925, may have been the origin of the Grand Ole Opry, he was not the first man to send country tunes rocking on the WSM airwaves out of Nashville. Three weeks earlier, at the Ryman Auditorium, later the Opry's most famous home, a broadcast benefit show for the city's police force had presented not only Uncle Dave Macon, singing and picking his banjo, but a small-town doctor who "directed his old-time orchestra [in] . . . several numbers of old time and popular music."

In fact Dr. Humphrey Bate and his friends had been playing on both WSM and another Nashville station, WDAD, for several months beforehand. And in the early days of the WSM Saturday night barn dance, before it acquired the name of the Grand Ole Opry, Bate's was one of the bands most often heard.

Playlist
•• *Nashville—The Early String Bands Volume Two* (County CD-3522): "Billy Wilson," "Karo," "Uncle Jimmy's Favorite Fiddling Pieces" •• *The Cornshucker's Frolic Vol. 2* (Yazoo 2046): "Lynchburg"

Dr. Humphrey Bate band, some time before 1920. Left to right: A. C. Womack, Bate, Sewall (Rabbit) Chenault, (first name unknown) Womack, P. D. "Boss" Belote. (Author's collection)

Left to right: Gale Binkley, Walter Ligget, Bate, Raymond Ligget, Bill Barret, Burt Hutcherson, Monroe Hooberry. (OTM collection)

Their records, a dozen sides cut at a single session in 1928, show us why. The rustic vocal refrains, fiddling, and banjo-picking are commonplace ingredients of old-time stringband music, but Oscar Albright's bowed bass playing gives the group thrust, and Bate's deft and delightful harmonica playing ripples through the plain fabric like a thread of silver. We ought to be happy that we have their versions of "Ham Beats All Meat," "Throw the Old Cow over the Fence," or "Take Your Foot Out of the Mud and Put It in the Sand"—indeed, we should be quite glad just to have those *titles*—but we must regret missing so much else. Some years later Bate wrote out a list of the tunes he knew for the Opry's music librarian. It ran to 125 pieces.

He was born in Sumner County, Tennessee, took his degree in medicine at Vanderbilt University, served in the U.S. Medical Corps during the Spanish-American War, and then inherited his father's practice in Castalian Springs, some thirty miles northeast of Nashville. When not driving round Sumner County with his black bag, he liked to hunt, fish, or play the harmonica. "I have heard him say," his daughter Alcyone recalled, "that most of the tunes he learned, he learned from this old Negro who

was an old man when he was a little boy." At least as early as 1919 he was playing in a local band, and there exists a wonderful photograph of them from about that time, frock-coated, stiff-collared, and bow-tied.

Several pictures of Bate's bands have survived, and they are informative as well as charming. One in which Bate sits with a guitar between his knees is comically, and deliberately, hokey. You would hardly recognize these rubes as the men in sober dark suits who fill most of the other photographs. It is an early example of country music image making, evidently instigated by the Opry's publicists, who played down Bate's medical qualifications while playing up his rural pastimes such as hunting. That explains the angle of a 1930 feature in *Mastertone*, the magazine of the Gibson guitar company, headlined "Keeping a Southern Custom Up-to-Date":

A loud crash, like men running through pine needles, and crackling brush; a lusty shout from the hound's master, urging the animal to "talk to him boy;" a thunder of feet on the bare earth of a little salt lick, and half a dozen panting joyous men burst into the open, and you see them for the first time.

(OTM collection)

The 'possum hunters.

To a native of the South, the scene is familiar. It suggests 'possum and sweet potatoes. It has become more familiar in the last year or two, since the inauguration of the "Grand Ol' Opry." . . . Dr. Humphrey Bate hits the trail in the wake of the old "Pot licker" hound with his "Possum Hunters." . . . To make their enactment of the great Southern sport authentic, Dr. Bate and his Hunters don the characteristic garb of a 'possum hunter of yore, and start whooping things up just as darkness falls, which is 8 o'clock, Central Standard Time, every Saturday night.

The Opry, like the country music business as a whole, changed rapidly in its first decade. Some of the old-time bands were soon dropped from the roster, but the Possum Hunters stayed, and even participated in the first tour organized by the WSM Artists Service Bureau, in 1931, playing in cities as far west as Des Moines, Iowa. "The act was real simple," Alcyone remembered. "My aunt and I"—who sang and danced—"wore little country dresses. . . .

Father wore work pants and suspenders. We stopped the show every time."

The Possum Hunters were still playing on the Opry when Dr. Bate died, and a lineup under that name was maintained until the mid-'60s, when the survivors, Alcyone and guitarist Staley Walton, merged with the Opry's other harmonica-led band, the Crook Brothers.

Playlist
•• *Nashville—The Early String Bands Volume One* (County CD-3521): "Eighth of January," "Green Backed Dollar Bill," "My Wife Died Saturday Night," "Throw the Old Cow over the Fence" •• *Raw Fiddle* (Rounder Select 1160); "Billy in the Low Ground" •• *Black & White Hillbilly Music* (Trikont US-0226): "Ham Beats All Meat," "How Many Biscuits Can You Eat" •• *Harmonica Masters* (Yazoo 2019): "Take Your Foot Out of the Mud and Put It in the Sand"

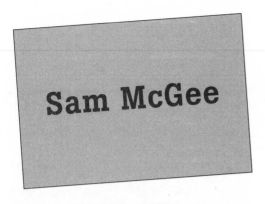

Sam McGee

(1894–1975)

Sam McGee recorded country music's first guitar instrumentals. The fact is unarguable, a matter of historical record in both senses, but the modern listener is entitled to wonder if the recordings are by now merely quaint. After all, it was over eighty years ago that the quiet farmer from Franklin, Tennessee, sat down in a New York studio and played "Buck Dancer's Choice" and "The Franklin Blues."

In fact they have lost little of their power to impress, whether it is a guitarist listening or just a music lover. Sam McGee played with exemplary speed, accuracy, and vigor on tunes that country pickers still think of as test pieces. Neither "The Franklin Blues" nor "The Knoxville Blues," another guitar solo he cut a few days later, actually is a blues; the titles were assigned by the record company, looking to cash in on the still-fresh blues craze. Both are neat packages of guitar tunes current in the early years of the twentieth century, quick-change medleys of rags, waltzes, and pieces from the common stock shared by white and black musicians such as "Poor Boy" and "Railroad Bill."

Even in these pre-blues tunes, however, McGee exhibits bluesy touches, and when, eight years later, he cut his "Railroad Blues," it was a superb example of blues picking, replete with slides, pulled notes, and even a guitar imitation of his Grand Ole Opry colleague DeFord Bailey's harmonica playing. Along this brilliantly executed guitar line he strung a series of humorous blues verses, culminating in a splendid image: "I met a little

Sam McGee (left) with Fiddlin' Arthur Smith and Kirk McGee. (Author's collection)

gypsy in a fortune-telling place—she read my mind, then she slapped my face."

Between those sessions in 1926 and 1934 McGee spent much of his time as the sidekick of Uncle Dave Macon. They had met in the early '20s.

I'd quit farming and I'd taken a notion that I'd want to run a blacksmith shop. So I got started shoeing horses and repairing old wagons and things. I went to Franklin one day to pick up some materials, and Uncle Dave was playing at the courthouse here. And he was throwing that banjo around and picking, you know, and passing the hat and people throwing in money. And I thought, well, that's pretty good. I believe I could do that.

A couple of months later him and Fiddling Sid Harkreader came up and put on an entertainment at the school here, which was adjoining my place. Just as quick as the entertainment was over, I made a break up to the stage to invite him to come spend the night with me. He says, "Yes, we'd be glad to." So we went on to my house and he looked over in the corner and I had an old rusty Martin guitar. And he says, "Mr. McGee"—he called me that then, you know—"Mr. McGee, I see you got a guitar there. You play?" I says, "Well, I play a little sometimes to entertain myself and my friends." He said, "Well, get it and play a number for me." So I played "The Missouri Waltz." Hadn't been out but a little while and people loved it. And he'd never heard nobody play an instrumental number with a guitar. He says, "That's great. Would you consider playing some dates with me?" So we played those dates and he liked me fine. So then we bought us a car and we played together for about twenty years.

McGee played on many of Macon's recordings, either guitar or banjo—or the two in one, a six-string banjo tuned like a guitar. Sometimes they were joined by Sam's brother Kirk, who was adept on several instruments and a fine singer besides. During one of Uncle Dave's sessions in 1927 the brothers were let loose on a dozen old-time songs ranging from "Salty Dog Blues" to the comic song "C-H-I-C-K-E-N Spells Chicken." The following year Sam indulged in a couple of picking displays with his banjo-guitar, "Easy Rider" and "Chevrolet Car," which hammered home his claim to be a blues musician of the first class.

Later in the '30s Sam and Kirk joined the fiery Tennessee fiddler Arthur Smith to create one of the most instrumentally talented trios of their day. The brothers had been associated with the Grand Ole Opry practically since its start and never lost their membership of its cast, though in later years they were scarcely regarded as headliners. In the '70s, however, thanks to his reputation as a pioneer figure of American vernacular guitar, Sam was invited to several major festivals and made a handful of albums. He continued to live in Franklin, play guitar, and work on his farm up to his death.

Playlist

• *Sam McGee (1926–1934)* (Document DOCD-8036)
• *Country Guitar* (Arhoolie CD 9009) [later recordings]
•• *Old-Time Mountain Guitar* (County CD-3512): "Buck Dancer's Choice," "The Franklin Blues" •• *Nashville—The Early String Bands Volume One* (County CD-3521): "Charming Bill" (McGee Brothers), "Chevrolet Car," "Salt Lake City Blues" (McGee Brothers) •• *Nashville—The Early String Bands Volume Two* (County CD-3522): "Brown's Ferry Blues," "Old Master's Runaway" (both McGee Brothers) •• *Old-Time Mountain Blues* (County CO-CD-3528): "Easy Rider," "Railroad Blues" •• *Close to Home: Old Time Music from Mike Seeger's Collection* (Smithsonian/Folkways SF CD 40097): "Black Mountain Rag" (with Arthur Smith & Kirk McGee) •• *Hard Times Come Again No More Vol. 2* (Yazoo 2037): "The Tramp" (McGee Brothers)

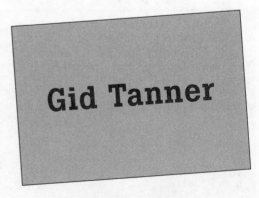

Gid Tanner

(1884/5–1960)

Splendid old hayseed though he was, Gid Tanner is more of a name in old-time music than he quite deserved to be. Lovers of stringband

They still dance the quadrille to "Turkey in the Straw" and "Old Zip Coon" down in some parts of Georgia, and we have with us a picture taken at the Convention of the Old Time Fiddlers, held in Atlanta. These men are mountaineers, and they are champions. In the centre is "Uncle" Billy Porterdale, 85 years young, and still doing the buck and wing as well as any youngster in the State.
Copyright by Shannon-Holloman.

There is a possibility that you can look at this picture without laughing. In that case, please line up with the iron-faced persons behind "Gid" Tanner, the famous Georgia fiddler, who is seen here playing and singing "When Hell Broke Loose in Georgia."
(C) Shannon-Holloman.

This is a photograph of Mrs. Charles Pergler, wife of the Commissioner of the Czechoslovak Republic, and her interesting family.
(C) Harris & Ewing.

This Is the Month of Roses in Pasadena, and This Picture Shows a Prize-Winning Float in a Recent Tournament There.

You May Not Believe It, but the Persons in This Photograph Are All Boys, Every One of Them. The Picture Is a Scene from "The Mikado," Recently Produced at the Riverdale Country School, at Which $500 Was Raised for the Fund for Relief in the Near East.

Pictorial news from round the world, *The Daily Oklahoman*, March 30, 1919. Top left: Standing behind "Uncle" Billy Porterdale, left to right: Unidentified, Fiddlin' John Carson, Land Norris, Earl Johnson. Top right: Gid Tanner. (Author's collection)

music, particularly the hectic, swirling kind made in north Georgia, rate the band billed as Gid Tanner & His Skillet-Lickers among the finest of their era, yet the nominal leader was regarded by some of the group's members as something between a passenger and a joke.

Unlike them, James Gideon Tanner belonged to the older entertainment tradition of the minstrel and medicine shows. He wore funny hats, cracked jokes, and sang crazy old songs about moonshine and chin whiskers. The *Atlanta Journal* paints a vivid picture of him performing at a fiddlers' convention in the city in 1914:

Perhaps the greatest novelty of the evening was Gid Tanner, a husky youth with a tan face and shoes, roan hair, a mouth as flexible as a minstrel show coon's, and a voice which ranged from a high falsetto to a rambling [rumbling? TR] bass. Mr. Tanner fiddled and sang "Everybody Works but Father," introducing under pressure of applause a series of parodies, introducing Decatur street types and the well known Judge Brayles, whose fame has penetrated to the wiregrass. His reception was so enthusiastic that it was with difficulty the performance was permitted to proceed.

Tanner first recorded in 1924, in a duo with Riley Puckett, and the success of those discs persuaded their record company, Columbia, to invest heavily in hillbilly music. It also explains why, when the Skillet-Lickers entered the recording arena in April 1926, Tanner was credited as their leader, though Puckett's name also appeared on the labels in recognition of his role as the primary singer. In fact, an outfit variously called the Lickskillet Orchestra or the Lick the Skillet Band, of which Tanner was not a member, had already been playing on Atlanta radio for a couple of years.

The Skillet-Lickers may be the first instance in country music of a group created primarily for the medium of records. Their repertoire perfectly fitted the phrase Columbia used for its hillbilly catalog, "Old Familiar Tunes," being stuffed with hoary pieces like "Turkey in the Straw," "Alabama Jubilee," and "Watermelon on the Vine." What distinguished their recordings from other, plainer renditions was the orchestration: two or three harmonized fiddles, Puckett's rich vocals and eccentrically swinging guitar lines, Tanner singing a falsetto harmony like a crow on helium. Nothing quite so deliberately hokey had been committed to disc before. Their first release, "Bully of the Town" coupled with "Pass around the Bottle and We'll All Take a Drink," sold over 200,000

copies and would be the fourth best-selling disc in Columbia's hillbilly list. The four discs produced at that April 1926 session achieved total sales of more than half a million. These were figures to make even the most blasé of record company executives blink and sit up.

Then some of the band put their heads together and devised rustic playlets such as "A Corn Licker Still in Georgia," in which the musicians make and sell—and drink—moonshine whiskey, interrupting their work only to bribe local law officers with free samples and impromptu music. These comic skits sold very well, too: the first "Corn Licker Still" racked up sales of more than 160,000, and was succeeded by six more two-part discs on the same topic, as well as a further eleven double-sided rural dramas like "Hog Killing Day," "A Day at the County Fair," "A Bee Hunt on Hell for Sartin Creek," and "Prohibition—Yes or No," which gave the impressionists in the band the opportunity to vent their imitations of greased pigs, angry bees, and temperance lecturers.

Tanner probably had little to do with the composition of these sketches, which are likely to have been conceived and at least partly written by the fiddlers Clayton McMichen and Bert Layne, perhaps with occasional help from Dan Hornsby, an Atlanta radio personality who participates in several of them. But even if they were complicit in their creation, younger members of the band like McMichen and Layne may not have taken much satisfaction from the Skillet-Lickers' comedy records. McMichen in particular was bent on turning the old-time fiddle band into an up-to-the-minute swing unit, capable of delivering country and pop songs with equal panache. Playing fiddle while Tanner chanted "Old McDonald Had a Farm" was not his idea of a good time. It was an uneasy collaboration of talents.

But for a while it worked: the Skillet-Lickers were successful enough, and made enough money—session fees alone netted the principal members about $1,000 a year—to keep the team working together more or less amicably throughout the heyday of hillbilly recording in the late '20s and early '30s. The younger men satisfied their different ambition by forming splinter groups to play fancy fiddle harmonies in waltz time on tunes like "Sweet Bunch of Daisies," while Tanner and his ally Fate Norris, the band's banjo player, made occasional outings as a rustic duo.

The group finally broke up in 1931, but Tanner evidently retained the right to the name, because three years later he led a new Skillet-Lickers lineup for Bluebird at a high-spirited farewell session. Puckett was still on the team, and Gid was joined in the fiddle section by his son Gordon. A couple of their recordings from that date, the effervescent breakdowns "Down Yonder" and "Back Up and Push," did amazing business: they were still in catalog in the '50s, and even appeared on a 45-rpm single.

After the glory days Gid went back to farming and did no more public music making that we know of. In the '70s Gordon, who had become a respected fiddle maker in their home town of Dacula, created a Junior Skillet-Lickers in his father's memory, and a third-generation lineup plays the old tunes there still. The Skillet-Lickers' music has also been preserved in the affectionate re-creations of later groups like the Highwoods String Band and the Freight Hoppers.

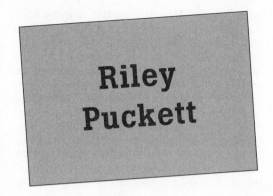

(1894–1946)

Eighty years later, musicians still argue about how Riley Puckett came by his unique style of guitar playing. A great deal of his work in the 1920s was with fiddlers, north Georgia associates like Gid Tanner and Clayton McMichen, or stringbands like the Skillet-Lickers, in which all three played. Guitarists in that kind of backup role typically play chords and occasional runs. Puckett disdained anything so obvious. Much of the time he simply didn't bother to play chords. Instead he

Playlist
• *Old-Time Fiddle Tunes and Songs from North Georgia* (County CD-3509) (Skillet-Lickers)
• *The Skillet Lickers Volume 1* to *Volume 6* (Document DOCD-8056 to 8061) [complete except for "A Corn Licker Still in Georgia"]
• *A Corn Licker Still in Georgia* (Voyager VRCD 303) [the full sequence of "A Corn Licker Still in Georgia," Parts 1 to 14]
•• *Serenade in the Mountains* (JSP JSP 7780 4CD): "Three Nights Drunk" (with Riley Puckett) •• *Old Mountain: Stringband Songs & Tunes* (Living Era CD AJA 5577): "Molly, Put the Kettle On" (Skillet-Lickers) •• *Good for What Ails You: Music of the Medicine Shows 1926–1937* (Old Hat CD-1005 2CD): "It Ain't Gonna Rain No Mo'" (Skillet-Lickers), "Tanner's Boarding House" (with Riley Puckett) •• *Bluegrass Bonanza* (Proper PROPER-BOX 29 4CD): "Hawkins Rag," "On Tanner's Farm," "Tanner's Boarding House" (Skillet-Lickers) [1934 recordings] •• *The Story That the Crow Told Me Vol. 2* (Yazoo 2052): "Devilish Mary" (Skillet-Lickers)

(Special Collections & Archives, Georgia State University Library)

Puckett plays with A. A. Gray. (OTM collection)

swung into single-note runs on the lower strings, obeying his own sense of time and melody, listening, as they say, to a different drummer.

But the effect was wonderful. While the fiddlers are strutting their stuff in familiar breakdowns, Puckett plays the traitor in their midst, lighting fuses for small explosions that rock the music on its heels. "Riley?" said another Skillet-Licker, fiddler Lowe Stokes. "He was hard to play with."

Self-willed, independent—it is no more than you would expect of a blind man in rural Georgia in the early twentieth century. George Riley Puckett was born in Alpharetta, a small town some fifteen miles from Atlanta, and lost his sight in childhood after incompetent treatment of an eye infection. About the age of seven he went to the Georgia Academy for the Blind in Macon, but after that we lose track of him until his name begins to appear in Atlanta radio logs in 1922. He is said to have learned banjo at the age of twelve, and then guitar. Music was one of the few occupations open to a blind Southerner, and in his teens and twenties he probably made his living from it, traveling from small town to small town, singing on street corners for small change from passers-by.

If he had been born only a guitar player,

Puckett would barely have survived, but he was much more. Many of the earliest country records were by fiddlers or stringbands, and if there was any singing at all, it was incidental. What vocal recordings were made were generally for the sake of the song rather than the singer. Puckett changed all that. When he opened his mouth, a gorgeous sound came out, a warm friendly baritone that could take on anything—love songs and ballads, comic numbers, hoedown verses, blue yodels—and make it beautiful. He never sounded anything but country, but his diction was excellent, and the microphone loved him. He was country music's first singing star. When Jimmie Rodgers appeared on the scene in 1927, Puckett had already been making best-selling records for three years, songs like "Blue Ridge Mountain Blues" and "Rock All Our Babies to Sleep."

He began recording in March 1924, and at two sessions for Columbia that year he and Gid Tanner, who partnered him, cut more than fifty sides, the majority featuring Puckett as vocalist. He continued to be one of Columbia's mainstays, recording solo, as a guitar accompanist to fiddlers (Tanner, McMichen, Stokes, Bill Helms) and to singer Oscar Ford, in vocal duets with "Bob Nichols" (McMichen under a pseudonym) and Hugh Cross, as guitarist for

Riley Puckett on WNOX, Knoxville, Tennessee. (Special Collections & Archives, Georgia State University Library)

McMichen's Melody Men and others of Mac's bands, and especially as a linchpin of the Skillet-Lickers, in both their regular band recordings and their comedy sketches. His vocals with the Skillet-Lickers were crucial. "Riley proved the people wanted to hear singin'," said McMichen. "And if he didn't sing on the records, why, they didn't sell much."

Altogether, of the nearly 800 releases in Columbia's hillbilly list, Puckett had a part in almost 150—an unrivalled 19 percent of the entire catalog. Even putting aside the Skillet-Lickers' discs and the sketches, Puckett's sixty-six solo and duet records amassed sales of almost one and three quarter million. Only Vernon Dalhart did more for Columbia's balance sheet.

So when the Skillet-Lickers broke up in the early '30s, Puckett was sufficiently well known to work as a single, and he broadcast on radio stations from West Virginia to Chicago. He did make a last appearance with a Skillet-Licker lineup, at a 1934 Bluebird session with Tanner and mandolinist Ted Hawkins, which added another four dozen sides to his tally. But most of his own eighty-odd recordings in the '30s and early '40s were solo, or with one or two accompanying musicians, and he took the opportunity to cast his song-catching net still

wider. McMichen might allege that Puckett was behind the times, but his discography indicates otherwise, for it is packed with contemporary material: Tin Pan Alley hillbilly songs like "Ole Faithful" and "Take Me Back to My Boots and Saddle," out-and-out pop like "When I Grow Too Old to Dream" and "Ma! (He's Making Eyes at Me)," even the British compositions "South of the Border" and "Red Sails in the Sunset." He listened, his daughter Blanche remembered, to "anything and everything. The radio was the first thing that went on in the morning. He could sit and listen to a song one time and just pick it up and sing it all the way through."

Playlist
• *Old Time Greats Volume 2* (Old Homestead OH-4174)
•• *When the Sun Goes Down Vol. 10: East Virginia Blues* (Bluebird 60085): "Nobody's Business" •• *Hillbilly Blues 1928–1946* (Frémeaux FA 065 2CD): "Chain Gang Blues" •• *Guitare Country 1926–1950* (Frémeaux FA 5007 2CD): "The Darkey's Wail" (as "John Henry") •• *Sounds like Jimmie Rodgers* (JSP JSP 7751 4CD): "Away Out on the Mountain," "Back on the Texas Plains," "The Moonshiner's Dream," "Peach Pickin' Time in Georgia," "Sleep Baby Sleep," " 'Way Out There" •• *Serenade in the Mountains* (JSP JSP 7780 4CD): "The Boston Burglar," "Don't Let Your Deal Go Down," "Everybody Works but Father," "Short Life of Trouble" •• *Howdy!: 25 Hillbilly All-Time Greats* (Living Era CD AJA 5140): "Red Wing" •• *American Yodeling 1911–1946* (Trikont US-0246): "Sauerkraut" see also Clayton McMichen, Gid Tanner

Clayton McMichen

(1900–70)

People talk about progressive country as if it were a new idea, but as far back as the mid-1920s there were players dedicated to exchanging hillbilly overalls for pressed pants. "That [term] 'hillbilly,' we fought it, teeth and toenails," said fiddler Clayton McMichen. "Took every insult ever slurred that you could possibly send towards anybody. And fought the pioneer trail for it, to bring it in, make somethin' out of it. Make it popular."

Mac said that in a long, candid interview he gave in 1959. Looking back on his time with the most popular stringband of the '20s, the Skillet-Lickers, he brusquely dismissed their banjoist Fate Norris and their nominal leader, fiddler Gid Tanner. "I didn't like playing with them, because they just was about thirty years behind us, or forty, in the music business. No use to sit here and lie about it—I had two or three in there couldn't play." He had some respect for the band's singing guitarist Riley Puckett. Oddly, he never mentioned Lowe Stokes, the other lead fiddler on many of their records, and one of the finest players of his time.

Mac himself, a fiddler since the age of eleven, was a skilful purveyor of the standard fiddle tune repertoire, but he never particularly cared for it. As early as 1922, when he made his first broadcast on Atlanta's WSB with the Home Town Boys—himself and the Whitten and Hawkins brothers, on that occasion, but the group had numerous configurations—he declared his musical interests in a selection of popular numbers such as "Dapper Dan," "Alabama Jubilee," and "The Sunshine of Your Smile." On another broadcast two days later he played "Ring Waltz," "Sweet Bunch of Daisies," and "St. Louis Blues." Not a hoedown tune in sight.

Hardly surprising, then, that Mac's sophisticated nose was put out of joint by Tanner's "hollerin' and singin' that falsetto voice and

foolishness." It was a further source of irritation that the band he helped to create didn't, at first, even acknowledge him: the initial releases were billed as by "Gid Tanner & His Skillet-Lickers with Riley Puckett." "I finally raised so much Hell about it," Mac wrote to the Australian researcher John Edwards in 1958, "that Frank B. Walker [Columbia's A&R man] put my name on all the records but the damage had already been done and Gid was starting to be known as the greatest old time fiddler in the country."

Once Mac was ratified as a significant member of the Skillet-Lickers, with his name on the record labels, he persuaded Columbia to sponsor him as a crossover artist, playing stringband arrangements of pop tunes like "Wabash Blues" and "Ain't She Sweet?" with two or three harmonized fiddles and the teenaged "Stranger" Malone on clarinet. Frank Walker was dubious at first, telling Mac that if he wanted music like that, all he had to do was stick his head out of the window of his New York office and holler, but the first release by McMichen's Melody Men, "Let Me Call You Sweetheart" and "Sweet Bunch of Daisies," sold almost 100,000 copies, and several of its successors were strong sellers.

Perhaps at Walker's urging, though, Mac continued to record old-time tunes, usually as fiddle–guitar duets with Puckett. At the beginning of "Rye Straw," a tune with an indelicate story behind it, he even offers a little fiddle scholarship:

"Folks, gon' play you a little tune here, me and old Riley. You know up in St. Louis they call this tune 'The Lady's Fancy,' and around Chicago they call it 'The Joke on the Puppy.' Down here in Georgia where we live, we just call it just plain old 'Rye Straw'—and Riley, I just *dare* you to sing the verse in it."

"Boy," says Riley, "I'm sure gonna sing it."

"Well, let your conscience be your guide."

In 1931, when the Skillet-Lickers finally split under the pressure of its members' mutual antagonism, Mac formed the first of a series of groups called the Georgia Wildcats, trading on an epithet awarded years before when he won a fiddlers' contest and a newspaperman dubbed him "The North Georgia Wildcat." The group backed Jimmie Rodgers at a session in 1932, where Mac provided Rodgers with one of his prettiest songs, "Peach Pickin' Time Down in Georgia." Over the next few years, younger players like guitarist Slim Bryant and fiddler Carl Cotner

The Home Town Boys, 1922: McMichen and the Whitten brothers. (Author's collection)

Another Home Town Boys line-up, early 1920s: McMichen, Robert Stephens Jr. and Sr., Lowe Stokes. (Author's collection)

helped Mac to design a polished modern country music with no debts whatsoever to the boisterous old-timey sound of the Skillet-Lickers. No more "Ya Gotta Quit Kickin' My Dog Around," but the Western styling of "Little Darling, I'll Be Yours" and the almost Western Swing of "Frankie and Johnnie." "St. Louis Blues," which he had recorded, soberly enough, as a fiddle solo in 1927, was brusquely updated in the song "St. Louis Woman (Got Her Diamond in the Hock Shop Now)." His policy was epitomized in the lyrics of one of his songs, where he declared, "I don't give a heck about corny fiddlin'—it's drivin' me insane! I'm a-gonna learn to swing!"

During the '30s and early '40s the Georgia Wildcats could be heard from a variety of radio stations in the East and South, where younger artists such as Spade Cooley and Pee Wee King listened attentively to their uptown swing stylings. Cooley later told Mac that when he first heard the Wildcats' recording of "Farewell Blues," he "sat up and burned a pan

Playlist
• *The Legendary Fiddler* (BACM CD D 081)
• *The Legendary Fiddler Vol. 2* (BACM CD D 142) [the better of the two BACM CDs]
•• *The Columbia Label: Classic Old Time Music* (BACM CD D 057): "House of David Blues" (McMichen's Melody Men) •• *Serenade in the Mountains* (JSP JSP 7780 4CD): "The Original Arkansas Traveler, Parts 1 & 2" (with Dan Hornsby), "Slim Gal" (with Riley Puckett) •• *Bluegrass Breakdown* (Vanguard VCD 77006): "Alabama Jubilee," "Sourwood Mountain" [from the 1964 Newport Folk Festival] •• *The Rose Grew Round the Briar: Early American Rural Love Songs Vol. 2* (Yazoo 2031): "Grave in the Pines" •• *Hard Times Come Again No More Vol. 2* (Yazoo 2037): "The Arkansas Sheik" (with Riley Puckett) •• *The Story That the Crow Told Me Vol. 1* (Yazoo 2051): "Old Molly Hare" (with Riley Puckett)

(Author's collection)

of midnight oil" over it. "I just set up the style of my band from that record."

From 1934 to 1939 Mac was a seldom toppled National Fiddling Champion, and although he quit full-time music in the '40s, he kept his hand in on the fiddle. He was still playing well in the '60s when he appeared at the Newport Folk Festival. But age did not mellow his view of the past. A few months before his death he wrote to the historian Norm Cohen, who had been quizzing him about the old days, "Don't ask me any more questions about that bunch of nothing down there in Atlanta. They were all a bunch of stab-you-in-the-back no-goods, . . . and the more I can forget them, and the longer I can keep them forgotten, the better."

A mid-1930s line-up of the Wildcats, with fiddler Bert Layne (left). "Slim" Bryant stands on the right. (OTM collection)

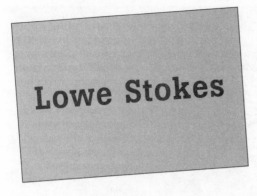

Lowe Stokes

(1900–83)

tive twin fiddling that was one of the group's trademarks.

But Lowe Stokes was no mystery man. He led several recording bands in his own name, such as his North Georgians and Pot Lickers, cut some brilliant versions of fiddle tunes with Puckett or guitarist Mike Whitten, and participated in many of the comedy sketch recordings that were such a craze in the late 1920s, like the "Corn Licker Still in Georgia" series, where his gruff voice, rough as a corn-cob, is instantly recognizable.

Unlike his fellow Skillet-Lickers Riley Puckett, Gid Tanner, and Clayton McMichen, Lowe Stokes seldom had his name on the labels of the band's records, but for much of its recording life he was a crucial component in its sound, combining with McMichen to produce the skillful, exhilarating, and innova-

He was born Marcus Lowell Stokes in Elijay, Georgia, and learned his fiddling from his father and older brother and the locally celebrated Joe Lee—"the best fiddler I ever heard." One of the tunes he got from Lee was "Katy Hill"—"I'd win most of my prizes on that"—and in due course he recorded it. Lee bought the disc and told his pupil proudly, "That sounds just like me!" In 1924 Stokes made his name by beating all comers at an Atlanta fiddlers' convention.

Lowe Stokes (2nd left) with (left to right) Bert Layne, unidentified, Clayton McMichen, Claude Davis. (OTM collection)

Unusually, it is not just fading newspaper cuttings and hazy microfilm that commemorate this event. Following an amused article in the magazine *Literary Digest*, the poet Stephen Vincent Benet published a long narrative poem called "The Mountain Whippoorwill, or How Hill-Billy Jim Won the Great Fiddlers Prize." Young Jim defeats the reigning champion, "Old Dan Wheeling," a character possibly inspired by Fiddlin' John Carson, who used to feature Stokes in his shows as "the little guy who beat me." "If I can't be the best," Carson would say, "I'll carry the best with me!"

In the late '20s Stokes hung out with McMichen, Bert Layne, singer-guitarist Claude Davis, and other fellows in the Skillet-Lickers' orbit. Like Mac, he got a lot of session work, backing singers or strengthening the sound of a band. His own discs with his North Georgians, like McMichen's with his Melody Men, can fairly be described as the progressive country music of their day. They are rags, blues, old pop songs like "Sailing on the Robert E. Lee"—anything but what we think of as "old-time." "Left All Alone Again Blues," for instance, is a tune by Jerome Kern, and "Everybody's Doing It" by Irving Berlin, while "Take Me to the Land of Jazz" and "Wave That Frame" have take-off guitar solos that could almost have been played by the jazzman Eddie Lang, but were in fact by Perry Bechtel, an Atlanta guitarist and banjoist who used to appear on radio billed as "The Boy with a Thousand Fingers."

Perhaps Stokes's choicest record, though, is the Brunswick disc of "Swamp Cat Rag" and "Citaco," issued under the name of The Swamp Rooters. Stokes and A. A. Gray, an older fiddler from Tallapoosa, Georgia, negotiate a pair of red-hot hoedown tunes with the speed, skill, and daring of racing drivers.

Just six weeks later, on Christmas Day 1930, Stokes was injured in a shooting accident, in the worst way possible for a fiddler. Bert Layne was visiting not far away.

Some fellow said, "Bert, did you know Lowe Stokes got his hand shot off?" And I says, "Well, my God, let's go," and I broke for Cartersville. That was the town. He'd got shot the day before. And an old doctor drank a half a pint of whiskey and so did Lowe, and they sat down in a chair out in the yard, and that old doctor took that hand off and dressed it up, right out there in that yard. And about an hour or so after that, when I got in there looking for him, he was sittin' up in a barber chair getting a shave. I never saw a man with such a nerve in all my life.

Almost incredibly, he learned to play again. Layne and a mechanic friend made a hook for him so that he could hold a bow, and within a year or so he was back in music professionally. He stayed in the business, either playing or as a booking agent, for another twenty years before retiring.

Then in 1981 someone gave him a fiddle for a Christmas present. He became interested again and started playing locally, around Chouteau, Oklahoma, where he now had his home. He lived just long enough to be reunited with a couple of old Skillet-Licker friends at the 1982 Brandywine Mountain Music Convention.

Playlist

• *Lowe Stokes—Volume 1 (1927–1930)* (Document DOCD-8045)
•• *Old-Time Mountain Guitar* (County CD-3512): "Take Me to the Land of Jazz" •• *Hard Times in the Country* (County CO-CD-3527): "Prohibition Is a Failure," "Wish I Had Stayed in the Wagon Yard" •• *Old-Time Mountain Blues* (County CO-CD-3528): "Left All Alone Again Blues" •• *Mountain Blues* (JSP JSP 7740 4CD): "Bone Dry Blues," "Left All Alone Again Blues," "Unexplained Blues" •• *Times Ain't Like They Used to Be Vol. 3* (Yazoo 2047): "Billy in the Low Ground" •• *Times Ain't Like They Used to Be Vol. 5* (Yazoo 2063): "Citaco" (as The Swamp Rooters) •• *Times Ain't Like They Used to Be Vol. 6* (Yazoo 2064): "Swamp Cat Rag" (as The Swamp Rooters) •• *The Stuff That Dreams Are Made Of* (Yazoo 2202 2CD): "Chicken Don't Roost Too High," "Up Jumped the Rabbit" (both as Georgia Pot Lickers)

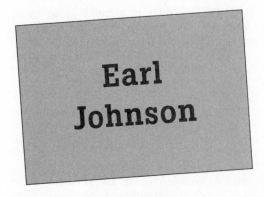

Earl Johnson

(1886–1965)

In the few pictures of Earl Johnson he is almost always wearing a sober dark suit, as if he were about to leave for his legal practice or undertaker's office. Yet nothing could be more lawless or vivacious than the fiddling that helter-skeltered through the records Johnson made in the 1920s and early '30s, discs that match the Skillet-Lickers' in exuberance. Indeed, Johnson's stringband, variously called his Clodhoppers or his Dixie Entertainers, was put up by OKeh Records as a direct rival of the Columbia label's band.

Robert Earl Johnson was born in Gwinnett County, not far from Atlanta. He learned his music partly from his father, whose fiddle he would surreptitiously play while its owner was at work on his farm, and partly through a correspondence course with a music school in Chicago, becoming equally capable with old-time breakdowns, popular songs, hymns, and light classical material.

He played with two of his brothers, Albert on banjo and Ester on guitar, and they made a name for themselves in and around Atlanta until Albert and Ester died in an epidemic in 1923. Earl then hooked up with the celebrated Fiddlin' John Carson. In the late '20s his demonic fiddling would be heard on many of the records by Carson and his Virginia Reelers, but by then he had opened his own recording account with ferocious versions of old favorites like "Ain't Nobody's Business," "Dixie," and "Shortenin' Bread," banjo player Emmett Bankston singing a shrill falsetto part in the style of Gid Tanner. The guitar role was taken by either Byrd Moore, a lean Virginian who worked with several old-time recording artists, or Lee "Red" Henderson, or perhaps sometimes both of them. Whatever the composition of the band, it underpinned Johnson's gleeful singing and fiddling with a furious and unremitting rhythm that made the Skillet-Lickers sound almost sedate.

(These OKeh sides, though the first to place Johnson's name in the foreground, were not his debut recordings. A couple of years earlier, in 1925, he had participated in a session for Paramount involving Henderson, Gid Tanner's brother Arthur, and other, uncertainly identified musicians, but the records give only a faint impression of his playing.)

At further sessions for OKeh and one for Victor, between 1927 and 1931, Johnson wrote many excellent entries in his recording log. There was a sprightly blues, "All Night Long," with strutting guitar breaks by Moore, and a more dignified slow one, "Wire Grass Drag." Skidding versions of "Mississippi Sawyer," lightly disguised as "Mississippi Jubilee," and "Johnnie, Get Your Gun." A wonderful "Arkansaw Traveler" with comic spoken exchanges by Johnson and Henderson—

"Ain't you got no knives?"
"No, sir!"
"Ain't you got no forks?"
"No, sir!"
"How'd you do, then?"
"Tolerable well, thank you. How are you?"

There was also a strange session when vivacious renditions of "Nigger in the Cotton Patch," "G Rag," and other breakdowns were repeatedly interrupted by mad laughter—a

Earl Johnson (seated) with (left to right) Byrd Moore, Lee Henderson, Emmett Bankston. (OTM collection)

Earl Johnson & His Dixie Entertainers, Victor Records, 1929. (Author's collection)

throwback to the brief vogue, in the earliest days of recording, for laughing records. But many of Johnson's disc selections were the grizzled comic songs that Georgia musicians seem to have been specially attached to: "Buy a Half Pint and Stay in the Wagon Yard," probably a cover of Lowe Stokes's recording, made a year before; "He's a Beaut," which shares the tune of "I Don't Reckon It'll Happen Again for Months," also done by Bill Chitwood and Bud Landress; the carefree "I Lost My Girl," or the chicken-stealers' anthem "They Don't Roost Too High for Me."

Occasionally he chose a more serious subject. "The Little Grave in Georgia," also recorded by Carson as "The Grave of Little Mary Phagan," concerned a shocking Atlanta murder of 1913, while one of his last discs was the hymn "I Know That My Redeemer Liveth," which he sang as a duet with his wife Lula Bell and fiddled with much fancy fingerwork.

Between fiddling contests and occasional radio appearances, Johnson kept up a semi-professional musical career until the '30s or '40s, though latterly without the comradeship of Emmett Bankston, who committed suicide. He was still playing in May 1965, not far off his eightieth birthday, when he participated in the Stone Mountain Fiddlers' Convention. He died a few days later from a heart attack.

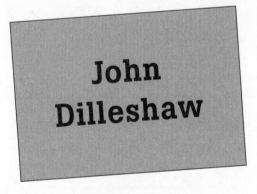

John Dilleshaw

(1896–1941)

I want to hear 'Soldier's Joy,'" grunts the drunk, lurching against the bandstand. "Can't you play 'Soldier's Joy' for me?"

"I'm playing 'Soldier's Joy' now, buddy," the bandleader replies brusquely.

"Doesn't sound like 'Soldier's Joy' to me," mutters the drunk. "I want to hear 'Soldier's Joy.'"

"Quit blowing your breath in my face," retorts the musician. "You smell like Fido."

Undeterred, the drunk keeps staggering back to the bandstand with his refrain "I want to hear 'Soldier's Joy.'" Eventually, losing patience, the leader waves the band to a halt, puts down his guitar, and slugs the troublemaker on the head with a bottle. As the

stunned figure is dragged out, the musicians strike up "Soldier's Joy" again.

A few minutes later the drunk returns with some of his friends. By now the band has moved on to another old-time breakdown, "Liberty." The resulting fracas involves more bottles, and a gun. Amid thuds, shots, and shrieks from the womenfolk, the drunk is carried out once more, moaning, "My head's done cut open here!"

"Well," says the bandleader, "I guess I cleaned that bunch out. On with the dance!"

Talk to old-time musicians and you will hear a lot of dance hall stories, but that one is purely imaginary. It all happened, if you can believe it, on a record: "The Square Dance Fight on Ball Top Mountain," by a gang of musicians who called themselves Seven Foot Dilly and His Dill Pickles.

John Dilleshaw was not quite a seven-footer, but he was a tall man, even among the rangy hillfolk of north Georgia. He was born near New Hope, in Paulding County, to the northwest of Atlanta. In his late teens he injured his foot in a shooting accident, and while recuperating he began to take an interest in the guitar, encouraged by a local black musician named Bill Turner. Soon he was playing with other Paulding County musicians. "You ain't never heard a guitar picker like him," recalled a friend from those days. "He wasn't no extra singer, but he was real on the guitar. Them old timers didn't go in for foolishness. They went for the sound of them boxes."

By 1925 he was broadcasting on Atlanta's WSB, paired with guitarist Charles S. Brook as the "Gibson Kings." Brook (or Brooks: the sources are skittish about the correct spelling of his name) was frequently heard on WSB in the second half of the '20s; a cabinet maker by profession, he devised a "broomophone," a novelty fiddle made out of a broomstick and a cigar box, and often played it on air. Dilleshaw's day job was with the city's Fire Department. As well as their duet act, the two men appeared in a quintet called the Dixie String Band, which probably gave Dilleshaw the idea of forming his own musical organization; at any rate, by 1929 he had put one together with a young fellow Paulding Countian, Harry Kiker, on fiddle, and the father and son team of Pink and Shorty Lindsey, Pink playing bass and Shorty tenor banjo.

In March that year OKeh Records sent a crew to Atlanta to record local talent and Dilleshaw made his first record, credited to

JUNE RELEASES OF
OLD·TIME·TUNES
ON VOCALION RECORDS
All Vocalion Records 75c each

Record No. 5419

Featuring

Seven Foot Dilly
(Guitar)

Bill Kiker
(Fiddle)

Shorty Lindsey
(Banjo)

Pink Lindsey
(Bass)

NOVELTY

The Square Dance Fight on Bald   5419
     Top Mountain--Part 1   75c

The Square Dance Fight on Bald
     Top Mountain--Part 2
     Descriptive Novelty Featuring:
     Seven Foot Dilly, Pink Lindsey,
         Shorty Lindsey, Bill Kiker

*This record introduces Seven Foot
Dilly and his Company from Georgia—
you're going to here from him a lot on
Vocalion Records—watch for him.*

VOCAL

San Antonio   5422
Back to Old Smoky Mountain   75c
    Vocal with Guitars, Banjo, Violin
      Smoky Mountain Ramblers

If You Think I'm Not Worthy   5423
Jack and May   Vocal with Guitar   75c
            Bess Pennington

I'm Sad and Blue   .   .   5425
Maudaline   Vocal with   75c
    Zither-Guitar and Harmonica
      Perry County Music Makers

"Gibson Guitar Kings" Popular at WSB

JOHN DILLESHAW, HEFTY FIRE-FIGHTER, with his talka-
tive guitar, and C. S. Brook, guitarist, and broomophone artist, form
one of the most popular combinations ever heard from WSB. Their
joint harmonies have brought scores of requests and messages of com-
mendation. Both are well versed in the art of entertaining the public, and have made innumerable friends among The Journal's radio
audience. They will be heard again before long at some scheduled
hour.

(OTM collection)

"John Dilleshaw & The String Marvel." The anonymous wonder-picker, possibly Brook or Pink Lindsey, may play the lead in the gorgeous guitar duet rendition of "Spanish Fandango." Then in 1930 the four-piece band made a bunch of sides for another visiting recording team, this time from Vocalion. In the wake of the Skillet-Lickers, every label wanted a versatile stringband that could provide both dance music and comedy sketches, and it seems likely that in the Dill Pickles Vocalion thought they had found one.

Some of the discs were two-part playlets with music: the "Square Dance Fight," a fiddling contest, a barbecue cookout. "A Fiddler's Tryout in Georgia" features the distinguished Tallapoosa fiddler A. A. Gray and another strong old player, Fiddlin' Joe Brown from Burnt Hickory in Paulding County, who recorded nowhere else. There was also a pair of breathtaking fiddle and guitar duets by Dilly and Gray, "Tallapoosa Bound" and "Streak o' Lean—Streak o' Fat." A couple more were by Dilly on his own, picking guitar and talking the blues, somewhat in the style of Chris Bouchillon but with a rich vein of extravagant nonsense that was all Dilly. "I was goin' along down the road, not thinkin' of a thing in the world. I walked into a store. Bought myself a Brogan hat, Stetson pair of shoes, box-toed pair of socks. All dressed up and nowhere to go. Ain't it awful?"

The rest were stringband hoedowns by the Dill Pickles with titles like "Lye Soap" and "Bust Down Stomp," driven by Dilly's muscular left-handed guitar runs and Pink Lindsey's bowed bass and enlivened by Dilly's stream-of-consciousness monologs about farming conditions, the weather, pigs, baseball, and getting off with other men's wives. In "Pickin' off Peanuts" he apologizes for arriving late because he had to get his mule shod and do some shopping for his old lady. As "Lye Soap" draws to a close he remarks, "I ain't heard anybody say anything about money yet." "Say," he exclaims somewhere else, "can you reach over here and blow my nose?"

There is nothing else remotely like this in old-time music. Seven Foot Dilly was unique, a hillbilly stand-up comedian who also played hot guitar.

Playlist
• *John Dilleshaw (1929–1930)* (Document DOCD-8002)
•• *Old-Time Mountain Guitar* (County CD-3512): "Spanish Fandango" •• *Guitare Country 1926–1950* (Frémeaux FA 5007 2CD): "Spanish Fandango" •• *Old Mountain: Stringband Songs & Tunes* (Living Era CD AJA 5577): "Lye Soap" •• *Down in the Basement* (Old Hat CD-1004): "The Old Ark's a'Moving" (with A. A. Gray) •• *The Roots of Rap* (Yazoo 2018): "Pickin' Off Peanuts" •• *The Cornshucker's Frolic Vol. 1* (Yazoo 2045): "Sand Mountain Drag" •• *The Cornshucker's Frolic Vol. 2* (Yazoo 2046): "A Fiddler's Tryout in Georgia Parts 1 & 2" •• *Times Ain't Like They Used to Be Vol. 7* (Yazoo 2067): "Bust Down Stomp" •• *Times Ain't Like They Used to Be Vol. 8* (Yazoo 2068): "Sand Mountain Drag"

Georgia Yellow Hammers

George O. "Bud"
Landress (1882–1966) •
William H. (Bill)
Chitwood (1888–1961) •
Charles Ernest
Moody (1891–1977) •
C. Philip Reeve (1897–1949) •
F. Clyde Evans (1906–74)

If you want to peer into the workings of the early country music record business, actually see the wheels go round, you can hardly do better than hold the magnifying glass of hindsight over Gordon County, Georgia. Between 1924 and 1931 this northwestern segment of the Peachtree State blossomed with stringbands, gospel groups, fiddle–guitar duos, and a brother trio, making every kind of old-time music from standard dance tunes to Sacred Harp hymns, by way of blues, gospel quartet numbers, heart songs, and comic novelties.

The first we hear of Gordon County's musicians is the ten sides made in November 1924 by the fiddler Bill Chitwood and the singer and banjo player Bud Landress. Earlier that year, Columbia Records had waxed a number of songs and tunes by the Atlanta-based duo of Gid Tanner and Riley Puckett, and Chitwood and Landress were Brunswick's response. These were all pre-electrical recordings and dim at best, but Brunswick's sounded even more like mice in a matchbox, and the Gordon County pair were not recalled to their New York studios. But they did drive down to Atlanta a few months later to play on the radio. "You Are Invited," ran an ad in the *Calhoun Times* on Thursday, April 2, 1925, placed by the Calhoun Radio Distributing Co., "to visit our radio demonstration room and hear WSB, Atlanta, broadcast the Gordon

The Georgia Yellow Hammers, c. 1927. Left to right: (standing) Phil Reeve, Ernest Moody; (seated) Bud Landress, Bill Chitwood. (Courtesy of Dixie Landress)

County Program, Friday noon and Friday night at 10:45."

Two years on, however, thanks to a combination of new technology and a strategically clever producer, Landress and Chitwood had another shot. Teamed with a couple of acquaintances, they ran out on to the field in the colors of Victor Records and the name of the

The Georgia Yellow Hammers attend the Victor Elyea Sales Convention, Atlanta, August 27, 1928. Standing, right to left: Lawrence Moss (manager of the L. Moss Music Co., Calhoun), Bill Chitwood, Ernest Moody, Phil Reeve, Bud Landress. Most of the other guests are unidentified, but seated third from left is a clearly recognizable Jimmie Rodgers. (Courtesy Georgia Archives, Vanishing Georgia Collection, ful0517)

Georgia Yellow Hammers. The band's first two sessions, in February and August 1927, with repertoire choices like "Pass around the Bottle" and "I'm S-A-V-E-D," showed how attentively they, or their producer Ralph Peer, had studied the previous year's Columbia releases by the Skillet-Licker circle. The band gave Victor several strong sellers and, in Landress's departed-mother song "The Picture on the Wall," a solid hit. Over the next couple of years the Yellow Hammers were among the stalwarts of Victor's hillbilly catalog—and of other companies', too, as they turned out for OKeh calling themselves Bill Chitwood & His Georgia Mountaineers and for Columbia as the Clyde Evans Band.

The most prominent member of the group was Bud Landress, who wrote or reset most of their songs, usually sang lead, and could switch from banjo to fiddle if necessary; he plays fiddle throughout the August '27 and February '28 sessions, which Chitwood didn't attend. But the Yellow Hammers were truly a team, in a way the Skillet-Lickers never managed to be: everyone had a role. Chitwood, when he was there, played twisting fiddle lines and sang bass in the quartet choruses that were the group's specialty. Ernest Moody strummed his uke and arranged the harmony. Phil Reeve punctuated the melodies with swoops of slide guitar, was quite an adept yodeler, and looked after the band's business. His day job was at the L. Moss Music Store in Calhoun, the county seat, where many of the area's musicians lived, and his knowledge of the record trade enabled him to build a good relationship with Ralph Peer.

Reeve ensured that their original material was copyrighted, yielding a regular income in royalties. At the height of their popularity, Landress told a reporter from the *Atlanta Journal and Constitution* in 1953, "I received about $400 every three months from royalties alone . . . and that was back when a dollar looked as big as a wagon wheel." Reeve also entered into management contracts with other local musicians, notably Andrew and Jim Baxter, an African-American father and son team from Calhoun who made a dozen remarkable records of fiddle tunes and blues.

Moody, too, was an active fixer, his position as president of the Gordon County Singing Convention enabling him to organize singing groups to record sacred music for Paramount and Vocalion. But the full extent of Gordon County entrepreneurism would make too long a story for this book, and we must return to the Yellow Hammers, if for no other reason than to celebrate songs like "Fourth of July at a Country Fair," a Munchausenesque tale of balloon rides and horse thieving, or the solemn quartet singing on the Victorian parlor piece "Kiss Me Quick"—or the ludicrous effect of that frock-coated harmony when applied to the words of "Song of the Doodle Bug": "doodle doodle doodle, bug bug bug . . ." The Georgia Yellow Hammers are the great absurdists of old-time music.

For that, certainly, we must thank Landress, who must have dredged some of these strange songs from the silt of half-forgotten sheet music and "pocket songsters." Everyone in Gordon County who remembers him—and there are not a few, still, who do—acknowledges him as a born comedian and master-of-ceremonies, in his element when the band performed on summer Saturday evenings at Calhoun's Gentlemen's Park, by the railroad tracks. (There was a Ladies' Park across the street, but it isn't clear whether string music—or at least *this* kind of string music—was acceptable there.) His charisma is attested, too, by stories in the *Calhoun Times*, which report him presiding over fiddlers' contests and suchlike entertainments. Commenting on the October 1927 fiddlers' convention staged by the American Legion at the Calhoun courthouse, the paper said: "Bud Landers [*sic*] added to his laurels as a one-man steering committee." In common with the other band-members, Landress didn't rely on music for a living. At different times he did railroad work, farmed, and was a prison guard and bloodhound trainer at the Fulton County jail. Chitwood farmed, and Moody taught school.

If the original lineup of the Yellow Hammers had a weakness, compared with the Skillet-Lickers, it was that they lacked a strong guitarist. They seem to have realized that themselves, and soon coopted Clyde Evans, who lent some muscle to their recordings, as well as his name to the Columbia coupling of "How I Got My Gal" and "All Gone Now," two of the group's strongest performances, recorded in early November 1929. Later that month the band made their last sides for Victor, though it was an oddly divided effort: first Landress recorded with a couple of musicians from outside the county, though still using the GYH billing, then the other "original" Yellow Hammers cut some sides without him. But if there were dissensions, they were healed by the following April, when Landress, Chitwood, Moody, and Reeve regathered to cut a record of sacred songs for Columbia as the Gordon County Quartet.

It was their last bow. The bleak climate of the Depression was as unfriendly to the Georgia Yellow Hammers as it was to so many of their contemporaries in hillbilly music. Phil Reeve moved away for a few years, working for the U.S. Agricultural Department; Bill Chitwood carried on farming; Bud Landress ran a café. Clyde Evans served in the Marines in World War II, then returned home to manage a clothing store. Ernest Moody organized the music for the Calhoun Presbyterian and First United Methodist churches, and wrote some 200 hymns; the best known, "Kneel at the Cross," became a standard. Perhaps only the peculiar musical atmosphere of the late '20s, when old-time songs and tunes briefly enjoyed the patronage of the recording industry, could have assembled this group of disparate personalities, but in those few years their work together was an eloquent expression of collective wit, ingenuity, and fun.

South Georgia Highballers

Melgie Ward (1882–1965) •
Vander Everidge (1886–1938) •
Albert Everidge (c. 1900–55)

The South Georgia Highballers cut just two discs, but if it weren't for their name on the labels you would hardly guess they were made by the same men.

"Green River Train" and "Mister Johnson, Turn Me Aloose" are by a trio of fiddler, guitarist, and saw player, the last bowing a handsaw to produce a sweet, otherworldly humming that anticipates the oscillating electronic sounds of the theremin. A few other old-time musicians played the saw, Asa Martin for one, but this is its only appearance on a 1920s hillbilly record. "Green River" is the popular old-time song "New River Train," while "Mister Johnson" is a "coon song" of the ragtime era.

But if those performances suggest a sort of hillbilly tearoom music, "Blue Grass Twist" and "Bibb County Grind" belong to the tavern, or the barbershop—anywhere men hang out and shoot the breeze. The guitarist who had played the steady rhythm on the trio tunes shows us what he can do when he's fingerpicking. As he releases a prodigal display of blues licks, the other two musicians put their instruments down and urge him on: "Quit your foolishness round here! . . . Go away from this country! . . . Kill yourself!"

"Old Vandy can win a woman's heart and make a bulldog jump a fence," interjects one of them approvingly in "Bibb County Grind," and on the other side, "That's the way them girls cry when he's pickin' for 'em."

"I'm gonna learn how to play one like that myself," he adds, "—'fore my old lady quits me."

The men who served this fascinating mixed menu of music were guitarist Vander (formally Vander Bilt) Everidge and fiddler Melgie Ward, who were in their forties, and Vander's twenty-seven-year-old nephew Albert, the saw player, all from around Macon, Georgia. As the Everidge family recall, the group was active in the '20s and early '30s, playing at

The South Georgia Highballers, 1927. (Courtesy of Big Boy Woods)

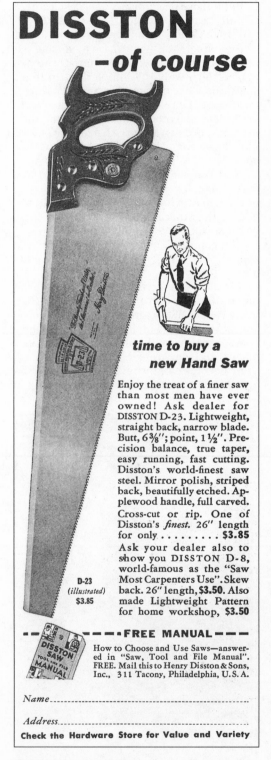

(Author's collection)

fiddlers' conventions and town halls all over Georgia, often in company with musicians like Fiddlin' John Carson, Gid Tanner, and Riley Puckett. Melgie Ward is a more shadowy figure, but we know that in March 1926 he placed second after Clayton McMichen in an old fiddlers' convention at Macon's city auditorium.

Unlike his older partners, Albert Everidge could compete in two categories, not only playing the saw but dancing the buck-and-wing, at which he was a champion. His son Rubin remembers how he once tried to go up against the fiddlers with his saw, but the officials running the contest ruled him out. One of the fiddlers interceded for him, adding, "If he can play a tune on that thing, I'll break my fiddle over this chair and give him any money I've made." Albert played "The Waltz You Saved for Me," and the fiddler did what he said he'd do.

"He could make a handsaw talk," says Al Everidge, another son. "He played anything. Waltzes like 'Fifty Years Ago Waltz' and 'Girl of My Dreams' . . . not dance music. Listening music."

"He would shop for a handsaw for half a day," adds Rubin. "Plucking it, bending it. . . ." His favorite brand was a Disston saw.

Not a lot of south Georgia musicians got to record. Probably the earliest were the fiddle and guitar team of George Walburn and Emmett Hethcox, who made about a dozen records between 1925 and 1931. Though remembered round Macon, they were from LaGrange in west Georgia. But the OKeh team that came to Atlanta in October 1927 must have been impressed by the varied skills of the Everidges. They would have had more: Albert was supposed to sing some numbers but had a bad cold. As his son Al points out, you can detect his sore throat when he talks during Vander's guitar solos. The talking, inci-dentally, was not devised for the record: they went through that routine in their stage act, too, peppering Vander's guitar music with asides like "Strut your stuff!" and "Get on down!" "It was like a family tradition," says Al.

OKeh were sufficiently taken with the novelty of "Blue Grass Twist" and "Bibb County Grind" that they hastened the disc's release: it was on sale before the end of November, barely six weeks after its recording. Produc-tion time was usually closer to three months. The trio disc followed in January 1928. Albert's widow remembered that Melgie Ward's foot-patting on that record was too loud, so the engineers had to hush it with a pillow.

In the '30s Albert started to raise a family and needed steady work, first as a tree surgeon, later a termite exterminator. The band broke up, and a few years later Vander died in a street accident, run down by a car on Macon's Broadway. But Albert's sons, Al, Rubin, and Alton, all took up music, singing and playing guitar. Rubin has been working in country music in upstate New York since the '50s, opening shows for many visiting stars, and is the director of the New York State Country Music Hall of Fame. Al, who has stayed closer to home, is proud to have sung the first country song on Macon's WMAZ-TV (Channel 13), in September 1953. (It was Webb Pierce's "Slowly.") He also initiated a Friday-night "Jubilee" at the Macon Farmers' Market, which still goes on, run by his son David.

The Cofer Brothers

Leon Cofer (1899–1968) • Paul Cofer (1901–67)

Boy, I'm sore today."
  "What in the heck are you sore about?"
  "Old Keno the rent man. He's as mean as h— . . . as he can be."

After this surly snatch of dialog, the Cofer Brothers strike up a jerky ten-bar blues dedicated to "Keno, the Rent Man." The ragged voices, sharp-cornered fiddle, and stuttering guitar evoke the gaunt hillbillies of Depression

---

Playlist
•• *Old-Time Mountain Guitar* (County CD-3512): "Blue Grass Twist" •• *Old-Time Mountain Blues* (County CO-CD-3528): "Bibb County Grind" •• *Guitare Country 1926–1950* (Frémeaux FA 5007 2CD): "Blue Grass Twist" •• *Mountain Blues* (JSP JSP 7740 4CD): "Bibb County Grind," "Blue Grass Twist" •• *Serenade in the Mountains* (JSP JSP 7780 4CD): "Mister Johnson, Turn Me Aloose"

Paul and Leon Cofer. (Author's collection)

The Georgia Crackers, from a 1927 OKeh catalog. (OTM collection)

photographs no less keenly than the song's grim narrative of being stomped into the dirt by a debt collector. In another version of the theme, "Riley the Furniture Man," the brothers watch disconsolately as their household effects are repossessed: "Riley's been here, got my furniture, and gone." Rubbing their noses in their shame, Riley orders their very beds to be dragged out and thrown on to his cart by his black assistant.

Gene Wiggins, historian of old-time music in Georgia, who discovered much of what we know about Leon Cofer and his fiddling brother Paul, remarked that the music of the Hancock County duo "evoked a vision of carefree, amoral poor whites or blacks—fugitives from an Erskine Caldwell novel. . . . The truth is that the Cofer Brothers were not that sort of people at all." No, indeed: their father was a Methodist minister, singing teacher, and sawmill owner. But, fortunately for those who like their music gamey, "people they knew as friends were that sort, and the most special kind of music the Cofers had to offer . . . was the music of those friends."

But if we are to read the Cofers as interpreters of lives different from and harsher than their own, we can still see the unplaned edges of their music as unfaked signs of authenticity. For one thing, it is profoundly bluesy, and Wiggins reported that the Cofers did learn from black musicians in their predominantly African-American mid-Georgia county. Among the other numbers they recorded, whether as a duo or with an added friend, guitarist Ben Evans, under the name of the Georgia Crackers, were black songs like "Diamond Joe" (which Bob Dylan has revived, though probably not from the Crackers' recording) and "The Georgia Black Bottom," one of the innumerable variations on "Deep Elm Blues."

Altogether, at three sessions in 1927 and '29, the Cofers cut fourteen sides. The first tune they committed to record was a faded postcard from a Victorian scrapbook—"I remember, I remember, the place where I was born, where the morning glories twine around my door at early morn"—but their abrasive harmony prepares the listener for funkier narratives: old-timey favorites like "The All Go Hungry Hash House" or "The Georgia Hobo," their version of the widespread theme that Jimmie Rodgers reworked for "Waiting for a Train"; the chainsaw fiddling of "Rock That Cradle Lucy"; and a gritty chunk of cracker elbow-nudging called "How Long?" "I got a girl, she's long and tall, got a hump on her back'd make a panther squall. How long? Wooh! How long!"

Playlist

• *Georgia Stringbands—Vol. 1 (1927–1930)* (Document DOCD-8021) [includes all the recordings by the Cofer Brothers and Georgia Crackers]
•• *Hard Times in the Country* (County CO-CD-3527): "Riley the Furniture Man" •• *Mountain Blues* (JSP JSP 7740 4CD): "Stockade Blues" •• *O Brothers! Family Harmony in Old-Time Music & Bluegrass* (Living Era CD AJA 5467): "Keno, the Rent Man" •• *Times Ain't Like They Used to Be Vol. 2* (Yazoo 2029): "Riley the Furniture Man" •• *Hard Times Come Again No More Vol. 1* (Yazoo 2036): "The Georgia Hobo" •• *Hard Times Come Again No More Vol. 2* (Yazoo 2037): "Keno, the Rent Man" •• *My Rough and Rowdy Ways Vol. 2* (Yazoo 2040): "The Georgia Black Bottom" •• *The Cornshucker's Frolic Vol. 2* (Yazoo 2046): "Rock That Cradle Lucy"

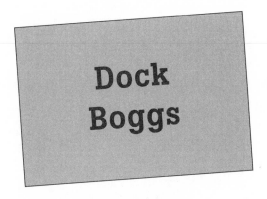

Dock Boggs

(1898–1971)

Certain voices from country music's past speak to us of times and places we can barely imagine. In a thoughtful essay accompanying one of Dock Boggs's albums, Jon Pankake observed that his life "is measured out not only in decades but in entire cultures. When he was a child, he often followed a local Negro musician up and down the dusty roads pestering the man to play a tune on the banjo. . . . Dock can still vividly describe the passion with which he heard music as a child, the vision it became to him, the preciousness and rareness of its sound.

"Today Dock in his old age moves easily through the modern world of . . . Carnegie Hall audiences and Newport ovations and television interviews. A long way from the dusty road. But the passion of the child hearing his first precious notes of music remains to awe us, we whose brains are so chock full of electronic echoes and broadcast jangle that we will never, never hear music the way Dock heard it from that banjo player."

Pankake wrote that over forty years ago, little knowing how much more of "electronic echoes and broadcast jangle" would besiege a music enthusiast in the twenty-first century. If Dock Boggs was remote then, he seems almost prehistoric now—a man of the Cumberland Mountains, from farming and hunting people who were turning reluctantly to a different life as they left the backwoods for the dusty hell of the coal mines.

Moran Boggs worked as a miner for forty-five years, from the age of twelve. He knew at first hand the battles between the mine owners and the unions, the violence of a society where even peaceable men carried .38 Specials, the chill wind of mechanization, the long shadow of premature unemployment. And in his last years he returned to the music he had made as a young man, the ballads, blues, and banjo tunes for which he was once well enough known to put them on records. He made only a dozen sides in the 1920s, but in pieces like "Country Blues," "Pretty Polly," and "Down South Blues" he effected an eerie musical union between the dispassionate narratives of hillbilly balladry and the personal testimonies of the blues.

"Blues" figures in the titles of six of his recordings. Only one, "Down South Blues," has a conventional blues structure (he learned it, he said, from a record by one of the early black women singers: probably Clara Smith's 1923 disc with the same title, which contains four of his five verses), and "Hard Luck Blues" is not much more than a couple of jokes set to a jogalong banjo tune. But it is not their shape or even their words that give these songs their blues character, it is what Boggs adds of himself: the steadfast gaze of the famous studio portrait of 1927, a vision of a way of life changing too fast for comfort. One of the things blues are about is impermanence, and Boggs had a clear view, too clear for his peace of mind, of the disappearing landmarks of his world. "Thinking of those good times gone by me, knowing that I once had a home. . . ." Whatever the form his song takes, Boggs invests his interpretation with

Dock Boggs, 1927. (Courtesy of Mike Seeger)

a sense of the sorrow that lies beyond the words one can find. "Done all I can do, I've said all I can say": it is the summing-up not of a despairing but of a frustrated man—not capitulating to fate but beating, unbeaten, at its door.

Some time during the Depression, he pawned his banjo. When Mike Seeger tracked him down in 1963 Boggs had begun to play again, but he often brooded over his years of silence. He worried, too, whether a truly God-fearing man had any business with what many in his community called sinful music. Yet there's little in Dock Boggs of the roistering, hell-raising spirit of Charlie Poole, none of the sly suggestiveness of Jimmie Rodgers. His songs, especially the ones he recorded in his sixties on albums for Folkways, are redolent of hard old times: bandits and drunkards, prisoners and prodigal songs and pit disasters. "Sometimes," he said to Seeger, "I get tears in my voice." They were tears not of self-pity but of sadness for all the troubles in the world.

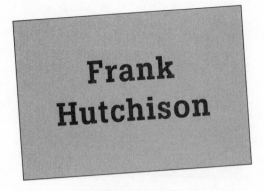

Frank Hutchison

(1897–1945)

Playlist
• *Country Blues: Complete Early Recordings (1927–29)* (Revenant RVN 205)
• *His Folkways Years 1963–1968* (Smithsonian Folkways SF 40108 2CD) [the contents of three Folkways LPs recorded in the '60s]
•• *Old-Time Music from South-West Virginia* (County CO-CD-3523): "Country Blues," "Danville Girl," "Down South Blues," "Old Rub Alcohol Blues," "Pretty Polly" •• *Old-Time Mountain Blues* (County CO-CD-3528): "Down South Blues" •• *Close to Home: Old Time Music from Mike Seeger's Collection* (Smithsonian Folkways SF CD 40097): "Sugar Baby" •• *Prayers from Hell* (Trikont US-0267): "Country Blues," "Down South Blues," "New Prisoner's Song," "Pretty Polly," "Sugar Baby" •• *The Rose Grew Round the Briar: Early American Rural Love Songs Vol. 1* (Yazoo 2030): "False Hearted Lover Blues" •• *The Rose Grew Round the Briar: Early American Rural Love Songs Vol. 2* (Yazoo 2031): "Lost Love Blues" •• *The Stuff That Dreams Are Made Of* (Yazoo 2202 2CD): "Old Rub Alcohol Blues"

In a makeshift recording studio in a New York hotel room, a slim, hesitant-looking young man bends over his guitar, weaving a dense pattern from the threads of an old melody. His fingers move fast, and for a couple of minutes he improvises deftly. Then, reaching the end of a chorus, he looks up and leans back a little. Perhaps he smiles faintly at the recording engineers. It seems to be a good take, but he is not done yet.

"All right, boys," he says. "This is Frank Hutchison, sittin' back in the Union Square Hotel, just gettin' right on good red liquor." His fingers twitch on the strings. "All right, Frank, step on it!"

He picks up the melody again, tosses it about for another minute, lets it fall. It is July 9, 1929. The Wall Street Crash is only weeks away, and although none of the men in the hotel room is aware of it, Frank Hutchison has just made his last solo recording.

"K. C. Blues"—as the tune will be titled when the record is issued; in fact it's "John Henry" without the words—is a fine ending to a day's work and a life's record making. Since his debut almost three years earlier Hutchison has recorded over thirty songs and tunes, and has become one of the OKeh label's main hillbilly attractions. He sings crusty versions of old-time songs like "Burglar Man" and "Cumberland Gap," and ballads such as "Stackalee," which, nearly seventy years later, Bob Dylan will record in a remarkably faithful rendition. But his big thing is blues. "Just blues of all kinds," remembered Aunt Jennie Wilson, a banjo-playing contemporary. "He always specialized in the blues. He could really play them, too."

She was right about that. Hutchison's first record was a blues double-header, the defiant "Worried Blues"—"got the worried blues, got no heart to cry—if the blues don't kill me, boys, I'll never die"—and "Train That Carried

(OTM collection)

the Girl from Town," which rolls, smooth as polished steel, on the rhythms of Hutchison's flashing slide guitar. Another slide number, "Cannon Ball Blues," is reminiscent of a similarly titled song by the Memphis bluesman Furry Lewis. Another, "Logan County Blues," proves to be "Spanish Fandango," a favorite tune of turn-of-the-century parlor guitarists. He also played fast finger-picked ragtime tunes like "The West Virginia Rag," which he subsequently set words to and recorded as "Coney Isle" (turned into a big hit in 1960 by Cowboy

(Author's collection)

During the Depression Hutchison tried playing on riverboats on the Ohio. He and his wife moved up into Ohio, then back to West Virginia to run a store. By the end of the '30s he had given up music. He died in Ohio from liver cancer.

Playlist
• *Frank Hutchison—Volume 1 (1926–1929)* (Document DOCD-8003)
• *Old-Time Music from West Virginia (1927–1929): Williamson Brothers & Curry, Dick Justice, Frank Hutchison* (Document DOCD-8004) [contains the eight recordings by Hutchison which could not be fitted on to the preceding CD, as well as the work of a West Virginia contemporary, singer-guitarist Dick Justice]
• *Worried Blues* (JSP JSPCD 7743 4CD) [duplicates the Document CDs and adds material by Kelly Harrell and others]
•• *Old-Time Mountain Guitar* (County CD-3512): "Logan County Blues" •• *Old-Time Music of West Virginia Volume One* (County CD-3518): "The Miner's Blues," "The West Virginia Rag" •• *Old-Time Music of West Virginia Volume Two* (County CD-3519): "The Last Scene of the Titanic," "Worried Blues" •• *Hard Times in the Country* (County CO-CD-3527): "The Miner's Blues" •• *Old-Time Mountain Blues* (County CO-CD-3528): "Cannon Ball Blues" •• *Guitare Country 1926–1950* (Frémeaux FA 5007 2CD): "K.C. Blues" •• *Prayers from Hell* (Trikont US-0267): "Hell Bound Train," "Stackalee" •• *The Roots of Rap* (Yazoo 2018): "Back in My Home Town" •• *Times Ain't Like They Used to Be Vol. 3* (Yazoo 2047): "Worried Blues" •• *Times Ain't Like They Used to Be Vol. 8* (Yazoo 2068): "The Train That Carried the Girl from Town"

Copas, retitled "Alabam' ") and then again, with different words, as "Johnny and Jane."

Where did Hutchison learn to play like this? In the notes to the (now deleted) CD *White Country Blues*, Charles Wolfe located him in "a rough, isolated mountain community in Logan County, West Virginia, a mining area where miners both black and white found themselves living in company towns and doing some of the most dangerous work in the country. The miners led lives as desperate as sharecroppers in the Mississippi Delta, and many of them, white and black, were drawn to the blues."

Hutchison had been a miner himself, but according to Aunt Jennie Wilson he was slightly disabled, which may have forced him out of the mines and into music. The fiddler Sherman Lawson, who played and recorded with him, said that he got much of his blues knowledge from another disabled man, a black singer and guitarist from Logan County named Bill Hunt. According to Lawson, Hunt gave Hutchison the idea of playing with a slide—"makin' it cry"—and furnished him with both the songs on his debut record.

Entrancing though Hutchison's guitar pieces are, they represent only part of his skill. Several of his early sides were old tunes like "The Wild Horse" and "Long Way to Tipperary," played on guitar and rack harmonica—like Henry Whitter, but good. He was evidently a capable entertainer. "He could put on a pretty good show," said Lawson. "He knowed how to get it on there!"

Tom Darby & Jimmie Tarlton

Tom Darby (c. 1890–1971) • Jimmie Tarlton (1892–1979)

Sweet, sexy, or stinging, the sound of the steel guitar is intrinsic to country music, and always has been. Eighty years ago, when today's gleaming electric ironing boards were unimaginable, the shimmering effects of the pedal steel were obtained on a regular guitar, by a steel bar sliding on a string, with only the natural amplification of the guitar's body.

What brought this sound to country music was the Hawaiian acts on vaudeville shows in the early years of the twentieth century. The music of the islands proved to be an enduring fad, and the record industry promoted it vigorously, employing guitarists like Frank Ferera and troupes like Irene West's Royal Hawaiians to make thousands of discs, initially of genuine Hawaiian melodies but gradually embracing the standard forms of American popular music.

Ferera passed on some tips to a young migrant worker from South Carolina, Johnny James Tarlton. A few years later, now working in a textile mill in Columbus, Georgia, Tarlton teamed up with a local singer and guitarist, Tom Darby. Impressed by their music, a Columbus record store owner arranged an audition with Columbia Records on the company's next recording trip to Atlanta, in April 1927. They passed, made a record, and were invited back to a second session in November, when they cut one of the biggest hillbilly hits of the era, "Birmingham Jail" and "Columbus Stockade Blues." It sold almost 200,000 copies, the kind of sales figure normally reserved for Jimmie Rodgers or, on a good day, The Carter Family.

The songs themselves were antiques. The "Blues" attached to "Columbus Stockade" was

Tom Darby (right) & Jimmie Tarlton, c. 1927. (Bear Family Records)

Tom Darby. (Bear Family Records)

merely a nod to fashion: the verses are in a conventional four-line form and the lyrics deploy motifs decades old: "Go and leave me if you wish to, never let me cross your mind. . . ." What sold them was the combination of plaintive harmony singing and Tarlton's swooping slide guitar. The magic continued to work, and over the next five years the duo recorded more than sixty sides. Their favorite material was nineteenth-century heart songs like "The Black Sheep," "I Left Her at the River," or "Maple on the Hill," of which theirs was the first country recording, but they also liked train and hobo numbers, and blues—genuine blues. Tarlton was an outstandingly expressive blues guitarist and singer, and performances like "Sweet Sarah Blues," "Slow Wicked Blues," and "Rising Sun Blues" are among the finest of their kind. Another exceptional piece is Tarlton's solo recording "Lowe Bonnie," a version of the Old World ballad "Young Hunting," which he learned from his mother.

The pair's records sold consistently well. "Birmingham Jail No. 2," coupled with "Lonesome Railroad," and the blues double-header of "Traveling Yodel Blues" and "Heavy Hearted Blues" were Columbia's second and third biggest sellers of 1929, and later in the year, when sales were dropping fast, "Sweet Sarah

Blues" scored above-average sales. In 1930, when most of Columbia's hillbilly releases were lucky to sell three or four thousand, Darby & Tarlton's "My Little Blue Heaven" and "On the Banks of a Lonely River" topped 17,000, one of only two Columbia discs that year to sell in five figures. (The other—curiously, we may think—was a gospel coupling by a quartet from Lubbock, Texas, who never recorded again.) For a while they might have made a lot of money, had Darby not insisted on their being paid a flat fee rather than royalties. But, like so many of their contemporaries, they had too rugged and unpredictable a style to fit comfortably into the smooth radio-dominated format of '30s country music, and soon they disappeared from the scene.

But not finally. Almost thirty years later, collectors made contact with both men. Darby was still living in Columbus, and still regretting that flat fee decision. "He was rather bitter that he'd never received credit for a lot of his songs," reported his interviewer Robert Nobley, "[but] . . . seemed hopeful of recording again." The following year Nobley and a friend visited Tarlton in Phenix City, Alabama. Though in poor health and nearly blind, he proved to be singing and playing almost as well as ever. He went on to cut an excellent album for Testament, appeared at the Newport and Chicago Folk Festivals, and even filled a week-long engagement at the Ash Grove folk club in Los Angeles.

Playlist
- *Ooze It Up to Me* (Acrobat ACMCD 4016) [emphasizes their blues repertoire]
- *Complete Recordings* (Bear Family BCD 15764 3CD)
- *On the Banks of a Lonely River* (County CD-3503)
- *Tom Darby & Jimmie Tarlton Also Starring Chris Bouchillon* (JSP JSPCD 7746 4CD)
- *Steel Guitar Rag* (HMG HMG 2503) [Tarlton's Testament LP, recorded in 1963–65]

The Carter Family

A. P. Carter (1891–1960) • Sara Dougherty Carter (1899–1979) • Maybelle Addington Carter (1909–78)

In 1936, when I was three years old, we lived on a cotton farm at Dyess, Arkansas, about forty miles from Memphis. And I became a fan of the Carter Family. We bought a radio from Sears Roebuck that year, and I glued my ear to it, and learned every song that Maybelle, Sara, and A. P. recorded. As long as the battery lasted, that is. We had no electricity.

Johnny Cash was just one of hundreds of thousands of Southerners who grew up to the sound of guitar, autoharp, and old-time harmony: instantly recognizable, quickly unforgettable, the music of The Carter Family.

The original trio spanned American life from the pre-Crash 1920s until World War II. In that decade and a half, while they traveled round small mountain towns or sang into the crackly ether, the nation sank into the Depression and hauled itself out again. In some ways, the Carters changed with those changing times; a discreet polish began to show on their music, a knowingness that derived from experience and success. But at its core The Carter Family's music was a rock of old values around which fashion and progress bobbed and ducked without avail. Their audience could turn to it as they might turn to the family Bible, for reassurance and guidance, truth and peace.

For the younger or more restless listener, however, there was enticement and challenge: the rippling guitar melodies of "Wildwood Flower" or "Cannon Ball Blues," the crisscrossing call-and-answer harmonies of "Lonesome Valley" or "Will You Miss Me When I'm Gone," the stories in song of "Little Joe" or "Black Jack David." Ballads and blues, heart songs and hymns, the repertoire of the Carter Family is a microcosm of old-time music itself.

When Alvin Pleasant Carter was born, there had been Carters in Scott County, Virginia, for a little over 200 years. His family was wrapped in music: his father played banjo in his youth, his mother sang old ballads, and her brother was a music teacher and choir leader. A. P. and his brothers and sisters all learned to sing and play. So too, in adjoining Wise County, did Sara Dougherty, and it became part of family lore that A. P. was attracted to the young woman when, traveling through her section selling fruit trees, he heard her playing her autoharp and singing "Engine 143." They were married in 1915. Among the extended family to which A. P. was now connected was Sara's young cousin Maybelle Addington. In due course she began playing guitar and singing with A. P. and Sara, and in 1926 she came farther into the family circle by marrying A. P.'s brother Ezra.

In July 1927 the Carters heard that Victor Records had dispatched a team to Bristol, Tennessee (strictly, Tennessee–Virginia: the state line runs along the middle of the main street), to check out local talent. Undeterred by an unproductive audition with Brunswick a year earlier, A. P. decided to try again. Gladys Carter Millard, his and Sara's first child, remembered the occasion:

Daddy loaded up the old A Model [Ford] with the guitar, harp, Mother, Maebelle [sic], Joe, my 7 month old brother (who was on my Mother's breast) and me a little eight year old girl to mind the baby. . . . It took us almost the whole day to get the 25 miles from our house to Bristol. Dirt roads all the way, creeks to cross, and poor Daddy had three flat tires. It was so hot, the patches melted off almost as fast as he could put them on. . . . We got to Aunt Vergie's house about dark. That would give them the night to rest, tune the instruments, rehearse the songs, and walk the floors and wait for day light and the big day.

On August 1 they cut "Bury Me under the Weeping Willow" and three other songs, and the following day two more. Ralph Peer, the recording supervisor, said years later: "As soon as I heard Sara's voice . . . that was it. . . . I knew that was going to be wonderful." He discovered, too, that the family had a large stock of songs that met his two basic requirements: they had not been on record before, and they were not—or not identifiably—existing copyrights, which meant that Peer could acquire the publishing rights for his company Southern Music.

What Peer was always looking for, both for Southern Music and for Victor's catalog of "Old Familiar Tunes," was songs that had some patina of age or tradition but had been worked over by the artist, rewritten and rearranged to give them an identity of their own. In A. P. he had happened upon a song collector and song fixer who could supply such material by the wagonload: some from collecting trips into the mountains, others from a group of local contacts, some, as the family became better known, from people much farther away. The words of "The Winding Stream," a drowsy story of love in a canoe, were sent to them by a fan in British Columbia.

The Carters became regular Victor artists, releasing between six and ten records a year. "Three years [later]," Peer would recall, "they were very prosperous people indeed. . . . They didn't do anything like Jimmie Rodgers, but they did make a tremendous amount of money comparatively through the years." But by the mid-'30s Victor appeared to have lost interest in them, or they in Victor—they did not get on so well with Eli Oberstein, Peer's successor as recording supervisor—and, encouraged by Peer, they moved elsewhere. If their sides for ARC seem a little drab and self-repeating, they are more than redeemed by the work that followed for Decca. The recording is close and warm, Maybelle's singing snaps into focus, and their repertoire is refreshed by lovely new songs like "My Dixie Darling" and "You Are My Flower."

The Carter Family at the time of their first recordings, 1927. (Author's collection)

Music store ad, *Charleston Gazette*, May 3, 1929. (Author's collection)

Record making occupied no more than a week or two in any year. The rest of the time they gave concerts in Virginia, Tennessee, North Carolina, and sometimes farther afield, typically in schoolhouses, churches, or courthouses. Sometimes, assisted by other members of the clan, they held instrumental tuition courses in schools. Or they might make promotional visits to record stores. "The famous Carter Family . . . will be in the city tomorrow," the *Kingsport Times* announced on Friday, March 29, 1929, "performing at Lamb Company's music store," and on the Sunday the paper reported that "a large crowd of people was present at the affair, several standing far back into the street in front of the store." A week later they were at nearby Horse Creek High School. In November 1931 they were engaged to give a one-hour program at the Kingsport Athletic Club—before an evening of boxing.

By the late '30s the original trio had been expanded, first by A. P. and Sara's daughter Janette, then by Maybelle and Ezra's daughters Helen, June, and Anita. The youngsters received on-the-job training during the family's stints in Texas, where from 1938 to 1942 they spent the winter months at the border station XERA in Del Rio, making weekly transcription discs for stations carrying programs sponsored by their employer, the Consolidated Royal Chemical Corporation, manufacturers of Peruna tonic and Kolorbak hair-dye. Many of these transcriptions survive and have been issued on CD, and if they reveal the second-generation Carters as nervous and somewhat erratic performers, they compensate by showing us aspects of the elder Carters only sketchily described by their other recordings, such as instrumentals by Sara and Maybelle and solos by A. P., as well as the breezy introductions of announcer "Brother Bill" Rinehart.

In 1942 the Carters moved to WBT in Charlotte, North Carolina, but after less than a year the original family split, never to be re-united. Sara, who had divorced A. P. in 1939 after several years of separation, moved with her new husband Coy Bayes to California and semi-retirement, while Maybelle and her daughters embarked on a long cruise of southern radio, finally anchoring in 1950 in Nashville, where June later married the family's one-time radio fan Johnny Cash. A. P. returned to Maces Spring, but continued to write songs and sometimes performed with other family members. There were several recorded reunions and regroupings in the

'50s and '60s, and Maybelle pressed on into the '70s, taking part in the iconic album *Will the Circle Be Unbroken*. The dynastic line has continued through third-generation members like Rosanne Cash and Carlene Carter. The Carters have a lot of history, and it is not over yet. But the heart of their legacy is the 200-odd recordings of the original trio, stately, serene, and imperishable.

Playlist

• *On Border Radio, Vol. 1* (Arhoolie CD 411), *Vol. 2* (Arhoolie CD 412), *Vol. 3* (Arhoolie CD 413) [1939 transcriptions as broadcast on XET, Monterrey]
• *In the Shadow of Clinch Mountain* (Bear Family BCD 15865 12CD) [magnificent boxed set of their recordings from 1927 to 1941 (excluding the border radio transcriptions) with illustrated book]
• *Can the Circle Be Unbroken* (Columbia/Legacy CK 65707)
• *Clinch Mountain Treasures* (County CCS-CD-112) [1940 session]
• *Wildwood Flower* (Living Era CD AJA 5323) [serviceable 25-track selection]
• *RCA Country Legends: The Carter Family* (RCA/BMG Heritage 59266)

phonograph records are unlikely to have been purchasable across a single store counter—but there is truth at its core: Rodgers's records did become staple shopping items in innumerable homes. Few Southerners would have grown up in the late 1920s and '30s unacquainted with that warm, hail-fellow voice, rising and falling at the end of each verse in the cadences of a merry or mournful yodel.

Rodgers was the first country music artist to be the subject of a biography—*My Husband Jimmie Rodgers* by his widow Carrie, published in 1935—and there has been plenty of time for his life's story to become encrusted with anecdotes and adjusted facts. The plain tale, briefly, is that Rodgers was born and raised in Meridian, Mississippi, and spent part of his twenties as a railroad worker. Invalided out of that profession by tuberculosis, he moved to Asheville, North Carolina, whose clean mountain air had made it a popular resort for people with pulmonary and respiratory conditions. There he did odd jobs and hung out with local musicians. Some of the time he played with three other men in a stringband, the Jimmie Rodgers Entertainers, and it was in such company that he rolled up to Bristol, Tennessee, in August 1927 to audition

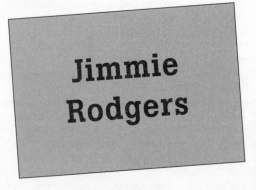

Jimmie Rodgers

(1897–1933)

It is anywhere in the South, *circa* 1930. A customer goes into a store and asks for a pound of butter, a dozen eggs, and the latest Jimmie Rodgers record.

It's one of the oldest stories in old-time music. No doubt it's apocryphal—produce and

(OTM collection)

(OTM collection)

for the visiting team from Victor Records, but Ralph Peer preferred him on his own, singing and yodeling with just his guitar.

His first release, "The Soldier's Sweetheart" and the yodel song "Sleep Baby Sleep," sold only moderately, but Peer saw great things in the lean thirty-year-old and booked him for another session a few months later at one of the company's principal studios, the former Trinity Church in Camden, New Jersey. "Blue Yodel" ("T for Texas, T for Tennessee . . .") initiated a symphony of ringing store tills and ran up a sales total in six figures, a feat Rodgers would repeat over and over again during the next five and a half years, with blue yodels, heart songs, hobo and railroad songs, and, cannily, landscape songs: as well as four compositions about Mississippi, he recorded pieces dedicated to seven other states, plus Memphis and New Orleans, besides several generic southern songs like "Somewhere Down Below the Mason Dixon Line," the last-but-one title he recorded, just days before his death.

When cultural commentators identify a new movement and open a window for observation, adherents and critics alike soon fog it up with heated arguments about definition and priority. For some historians of country music, its father figure is Vernon Dalhart, who disseminated long before anyone else songs that have become staples of the repertoire. Popular music historian Jim Walsh argued that case half a century ago, and it is promulgated today by Dalhart's biographer Jack Palmer. For most judges, however, Dalhart's distant relationship with their conception of country music style forbids his being recognized as anything more than a historical accident: coming first, but in a different race. For them, Dalhart is a faded leaf pressed between the pages of a Victorian songbook, and the artist who truly puts country music on the map—not locally, like a Fiddlin' John Carson, but nationally—is Jimmie Rodgers: a performer whose background, worldview, and expressive style jibe, as Dalhart's do not, with what they take country music and its performers to be like, to be *about*.

It's far from certain that Rodgers would have welcomed that kind of support. For him, the distance between himself and Dalhart may have been no more than the width of a New York street separating one recording studio from another. Both men were keenly aware of musical developments around them. Neither seems to have had much empathy with the southern fiddle-band sound, but both took an interest in Hawaiian music, and both worked happily, when required to, with musicians from the world of the dance band and the theater pit orchestra. Above all, both men saw themselves as gardeners in the broad parkland of popular music rather than the backyard plot of hillbilly.

Although Rodgers made his name with blue yodels and other rowdy songs, he was steadily moving away from them, exchanging their homely humor for a less demotic, more calculated music, the Tin Pan Alley romanticism of "Dreaming with Tears in My Eyes," "Miss the Mississippi and You," or "Prairie Lullaby." He was, in a sense, coming home, for his first models had been men like Gene Austin, the "Sweet Singer of the Southland," or the guitar-playing pop troubadour Nick Lucas, artists who balanced downhome and uptown, rural simplicity and urban sophistication, and if he had lived longer he would have continued to draw closer to them, glad to have escaped the stockade of "old familiar tunes," free from the chain gang now.

But he did not, and the recordings he did make, rather than those we might speculate about his making, tell another story. What prevented him from turning into a rustic Rudy Vallee was his singularly developed taste for black music. More than any popular

(OTM collection)

singer of his time, more even than knowledgeable admirers of black idioms like Bing Crosby or the Boswell Sisters, Rodgers had an instinctive rapport with the blues. It sat on his shoulder like a devil in a Medieval allegory, whispering hotly of high-stepping mamas and pistol-packing papas, telling tall tales of gamblers and spenders, of whistling freight trains and rooting groundhogs, and whatever it was that everybody did in Hawaii. And that made all the difference. Rather than pushing him toward a cameo in *Gold Diggers of 1930something*, it pulled him back to the South, where people were used to that kind of talk, and liked their singers to address them in it.

Rodgers was the first white performer to be aesthetically convincing as an interpreter of the blues. We don't know whether he listened to the artists who preceded him on record with approximately kindred material, men like the yodeler Frank Kamplain or the blackface "coon" singers Emmett Miller and Al Bernard, but if he did, it was only to learn what not to do: he knew too much about African-American speech to adopt their caricatures of it. "Gambling Polka Dot Blues," for instance, with its appropriately swaggering piano accompaniment, is first-rate vaudeville blues singing, as authentic to that idiom as many such performances by black singers.

It's significant that black musicians seem to have felt comfortable about him: they often remembered his records (a thing unusual in itself), sometimes well enough to sing them years later. And they were comfortable around him, too: several Mississippi bluesmen have claimed that he hung out or played with them.

Even his white contemporaries felt that he had some special understanding of black style. "He crossed that leg," said Cliff Carlisle, "—well, his leg didn't do like mine does; my leg won't hang down . . . he put one leg over the other, and it was hangin' right down . . . and he opened that mouth—and he had a long face, you know, long jaw, like—anyhow, it just flopped. Jimmie, he reminded me more of a colored person, or a Negro . . . than anybody I ever saw, in a way."

Scores of white singer-guitarists like Carlisle were inspired by Rodgers's example to break their connection with the narrative ballad and the melodrama of the nineteenth-century heart song and plug into the blues. In doing so they signaled a shift in performance style, as if donning a new costume, or a mask. To step out as a blues singer is to step out of line. Blues confers a license to break rules, defy taboos, say the unsayable, create its own dark carnival. That revelation was a large part of Jimmie Rodgers's unique legacy to country music.

But it was not all of it. Beguiled by Rodgers's way with a blues, we may risk forgetting how effective he was with other kinds of material: songs of unstrained affection like "You and My Old Guitar," "Old Pal of My Heart," or "Any Old Time," the prisoner's meditation "Moonlight and Skies," the manly nostalgia of "Down the Old Road to Home." Several of these have blossomed over the decades into standards, their uncomplicated emotional messages serving as reaffirmations of moral truths that are intrinsic to country music. Hold on to your friends. Be as good as your word. Leave home if you must, but don't forget it.

With his unique ability to stand on both sides of the tracks, to fashion anthems alike for the footloose and the settled, for the playboy and the parent, Rodgers is country music's first Everyman. And this is why he seems—more, perhaps, than anyone else in this book—so undated, so available. He stretches his arm across the decades to shake hands, grip us by the elbow, pat us on the back. "Right here for you, partner. Dee-yodel-ay-ee-hee!"

Bridge: The Great Divide

Victor Records' two weeks of location recording in Bristol, Tennessee, in July-August 1927 would prove to be the most momentous session in the history of country music. On Monday, August 1, the crew cut the first sides by The Carter Family; on Thursday, August 4, their heavy wax discs captured the debut performances of Jimmie Rodgers.

There is something extraordinarily fateful about this, for no two acts testify more explicitly to a deep-cut dichotomy in country music. It's as if a wild, muddy river, itself funded by the tributes of many tiny streams pouring into it, were suddenly to divide itself in half, flowing one way past green hillsides and leafy valleys, the other through hot flatlands and dusty prairies, by railroad yards and waterfront bars.

What Jimmie Rodgers stands for in country music you may glimpse in many of his photographs. He leans nonchalantly against a bright new automobile, sharply suited, diamond-ringed; he stands, shoulder to self-assured shoulder, alongside the much-loved humorist Will Rogers; he suns himself on the boardwalk at Atlantic City. The Carter Family do not present themselves like that. They were never photographed in their true milieu. We ought to see them giving a concert in a mountain village schoolhouse; or, better yet, in an old-fashioned front parlor, the sun filtering through muslin curtains onto the quiet group around the harmonium. In their values, their repertoire, and their style, The Carter Family evinced another attitude toward their times than Rodgers's. He was at home with the roaring '20s, with flappers and flivvers and the fast life. They, speaking for the old cottage home and the church in the wildwood, emphatically were not: "These are the latter days, we know."

Nonetheless, Ralph Peer persuaded his two star acts to engage in a couple of recorded meetings, the sketches "Jimmie Rodgers Visits The Carter Family" and "The Carter Family and Jimmie Rodgers in Texas." Just as you would expect, Rodgers, whether on his own turf or visiting, is entirely at home, but the Carters, especially the women, are as uncomfortable as if they had had to do the routine in swimsuits. Winding up his imaginary trip to Virginia, Rodgers proposes "a little old sure enough ridiculously harmonizing" and launches into "Hot Time in the Old Town Tonight," a song just about compatible with his own approach but laughably ill-suited to the Carters, who la-la everything but the tagline: they're like a quartet made up of a fox and three chickens. It's not just that the text is not from the Carters' customary breviary. This

This ad for the Rodgers–Carter record appeared in numerous papers in October 1931. (Author's collection)

brief *entente*, cordial though its participants are to each other, reveals how far apart they stood on the stage of early country music: Rodgers the soloist, atomized twentieth-century man, singing for ramblers, gamblers, and other loners; the three Carters making music together (whatever their personal disharmonies), evoking family, community, and continuity.

Rodgers's legacy to country music is clear. He heads a line that descends through copyists like Gene Autry and Jimmie Davis, through Western Swing (Bob Wills recorded at least ten of Rodgers's songs) and honkytonk singers like Rex Griffin and Ernest Tubb, to Hank Williams, Willie Nelson, outlaw country and beyond. The Carters' mark is no less plain. They originated much of the bluegrass repertoire, and stamped their style on the folksong movement of the '50s and '60s. It is the simple, sober delivery of Sara Carter that echoes in the singing of Gillian Welch.

So, within the space of four days, Ralph Peer and Victor had secured what would prove to be the two most influential acts in their idiom. It is so fitting, so artistic a coincidence that you almost want to believe it was something more.

Birmingham and Atlanta. But some of the local players were a match for those out-of-towners, and none more than a pair of brothers from nearby Sewanee, Austin and Lee Allen.

Austin picked the four-string tenor banjo and did most of the singing. Lee played the guitar and blew blaring blues choruses on his kazoo. It was the blues that made their name: their first recording, for Columbia in 1927, was "Salty Dog Blues," and when they moved over to Victor a year later they started with a coupling of "Frisco Blues" and "Tiple Blues." It was a substantial seller, and for the rest of their seven-year recording career they kept on coming back to the blues.

"We lived in those days when people, that's about all they knew," Lee Allen remembered, and his wife Edith chimed in, "Yes, people all over the state of Tennessee liked the blues."

"Tiple Blues" was inspired by a coal tipple in Lynch, Kentucky, that was reputed to be the largest in the world. "I think they were sending out about 125 carloads of coal in one day," said Lee Allen. "And that was something for the time. It was hard, dangerous work—a lot of people would get killed in those mines up there—and we decided that would be a good thing to make [a record about]."

Their longest-running hit was a remake of their first record, titled "A New Salty Dog," a rowdy little song with a familiar ragtime chord progression. Coupled on a Bluebird disc with

The Allen Brothers

Austin Allen (1901–59) • Lee Allen (1906–81)

Most people know it best for its famous choo-choo, but in the 1920s and '30s the city of Chattanooga, Tennessee, on a bend of the Tennessee River close to the state lines of Alabama and Georgia, was a mainline station for music too. Old-time fiddlers' conventions met there, attracting the best musicians from

Take Part in "Bushwhacker"

AUSTIN AND LEE ALLEN

The Allen brothers, Chattanoogans, who have achieved fame in the world of "blue" music and mountain melody through their phonograph records and radio work, are appearing in person all next week as members of the cast of "The Bushwhacker," with the Peruchi Players at the [Bijou]. As a result of the week's run of "The Bushwhacker," a Chattanooga cast is expected to go to New York in May to represent this city [in the] national Little Theater tournament.

(Norm Cohen collection)

(Author's collection)

another suggestive number, the Delmore Brothers' "Brown's Ferry Blues," it made probably the best-selling hillbilly two-header of its era. But what is it about? According to Lee Allen, "a salty dog was somebody that was just a little low-down, not too much. They just wanted to have a good time . . . they were drinking people and that's about all they had on their mind."

During Prohibition determined drinkers could get a kick from potions that contained alcohol but evaded the law by being sold as medicines or tonics. One such was Jamaica Ginger, popularly known as "jake." In 1930 a batch of jake was put on the market that had been dangerously adulterated, and thousands of Southerners were partially paralyzed after drinking it. The condition, which proved to be irreversible, gave the sufferer a distinctive hobbling gait, the "jake walk." The Allens responded with a blackly humorous composition, "Jake Walk Blues," and it was one of Victor's biggest-selling country discs that year. (Several other hillbilly and blues artists recorded jake songs, which have been collected on a CD, *Jake Leg Blues*.)

The Allens wrote other topical songs, such as "Price of Cotton Blues" and "New Deal Blues." "That's the way you wrote music back then," Lee Allen told the Nashville *Banner* in 1976. "People liked that kind of thing. . . . We always wrote our songs on things that happened—things that made newspaper headlines." In "I've Got the Chain Store Blues" they contributed to a campaign that was being vigorously waged by the populist W. K. "Hello, World" Henderson, owner of the powerful station KWKH in Shreveport, Louisiana, who used his access to southern homes to proselytize for the independent store and defy the encroaching power of national chains. But mostly the Allens sang about moonshine whiskey—their "Fruit Jar Blues" (which, coupled with "Jake Walk Blues," was one of the first releases in the new Bluebird catalog in 1933) foresaw the end of Prohibition—or about gals with red pajamas, warm knees, and misbehaving ways. "Stay in one line," producer Ralph Peer advised them, "and you'll do better." They seldom varied their instrumental format, except for a few talking blues with guitar, like "Maybe Next Week Sometime."

Though they sold considerably more records than most hillbilly acts, perhaps as many as a quarter of a million altogether, the Allens could not make a living from them. They worked on medicine shows, played for dances in the mountains of East Tennessee and West Virginia, had a weekly radio show in Chattanooga: the usual scuffle. By the mid-'30s, after a last batch of recordings for Vocalion which didn't sell very well, they were on their way out. But one of their songs lived on after them. "Salty Dog," reshaped by the Morris Brothers, became a staple of the early bluegrass repertoire.

Fleming & Townsend

Reece Fleming (1909–58) • Respers Townsend (1909–74)

A good deal of early country music is currently available in modern formats: at the time of writing, probably about 5,000 items, amounting to something like a quarter of all the recordings that were issued between the early 1920s and the early '40s. So you might suppose that we have a fairly representative sound-picture of country music's First Age. In fact—for a number of reasons, but chiefly because of the tastes of the small group of collectors who are largely responsible for reissuing old-time music—it's not so. You can find on CD any number of obscure bands from Kentucky or West Virginia whose few 78s sold in the hundreds, but until quite recently you would have searched unsuccessfully for any recording at all of a duo who made more than

sixty, for three companies, over seven years and scored a couple of certifiable five-figure hits.

Reissues, then, rewrite history, and the historian is required to stake a claim for the artists who have been written out—such as the blue yodeling, guitar and mandolin picking duo of Reece Fleming and Respers Townsend.

Both men were from around Covington, Tennessee, about thirty miles north of Memphis on Highway 51. Lee Respers Townsend was born in the nearby small community of Elm Grove. A family friend suggested his unusual forename, which is exceptionally rare in the United States: genealogical records of more than 70 million twentieth-century Americans furnish only one other example, though the Townsend family recall that the name was shared by someone else in their community. Respers' friends preferred to call him Rusty. According to his son Ted, "he left home early in his life due to an unhappy home life. His step mom agreed to raise two other boys outside of the immediate family and Dad sort of felt neglected. . . .

"Back in those days people didn't have very much money at all. Tipton County was mostly a farming community and people would work all day for only a dollar. . . . [They] basically had to entertain themselves to pass the time. So that was the beginning of Fleming & Townsend. They started out playing in different communities for dances. Later on they became very popular and started playing on radio. Several country grocery stores had radios and they put up speakers and folks around the community would come and listen to them play and sing." They also performed at Covington's theatres, the Ritz, Gem, and Ruffin, and at clubs in Covington and Memphis.

By 1930 they had enough cachet to win a recording session with Victor. "I believe that Dad and Reece sang on WREC radio [in Memphis]," says Ted Townsend, "and were discovered by Victor doing so." Their first release, "She's Just That Kind" and "Just One Little Kiss," sold over 20,000 copies. Then only Jimmie Rodgers, The Carter Family, and Carson Robison & Frank Luther were providing Victor with sales of that magnitude. Fleming usually sang lead and played guitar, while Townsend sang harmony and played mandolin, second guitar, harmonica, and kazoo. His blues phrasing on harmonica occasionally makes you wonder if he had heard Noah Lewis, who played so eloquently on records by Cannon's

Reece Fleming (right) & Respers Townsend, 1934. (Courtesy of Ted Townsend)

Jug Stompers, and lived in Ripley, only a few miles away. Both Fleming and Townsend could yodel, and they seem likely to be the first significant yodeling duet in country music. "Everyone here at home that remembers them," says Ted Townsend, "talks of how great their voices blended in harmony."

Their next release, "I'm Blue and Lonesome" and "Little Home upon the Hill," sold somewhat less than 11,000, but for the time—

Garland, Tennessee, baseball team, with Reece Fleming (center row, first left) & Respers Townsend (back row, far right). (Courtesy of Ted Townsend)

late 1930, with the Depression tightening its hold—that was more than respectable, and probably explains why Victor persisted in recording them. The company also passed some of their compositions to another duo on their books, Gene Autry and Frank Marvin, and in April 1931 they recorded three of them, "She's Just That Kind," "She's Always on My Mind," and "I'm Blue and Lonesome." (Versions of "She's Just That Kind" were later recorded by the Callahan Brothers and Hank Penny.)

Fleming & Townsend had further sessions for Victor in 1930–32, and although sales of their later releases were low, the company recouped some of their investment a few years later by reissuing most of the duo's recordings on Bluebird. There were subsequent dates for ARC in 1934 and Decca in 1937, both in New York. For one of those sessions the record company sent them travel money, but the pair gambled it away the night before and had to borrow from the bank to buy their train tickets.

"They both were a little on the wild side,"

says Ted Townsend, "sort of like Hank Williams Jr. today." Some of their most popular numbers, such as "She's Just That Kind" and "Gonna Quit Drinking When I Die," do have a dissolute air, but at least as many of their songs are about restlessness and movement, and so not all that different from the repertoire of contemporaries like the Delmore Brothers.

The last known trace of the double act is an ad in *Billboard* in February 1946: "At Liberty. Fleming and Townsend—Former Recording Artists for Decca And Bluebird—Have a Number of New Hot Hillbilly Songs Ready for Recording." The offer appears to have fallen on uncaring ears, for they did not record together again, though they continued to play at home and enjoyed fishing and quail hunting together. Ginger Townsend, Ted's wife, remembers how Rusty liked to visit with them and their friends, bring an armful of his records, play them, and then leave. "He was proud of his music," says his daughter Ada Lee. "He loved it day and night."

He returned to farming, and later worked as a supervisor of heavy equipment on the Mississippi River. Fleming hung on in music, running a band in the late '40s and '50s, and worked with a fellow Covingtonian, singer Malcolm Yelvington, in The Tennesseans (later The Star Rhythm Boys), playing in local clubs and on radio. In 1954–55 the band recorded for Sun, and Fleming's piano playing can be heard on "Drinkin' Wine Spo-Dee-Odee." He died of an aneurysm after a night's coon hunting. His old partner survived him for a while before dying of lung cancer.

Chris Bouchillon

(1893–1968)

Early in his career, Bob Dylan performed a few pieces that are not sung but spoken— loose bundles of anecdotes, jokes, and throwaway reflections strung together with a raggy guitar accompaniment, compositions like "Talkin' New York" or "Talkin' Bear Mountain Picnic Massacre Blues." In work like that Dylan was tipping his cap, not for the only time, to Woody Guthrie, who frequently used the form to comment on the world about him, sometimes humorously, sometimes, as in his *Dust Bowl Ballads*, with a sharper edge. Many of Dylan's listeners know that, but what they may not know, and perhaps Dylan did not

know either, is that the lineage of such pieces extends far beyond Guthrie—back to the 1920s, in fact, and to a bespectacled South Carolinian named Chris Bouchillon, the first man to use the phrase "talking blues."

Or so we believe. The combination of the two words seems to have had its first airing in print on the label of Bouchillon's "Talking Blues," recorded in November 1926 and issued early the following year. The concept, however, must surely have existed beforehand. Frank Walker, who signed Bouchillon to Columbia and chose "Talking Blues" as his debut release for the label, used to tell a story in later years about how Bouchillon's singing was so thin that he, Walker, suggested he talk instead—and so the talking blues was born. The evidence is against it. On the flipside of "Talking Blues," an old vaudeville piece called "Hannah," Bouchillon sings the lyrics quite competently, and besides, people who knew him say he always did talking pieces, and got the idea from local black musicians.

After that, several other hillbilly artists contributed to the genre, but they, or their record labels, seem to acknowledge Bouchillon as its instigator. When the washboard player and bandleader Herschel Brown, at an OKeh session in July 1928, put aside his board, had his guitar player pick a tune, and started in on a comic narration, the performance was titled "New Talking Blues," a plain nod to Bouchillon's original. The talking blues recordings made in the '30s by artists like Curly Fox, Jesse Rodgers, and the Tennesee Ramblers are all, to some degree, spin-offs from Bouchillon's records.

Chris Bouchillon in Columbia's "Old Familiar Tunes" catalog, 1927. (Author's collection)

Music store ad, *Burlington Daily Times*, January 27, 1928. (Author's collection)

But whatever credit we might want to give to Bouchillon as a musical architect, we needn't suppose that he also made the bricks. Take, for example, "Born in Hard Luck," one of his best pieces. The jokes in it, like the one about the shoe store clerk who had to fit shoes on ladies' feet but got above his job, or the man who was checking the level in his gas tank and lit a match to see better, were surely bewhiskered by 1927. What Bouchillon was doing here and elsewhere was creating a kind of hillbilly comedy routine, stringing public domain jests about wives and mothers-in-law into three-minute narratives.

As such they are well delivered, and the listener with a taste for old jokes may find them still amusing, but what gave them a sheen of novelty at the time was the guitar accompaniments, adeptly picked improvisations by Bouchillon's brother Urias, patchworks of ragtime and blues licks. They were a musical family: another brother, Charlie, played fiddle, and the first recording to bear a Bouchillon name, made for OKeh a year and a half before "Talking Blues," was by the three of them, doing a vaudeville song about a girl who played saxophone, "She Doodle Dooed." The family originated in Oconee County, the western tip of South Carolina that juts into northeast Georgia, but the brothers grew up in Greenville. The name Bouchillon is of French origin, and evidence from public records suggests that Chris may have been christened Christophe. In later years he's believed to have run a Greenville dry-cleaning store, then moved to Florida during World War II to work in the Jacksonville shipyards.

Bouchillon had eleven releases on Columbia, and the later ones show some development, away from strings of jokes and toward themed pieces like "Speed Maniac" and "Girls of Today," wry commentaries on contemporary manners. But he never matched the sales of his early sides like "Talking Blues," which sold over 90,000 copies, or "Born in Hard Luck"—whose flipside, "The Medicine Show," acquired a curious afterlife, turning up slightly modified in Buddy Jones's 1937 record "Huntin' Blues" and then again in the '50s as "The Great Medical Menagerist" by an eccentric one-man-band from Mississippi, Harmonica Frank Floyd.

Where Guthrie fits into all this is uncertain. Possibly he was acquainted with Bouchillon's records. Maybe he tuned into the Grand Ole Opry one day and heard Robert Lunn, "The Talking Blues Man," another exponent of comic-storytelling-with-guitar in the Bouchillon mode. Whatever his inspiration, he gave the talking blues a characteristic twist, exchanging the joke-book cracks for political satire, leaving a signpost to be followed by his young admirer from the Minnesota Iron Range. Bouchillon was still living, in a Florida retirement home, when Dylan's early albums came out; perhaps a grandson brought one of them over and played it to him. It is pleasant to imagine the old man hearing Bob drawl "Talkin' New York" and allowing himself a small, knowing smile.

Playlist

• *Tom Darby & Jimmie Tarlton Also Starring Chris Bouchillon* (JSP JSPCD 7746 4CD)

•• *Good for What Ails You: Music of the Medicine Shows 1926–1937* (Old Hat CD-1005 2CD): "Born in Hard Luck," "Hannah"

Ed Haley

(1883–1951)

Not all the important figures of old-time music spread their influence by records. Blind Ed Haley's only discs were home recordings, done in his dining room and distributed after his death among his six children. Yet in the hills and hollows of West Virginia and eastern Kentucky his fiddling echoed for much of the twentieth century in the repertoire and playing of dozens of musicians, some of them still living.

Blinded by measles as a baby, he devoted himself to the fiddle, playing at house dances and county fairs. In his later years he attended a few fiddling contests but disliked the razzmatazz of public competition, especially when up against trick fiddlers like the notorious "Natchee the Indian." He preferred to travel the country with his wife Martha Ella, also blind, who accompanied him on mandolin, or one or two of his children, exchanging his music for a night's hospitality. Though born in West Virginia—in Logan County, like Frank Hutchison—he settled, after his marriage in 1914, in Ashland, Kentucky, but evidently ranged widely in both states.

"It was an event of major importance," write the fiddle scholars Mark Wilson and Guthrie T. Meade, "when the Haleys came to visit an isolated mountain town. . . . Virtually every evening a dance would be scheduled at someone's house. Ed had great endurance and would often play continuously all night, without even pausing between sets. If someone gave him a dollar to play a special tune, he might play it for ten minutes or more. Before the Depression, Ed made as much as twenty dollars a day . . . [and] the Haleys managed to put all of their six children through school and to maintain a stable home."

Some of the younger men who listened and learned from him would take his tunes into the larger world, fiddlers like Clark Kessinger or Georgia Slim Rutland. Kessinger, a tough judge of other musicians, called him "a great fiddler . . . I thought he was the best." Others simply absorbed his music and preserved it for decades after he was gone, to play it into the tape-recorders of old-time music researchers and fiddle buffs. Listen to the fiddling of Wilson Douglas or J. P. Fraley, or some of the players on Rounder's CDs of *Traditional Fiddle Music of Kentucky*. For such men, Haley was the brightest comet ever to flash across their skies.

For a while it seemed as if his music survived only at second hand, but then portions of his home-recorded legacy turned up, and in the '70s Rounder had enough for an LP. Now over a hundred pieces have been recovered, from a collection that was once maybe three times as large, and many of them have been gathered on two double CDs. Some of the discs are worn and hard to listen to, but there is more than enough evidence to back up Haley's word-of-mouth reputation.

It is fiddling in the grand old style. Many of Haley's tunes are rare and fascinating, but even common ones like "Green Mountain Polka" or "Flop Eared Mule" are complex versions, often with unfamiliar parts or in unusual keys. "I like to flavor up a tune," he said, "so that nobody in the world could tell what I'm playing." Fast, fierce, and pungent, his fiddling evokes an older, tougher world, when tunes and their names—"Yellow Barber," "Three Forks of Sandy," "No Corn on Tygart"—often commemorated events and places, embodied local history in music. "Brushy Fork of John's Creek," for example, refers to a Civil War battle site.

Haley's fiddling language, wrote John Hartford in the CD notes, is "highly sophisticated. . . . The hand written script of the bow is so elegant and is deeply rooted in the Scotch-Irish experience." Tunes like "Humphrey's Jig" or "Salt River," traced back through their many adaptations and name changes, remove us from Appalachia to eighteenth-century Britain, while other strains descend from the minstrel stage or the African-American tradition. To listen to Ed Haley is to hear an American music creating itself.

Postscript: The account given above of Ed Haley's home recordings is based on Wilson and Meade's statement that he made them only for himself and his family. This has been the generally accepted story, but recent research in West Virginia newspapers provides grounds

(OTM collection)

for questioning it. In the *Charleston Gazette* of September 27, 1930, appeared this classified advertisement:

MOUNTAIN MUSIC—Ed Haley, champion fiddler of the West Virginia and Kentucky hills, will broadcast over WOBU, Charleston, Saturday night, the 27th, at 9.30. . . . Tune in and if interested, either as a seller or user, in 10-inch double-faced Phonograph Records, made by him, price 35 cents each, write Ed Haley Co., Huntington, W. Va.

Playlist
- *Forked Deer* (Rounder CD 1131/1132)
- *Grey Eagle* (Rounder CD 1133/1134)

Clark Kessinger

(1896–1975)

Clark Kessinger was to old-time fiddling almost what Louis Armstrong was to jazz. He soared beyond the confines of a local idiom to create a superstyle that impressed and was imitated by musicians everywhere.

Between 1928 and 1930 Kessinger and his guitar-playing nephew Luches, billed as the Kessinger Brothers, made sixty-eight recordings: everything from venerable dance tunes

Clark Kessinger (center) with Luches Kessinger (right) and dance-caller Ernest Legg (left). (Author's collection)

Music store ad, *Charleston Gazette*, November 3, 1929. (Author's collection)

like "Hell among the Yearlings" or "Ragtime Annie" to song tunes like "Steamboat Bill" and novelties such as "Pop Goes the Weasel." Or almost everything: he appears to have been deaf to the siren song of the blues.

Whatever the piece, Kessinger played it with a smooth, unhurried elegance, nonchalantly adding decorative curlicues that most other fiddlers could bring off only in their dreams. His approach was the antithesis of the devil-may-care scraping of a Gid Tanner or Fiddlin' John Carson. It was playing of a technically high order, admired by the classical violinist Joseph Szigeti, as it was too by rural fiddlers from Appalachia to Texas.

Clark Kessinger grew up near Charleston, West Virginia, listening to local players like Ed Haley and becoming so successful at fiddling contests that many of his peers refused to compete with him. By 1926 he and Luches ("Luke, we always called him"), who was about nine years younger, were playing on the local radio station. The *Charleston Daily Mail* reported, on January 31, 1928: "A varied vocal and instrumental program will be broadcast [tonight] over station WOBU between 9:30 and 10:30 o'clock, sponsored by the Woodrum Home Outfitting company. The hour will be chuck-full of music. . . . The Kessinger brothers, 'old-time fiddlers' who recently were contracted to make recordings for the Brunswick phonograph company, and Richmond Houston, violinist, will have an important part in the musical hour. The program is one of the most elaborate ever to be broadcast over the local station."

Soon afterward the Kessingers cut fourteen sides for a Brunswick location recording crew in Ashland, Kentucky. They gave the company a substantial hit with their first release, a graceful cover version of the Leake County Revelers' hugely popular "Wednesday Night Waltz," coupled with the "Goodnight Waltz." "I'd rather play a waltz," Clark said in later years. "They're harder to play, for the time [i.e., timing]." Other early sides were aimed at the square-dance audience, and some had an extra man calling the sets, but this policy was soon abandoned and thereafter Kessinger's fluent fiddling could be heard without distractions.

Some of his finest performances were captured in New York in the summer of 1929, during a session that spread over three days and produced twenty-four issued titles—some rather bizarrely titled at that, like "Hot Foot," "Josh and I," or "Rat Cheese under the Hill," usually explained as a Brunswick staffer's mishearing or miswriting of "Natchez under the Hill," though that isn't the tune Kessinger plays. "Sopping the Gravy" is the melody of the Civil War song "Year of Jubilo" (which, with its words restored, also became Sam & Kirk McGee's "Old Master's Runaway"). Other titles are more readily decodable: "Going Up Brushy Creek" is the old favorite "Cripple Creek."

Interviewed in later life, Kessinger recalled playing for "picnics and dances on the Fourth of July, Labor Day . . . just build a stage in a grove, square dance all day, eating and everything on the ground . . . never got a dime for it, just be playing just for fun." This sylvan and carefree picture must come from his youth, because by the time he was a radio and recording artist he was making serious money with his fiddle, playing for dances and other functions. Snapshots of the Kessingers' professional life are scattered through the Charleston papers of the late '20s. On January 24, 1929, the *Charleston Daily Mail* carried an advance notice, wedged beneath an ad for Red Top Malt Extract ("Taste it! Smell it! It's *ENTIRELY* Different!"), for an "Old Time Barn Dance and Shin Dig at Pleasure Hall on Malden Road. Friday Night from 8 to 12. Music Furnished by Kessinger Brothers." Three weeks later the *Charleston Gazette* curtly announced: "Usual Barn Dance Friday. Music by Kessinger Brothers."

After the Depression took hold, however,

Playlist

• *Kessinger Brothers—Volume 1 (1928–1929)* (Document DOCD-8010)
• *Kessinger Brothers—Volume 2 (1929)* (Document DOCD-8011)
• *Kessinger Brothers—Volume 3 (1929–1930)* (Document DOCD-8012)
• *The Legend of Clark Kessinger* (County CO-CD-2713) [Kessinger considered the recordings of his youth far inferior to his mature playing and would probably have preferred to be remembered for an album like this, recorded soon after his reemergence, with vigorous bluegrass-style accompaniment by banjoist Wayne Hauser and guitarist Gene Meade]
• *World Champion Fiddler* (Tri-Agle-Far TR-701) [similar to above]
• *Last Fiddle Album* (Tri-Agle-Far TR-707)
•• *Old-Time Music of West Virginia Volume One* (County CD-3518): "Garfield March," "Sally Goodin" •• *Old-Time Music of West Virginia Volume Two* (County CD-3519): "Boarding House Bells Are Ringing," "Richmond Polka" •• *Old Time Music: The Essential Collection* (Rounder Heritage 11599): "Red Bird" [1971 recording] •• *Times Ain't Like They Used to Be Vol. 4* (Yazoo 2048): "Salt River"

there were fewer engagements, and after a final session in 1930 no more recordings. They continued to appear on radio till Luches died in 1943, and thereafter Clark played only for neighborhood dances, making his living as a painter and decorator. Then, in the early '60s, old-time enthusiast Ken Davidson reintroduced him to the fiddling contest circuit, and Kessinger discovered he could still win as effortlessly as he used to. His Indian summer decade produced a handful of albums that found him in excellent fettle. He continued to play at fiddlers' conventions and folk festivals until his death.

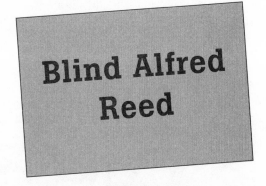

Blind Alfred Reed

(1880–1956)

Ry Cooder, Bruce Springsteen, David Lindley . . . Blind Alfred Reed could not remotely have imagined the hands his songs would fall into, decades after his death. Yet even when he recorded it, in December 1929, his composition "How Can a Poor Man Stand Such Times and Live" must have seemed out of the ordinary. "There was once a time when everything was cheap," he begins. "But now prices almost puts a man to sleep. When we pay our grocery bill, we just feel like making our will. Tell me, how can a poor man stand such times and live?"

Over the next seven verses the forty-nine-year-old singer and fiddler lays into swindling tradesmen, worthless schools, over-zealous revenue officers, insincere clergymen, and fraudulent doctors: a catalog of the forces that Depression-hit rural Southerners blamed for their problems, its bitterness in vivid contrast with the buoyancy of Broadway songs like "We're in the Money." Some of the song's points—about the school system, for example—are still replicated in American political debate. No wonder it has attracted inquisitive musicians like Cooder and Springsteen.

"How Can a Poor Man Stand Such Times and Live" is wholly serious, but it might be asked whether all Reed's songs should be taken at their solemn face value. His favorite topic was Women: Mad, Bad, and Dangerous to Know. He was the Kingsley Amis of hillbilly music. He disliked the flappers' short haircuts so much that he wrote two songs called "Why Do You Bob Your Hair, Girls?":

> Why do you bob your hair, girls? You're
>   doing mighty wrong.
> God says it is a glory, and you should wear
>   it long.
> You'll spoil your lovely hair, girls, to keep
>   yourself in style.
> Before you bob your hair, girls, just stop
>   and think a while.
>
> Why do you bob your hair, girls? It is an
>   awful shame
> To rob the head God gave you and wear
>   the flapper's name.

> You're taking off your covering, it is an
>   awful sin.
> Don't never bob your hair, girls, short hair
>   belongs to men.

There was also a lugubrious lament about marriage, "Black and Blue Blues," and an extraordinary attack-on-every-front number on the theme "God made woman after man, and she's been after man ever since." Present-day listeners may be inclined to wonder if, now and then, Blind Alfred Reed deliberately went a little over the top. In "We've Got to Have 'Em, That's All," where he finally resigns himself to the presence of a second sex and sings, "Every fellow knows his mother is a woman . . . Man should not be angry with his wife at all"—do we detect the faintest suggestion of a twinkle in the minister's eye?

Perhaps. Other songs in his repertoire, however, take an unquestionably sober view of life and death. Several were derived from stories in the papers or on radio, like "The Wreck of the Virginian," about a train crash not far from his home in Princeton, West Virginia, or "Fate of Chris Lively and Wife," who were killed when a train ran into their car on a crossing.

Blind Alfred Reed (center) with Fred Pendleton (fiddle) and Arville Reed (guitar). (Rounder Records)

He had some of these compositions printed on cards and sold them for ten cents each.

Reed made his living playing for dances and church meetings and giving music lessons; sometimes, when money was tight, he'd walk down to town and play for passers-by. "Many times he would walk all the way back home without having earned a nickel," recalled his son Collins Reed. "On more successful occasions he would pick up some groceries on the way back. Six or seven cents was enough to buy a pound of bacon."

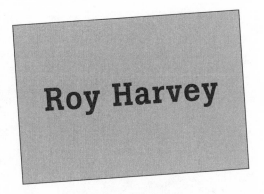

Roy Harvey

(1892–1958)

For much of country music's history there has been one group of people making the music and another doing the business. Roy Harvey belongs to an era before that demarcation line was drawn. He was a musician who made music his business.

It wasn't that he needed to compensate for a slight talent, for he was a good singer and an excellent guitarist. All this genial, bespectacled man lacked was pizzazz, and by chance he fell in with a musician who had that to spare. If he

Playlist
• *Blind Alfred Reed (1927–1929)* (Document DOCD-8022)
•• *The Bristol Sessions* (Country Music Foundation CMF-011-D 2CD): "Walking in the Way with Jesus," "The Wreck of the Virginian" •• *Old-Time Mountain Ballads* (County CD-3504): "Fate of Chris Lively and Wife" •• *Old-Time Music from West Virginia Volume One* (County CO-CD-3518): "Explosion in the Fairmount Mines," "You'll Miss Me" •• *Hard Times in the Country* (County CO-CD-3527): "How Can a Poor Man Stand Such Times and Live" •• *RCA Country Legends—The Bristol Sessions Vol. 1* (RCA/BMG Heritage 65131): "You Must Unload" •• *Times Ain't Like They Used to Be Vol. 2* (Yazoo 2029): "Beware" •• *The Rose Grew Round the Briar: Early American Rural Love Songs Vol. 1* (Yazoo 2030): "The Old-Fashioned Cottage" •• *Hard Times Come Again No More Vol. 1* (Yazoo 2036): "How Can a Poor Man Stand Such Times and Live"

Roy Harvey (seated) with Earl Shirkey. (Kinney Rorrer collection)

Roy Harvey (standing, left) with (standing, left to right) Odell Smith, Lonnie Austin, E. D. Terry, Lucy Terry; (seated) Hamon Newman, Earl Shirkey. Beckley, West Virginia, 1929. (Kinney Rorrer collection)

had done nothing but play guitar behind the charismatic Charlie Poole, Roy Harvey would have his share of fame, but he guided Poole's career for most of its hectic five-year heyday, picking up enough know-how to develop a series of profitable record business associations for himself.

The first few recordings by Poole's North Carolina Ramblers in 1925–26 created such a stir that every other label wanted a piece of North Carolina stringband action. Since Poole was chary of breaking his contract with Columbia, Harvey took over the band's name, replaced the leader with the singer and banjo-mandolin player Bob Hoke, and briskly set up sessions with Gennett, Paramount, and Brunswick. Thanks to the presence of Posey Rorer, the Ramblers' fiddler, all these recordings are well worth hearing, but there's no concealing the fact that without Poole they lacked a magic ingredient. Listen to songs first recorded by the Harvey-led Ramblers and later by the group with Poole, such as "Bill Mason" or "Sweet Sunny South." The earlier versions are evocative, well-played, touching; they have almost every virtue you would look for in that

kind of music. But when Charlie Poole took on a song he took it over, dousing it in the vinegar of his personality, and after you have heard his version, anyone else's seems a little bland.

Unlike the North Carolinian Poole, Roy Harvey was born and bred in West Virginia. He began playing guitar as a boy. From the age of nineteen he worked on the Virginian Railroad, first as a fireman, then as an engineer, but in 1923 he was laid off after a strike. (He later wrote and recorded a song about it, "The Virginian Strike of '23.") For part of the period when he was associated with Poole he worked as a salesman at a music store in Beckley, West Virginia, which put him in touch with local musicians and led to collaborations on record with the fiddler and guitarist Jess Johnston, the Beckley guitarist Leonard Copeland, the singer and yodeler Earl Shirkey, and the duo of banjoist Ernest Branch and fiddler Bernice Coleman. Aware of changing fashions in the market, he calculatedly formed teams so as to offer recording companies any kind of old-time music they wanted: stringband songs with Branch and Coleman, sacred numbers with Hoke and Rorer, guitar duets with Johnston or

Copeland, comic sketches with Poole and friends, yodel songs with Shirkey. In less than five years Harvey appeared on the best part of 200 recordings.

Some of them were more than averagely successful. His first collaboration with Shirkey, "When the Roses Bloom for the Bootlegger," a Prohibition-era parody of the turn-of-the-century popular song "I'll Be with You When the Roses Bloom Again," was Columbia's sixth best selling disc of 1928, moving more than 72,000 copies. The elegant guitar duets with Copeland had a more restricted appeal in their day, but have been greatly esteemed by later listeners. Others of Harvey's recordings, like the 1931 sides with Johnston for Gennett and with Branch and Coleman for OKeh, came out at a time when hillbilly record sales were counted not in tens of thousands but in low hundreds, and the original discs are consequently very rare; one or two of them seem not to have survived at all.

Playlist
• *Roy Harvey—Volume 1 (1926–1927)* to *Volume 4 (1931)* (Document DOCD-8050 to 8053) [Harvey's complete recordings, including those with Leonard Copeland (on *Volume 2* and *3*), Jess Johnston (on *Volume 3* and *4*), and Branch and Coleman (*Volume 4*)]
• *Early String Band Favorites* (Old Homestead OH-4017)
•• *Old-Time Mountain Guitar* (County CD-3512): "Guitar Rag," "Jefferson Street Rag" (both with Jess Johnston), "Back to the Blue Ridge," "Greasy Wagon," "Lonesome Weary Blues" (all with Leonard Copeland) •• *Old-Time Music of West Virginia Volume One* (County CD-3518): "Beckley Rag," "Underneath the Sugar Moon" (both with Leonard Copeland) •• *Old-Time Music of West Virginia Volume Two* (County CD-3519): "Good-Bye Maggie, Good-Bye Darling" (with Jess Johnston) •• *Guitare Country 1926–1950* (Frémeaux FA 5007 2CD): "Guitar Rag" (with Jess Johnston), "Just Picking" (with Leonard Copeland) •• *The Rose Grew Round the Briar: Early American Rural Love Songs Vol. 2* (Yazoo 2031): "George Collins" •• *Times Ain't Like They Used to Be Vol. 5* (Yazoo 2063): "No Room for a Tramp," "Railroad Blues" (both with Jess Johnston) •• *Times Ain't Like They Used to Be Vol. 6* (Yazoo 2064): "Milwaukee Blues" (with Jess Johnston) •• *The Stuff That Dreams Are Made Of* (Yazoo 2202 2CD): "John Hardy Blues" (with Jess Johnston)

The country music scene of the later '30s offered few openings to old stagers like Harvey. He worked for a while as a policeman in Beckley, then in 1942 moved to Florida and took a railroad job, thereby returning to his first profession. He gave up music entirely, and when he died he didn't even own a guitar.

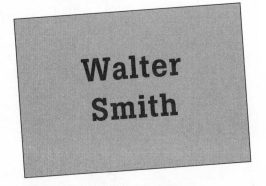

Walter Smith

(1895–1978)

A clique gathered in the 1920s and early '30s around the singer, banjoist, bandleader, and hell-raiser Charlie Poole. They were musicians from his neck of the woods, a section approximately enclosed by Patrick, Henry, and Pittsylvania Counties in southwestern Virginia and Rockingham County in northwestern North Carolina. What they also had in common was a penchant for elegant, affecting string-band music and, thanks to Poole's early success, well-developed lines of communication with recording companies that dealt in hillbilly music.

One of the most active and interesting of these figures was the singer and songwriter Walter Smith. He was originally from Carroll County, Virginia, but moved into Poole's orbit at some point in the '20s. He'd worked in sawmills and cotton mills and done a little boxing, earning the nickname "Kid," but his chief interest was singing old-time songs.

He fell in with Posey Rorer and Norman Woodlieff, fiddler and guitarist, respectively, in the original lineup of Poole's North Carolina Ramblers, though they had since parted company with him. Rorer fixed a recording date with Gennett and in spring 1929 Smith made his first recordings, a mixture of late-nineteenth-century sentimental songs like "I'll

Walter Smith (standing, left) with Lonnie Austin and (seated) Hamon Newman, Dorothy Smith, and Thelma Smith. (OTM collection)

Remember You Love in My Prayers" and old comic pieces like "The Bald-Headed End of a Broom" ("you'll find, when you're wed, that she'll bang you on your head with . . ."). Some of these sold rather well, launching Smith on a career that would last nearly eight years. But when he next recorded, a year later, he had a song of his own to promote.

On Christmas Day, 1929, Charlie Lawson, a prosperous farmer in Stokes County, North

Carolina, took his shotgun and shot or clubbed to death his wife, their four daughters, and two of their three sons. He laid out the bodies, closed their eyes, placed a stone under each head, then turned the gun on himself. A postmortem revealed that he was suffering from a brain tumor, probably caused by an earlier accident.

Using newspaper reports, Smith wrote a song, "The Murder of the Lawson Family," and recorded it with Rorer, banjoist Buster Carter, and guitarist Lewis McDaniels as the Carolina Buddies. It was one of Columbia Records' hit hillbilly songs of 1930, and is still occasionally sung by old-time and bluegrass bands.

Later that year Smith and McDaniels made further recordings for two other labels. They were attractive performances but didn't sell particularly well, and when, in 1931, Columbia asked for more Carolina Buddies recordings, Smith provided different musicians, his old friend Norman Woodlieff and the young (and unrelated) fiddler Odell Smith, who had played on some of Poole's records. The session elicited such quirky pieces as Smith's "My Evolution Girl," about a subject then (as

(OTM collection)

now) widely debated in the South, and Woodlieff's "He Went In like a Lion (but Came Out like a Lamb)." The best remembered song from the date is "Otto Wood the Bandit," Smith's composition about a local gangster, set to a lively tune.

"Kid, now, he was really a clown," Lewis McDaniels would remember. "He'd have made a good comedian." Which is exactly what he did. He enlisted his young daughters Thelma and Dorothy to play guitar and ukulele and sing, and they traveled quite widely in the southeastern states, accompanied by Woodlieff and Odell Smith. Photographs sometimes show Smith in the traditional hillbilly clown garb of check shirt and bib-and-brace overalls, with one front tooth blacked out.

A classified ad that Smith placed in the Danville *Bee* on February 7, 1931, wedged between "Nice Fat Turkeys" and "Store Room for Rent," read: "Musicianers and Singers want job broadcasting or stage." Times were hard for "musicianers" and farmers alike, but Smith's family band did get a recording opportunity in

Walter Smith and his daughters with Norman Woodlieff (guitar), 1931. (Kinney Rorer collection)

May, though it yielded only two sides. They returned home just in time for Walter to see his friend Charlie Poole before he died after one of his alcoholic binges. Smith promptly wrote a song, "The Life and Death of Charlie Poole," and premiered it for Poole's widow at their house. As Posey Rorer's grandson Kinney Rorrer recounts, Smith "was to deliver the song before a crowd of neighbors who had gathered on the front porch. However, before he could complete the third verse, the neighbors, Mrs. Poole, and even the musicians themselves had broken into hysterical weeping." Smith sold printed copies of the song, which was occasionally performed by The Carter Family, but it had to wait forty years to get on record, played by a local bluegrass band, Ted Prillaman & The Virginia Ramblers.

Poole's death stimulated recording activity in his circle, first by Roy Harvey and then by Posey Rorer with Buster Carter and guitarist Preston Young. Smith, curiously, had no part in this. His only other recording date was five years later, when he and his daughters made a few sides in a somewhat Carter Familyish style.

Playlist

• *Walter Smith & Friends Vol. 1 (1929–1930)* to *Vol. 3 (1931–1936)* (Document DOCD-8062 to 8064) [these contain, as well as all the recordings in which Smith himself was involved, sides by Buster Carter & Preston Young, Lewis McDaniels, and Norman Woodlieff]
•• *Cotton Mills and Fiddles* (Flyin' Cloud FC-014): "Little Bessie," "Long Eared Mule" (as Dixie Ramblers), "The Murder of the Lawson Family" (as Carolina Buddies) •• *Good for What Ails You: Music of the Medicine Shows 1926–1937* (Old Hat CD-1005 2CD): "The Bald-Headed End of a Broom," "The Cat's Got the Measles, the Dog's Got the Whooping Cough" •• *How Can I Keep from Singing Vol. 1* (Yazoo 2020): "It Won't Be Long Till My Grave Is Made" (with Norman Woodlieff) •• *My Rough and Rowdy Ways Vol. 2* (Yazoo 2040): "Otto Wood the Bandit" (as Carolina Buddies) •• *The Half Ain't Never Been Told Vol. 1* (Yazoo 2049): "There's a Beautiful City Called Heaven" (as Virginia Dandies) •• *The Half Ain't Never Been Told Vol. 2* (Yazoo 2050): "God's Getting Worried" (as Virginia Dandies) •• *The Story That the Crow Told Me Vol. 1* (Yazoo 2051): "The Story That the Crow Told Me" (as Carolina Buddies)

He continued to work as a comedian in tent shows and on radio, and by 1940 had settled in Fredericksburg, Virginia, where he had a daily program on WFVA. In 1947 he married another circuit veteran, a singer and guitarist known as Texas Tona Lee, and they headed a show that also included "Little Dot, America's No. 1 Contortionist" and "Tom Dooly, the Yodeling Dog." Smith eventually retired in 1969.

Asa Martin

(1900–79)

It was the talkies that pushed Asa Martin into country music.

Maybe he would have gone that way eventually. His background was copybook: he grew up in Winchester, Kentucky, in a family fond of music. His mother played guitar and taught piano, his father was something of a fiddler, and they both loved old songs. But when he himself started to play music for money, having

FIDDLING DOC ROBERTS TRIO

(OTM collection)

(Author's collection)

been forced by his straitened circumstances to drop out of medical school, Martin played his guitar in dance bands and sang the popular songs of the day. In the early 1920s a common engagement for that kind of musician was playing intermission and background music for silent movies. When talking pictures revolutionized the experience of movie-going, Martin was one among thousands of musicians on the fast track to obsolescence. He remembered, "I thought music was about done."

But thanks to another technological development, a new door was about to open. The recording of old-time music had begun a few years earlier, and by 1925 it was no longer a novelty. Every company in the business realized that it had to have country product, though neither "country" nor "product" would have been words they used. "Old time tunes" or "songs from Dixie" was how they described these early records of solo fiddling, harmonica-and-guitar one-man-bands, and Victorian parlor songs.

Some players from Martin's neck of the woods had already made recordings, like the fiddler Doc Roberts and the singing schoolteacher Welby Toomey. Martin hitched up with Roberts at a fiddlers' contest in Win-

chester soon afterward. They not only became friends but swept the board of prizes at the contest. Roberts had had other guitarists backing him on his records, including the African-American Booker brothers, but in May 1928, when he traveled up to Richmond, Indiana, for his annual session with Gennett Records, Martin was installed as his guitar accompanist. It was a partnership that would endure for at least six years.

A successful one, too. There were more than fifty of their exciting fiddle and guitar duets like "Billy in the Low Ground" and "Brick Yard Joe," and they sold consistently well. And Martin found another role. At that first session he was demonstrating to another singer how "The Knoxville Girl" should go. "You seem to be doing all right with it," commented the recording manager. "Why don't you sing it?" He quickly became one of Gennett's best-selling old-time artists with numbers like "The Dying Girl's Message," "The Old Fashioned Picture of Mother," and "There Is No Place like Home for a Married Man." When he and Roberts switched labels to ARC in 1931, it was the vocal duet pairing of Asa and Doc's teenaged son James that caught the ears of the public, with records like

"A Letter from Home Sweet Home," "There's a Little Box of Pine on the 7:29," and—a particularly good seller—the prison song "Ninety-Nine Years (Is Almost for Life)."

Recording sessions were merely incidents in a working musician's life. Martin put in many hours at the radio microphone, at stations in Louisville, Lexington, and Cincinnati. He began to book other acts, like the all-female Girls of the Sunny South, which at one point included Lily May Ledford, later leader of the Coon Creek Girls. For his own stage act he learned to play a few tunes on the musical saw.

In the '40s and '50s he was out of music, working at a steel plant in Ohio. When he returned to Kentucky he bought land outside the small town of Irvine, in Estill County, next door to Clark County, where he had been born. It would be his home for the rest of his life.

Asa Martin was slow to age. Old-time music enthusiasts, researching the music in the '60s and '70s, found him an exhilarating person to visit: his memories were sharp and he had held on to a lot of interesting old stuff. When he wasn't looking after his tobacco crop or working on one of his two houses, he was still playing with a bunch of friends, as "Asa Martin and the Cumberland Rangers," on the local radio station and at festivals both within and beyond Kentucky. The band also cut an album for Rounder, *Dr. Ginger Blue.*

Asa Martin died from a heart attack one summer afternoon in his garden, where he'd gone to pick cucumbers.

Dick Burnett

(1883–1977)

I'm a long ways from bein' dead," said Richard D. Burnett stoutly to country music historian Charles Wolfe on their first meeting. It was true enough. At the age of eighty-nine, although blind, he could still earn money from making chairs. He even played a little music yet, and his memory was as sharp as a tack. He sang along faultlessly to his old discs like the archaic ballad of "Willie Moore," which he and his partner Leonard Rutherford had recorded almost half a century before.

To this day, there are older people in Tennessee and southern Kentucky who can talk admiringly about the music of Burnett and Rutherford, preserved in memories of their playing in coal camps and courthouse squares and in a small pile of pre-Depression 78s.

Rutherford, who was by some fifteen years the younger of the two, was one of the prettiest of old-time fiddlers and he could sing too, but as his colleague recalled with amusement, "There wasn't no monkey work about him at all. He wouldn't do it. He could play that fiddle, he was the best in the world, but he wouldn't do nothin' else. You've got to have showmanship." It fell to Burnett, as the showman, to execute the decorative flourishes on their records—dance-calls and imitations of a jew's harp—as well as picking the guitar or banjo.

The two men's empathy was extraordinary. "We played every note right together," said Burnett. "I wanted to play the same notes on the banjo that he was playin' on the fiddle. Other people cut their music up so much with the fiddle bow, cut it all to pieces, till it didn't sound good."

Burnett and Rutherford traveled together for thirty-five years, "plumb through West Virginia and Old Virginia and Florida and Georgia and everywhere else. Played all those coal camps in Harlan County. . . ." It was in a coal

Playlist
•• *Jake Leg Blues* (Jass J-CD-642): "Jake Walk Papa" •• *Mountain Blues* (JSP JSP 7740 4CD): "Lonesome, Broke and Weary" •• *Old Time Music: The Essential Collection* (Rounder Heritage 11599): "Death of J. B. Marcum" [1972 recording] •• *When I Was a Cowboy Vol. 1* (Yazoo 2022): "The Roundup in the Spring" •• *Times Ain't Like They Used to Be Vol. 4* (Yazoo 2048): "Havana River Glide" (with Roy Hobbs, mandolin) •• *Kentucky Mountain Music* (Yazoo 2200 7CD): "Gentle Annie," "Hot Corn" (Martin & Roberts), "I Must See My Mother" (with Roy Hobbs, mandolin), "Lillie Dale" (Martin & Roberts), "My Cabin Home among the Hills" •• *The Stuff That Dreams Are Made Of* (Yazoo 2202 2CD): "Wild Cat Rag" (with Roy Hobbs, mandolin)

Burnett & Rutherford, late 1920s. (Author's collection)

camp region of Virginia that they met a man who sold records in his store.

> We played some for 'em, and he said, "My goodness, why don't you fellers go and put them on records?" "Well," I said, "I been thinkin' about it, but I didn't know if I could or not." And he says, "Yes, you can. . . . I'm going to write a letter to Atlanta, Georgia, down there to the manager, and ask him to get you fellows to come and make records." And you know, he did, and we went, and put on records, and that man—I forgot how many he bought, dozens of our records.

Frank Walker of Columbia Records, auditioning them in 1926, remarked, "I've had a heap of people record for me here, but you two fellers are the two smoothest musicians that I ever had record for me." And he added, "You have some of the tantalizingest names for these records that ever I listened at." Among them were the skipping dance-tune "Ladies on the Steamboat," "A Short Life of Trouble" (later done by Buell Kazee, G. B. Grayson, Wade Mainer and Zeke

Morris, and the Blue Sky Boys), and the hobo fantasy "Little Stream of Whiskey."

At a later session for Gennett, joined by guitarist Byrd Moore, they played a lively, intricate version of "Cumberland Gap." In accordance with their usual marketing practice, Gennett issued it on subsidiary labels like Champion and Supertone with pseudonymous credits.

> And when it [the record] came back here [to Monticello, Kentucky], this here Johnny Powers over here, he'd ordered some of these records, bought 'em to sell. He had one of them records of "Cumberland Gap" and he was playin' that. And somebody said, "Listen there! Listen there! That's Dick and Leonard!" And the record said "Norton, Bunch and Bond" [actually "Norton, Bond and Williams"]. And he said, "Ain't no such stuff. I know who it is, it's Dick and Leonard." And it *was* us. They'd done that to try and sell more records. But it didn't fool the people—they knowed who it was, soon as they heard it.

Unfortunately Burnett never recorded one of the most powerful songs in his repertoire,

"Man of Constant Sorrow," which he had printed in a pamphlet of old-time songs that he sold for ten cents. But another Kentuckian, Emry Arthur, put it on disc, and later the Stanley Brothers turned it into a bluegrass standard. Burnett knew sorrow firsthand. He lost both parents before he was in his teens, and was blinded in a shooting accident in his early twenties. But he was no figure of pity.

> There was a man down here in Clinton County, where I used to drill for my wife's brothers in the oilfields. I was raised in the mountains a mile and a half from where they was raised and they knowed what a hard time I had had all my life, that I had worked hard all my life. Now I'd go down to Albany to play, and there was a man, old John Upchurch, lived on the road there, said he wondered what that Dick Burnett was doing ridin' up and down that road so much fur. And this Mrs. Bennet, friend of mine, said, "Why, he's goin' down there to put on an entertainment. He's a blind man, can't see to work now, he's tryin' to make a living." And he said, "He never worked when he could see. He never was no 'count, wouldn't give a nickel for the lot."
>
> So she told me about it and I said, "Well, I bet he ain't gonna get away with it none. I'm gonna have it anyhow." He claimed to be religious and he had a barrel of wine down in his cellar, and he'd go down there and get so drunk that he couldn't get back upstairs. He'd go to the Davis Chapel up there and he'd shout and his wife would shout and pray. And I made a song about it and sung it.

> Come all you rounders if you want to hear
> Story all about a revival held here
> Rounder Windy was the speaker's name
> Up in Davis Chapel where he won his
>   fame. . . .

I made a long song out of it and I sold three hundred of them on song cards, all around him down there, and they'd sing 'em goin' to milk and goin' to feed and everywhere.

People who knew Burnett in his later years regarded him primarily as a fiddler. "Actually I loved the fiddle more than the banjo," he said, and after Rutherford's death, around 1950, he played it more, though he stopped traveling and stayed at home in Monticello. His and Rutherford's exhilarating music lives on in the playing of a fellow-townsman, the superb fiddle and banjo player Clyde Davenport.

Playlist
• *Burnett & Rutherford (1926–1930)* (Document DOCD-8025)
•• *Old-Time Mountain Ballads* (County CO-CD-3504): "Pearl Bryan," "Willie Moore" •• *Old-Time Mountain Blues* (County CO-CD-3528): "Curley-Headed Woman" •• *Old Mountain: Stringband Songs & Tunes* (Living Era CD AJA 5577): "Ladies on the Steamboat" •• *Times Ain't Like They Used to Be Vol. 4* (Yazoo 2048): "Billy in the Low Ground" •• *Kentucky Mountain Music* (Yazoo 2200 7CD): "All Night Long Blues," "Billy in the Low Ground," "Cumberland Gap," "Curley-Headed Woman," "Grandma's Rag," "I'll Be with You When the Roses Bloom Again," "Knoxville Rag," "Ladies on the Steamboat," "Little Stream of Whiskey," "Lost John," "Pearl Bryan," "Ramblin' Reckless Hobo," "She Is a Flower from the Fields of Alabama," "Willie Moore"

John D. Foster

(1896–1984)

The story of fiddler Leonard Rutherford has another chapter, which has little to do with his first recording partner Dick Burnett. It is shared with his next associate, the singer and guitarist John Foster, and it can be told in Foster's own words. Following a visit to his home in Robbins, Tennessee, by Charles Wolfe and me, Foster was inspired to write an account of his times in the music business.

His first brush with the profession was in the 1920s, when a tent show came to town that featured "a comedian by the name of Jesse James."

John Foster (left) and Leonard Rutherford.
(Courtesy of the Foster family)

This is when I started with guitar. James was my instructor, and a good one. After three months' practice we went on the stage and we played a wide range of territory. All over Kentucky and Tennessee we entered many large state contests and won them all. Then we started playing high schools and theaters. We was getting more calls than we could handle. Then [1927] the Gennett Record Co. brought a portable recording [unit] to Birmingham, Alabama. They called me and Jesse James. We made our first recording. The Depression was coming on. Plants started closing down. We decided to move to Knoxville. We did lots of music programs there but times was growing worse daily.

At this time Burnett, Rutherford, and Byrd Moore was playing together. They was hired by Dennis W. Taylor to make a recording for Gennett, but Rutherford was a very smooth violinist and Burnett and Moore played a harsh accompaniment. They was no match for his music. The company advised Mr. Taylor they could not record this team any further unless he could find a man to match Rutherford.

Since they had my records I recorded in Birmingham, they chose me. I met Rutherford in Somerset[, Kentucky] on request. We went to a private room. I had about fifty numbers to choose from at that time. We picked the numbers for our first recording and played 24 hours on them. Then Rutherford called Taylor, advised him he had me and I was just what they needed. He called us right on up there. We immediately made our first recording, and we signed our first two years' contract.

Dennis W. Taylor was a wealthy farmer in Richmond, Kentucky, who acted as an intermediary for Gennett, scouting for musicians and sometimes, as with Rutherford and Foster, signing them to management contracts that guaranteed them a regular income; in exchange, Gennett paid him a share of disc royalties. He was involved with Asa Martin and Doc Roberts, banjoist Marion Underwood, singer Aulton Ray, the African-American fiddler Jim Booker and his guitar-playing sons, and numerous others. Some recordings by these musicians were even issued as by "Taylor's Kentucky Boys." The details of Taylor's activities are obscure, since his family was unresponsive to questions. Foster suggests a possible reason for their reserve.

Sears, Roebuck sent a representative to meet us at Mr Taylor's to hire us on WLS radio station. We made every test possible for him. He turned to me and said, "You know more ballets [old songs] than all the artists we have on WLS." He then said, "Are you under contract with Mr. Taylor?" I said yes. He said, "We want you all," and said if I would go there the company would buy me a home in Chicago and start my salary at $25,000, and would make an album of my life and sell it from their big catalog, and permit me to advertise all I wished over WLS.

I turned to Mr. Taylor. "Will you release me to go?" I knew he would not without a large commission. He said, "For ten thousand [dollars] annually, and this will have to be paid as long as you are on WLS." That was a very unfair offer. There was no way we could reach that offer. My last contract was up in six months from that date. I said to Sears' man, "I cannot accept this offer until my contract expires. We may see each other then." He said, "I hope so." I then turned to Mr. Taylor and said, "You could have let me take this job. I would guarantee to make you three recordings free and advertise all the records on WLS to help the sales." "No," he said, "I cannot do that." I said, "OK, you can do this, Mr. Taylor. We have made you a barrel of money that did not cost you a million dollars. I am quitting you now. I will not make another record. Do not call me." That closed this offer.

The notion of Sears, Roebuck, the owners of WLS, paying a five-figure salary to a hillbilly artist in 1929 is a little hard to swallow—perhaps, over the years, Foster's memory improved the offer somewhat—but Taylor's role in the story is quite plausible: other people's reminiscences imply that he ran his cadre of musician-employees in the style of a plantation owner.

Foster recalled several sessions with Rutherford, and Gennett files confirm they came to the studios four times in 1929, cutting fiddle tunes—among them a "Taylor's Quickstep," named for their manager while they were still getting along—and sturdy vocal duets on romantic, sentimental, and humorous material. "Yeah, they made a few records," said Dick Burnett dismissively, "but they never did amount to nothin'." Actually their recording of "Six Months Ain't Long," coupled on a 35-cent Champion disc with another prison song, "Birmingham Jail" by Byrd Moore and fiddler Melvin Robinette, was one of Gennett's top hillbilly sellers. But all the masters from their last two sessions are noted as "rejected," perhaps a consequence of their falling-out with Taylor.

Me and Rutherford stayed on together playing in theaters and high schools until our contract expired with Taylor. The day after it expired we was called to Atlanta, Ga., to record for the Brunswick Record Company. We made a good go on this recording. Then Rutherford became very sick and taken epileptic fits. He was no more good.

Foster had a final session in 1934. Then, he remembered,

a panic hit the recording work. Everything was terribly reduced. I did carpenter work up to 1943, when I signed up with the army to work at their security force at Oak Ridge. I worked as investigating officer until discharged. Since this time I have done carpenter work, and was self employed in the insurance work and etc. until I retired.

Our interview over, John Foster and his visitors sat and chatted on his porch. His children had borrowed my tape recorder and were playing a tape we had brought with us. An artistically shapely conclusion would have them captivated by the sound of their father, singing on a record made decades before they were born. In fact they were more taken with some blues they found at the end of the tape, and as the light faded into the shadows of the East Tennessee woods we listened not to John Foster singing "Six Months Ain't Long" but to "Ten Long Years" by B. B. King.

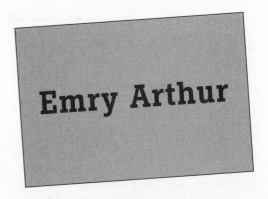

Emry Arthur

(1902–67)

When George Clooney leans into the microphone in the radio station sequence of *O Brother, Where Art Thou?* and sings, "I am a man of constant sorrow—I've seen trouble all my days," he is not only initiating one of the most captivating sequences in that ingenious movie but giving an incidental nod to a figure from another time and place: not the Depression, but earlier in the 1920s, and not the flatlands of Mississippi, where that section

(OTM collection)

of the movie is set, but the mountains of south central Kentucky.

That section of the country, particularly counties on the Tennessee line such as Wayne and Whitley, was once intensely musical terrain. In Whitley County there was an extraordinary nexus of banjo players, stringbands, and singing preachers. Monticello, in Wayne, boasted Dick Burnett and Leonard Rutherford. And out in the sticks of Wayne County was a family of Arthurs who liked to sing old songs.

Sam and Henry Arthur mostly played, but Emry, who had lost a finger in a hunting accident while a boy and could do little more than strum a guitar, concentrated on singing: ancient mountain chants, romantic Tin Pan Alley songs of the Victorian and Edwardian era like "I'll Remember You Love in My Prayers," newer gospel songs and hymns like "Love Lifted Me." It was a talent, but not a livelihood. There was not much to make a living from in Wayne County in those days, so in the mid-'20s he exchanged the mountains for the northern industrial city of Indianapolis.

Within three years his life was changed. Following a successful audition for Vocalion, he cut a stack of records during 1928: more than two dozen between January and August, some made in Indianapolis, others in Chicago. Brother Henry came up from Wayne County to play banjo and sing duets, and sometimes a local steel guitarist sat in. Emry also sang on a couple of sessions by a curious group of Indianapolitans who billed themselves as Floyd Thompson & His Home Towners and had plainly been listening carefully to the Broadway hillbilly music of Carson Robison and Frank Luther.

Arthur's sacred songs seem to have been the best sellers at the time, but there were other potent scripts in his portfolio, and one of them was "I Am a Man of Constant Sorrow." It is not the version of the song that came down to Clooney, or rather to Dan Tyminski, the bluegrass singer to whose voice Clooney is lip-synching. Tyminski's model was one of the magisterial versions recorded by Ralph Stanley, who says he heard it first from his own father. It might still have come from Emry Arthur, indirectly, but it probably didn't start there. Dick Burnett claimed he wrote it about 1912 and taught it to Arthur. Perhaps he did, or perhaps it was just around when they were both growing up, a floating text whose author was already forgotten.

Compared with later versions, Arthur's is sedate. All his work is notable for its calm and restraint, qualities that evidently appealed to Vocalion, who continued to record him in 1929, giving him the chance to extend his repertoire with blues and a couple of harmonica solos. The blues are somewhat in the Jimmie Rodgers manner, but lack his ease and humor, and Arthur's guitar-playing is ponderous. Then, that summer, he suddenly stepped into the world of one of his songs and learned at first hand the meaning of constant sorrow. His marriage broke up and he moved away to Illinois, leaving, as he wrote in a letter to a friend, "everything I had."

Soon afterward, however, he signed up with Paramount Records, not just as a recording artist but as a hand in their factory in Port Washington, Wisconsin. He recorded a further twenty songs for them, including another version of "Man of Constant Sorrow." Some were duets with Della Hatfield, whom he may have met in Indianapolis (though there are Hatfields aplenty in Wayne County), and whom he married. He also became acquainted with William Myers, a songwriter in Richlands, Virginia, who used to send lyrics to artists he admired, among them Mississippi John Hurt and Dock Boggs. (Many years later Hurt recalled and recorded two of them, "Richland Woman Blues" and "Let the Mermaids Flirt with Me.") Myers even ventured into the record business to disseminate his compositions. He must not have cared for the music of Jimmie Rodgers, for the Lonesome Ace label carried the challenging legend "Without a Yodel." Arthur made a record for Myers and played guitar on a couple by Boggs. As it turned out, those three discs would be Lonesome Ace's entire catalog.

Emry Arthur made his last records, for Decca, in 1935. By then he and Della were probably back in Indianapolis, but we know nothing of their later life, even though Della survived him by almost four decades.

Playlist

• *I Am a Man of Constant Sorrow* (Old Homestead OH-4190) [Vocalion recordings] •• *Old-Time Music from South-West Virginia* (County CO-CD-3523): "Careless Love," "Reuben Oh Reuben," "She Lied to Me," "Short Life of Trouble" •• *Appalachian Stomp Down* (JSP JSP 7761 4CD): "The Bootlegger's Lullaby," "The Broken Wedding," "Down in Tennessee Valley," "Ethan Lang," "Going around the World," "Goodbye, My Lover, Goodbye," "I Am a Man of Constant Sorrow," "I Shall Know by the Print of the Nails on His Hand," "I'm a Man of Constant Sorrow," "In the Heart of the City That Has No Heart," "The Little Black Train Is Coming," "Love Lifted Me," "Nobody's Business," "She's a Flower from the Fields of Alabama," "Shining for the Master," "The Wanderer," "Wandering Gypsy Girl," "Where the Silvery Colorado Wends Its Way" •• *Paramount Old Time Recordings* (JSP JSP 7774 4CD): "The Bluefield Murder," "George Collins," "Got Drunk and Got Married," "I Tickled Her under the Chin," "The Married Man," "There's a Treasure Up in Heaven" •• *The Music of Kentucky Vol. 2* (Yazoo 2014): "I Am a Man of Constant Sorrow," "Reuben Oh Reuben," "She Lied to Me," "Short Life of Trouble"

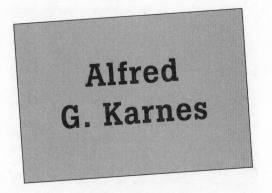

Alfred G. Karnes

(1891–1958)

The Victor session in Bristol, Tennessee, in July–August 1927 brought out of the shadows two acts that would dominate country music. But in the brilliant glare of Bristol's most famous discoveries one can all too easily be blinded to what else happened there. Jimmie Rodgers and The Carter Family recorded, between them, eight sides, but the Victor crew took home nearly eighty—by stringbands, gospel quartets, banjoists, church groups, all sorts. Buried in that lode was a small stack of discs by a former barber, now a Baptist minister, from Corbin, Kentucky, named Alfred G. Karnes.

The first time you hear Karnes's music, you will probably be riveted by the power of his guitar playing. The first reissue of a Karnes track, "I Am Bound for the Promised Land," was on an LP otherwise devoted to black religious music—not because the compilers were unaware of Karnes's color, but because his flatpicking and thumping bass-string runs seemed to align him less with hillbilly guitarists like Rodgers than with black players like Charley Patton or "Rabbit" Brown.

Karnes was actually playing an instrument he had only just bought, an expensive Gibson harp guitar. He might have chosen differently: since his boyhood in Bedford, Virginia, he had played banjo and fiddle. But the instrument he probably valued most was his voice, which was rich and true, polished by years of singing in barbershop quartets and, after he became a minister in 1925, by leading his congregation in church.

He had arrived in Corbin, his wife Flora's hometown, in 1920. It was no big place, but on a musical map of the South it has a significance far out of proportion to its size. The roster of Corbin artists who made records in the '20s and '30s includes the banjoist B. F. Shelton, singers Dick Parman and Ted Chesnut, the

Watchman, What of Night? Watchman What of the Night?

— PROPHECY AGAINST GOG —

Thus saith the Lord God: Behold I am against thee, O Gog. — Ezekiel 39:1.

In the light of the Bible, I feel very keenly the need of the hour, through many years of evangelical work, I never felt that time is so short, to set our house in order for the coming of the Lord.

No man or Angels know that day, or hour (Matt. 24:36.) but Jesus tells us of the events, and generation, and as sure as we know by the budding on the trees, that summer is nigh, we will know the coming of Christ in night. (Matt. 24:32.)

THE JEWS CHARACTERIZED
God said in many scriptures he would remove them from the Land he gave them, to all the Kingdoms of the earth. (Jeremiah 24:9-10). Also Jesus said, Jerusalem shall be trodden down of the Gentiles until the times of the Gentiles be fulfilled (Luke 21:24.). Now they are back as a nation after 2500 years. God promised he would gather them back, also in many Scriptures (Jeremiah 32:37) because God gave the land of Canaan to Abram or Abraham's children or seed. (Genesis 15:18).

RUSSIA CHARACTERIZED

We know that Russia's plan is to swallow up the world in atheistic Communism. Russia advances to this end by piece-meal aggression, and puts them under a protectorate (guard) Ezekiel 38:7. Now read the 10, 11 12 verses of this 38 Chapter: God is against Magog, the land of Gog. So Russia fits exactly, characteristically, geographically, and prophetically, the end of time, just before Christ comes for his saved. If true, Russia will not be conquered until the Saved are gone with Christ."
Have you received Christ as your Saviour and keeper of your Soul? Receive him now, by faith, before it's too late. John 1:12. John 3:16. John 3:36. Luke 21:36. Matt. 24:21.

IF YÒU WANT MORE COPIES WRITE ME:
REV. A. G. KARNES
Rt. 2, Box 109   Starke, Fla.

(Norm Cohen collection)

Holiness minister Ernest Phipps, and two fascinating stringbands, Alex Hood's Railroad Boys and John Walker's Corbin Ramblers. Shelton and Phipps, too, made the journey to Bristol, some 150 miles east by 1927's roads. Karnes would surely have known Phipps and, despite doctrinal differences, they might not have minded making music together. Some listeners hear Karnes's distinctive guitar on Phipps's records: wishful thinking, probably, but Karnes may be one of the hand-clapping congregation on Phipps's sides from the second Bristol session, held the following year and attended by both men.

In his two trips to Bristol Karnes recorded thirteen sides, eight of them issued. "To the Work" and "Called to the Foreign Field" were songs of missionary zeal: "I am called to bear a message to the heathen far away." Two from the second session, "Do Not Wait 'Till I'm Laid 'Neath the Clay" and "The Days of My Childhood Plays," were not sacred themes but heart songs, one echoing the sentiment of the blues, "Don't Bring Me Flowers While I'm Living," the other looking longingly back at lost innocence. "We Shall All Be Reunited" contemplates a final meeting "in that land beyond the skies, where there'll be no separation, no more parting, no more sighs." "I Am Bound for the Promised Land," another fine old song of hope in the afterlife, is arrestingly set to a melody reminiscent of Charlie Poole's "Don't Let Your Deal Go Down." "Where We'll Never Grow Old" and "When They Ring the Golden Bells" were popular sacred numbers that many artists recorded, but Karnes's versions have a sober, stately beauty.

Karnes never recorded again, but he had not deserted music. In the '30s, living near Berea, Kentucky, he formed a stringband with four sons and a daughter, who played guitars, mandolins, and bass while he led on the fiddle. They played on Sundays in the courthouse squares of townships like Mount Vernon, Broadhead, Lancaster, and Stanford. "When they came in front of the courthouse there were only a few people around," recalled a Lancaster resident, "but by the time they had done three or four songs the square was so full of people you could hardly drive through." He continued his ministry until felled by a stroke.

Buell Kazee

(1900–76)

My trouble," Buell Kazee remarked, "was that I made the records too good."

To say that Kazee was an old-time Kentucky mountain banjo player might suggest a lean, sunburned, high-booted farmer or a gaunt coal miner—men of the earth, happier around a gun or a dog than a schoolbook. But Buell Kazee grew up different in Magoffin County. He went to college, where he took formal voice training, and after graduating he worked as a music teacher in Ashland, Kentucky.

Browsing among the hillbilly discs in the town's music store one day, he let slip to the proprietor that he sang old songs and played banjo, which he had learned in his community when a child. He was persuaded to demonstrate. "Boy," said the store owner, "they'll throw their arms around you in New York." Three weeks later, in

Buell Kazee, Brunswick Records publicity photograph, 1927. (Southern Folklife Collection)

April 1927, Kazee was up there to make his first records.

What he meant by "too good" was that he started out singing in his trained voice, only to be told by the Brunswick Records people: "That just won't ring on the cash register." Country people wouldn't buy it. So he lapsed into a back-home accent, and over a rippling banjo accompaniment delivered some of the finest performances of traditional American ballads and mountain love songs to be heard on record. Two of them were "East Virginia" and "The Wagoner's Lad," which Joan Baez learned from him and recorded on her first and second albums, respectively. Others included "John Hardy," "The Butcher's Boy," "Little Bessie," and "Darling Cora." Reviewing Kazee's disc of "The Butcher's Boy" and "The Wagoner's Lad," Abbe Niles wrote in the September 1928 issue of the magazine *The Bookman*: "These two have all the mysterious pathos of the English ballad that finds itself far from home and on a strange tongue."

Kazee's repertoire is a well-stocked library of old Appalachian songs, and, apart from the Asheville lawyer and banjo-playing folksinger

Bascom Lamar Lunsford, nobody recorded more of them. But his appeal was not only to lovers of ballad tales. He sang pop songs like "You Taught Me How to Love You, Now Teach Me to Forget" in his "nice" voice and with studio musicians. He went for the Western song market with "The Roving Cowboy" ("I sold a lot [of that] in Texas") and "The Cowboy Trail," and even reluctantly recorded a couple of comic sketches. Looking back, he dismissed them as "pretty dumb." His discs sold in Canada, Australia, Ireland, and the UK.

On one of his New York recording trips Kazee met the dean of citybilly singers, Vernon Dalhart. "He looked me out to see if he had any competition," said Kazee. "He didn't have." Yet for all his correct diction and smooth delivery, which in truth he never succeeded in roughing up all that much, Kazee was a more convincing performer of southern song than Dalhart or concert folksingers of a later era like John Jacob Niles. As he observed, he had grown up with "the old, the genuine thing . . . I can almost go back to the original."

Kazee's recording career didn't outlast the Depression, but he didn't need it, since he was a Baptist minister. "They [Brunswick] wanted me to go to Texas and places like that and play the county and state fairs, and . . . go up the hollows to every picture show and popularize [the records]. I didn't have time for that. . . . My life was cast in a different direction, you see."

"My entire time is spent," he would write later, "in preaching and teaching the Bible, holding meetings and Bible conferences, and pastoring a young church here in Lexington, Ky." But from time to time he would give a recital, presenting mountain songs "with absolute conformity," as he explained to the folklorist Archie Green, "to the original styles of singing and playing, and never with any attempt to take them out of their settings or make them take on a classical or even conventional atmosphere." He sometimes appeared on that most purist of country shows, the Renfro Valley Barn Dance, and even guested at the 1968 Newport Folk Festival, though he didn't care for the radical politics of some of his fellow performers. But he may have set more store by his inspirational book *Faith Is the Victory* and his composition of operas and cantatas based on folk themes.

Playlist

• *Legendary Kentucky Ballad Singer* (BACM CD D 027)
•• *Old-Time Mountain Ballads* (County CD-3504): "The Wagoner's Lad" •• *Old-Time Mountain Banjo* (County CO-CD-3533): "The Orphan Girl" •• *Country* (Frémeaux FA 015 2CD): "The Butcher's Boy" •• *Folksongs* (Frémeaux FA 047 2CD): "East Virginia," "The Wagoner's Lad" •• *Kentucky Old-Time Banjo* (Rounder CD 0394): "The Blind Man's Lament," "John Hardy," "Soldier's Joy" [1972 recordings] •• *Before the Blues Vol. 1* (Yazoo 2015): "John Hardy" •• *When I Was a Cowboy Vol. 2* (Yazoo 2023): "The Cowboy Trail" •• *Times Ain't Like They Used to Be Vol. 1* (Yazoo 2028); "The Dying Soldier" •• *The Rose Grew Round the Briar: Early American Rural Love Songs Vol. 1* (Yazoo 2030): "A Short Life of Trouble" •• *Kentucky Mountain Music* (Yazoo 2200 7CD): "The Butcher's Boy," "The Cowboy Trail," "The Dying Soldier," "I'm Rolling Along," "The Orphan Girl," "The Roving Cowboy," "A Short Life of Trouble," "The Sporting Bachelors"

Raymond Render

(1906–59)

The channels by which old-time music reaches us are often wide, like great rivers coming down from the mountains of the past—the Poole, the Stoneman, the mighty Macon. There is so much music in them that we can bathe in it. But sometimes they are tiny: threadlike traces of a recording career that amounted to no more than one coupling—or even less than that, a single side of a 78 rpm disc. The annals of old-time music hold more than twenty of these short-short stories, giving us momentary sightings of the Pelican Wildcats from Louisiana or the Copperhill Male Quartet from eastern Tennessee, small-town groups whose bid for fame was reduced to a solitary song or tune.

Occasionally these hapless musicians couldn't even preserve their identity. A combination cumbersomely billed on the recording sheet as "The Tennessee Hillbilly with Ruth and Leo West" showed up for a Bluebird session in Charlotte, North Carolina, in 1937 and recorded eight songs. The only one that survives is tantalizingly fine, the aching valediction "Sleep On, Departed One," but when issued it was credited to the group on the other side of the disc, Mainer's Mountaineers. Similarly, the twenty-four-year-old singer and guitarist who traveled three hundred miles to Gennett's studios in the summer and fall of 1930, to make a trial recording and six finished performances, saw just one of them released, on a cut-price label with a bogus artist credit. If Gennett's files had not survived, we should probably never have known that "Frank Dunbar," who sang "Nobody's Darling on Earth" on Superior 2538, was actually Raymond Render, "The Dixie Yodeler," sometime "Radio Star" of Akron, Ohio, but originally from the coalfields of Ohio County in western Kentucky.

The mark Render left on old-time music history may be barely perceptible, but he has a role to play, all the same. He stands for many musicians like him, competent, personable performers who took hillbilly music to states like Ohio, Indiana, Illinois, or Missouri, finding niches for it in clubs and theaters and the schedules of small radio stations. So far as most of the companies dealing in hillbilly music were concerned, such men were off the map. Their only hope of making a record lay with the Indiana-based Gennett, whose ledgers are indeed littered with trial or rejected recordings that we shall never hear, by obscure hopefuls whose stories we may never be able to tell.

With Raymond Render, however, we are more fortunate, because he made a deep impression on his grandson Ron Whitehead, Kentucky memorialist, sometime college professor, associate of Hunter S. Thompson and Lawrence Ferlinghetti, and Ohio County's only Beat poet. "Every kind of music/we heard it all," he writes in "Music Saved My Life and Jesus Saved My Soul: The Impossible Dream."

Raymond Render. (Courtesy of the Whitehead family)

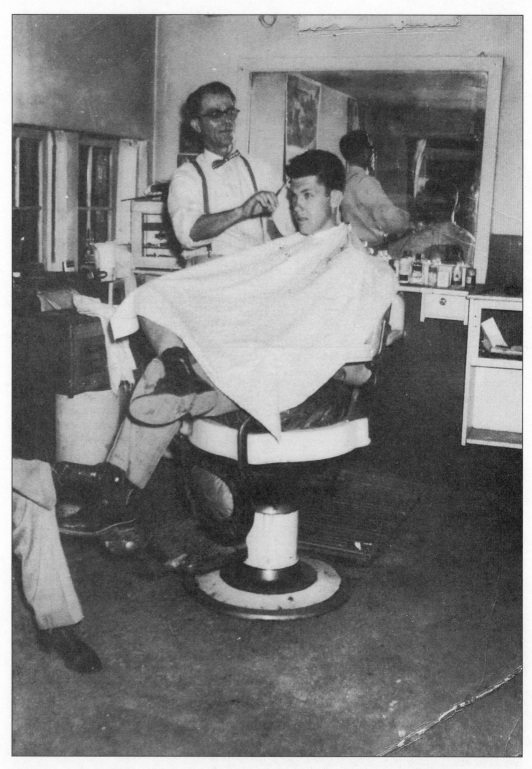

Ray Render styles William E. Boyd. "William E. come in the shop one night drunk & told grandaddy he wanted his head shaved," Ron Whitehead notes in the family album. "He shaved it & the next morning he was mad." (Courtesy of the Whitehead family)

. . . we listened to Jimmie Rodgers
and Hank Williams, Bill Monroe and
    Woody Guthrie
and Raymond Render and Mose Rager
and The Montgomery Brothers and
    Brother Matthew's Gospel Quartet
with Mrs Duncan bangin on that piano
    like I'd
never heard in no Baptist church and I
    got excited
Oh Lord can music make you feel this
    good?

In his collection *Beaver Dam Rocking Chair Marathon*, Whitehead fills out the picture of his grandfather:

Barber, handsome, coon hunter, daring, entertainer, recording star, played guitar, ukulele, drums, piano, tap dancer, artist, he had a painting in barber shop, he sang in womanless wedding dressed like woman, great gardener, inventor, builder . . .

Raymond Thomas ("Dick") Render grew up around Centertown, Kentucky, whose population then numbered in the low hundreds and is hardly larger today. In his early twenties he moved to Akron to work as a barber, a trade two of his brothers had already taken up. His daughter Greta Render Whitehead recalls that he always wore a white shirt and a bow tie. Away from the tonsorial parlor, he led Render's Southern Recording Entertainers ("Music furnished for all occasions"). A clipping in his family's possession, headed "Centertown Youth's Music Recorded" and probably dating from 1930, reports that he "has recently been spending much time in the studios of the Gennett Record Co., where many of his guitar selections have been placed on phonograph records"—a somewhat over-optimistic assertion—and that "he has also frequently appeared before the microphone at various radio stations." As his "Dixie Yodeler" billing implies, he loved the music of Jimmie Rodgers. He made a few home recordings in the '40s and most of them are yodel songs from the Rodgers folio such as "T.B. Blues," "My Carolina Sunshine Girl," or "Mississippi River Blues."

"He was always on the move, going going going doing doing doing," Ron Whitehead writes. He fathered thirteen children ("*known* children," Whitehead adds with a grin), farmed, and ran Centertown's Blue Bus Café—which was exactly that, a double-decker bus converted into a café. Later he worked in construction

around Louisville, building new highways, but on Saturdays he returned to Centertown to open the barbershop, where between haircuts he played guitar and sang with his daughters. Sometimes he visited with other local musicians, such as the celebrated guitarists Mose Rager and Ike Everly, who lived in Drakesboro in neighboring Muhlenberg County. (Rager, a fellow barber, and Everly, father of Don and Phil, were direct influences on Merle Travis, who took their bluesy thumb-picking style to the West Coast in the '40s and became famous.) In what time was left of his weekends Ray Render went out with his buddies, ostensibly coon-hunting but mostly sitting round a fire, deep in the woods, drinking and telling stories.

In the fall of 1959, while he was working on Louisville's Henry Watterson Expressway, his grader toppled on a steep incline and rolled over on him. He hung on to life for a week. The last words of this whiskey-drinking blue yodeler, described by his grandson as "untamed, wild, a gypsy, a free spirit," were "Go to church for me."

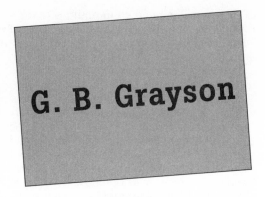

G. B. Grayson

(1887–1930)

Choosing the life of an old-time musician was no guarantee that a man would live to be old. Gilliam Banmon Grayson was only forty-two when he was killed in a car accident. But in his short life of trouble (to borrow the title of one of his songs) he became one of Appalachia's more famous musicians, and he left behind him, as well as a widow and six children, three dozen recordings of old-time songs and tunes that would be models for later artists like J. E. Mainer and the Stanley Brothers.

Though born in Ashe County in northwestern North Carolina, he spent almost all his life

(OTM collection)

in the prettily named community of Laurel Bloomery, in the northeastern tip of Tennessee. His was only the second American-born generation of his family: his grandfather, a shipwright, had emigrated to North Carolina from Scotland.

Accident or infection in babyhood permanently damaged Grayson's sight—the family story is that, left in his crib one winter day, he stared too long at the bright sunlit snow—and when he grew up he could find no work except as an itinerant fiddler, playing on the streets by day, for dances or schoolhouse concerts at night. In his travels and at fiddlers' contests he began to encounter musicians who had made records or were preparing to do so, and in 1927 he formed a partnership with one of them, the guitarist and singer Henry Whitter, then living in Warrensville, North Carolina, not far from Laurel Bloomery.

It was a lucky meeting for both men. Whitter's success in the record business had owed more to enterprise than to outstanding talent, and by this point it was to his advantage to team up with a musician like Grayson who, as it proved, could attain the kind of sales Whitter himself could no longer guarantee. Grayson, for his part, profited from Whitter's contacts, which gained them bookings with Victor and Gennett

only days apart in the fall of 1927, and subsequent sessions for both labels in 1928–29.

Unlike many of his contemporaries Grayson was not primarily a dance fiddler. He made a few records of dance tunes like "Old Jimmy Sutton," and of impressionistic fiddle pieces like "Cluck Old Hen," "Train 45," and "Going Down the Lee Highway" (usually known as "Lee Highway Blues"), but his specialties were murder ballads such as "Rose Conley" or "Banks of the Ohio" (which he called "I'll Never Be Yours"), or "Ommie Wise," one of the few '20s recordings of a ballad accompanied only by fiddle. Grayson also cut the first record of a song that would make the folk group The Kingston Trio a great deal of money many years later, "Tom Dooley." He had a family interest in the subject: some sixty years earlier, his uncle, Major James Grayson, had apprehended Dooley (actually Dula), who was on the run after murdering a young woman named Laura Foster.

Many of these songs tell stories, but there is more going on than plain storytelling. Grayson and Whitter decorate their recordings with snatches of dialog, commenting on the action or referring to their hometowns and other mountain communities they know. From time to time Grayson interjects a moral comment: "Take warning, girls, don't marry a drunkard," or "Why is man born to die?" In the background Whitter emits a plaintive hoot, like a far-off train whistle. The effect of these homely devices is to relocate the mythlike narratives of half-forgotten seductions and murders in the known present: to ground them in the familiar geographical, social, and ethical landscape of '20s Appalachia. That this terrain was itself shifting uneasily beneath the pressures of modern life was all to the point: their tales, Grayson and Whitter might have argued, were, in their essence, for all time.

They certainly endured among fellow musicians. Grayson and Whitter's records of songs like "Handsome Molly" and "Little Maggie with a Dram Glass in Her Hand" not only sold unusually well, but Grayson's concise texts and vigorously drawn melodies shaped later treatments for at least a quarter of a century.

Playlist

(all with Henry Whitter)
• *The Recordings of Grayson & Whitter* (County CO-CD-3517)
• *Grayson & Whitter—Volume 1 (1927–1928)* (Document DOCD-8054)
• *Grayson & Whitter—Volume 2 (1928–1929)* (Document DOCD-8055)
• *Appalachian Stomp Down* (JSP JSP 7761 4CD) [duplicates the Documents and adds tracks by other artists]
• *Early Classics Vol. I & II* (Old Homestead OH-157/165)

Clarence ("Tom") Ashley

(1895–1967)

I'm a backwoodsman," Tom Ashley used to say to the folksong fans who gathered round him in his later years. "I know a few songs in

the old tradition." And he would add, indicating his fellow musicians, guitarist Clint Howard and fiddler Fred Price, "We're just a group of farmers who play—pick and sing a little in the old country way. Nothing very modern."

The claim was slightly disingenuous. All three had been farmers, and Howard and Price, Ashley's neighbors in the small town of Shouns, Tennessee, outside Mountain City, still were, but Tom Ashley had also been a professional musician, on and off, for fifty years. He had made over sixty recordings in the 1920s and '30s: solos, duets with the harmonica player Gwin Foster, in guitarist Byrd Moore's Hot Shots, and as a member of the popular Carolina Tar Heels and a related group called the Blue Ridge Mountain Entertainers. He played on medicine shows alongside Roy Acuff, and traveled with Charlie Monroe and the Stanley Brothers as a blackface comedian. His beautiful recordings of "The Coo-Coo Bird" and the ballad "The House Carpenter" were among the finest stones in that diadem of early twentieth-century Americana, Harry Smith's Folkways *Anthology*. And it was on the two volumes of Folkways' *Old Time Music at Clarence Ashley's* that lovers of Appalachian song and music first heard the young Doc Watson.

Thomas Clarence were his given names; on his records he was always Clarence, but everyone who knew him called him Tom. His teens and twenties were an extraordinary apprenticeship in old-time music. He grew up, like Uncle Dave Macon, in a boarding house, which was patronized by railroaders and lumbermen, some of them musicians, and he began playing banjo and guitar before he was in his teens. At sixteen he joined a medicine show as it passed through Mountain City, taken on as a musician, roustabout, and, most important, comedian. He would work on the medicine show circuit for more than thirty years, traveling all over Appalachia and sometimes beyond, during the harvest season, when money could more readily be coaxed from a rural audience. At other times he farmed, put on shows in local schoolhouses, or roamed around with another musician or two, playing outside mines and mills, or at carnivals and fiddlers' contests. A frequent traveling companion was G. B. Grayson.

All the time he was picking up songs— dark tales of murder like "Naomi Wise," melancholy mountain lyrics like "Dark Holler Blues" or "Short Life of Trouble," whiskery old popular songs, scraps of minstrelsy, and always the blues. If his repertoire was

Clarence Ashley (right) with G. B. Grayson.
(Author's collection)

with the folklorist Ralph Rinzler at the Union Grove Fiddlers' Convention led to the sessions with Doc Watson, Howard, Price, and others, and for a few years Ashley's strongly flavored music was often heard at concerts and folk festivals. One of the specialties of the Ashley–Howard–Price–Watson team was singing hymns in unaccompanied four-part harmony, and their arrangement of "Amazing Grace," which was copied by Judy Collins, played a part in reacquainting the world with a half-forgotten hymn.

He even toured England, accompanied by the guitarist Tex Isley, in 1966. "All right, ladies and gentlemen," he would say by way of introduction, "you can readily see that we don't belong in this part of the country. We're from the good old United States, and if we can't come up with no song or no tune or anything that will meet with your listening pleasure, we sure come a long ways to disappoint you." He planned to return the following year, but died of cancer.

remarkable, so was his expressive range. His voice is not conventionally handsome: best suited, you might think, to chipper comic songs like "You Are a Little Too Small." Yet from a blues he could conjure a haunting air of lonesomeness, and in his renditions of ballads he achieves an unlooked-for but astonishing poignancy.

Medicine shows had lost their appeal by the '40s, but Ashley continued to make music, either leading his Tennessee Merrymakers or getting out his burnt cork and novelty pants and going on the road with Charlie Monroe or the Stanleys as "Rastus Jones from Georgia." Otherwise he worked with his son in a small trucking business, hauling coal, furniture, and produce. Then, in 1960, a chance encounter

Playlist

• *Greenback Dollar: The Music of Clarence "Tom" Ashley 1929–1933* (County CD-3520) [includes three tracks by the Carolina Tar Heels]

• *Doc Watson & Clarence Ashley—The Original Folkways Recordings: 1960–1962* (Smithsonian/Folkways CD SF 40029/30 2CD)

•• *Old-Time Mountain Ballads* (County CD-3504): "Dark Holler Blues" •• *Hard Times in the Country* (County CO-CD-3527): "Bay Rum Blues" (Ashley & Foster) •• *Old Time Mountain Banjo* (County CO-CD-3533): "The Coo-Coo Bird" •• *Hillbilly Blues* (Living Era CD AJA 5361): "Times Ain't Like They Used to Be" (Ashley & Foster) •• *Good for What Ails You: Music of the Medicine Shows 1926–1937* (Old Hat CD-1005 2CD): "Baby All Night Long" (Ashley & Foster) •• *Close to Home: Old Time Music from Mike Seeger's Collection* (Smithsonian/Folkways SF CD 40097): "Pretty Fair Damsel" •• *Before the Blues Vol. 3* (Yazoo 2017): "The House Carpenter" •• *Harmonica Masters* (Yazoo 2019): "East Virginia Blues" (Ashley & Foster) •• *The Rose Grew Round the Briar: Early American Rural Love Songs Vol. 1* (Yazoo 2030): "Dark Holler Blues" •• *My Rough and Rowdy Ways Vol. 1* (Yazoo 2039): "Little Sadie" •• *The Stuff That Dreams Are Made Of* (Yazoo 2202 2CD): "Bull Dog Sal" (Ashley & Foster)

Carolina Tar Heels

Clarence ("Tom") Ashley (1895–1968) •
Dock Walsh (1901–67) •
Gwin Foster (1903–54) •
Garley Foster (1905–68)

The Carolina Tar Heels were less a band than a brand. The three dozen recordings issued under their name were by three different line-ups, but someone—perhaps Dock Walsh, the fixed point of the group, perhaps producer Ralph Peer—ensured that the musicians never deviated from the Tar Heels' trademark sound of banjo and bluesy harmonica, trenchant guitars and laconic vocals. With good reason: they were a hit on records from the start.

The family tree of the group begins with Doctor Coble Walsh, a banjo-playing school-teacher, and Gwin Foster, a textile mill hand who entertained on guitar and harmonica. Both North Carolinians, they met in Gastonia, North Carolina, in the summer of 1926 and formed a band, the Four Yellowjackets, with guitarists Dave Fletcher and Floyd Williams. In February of the following year they auditioned for Peer in Atlanta. Peer, who may already have been aware of Walsh's work—he had cut some solo sides for Columbia in 1925–26—saw no future in the quartet but liked the sound of Walsh and Foster. He recorded four sides by them and, in an unusual move, issued them consecutively, "There Ain't No Use Workin' So Hard" and "I'm Going to Georgia" on Victor 20544 and "Her Name Was Hula Lou" and "Bring Me a Leaf from the Sea" on 20545. In further recordings that August, the Tar Heels flicked through more pages of a songbook that embraced Victorian sentimental ditties, vaudeville novelty songs, and African-American "reels." Soon they added the blues, but by then the group had undergone its first personnel shuffle.

Walsh's home was in Wilkes County in north-western North Carolina, Foster's a day's journey

The Carolina Tar Heels, c. 1928: Clarence Ashley, Dock Walsh, Garley Foster. (Author's collection)

south near Gastonia—too far apart to be able to work together efficiently. Besides, Foster had got something else going for him at Victor, recording with Dave Fletcher in a duo called the Carolina Twins. So Walsh found a replacement in a musician closer by, who happened to have the same surname. Garley Foster, too, played both harmonica and guitar, and in addition could whistle like a bird. According to their playbills, not just *a* bird: "Mr. Foster will really entertain you with his mockery of many, many birds, including Red Bird, Canary Bird, Mocking Bird, Wren, Pewee, Owls, Hawks, etc. Also imitation of a saw mill in operation." A specimen of his bird sounds opens the Tar Heels' "My Home's Across the Blue Ridge Mountains," and very plausible it is, too. He even made a record of "Imitating the Birds on the Mountain," in two parts, in 1931, but by then record companies were hesitating over issuing conventional performances, let alone men impersonating wrens, and Victor never uncaged it.

The group was swelled to a trio by Tom Ashley, playing guitar and singing lead on pieces as varied as "Rude and Rambling Man," which is based on an eighteenth-century British ballad, and "The Train's Done Left Me," a slow blues. By now the Tar Heels stood apart from most of their contemporaries in hillbilly music: in their cleverly varied repertoire, their blend of solo and harmony vocals, plaintive harmonica, and jaunty string music (but no fiddle), and their ability to weave provocatively between the vernal innocence of parlor song and the visceral allure of the blues.

The Tar Heels maintained the trio lineup into the spring of 1929, at least for recordings: generally Walsh and Foster worked as a duo, while Ashley rode the wagons of the medicine show trail. But when, after an interval of nineteen months, the band showed up in Memphis in November 1930, they were down to two again, Garley and Dock. Responding to their rural audience, they grimly cataloged hard times in "Got the Farm Land Blues," but balanced it with a saucy "Farm Girl Blues": "I climb her tree, I shake her apples down . . . we eat our breakfast and ride on back to town."

The last two sessions by a Walsh–Foster duo were by Dock and Garley in 1931, under the name of the Pine Mountain Boys, and by Dock and Gwin, reunited as the Original Carolina Tar Heels, in 1932. Now nearly all the songs were steeped in a blue dye, sometimes shot through with a scarlet streak of sex, like the "red hot mama" whom Walsh backs up against a wall: "She wiggled and she wobbled and she danced the Black Bottom, but she wouldn't hardly be still. She gave me a thrill—but she *wouldn't* be still."

Even hotcha mamas couldn't ring the cash registers in 1931: sales of "She Wouldn't Be Still" and the other swan songs of the Tar Heel crew barely toppled into four figures. Walsh and Garley Foster, who had both recently married, looked for more secure work, Foster in construction, Walsh in poultry farming. Ashley, more tenacious in seeking recording opportunities, hooked up with Gwin Foster and other North Carolina friends like fiddler Clarence Greene and autoharpist Will Abernathy in an outfit called the Blue Ridge Mountain Entertainers, and later recorded twenty-odd exquisite duet sides with Gwin Foster, encompassing blues, minstrelsy, and heart songs—the old Tar Heel recipe.

That September '33 session seemed to have closed the recording log of the four men who were the Carolina Tar Heels, but the ledger would be reopened almost three decades later, first by Ashley with the *Old-Time Music at Clarence Ashley's* LPs, then by Walsh and Garley Foster on an album for Folk-Legacy, where they were joined by Dock's son Drake on fiddle and cheerfully recreated the music of their youth.

Playlist

• *Carolina Tar Heels* (Old Homestead OH-4113)
•• *Hard Times in the Country* (County CO-CD-3517): "Got the Farm Land Blues" •• *Country* (Frémeaux FA 015): "Peg and Awl" •• *Mountain Blues* (JSP JSP 7740 4CD): "The Apron String Blues" (Pine Mountain Boys), "Farm Girl Blues," "I Don't Like the Blues No-How" •• *Serenade in the Mountains* (JSP JSP 7780 4CD): "Her Name Was Hula Lou," "I'm Going to Georgia," "My Mama Scolds Me for Flirting," "Shanghai in China," "Somebody's Tall and Handsome," "There Ain't No Use Workin' So Hard," "Your Low Down Dirty Ways" •• *Hard Times Come Again No More Vol. 2* (Yazoo 2037): "Got the Farm Land Blues"
see also Clarence ("Tom") Ashley

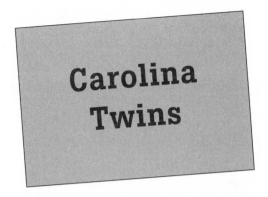

Carolina Twins

David O. Fletcher (c. 1900–58) • Gwin Foster (1903–54)

It isn't every day you go to a party and hear a fellow make train-whistle noises in his throat, or blow a harmonica with his nose, or play two harmonicas and a guitar all at the same time. Young A. O. Fletcher was impressed. This Foster character was good. He must tell his Uncle Dave about him. Dave was a musician too, sang and played guitar pretty well, but he didn't do tricks like that. Maybe they'd hit it off.

They did.

This was in Gaston County, North Carolina, around 1925 or '26. Dave Fletcher lived in Mount Holly, while Gwin Foster had his home a few miles away in Dallas and worked at the Globe Mill, between Mount Holly and Stanley. Gaston County is close to Charlotte, on the southern edge of the state: textile mill territory, which had recently been the scene of bitter showdowns between mill owners and workers.

The two men began to play for parties and civic functions in the area, Fletcher on guitar, Foster on guitar and rack harmonica, both of them singing. They also gathered other musicians around them: A. O. on guitar or ukulele, Gordon Buford on fiddle, Buck Bumgardner on mandolin, Fred Foster on banjo, and singer Avery Keefer. Despite its conventional string-band lineup, the group didn't have much taste for old-time songs, preferring to play modern pieces like "Lazy River" or "Five Foot Two, Eyes of Blue."

In 1926 Fletcher and Foster teamed up with Dock Walsh, traveling round the Southeast playing for dances and in barbershops. Once, A. O. told the music historian Wayne Martin, they met Riley Puckett and had so much fun jamming with him that they were late for their next engagement. But, like the Skillet-Lickers, the group had internal differences. Dock Walsh didn't share the interest of the other two in modern material, and although Foster attended a couple of 1927 recording sessions with him under the billing of the Carolina Tar Heels, by 1928 he was back working with Fletcher in Gaston County. The "Mount Holly

Gwin Foster (second left) with Gordon Buford (fiddle), Avery Keefer (singer), A. O. Fletcher (ukulele), and an unidentified farm owner. (Wayne Martin collection)

Dave Fletcher (center) and friends. (Wayne Martin collection)

Department" columnist of the *Gastonia Daily Gazette* on September 12, 1928, reported that they had played at a luncheon meeting of the Civitan club the day before, "delight[ing] the Civitans with a splendid musical number," and had then gone on to "render a musical program from WBT Charlotte" that evening. (The paper spells Foster's first name Gwen, as do his record labels, while other sources have him as Gwyn, but Gwin is how it's written on his gravestone.)

By then they had made their debut on disc, under the billing of the Carolina Twins. Victor liked them well enough to record them twice in 1928 and once in '29, eliciting altogether eighteen sides. Ralph Peer had little use for hillbilly renditions of current popular songs, so Fletcher and Foster had to bend to his will and concentrate on old-timey material. Their harmony singing is pretty, and they yodel in harmony too on several numbers, anticipating Fleming & Townsend—who are credited with originating the practice—by more than two years. The most arresting feature is Foster's bubbly playing at the high end of the harmonica, not easy to bring off with such grace. After a while they diversified from plaintive heart songs like "Off to the War I'm Going" (a.k.a. "Goodbye, Sweetheart, Goodbye") into livelier material such as the railroad song "Southern Jack" or "Gal of Mine Took My Licker from

Me," but they never really got rambunctious. Compared with the musicians who were most like them, Dock Walsh, Clarence Ashley, and Garley Foster, they seem rather mild: the Carolina Low-Tar Heels.

They were well enough received at the time—several of their releases sold in the 5–10,000 range, respectable for a regional act—but their recordings are hardly known today, whereas the Carolina Tar Heels' have been repeatedly reissued over more than forty years. The reason, surely, is that the Twins, unlike the Tar Heels, gave their songs only the palest wash of African-American music—except once. It was their last date for Victor, and they played a pair of elegant guitar duets, "Red Rose Rag" and "Charlotte Hot Step." The rag progressions, energized with blues phrasing, mark a shifting of their gears from nineteenth-century music making into something feistier and more modern, and Victor credited the record to "Fletcher & Foster," presumably to distance them from the rather different repertoire that by now was associated with the Carolina Twins brand.

During the couple of years they were making records, Fletcher and Foster covered some ground, basing themselves for a while in Bristol, Tennessee, where they played for parties thrown by wealthy bootleggers. In 1930 Fletcher moved to Richmond, Indiana—where the duo made their last few sides, for Gennett—and later he lived in Mansfield, Ohio, working in a machine shop. In the '50s he returned to Mount Holly, where he died.

Foster, however, hung on in the music business. After working in the early '30s with Clarence Ashley, he seems to have had radio engagements in various cities in North Carolina and Virginia. The mandolinist Shannon Grayson, who was with the Carlisle Brothers in the late '30s, told Wayne Martin that he thought he remembered running into Foster on WRVA in Richmond, Virginia, where he was playing with the Tobacco Tags—which sounds right, because Foster's last known recording, in 1939, has the Tags accompanying him on a remake of "Side-Line Blues," first done with Ashley, and a boisterous "How Many Biscuits Can I Eat?" He spent his final years at his home in Dallas, where he died one evening while listening to the news on the radio.

The Red Fox Chasers

Guy Brooks • Bob Cranford • Paul Miles • A. P. Thompson

Surry County in western North Carolina sits on the state line with Virginia. Its largest town is Mt. Airy, and a few miles north is Galax. These are names that make music lovers tingle, because this section of the country, and those towns in particular, is practically the headquarters of living old-time music. Festivals and fiddlers' conventions keep the music not only alive but competitive, as they have done for decades.

Eight decades, at least. It was at the 1928 fiddling convention in nearby Union Grove that two pairs of friends met and decided to form a band. Guitarist A. P. Thompson and harmonica player Bob Cranford had grown up together in Surry County, on either side of Pine Knob Mountain, and learned harmony singing from the traveling music teachers who would regularly visit mountain schoolhouses. Meanwhile, in neighboring Alleghany County, fiddler Guy Brooks and banjoist Paul Miles were learning the repertory of the dance floor.

It was Miles who organized the group and secured a recording date, in the spring of 1928, with Gennett Records. Brooks, who loved to hunt, gave them the name of the Red Fox Chasers. As a band they were well equipped to offer instrumental breakdowns—witness their sparkling versions of "Mississippi Sawyer" and "Did You Ever See the Devil, Uncle Joe"—but more often they displayed the craft they had learned in the singing schools by delivering the refrains in trio or quartet harmony, somewhat like their contemporaries the Georgia Yellow Hammers. "Stolen Love" is particularly charming, with its unusual switches from 4/4 to 3/4 time. Others, again, were done as vocal duets by Cranford and Thompson, and these include some of the most affecting records of old-time song that have come down to us, numbers like "Sweet Fern" and "Goodbye Little Bonnie."

The group also recorded gospel quartet numbers and even a four-part bootlegging sketch, patterned on the Skillet-Lickers' famous "Corn Licker Still" series, but mostly they stuck to what they did best, the heart songs of earlier generations that formed the bedrock of the old-time vocal repertoire preserved on disc in the '20s and early '30s. Anyone who recorded for Gennett saw their discs come out on a bewildering variety of labels, and for a few years there was a lot of the Red Fox Chasers' music around, more than forty titles dispersed on about fifty issues, but the Depression put paid to recording contracts and the band broke up. Music had never been full-time for them: Brooks and Thompson farmed, Miles was a mechanic, and Cranford worked for the R. J. Reynolds tobacco company in Winston-Salem. Miles, Cranford, and Thompson were still living, and singing and playing, in the late '60s, and so survived to see their music presented to a new audience on LP.

(Courtesy of Big Boy Woods)

Playlist
• *Classic Old Time Music from North Carolina* (BACM CD D 108)
•• *Old-Time Mountain Ballads* (County CD-3504): "Wreck on the Mountain Road"
•• *The Rose Grew Round the Briar: Early American Rural Love Songs Vol. 1* (Yazoo 2030): "Stolen Love" •• *The Rose Grew Round the Briar: Early American Rural Love Songs Vol. 2* (Yazoo 2031): "Little Sweetheart Pal of Mine"

Bascom Lamar Lunsford

(1882–1973)

For two weeks in March 1949, Bascom Lamar Lunsford was away from his home in South Turkey Creek, North Carolina, sitting before a microphone in the Library of Congress in Washington, D. C. He needed that long, because he was engaged in recording his "personal memory collection of folksongs," a treasury that would amount to more than 300 pieces.

Lunsford was a lawyer, teacher, traveling fruit-tree salesman, Democratic Party campaign manager, and much more, but he was always a lover of mountain music. He collected it, performed it, and organized what may be the oldest folk festival in the United States to promote it.

He was born in Mars Hill, North Carolina, where his father taught school. "My mother was a great singer of the old ballads," he recalled. "Early in life I acquired a repertoire of those things before I realized that there was any cultural value in it." He learned "cigar-box fiddle and tack-head banjo" and played them at country functions: "bean stringings, butter

stirrings, candy breakings, apple peelings, and corn shuckings."

As a teacher he began to learn the history and meaning of the old songs. He would spend a lifetime searching for people who knew them in the backwoods and hollows of Appalachia. When he was selling the fruit trees, he would exchange a tree for a night's lodging, then trade songs with his hosts. Years afterward he could recall in detail those evenings of storytelling and song-swapping. But it was not only from old men and women that he solicited songs. "I went to a one-teacher school on Roaring Fork, Madison County, in 1927," he told his biographer Loyal Jones. "I put up a prize for the one who would give me the best collection of traditional ballads. I got 'Sweet William and Lady Margaret' from a nine-year-old girl, Loretta Payne. . . . I learned 'Stepstone' in 1904 in Graham County, North Carolina, from a little girl named Lelia Ammons. She was about fifteen years old." Forty years later and 2,000 miles away, at a concert in California, he sang "Stepstone" to Ms. Ammons's daughter and grandson.

His own cultivated but grainy singing and banjo playing were heard on a handful of records in the '20s, such as the mountain blues "I Wish I Was a Mole in the Ground" and his own

(Lunsford Scrapbook Collection, Appalachian Room Archives of the Liston B. Ramsey Center for Regional Studies, Mars Hill College]

(Lunsford Scrapbook Collection, Appalachian Room Archives of the Liston B. Ramsey Center for Regional Studies, Mars Hill College)

humorous composition "Mountain Dew," popularized by fellow North Carolinian Scotty Wiseman (of Lulu Belle and Scotty) and later by Grandpa Jones. He also made a very strange record coupling parodies of a political address ("A Stump Speech in the Tenth District") and a sermon ("Speaking the Truth"). Burlesque oratory is not a form that is likely to weather seventy-five years of cultural change undamaged, but there are passages in "Speaking the Truth" that retain a transfixing weirdness:

Yes, the text says, "For they shall gnaw a file, and flee into the mountains of Hepsidam, where the lion roareth and the wang-doodle mourneth for his first-born." Now this doesn't mean the howling wilderness, whar John The Hard Shell Baptist fed on locusts and wild asses, but it means the city of New Orleans, where corn is six bits a bushel one day and nary a red the next . . . and where a strange woman once took up your beloved teacher and bamboozled him out of one hundred and

twenty-seven bucks in three blinks of the eye and the twinkling of a sheep's tail. . . .

He also cut LPs in the '50s for Folkways and Riverside. But these records were only a fragment of his repertoire, as he showed in his mammoth Library of Congress sessions—for he recorded his vast "memory collection" twice, first in 1935. Even earlier, in 1925, he had sung a portion of it, some eighty or so pieces, into the cylinder phonograph of the collector Robert W. Gordon, later the first director of the Library's Archive of Folk Song.

In 1928 he founded the Asheville Mountain Dance and Folk Festival, with contests for singing, fiddling, stringband music, and square-dance teams. Over the years the August event has been a gathering for local celebrities such as Samantha Bumgarner, George Pegram, and Obray Ramsey. This is the setting in which Lunsford will be best remembered, presiding over a stage full of pickers, singers, and cloggers. There would be a smile on his lips, but at times a faraway gaze behind his steel-rimmed glasses. Perhaps he was seeing those "rising generations" who, as he said at the end of his 1949 marathon, "I trust will avail themselves of what beauty may be found in these recordings. I give them somewhat in the spirit of the poet: 'I breathed a song into the air, it came to earth I know not where; but long years after from beginning to end, I found that song in the heart of a friend.'"

Playlist

• *Ballads, Banjo Tunes and Sacred Songs* (Smithsonian/Folkways SF CD 40082) [recordings from 1928 and 1949]
•• *Old Time Mountain Banjo* (County CO-CD-3533): "Italy" •• *Folksongs* (Frémeaux FA 047 2CD): "I Wish I Was a Mole in the Ground" •• *Serenade in the Mountains* (JSP JSP 7780 4CD): "Dry Bones," "I Wish I Was a Mole in the Ground," "Italy," "Kidder Cole," "Little Turtle Dove," "Lost John Dean," "Lulu Wall," "Mountain Dew," "Nol Pros Nellie" •• *The North Carolina Banjo Collection* (Rounder 0439/40 2CD): "Mr. Garfield" •• *Songs and Ballads of American History and of the Assassination of Presidents* (Rounder CD 1509): "Booth Killed Lincoln" (two versions), "Charles Guiteau," "Mr. Garfield," "Zolgotz" •• *Times Ain't Like They Used to Be Vol. 1* (Yazoo 2028): "Lost John Dean" •• *The Rose Grew Round the Briar: Early American Rural Love Songs Vol. 1* (Yazoo 2030): "Lulu Wall" •• *The Cornshucker's Frolic Vol. 1* (Yazoo 2045): "Kidder Cole" •• *The Half Ain't Never Been Told Vol. 2* (Yazoo 2050): "Dry Bones"

Leake County Revelers

R. O. Mosley (1885–1930s) • Dallas Jones (1889–1985) • Jim Wolverton (1895–1969) • Will Gilmer (1897–1960)

Leake County lies in the dead center of Mississippi, to the northeast of the state capital, Jackson. In 1927 you could hardly find a poorer place in the United States, as a Northern recording scout discovered. "The people are removed from education and from all sorts of social contacts," remembered Frank B. Walker of Columbia Records, who came searching for talent there. He was directed to the county's most popular band, which he named the Leake County Revelers—"a very highsounding name, and they were a pretty good sounding group, but they just played things that didn't have any sense to them at all."

Yet this senseless foursome, with their second release, provided Columbia with one of the decade's biggest hillbilly hits, "Wednesday Night Waltz" coupled with "Good Night Waltz."

Country music today has little place for the instrumental waltz, but in the late '20s it was big business. Practically every stringband that got behind a recording microphone cut some waltzes; several groups did little else. They were seldom the slow, melodramatic waltzes heard nowadays at fiddlers' conventions, or the sleepy ones executed by bands accustomed to playing for old folks. "Wednesday Night Waltz" moves at a fair clip, and twice breaks out of the 3/4 rhythm into the even brisker tempo of a breakdown.

The Revelers' disc sold almost 200,000 copies, setting off a chain reaction of cover versions. The Kessinger Brothers recorded it for Brunswick, a band from North Carolina played it on Hawaiian guitars for OKeh, while Carson Robison & Frank Luther put lyrics to it and did it for Victor, Brunswick, and Edison. In 1934, when the record business was beginning to

Left to right: Dallas Jones, R. O. Mosley, Jim Wolverton, Will Gilmer. (Courtesy of Big Boy Woods)

pull itself together after the Depression, the Revelers' disc was reissued, only to be covered again, instrumentally by the Stripling Brothers and vocally by Riley Puckett.

So far as the Revelers were concerned, the immediate aftermath of their success—other than being hired by Huey Long to play for his gubernatorial campaign in 1928—was regular recording sessions for four years. About a third of their forty-four sides were waltzes, but they also played vivacious breakdowns like "Johnson Gal" and "Leather Breeches," a coupling described in the Columbia catalog as "bright and sparkling as a mountain morning," "Monkey in the Dog Cart," "Bring Me a Bottle" (their version of "Pass Around the Bottle and We'll All Take a Drink"), and "Been to the East—Been to the West." Besides those there were blues, yodel songs, and ragtime tunes like "Georgia

Camp Meeting." They had a highly distinctive sound, the clean, bright fiddling of Will Gilmer often sharing the melodic lead with the tinkling mandolin of R. O. Mosley over an understated backing by banjoist Jim Wolverton and guitarist (and occasional singer) Dallas Jones. A delightful and unusual example is "Birds in the Brook," a lovely nineteenth-century melody played at the stately tempo of an Irish set dance.

It was all pretty music, with a lilt to it, and it seems a world away from the lopsided blues fiddling of their Mississippi contemporary Willie Narmour, let alone the tearaway stringbands of Georgia. With their sedate trio singing the Revelers seemed to evoke a less hurried era, a time before the flapper and the Model T Ford.

In their heyday the Revelers played all over central and southern Mississippi, and were heard on Saturday evenings on WJDX, in the

FAMILIAR MELODIES ON COLUMBIA NEW PROCESS RECORDS

In the Good Old Summertime

Here is a new release by the Leake County Revelers, makers of JOHNSON GAL and LEATHER BREECHES. On the other side s MY BONNIE LIES OVER THE OCEAN.
Columbia Record No. 15227—

RED WING
COME BE MY RAINBOW
Riley Puckett's Newest Record—No. 15226

HE'S COMING AGAIN
BEAUTIFUL HOME SOMEWHERE
Sacred Music by the Deal Family—No. 15214

FIFTY YEARS AGO
MY CAROLINA HOME
McMichen's Melody Men Record—No. 15224

JOHNSON'S OLD GREY MULE
UNCLE BUD
Gid Tanner and his Skillet Lickers with Riley Puckett and Clayton McMichen.—No. 15221

HEAR THESE RECORDS TODAY

M. B. Smith
"for your home come first"

Music store ad, *Burlington Daily Times*, March 16, 1928. (Author's collection)

Playlist
• *Leake County Revelers—Vol. 1 (1927–1928)* (Document DOCD-8029)
• *Leake County Revelers—Vol. 2 (1929–1930)* (Document DOCD-8030)
•• *Mississippi String Bands Volume One* (County CD-3513): "Dry Town Blues," "Mississippi Breakdown," "The Old Hat" •• *Mississippi String Bands Volume Two* (County CD-3514): "Johnson Gal," "Lonesome Blues," "Molly Put the Kettle On," "Wednesday Night Waltz" •• *Old-Time Mountain Blues* (County CO-CD-3528): "Leake County Blues" •• *Old Mountain: Stringband Songs & Tunes* (Living Era CD AJA 5577): "Wednesday Night Waltz" •• *American Yodeling 1911–1946* (Trikont US-0246): "Rockin' Yodel" •• *The Cornshucker's Frolic Vol. 1* (Yazoo 2046): "Leather Breeches"

state capital of Jackson. Inevitably, they did not outlast the Depression. Mosley, the oldest, died in the '30s, but even if they had not lost a founding member they could not have competed with the hotter music of popular '30s fiddlers like Arthur Smith or the tent-show high jinks of Mainer's Mountaineers. None of the Revelers had played music full-time: Mosley owned a hardware store, Wolverton was a farmer, and Gilmer was a footloose bachelor who never settled to anything for long.

Yet so strong were the family and community ties of the Leake County musicians that groups with something of the same flavor continued to play in the area for several decades. In the 1976 movie *Ode to Billy Joe*, based on the hit song by Bobbie Gentry, there is a sequence filmed at a county fair. Some of the background music is played by the Leake County String Band, led by fiddlers Morgan and George Gilmer, descendants of the man who had had the South dancing to the "Wednesday Night Waltz."

Narmour & Smith

William T. Narmour (1889–1961) • Shellie W. Smith (1895–1968)

One of the hot hillbilly records in the summer of 1929 was a blues—the "Carroll County Blues," played on fiddle and guitar by "W. T. Narmour & S. W. Smith," as they were rather formally credited on the label. It was a strange piece, two alternating strains of eleven bars, the first a piercing blues melody, the second seesawing on two low notes as if to give the ear a rest after the strident A part. On the other side was a tune called "Charleston

No. 1," but it was not at all the sort of thing you could imagine flappers cavorting to.

The titles, to anyone who knew their southern geography, gave a lead to where the tunes and the artists might come from. There is a Carroll County in central Mississippi, lying just west of old Highway 51, bracketed by the towns of Greenwood, in Leflore County, to the west, and Winona, in Montgomery County, to the east. The movie *Ode to Billy Joe* was partly shot in Carroll County locations. And Charleston is a central Mississippi town, maybe half an hour's drive north in Tallahatchie County.

Fiddler Narmour and guitarist Smith were native Carroll Countians. By the '20s they were well known in the area, playing for dances, picnics, county fairs, and other social occasions. Their contemporaries Hoyt Ming and Lonnie Ellis, also fiddlers, reported seeing Narmour at the fiddlers' conventions held regularly in Kosciusko, in neighboring Attala County. He was an unusually small man, Ming said, "between a midget and a medium-sized person."

Narmour and Smith also showed up at the fiddlers' conventions in Winona organized by Dr. A. M. Bailey. As well as his veterinary practice Bailey owned an electrical goods store that sold records and, like record dealers elsewhere, often scouted for local talent. He tipped off OKeh Records, and in February 1928 Narmour and Smith were summoned to Memphis to make their first records. Tunes like "Captain George, Has Your Money Come?" and "Who's Been Giving You Corn?" sold well, and in March the following year the duo were back before a recording microphone, this time in Atlanta. This second batch of discs also sold quite briskly, but it was the coupling of "Carroll County Blues" and "Charleston No. 1" that put the pair on the map.

"I believe the best piece he put out was 'Charleston No. 1,'" remembered Hoyt Ming. "I can play it, but I can't play it like he played it. It's hard to beat. And I know everybody that I've heard that talked about his playing, they'll mention that 'Charleston No. 1.'"

In September 1929, now established as stars of OKeh's "Old Time Tunes" catalog, Narmour and Smith appeared in a revue-on-disc called "The Medicine Show," where they lined up with other OKeh luminaries like Fiddlin' John Carson and Frank Hutchison to play excerpts of their current hits. They also capitalized on their most successful record by cutting a "Carroll County Blues No. 2" and a

"Charleston No. 2," and the following year they added a "No. 3" of each. They are all different tunes—one of the "Charleston"s is actually "Sailor's Hornpipe"—but similar in character to the originals.

In all, Narmour and Smith made thirty-two recordings for OKeh. Several are waltzes, which seem to have been particularly prized by Mississippi fiddlers and their audiences. Standard tunes are notable by their absence. The pieces called breakdowns are generally slower and less frenetic than those played by contemporary fiddlers in other parts of the South. A typical Narmour tune has a couple of choppy, bluesy strains, the implied dance steps those of the polka or the hornpipe. The melodies are often narrow in compass, and the effect of the insistent, repetitive phrasing on the two instruments can be hypnotic. Altogether, Narmour's repertoire is one of the most singular collections of Southern fiddle music preserved on record.

Their last OKeh record was issued in the summer of 1931, a dreadful time for the record industry, but they had a swansong, returning to Atlanta in July 1934, now at the bidding of

(Author's collection)

Bluebird Records, and cutting sixteen more titles. "More" is not quite the right word, though, because every tune repeated one they had made earlier, right down to the three versions of "Carroll County Blues" and "Charleston," and the remakes are almost indistinguishable from the originals.

With that Will Narmour and Shell Smith subsided into the daily life of Carroll County, where they died too early to be interviewed by researchers; the little we know of them comes from family members and from the black singer Mississippi John Hurt, who lived a few doors away from Narmour and sometimes played with him. But they are remembered by their tunes. Visiting central Mississippi almost half a century after the "Carroll County Blues" came out, I could not find a fiddler of any age who did not play it.

(1902–85)

Playlist
•• *Mississippi String Bands Volume One* (County CD-3513): "Avalon Quickstep," "Sweet Milk and Peaches" •• *Mississippi String Bands Volume Two* (County CD-3514): "Captain George, Has Your Money Come?," "Carroll County Blues," "Charleston No. 1," "Mississippi Breakdown" •• *Old-Time Mountain Blues* (County CO-CD-3528): "New Carroll County Blues No. 1" •• *Mountain Blues* (JSP JSP 7740 4CD): "Carroll County Blues," "Tequila Hop Blues" •• *Old Mountain: Stringband Songs & Tunes* (Living Era CD AJA 5577): "Carroll County Blues"

There's little that isn't fascinating in that treasury of early American vernacular music, Harry Smith's Folkways *Anthology*, but even in that company some tracks stand out for their transfixing singularity. "Indian War Whoop," credited to Floyd Ming and His Pep Steppers, is one of those quintessentially Mississippian fiddle tunes that are like watch movements, going round and round, tirelessly repeating themselves, fixed in a small, precise world of their own. But where it differs from a piece by, say, Narmour & Smith is that from time to time the fiddler emits an eerie holler, the war whoop of the title.

If the description sounds familiar, though the name of Floyd Ming means nothing to you, you are probably recognizing the tune from its use in *O Brother, Where Art Thou?*, where it was faithfully replicated by John Hartford to accompany the night-time procession of torchlit hillbillies marching bank-robber George "Baby Face" Nelson to the hoosegow. In fact, "Floyd Ming" *does* mean nothing. Someone at Victor Records misread someone else's writing. The fiddler and whooper was Hoyt Ming, a twenty-five-year-old potato farmer from Choctaw County, Mississippi.

He had been playing for about ten years, first with some of his six brothers, then with his wife Rozelle on guitar and her sister on mandolin, but when the news filtered out, early in 1928, that Victor were in Tupelo auditioning musicians, Hoyt's sister-in-law wasn't available, so his brother Troy took the mandolin chair. They passed, and a few weeks later made the trip to Memphis to record. Ralph Peer, Victor's talent scout, liked the way Rozelle beat time with her foot and placed the microphone so as to emphasize it. As well as "Indian War Whoop," the trio recorded the well-known "Whoa Mule," which Peer retitled "White Mule," and a couple of tunes Hoyt had learned from local fiddlers,

Hoyt Ming & His Pep Steppers, 1928: Hoyt Ming, A. D. Coggin, Rozelle Ming, Troy Ming.
(OTM collection)

"Old Red" and "Florida Blues," though Peer retitled that too. Feeling that it needed a more local name, he chose "Tupelo Blues." An acquaintance of the Mings from Nettleton, Andrew Coggin, furnished dance calls.

The hour or so they spent making records in the Memphis Auditorium would buy them a time-share at Immortality Court, but for the Mings it was just an episode between bookings. They played at fiddlers' contests, county fairs, political rallies, and rural picnics—and sometimes for dances, though they disliked the drinking that went on, and as soon as they had young children to bring up, they quit the dance halls. They also had a living to make outside music. Hoyt sold potato plants, partly direct to other farmers and farming cooperatives, but in high season, from April to the end of July, through small ads in papers like *Progressive Farmer* and *Southern Agriculturist*. He and Rozelle told me they once counted and bunched 30,000 plants in a day.

After World War II, playing music took a diminished role in their lives, and by the end of the '50s they had retired. Then, one day in early 1973, Hoyt Ming came across the photograph they had had taken soon after the recording session. A few days later, a letter arrived from David Freeman of County Records, the leading label for reissues of old-time recordings. Tickled by the coincidence, and realizing that 1973 marked both the fifteenth anniversary of his retirement and the forty-fifth of the Victor session, Hoyt replied.

That summer Freeman and some friends visited the Mings at their home in Ackerman, and soon afterward Hoyt and Rozelle, with their son Hoyt Jr. and James Alford on guitars, were booked for the National Folk Festival. They also cut the album *New Hot Times!* for Freeman's Homestead label. The following year they returned east for the Smithsonian Festival of American Folklife, and in 1975 they contributed to the soundtrack of *Ode to Billy Joe*. The renewed interest in their music also encouraged them to play at local events. It's curious to reflect that if Ralph Peer had not left researchers a clue in "Tupelo Blues," none of this might have happened.

Playlist
•• *Mississippi String Bands Volume One* (County CD-3513): "Indian War Whoop," "Tupelo Blues" •• *Mississippi String Bands Vol. 1 (1928–1935)* (Document DOCD-8009): "Indian War Whoop," "Old Red," "Tupelo Blues," "White Mule"

Dr. Smith's Champion Hoss Hair Pullers

The traveling recording men of the late 1920s quickly recognized that there were finds to be made in northern Arkansas. The region seemed to be thronged with vigorous, idiosyncratic stringbands. Within the space of a couple of years OKeh recorded the Arkansas Barefoot Boys, while Vocalion booked Luke Highnight's Ozark Strutters and the Reaves White County Ramblers—who arrived at the Chicago studio, found no piano there, and had to make do with an organ, which gave their records an odd, lumbering grace, like elephants dancing. Both labels got a piece of Fiddlin' Bob Larkan. But Ralph Peer at Victor aced his rivals by signing up Ashley's Melody Men, Pope's Arkansas Mountaineers, and the Morrison Brothers, all from Searcy County, and a curious aggregation from Izard County called Dr. Smith's Champion Hoss Hair Pullers. The annals of old-time music hold few stranger names—and their music was not exactly ordinary, either.

In tune with the times, this was a band brought to public notice by the spirit of promotion. Dr. Henry Harlin Smith was one of the most get-up-and-go spirits in Calico Rock, Arkansas. He persuaded the organizers of the

Dr. H. H. Smith, c. 1906. (OTM collection)

Izard County Fair to move it to Calico Rock from its logical home in Melbourne, the county seat. He opened a café that doubled as a cinema, showing movies six nights a week. And in January 1926 he put on a fiddlers' contest. From the musicians who turned up he assembled a stringband, headed by fiddler Bryan Lackey, and a vocal group, and by March he had them broadcasting on KTHS in Hot Springs. The station received more than 200 telegrams approving of the Hoss Hair Pullers and the Hillbilly Quartet, and within a few weeks the musicians were back for a second broadcast. This is how Smith introduced them:

It is indeed gratifying to know our program has made so many minds and hearts drift back to the earlier days when all was well, when the "hoss hair pullers" of old were in due form and all parties concerned were in a receptive mood for tipping of the fantastic toe. . . . We take this opportunity to boost the White River country and the Missouri Pacific Company [Smith's employers]. My aggregation from this district claim that their music and songs are not suggestive of anything except good and wholesome exercise. . . .

He ended his address with a fervent appeal to potential tourists:

So everybody come to the Arkansas Ozarks, where you can eat the best fruit in the world; where home-cured meat is found in the smokehouse and corn and hay in the barn; where you can juice your own cow, feed your own chickens, fish in the wonderful White River, meet these men of the Missouri Pacific and natives, and you will then say, "Yes, indeed, you have the most wonderful country in the world."

Apart from their occasional trips to Hot Springs, Smith's crew played mostly for local functions, but by summer 1928 they had evidently built enough of a reputation to attract the eye of a talent scout. Victor had had some success earlier that year with recordings by Pope's Arkansas Mountaineers, and Peer may have had similar hopes for the Hoss Hair Pullers' old-time songs. Possibly he saw them as an Ozark equivalent of a group he had been recording for more than a year, the Georgia Yellow Hammers, who also delivered their songs in four-part harmony; and perhaps he was remembering the Yellow Hammers' most successful song, "Picture on the Wall," when he had the Hoss Hair Pullers open their session with a piece called "Save My Mother's Picture from the Sale."

The song was contributed to the group's repertoire by their guitarist, and occasional singer, Leeman Bone, a singing school teacher and piano tuner. Another piece he brought was a rustic love song, "In the Garden Where the Irish Potatoes Grow." Probably the best known of the band's recordings today is "Going Down the River," a jaunty tune that shares its DNA with "Davy" by the Weems String Band from west Tennessee and "Boatin' Up Sandy" by Al Hopkins & His Buckle Busters. The least known are the "coon songs" "Just Give Me the Leavings" and "Nigger Baby," which, coupled on one disc, gave the purchaser a choice of stereotypes for seventy-five cents: on "Leavings" a philosopher with a watermelon, on "Baby" a psychotic with a razor. Extraordinarily, the latter song reappeared on record in the '60s, on the blues scholar Paul Oliver's documentary LP *Conversation with the Blues*, where it was sung, under the title "Kill That Nigger Dead," by a couple of black musicians from southern Louisiana, Butch Cage and Willie Thomas.

An odd repertoire, then, which the band's instrumentalists approach like Ozark cousins of the Leake County Revelers, loosing the pretty melodies in a sparkling cascade of fiddle and mandolin, while the singers deliver their antique burdens with stiff-collared severity. It's as if the elders of Calico Rock Baptist, seeking a quiet spot for the annual church picnic, had wandered into Arcadia.

The Hoss Hair Pullers lasted no more than a couple of years after the recording session. Victims of their own success, they accrued more bookings than they could fulfill; some of the members disliked the traveling, and even the by no means work-shy Smith found it hard to balance the roles of country doctor and stringband MC. In any case, he was struck down by a cerebral hemorrhage in 1931, at the age of fifty. One or two of the Hillbilly Quartet carried on singing in gospel groups, but in the absence of Smith's genial patronage the rest of the band dispersed into the obscurity of small-town life.

Playlist
• • *Echoes of the Ozarks Volume Two* (County CD-3507): "Going Down the River," "In the Garden Where the Irish Potatoes Grow"

Fiddlin' Bob Larkan

(1870–1942)

Bob Larkan was born, unusually for a hillbilly fiddler, in New York City, and learned to play fiddle, banjo, and guitar as a boy. In 1891 he and his wife Hattie moved west, settling first in Prairie County and then in adjoining Lonoke County, Arkansas. While working as a farmer he continued to play the fiddle, accompanied by Hattie on the organ. In due course some of their children joined them

(they had nine daughters and five sons), and the Larkan family band became well known at local entertainments in the 1910s and '20s.

They also performed on some of the small radio stations that were springing up in northern Arkansas, such as KGHI and KGJF in Little Rock. Winning a broadcast fiddlers' contest, Larkan took home $12 in cash, a barrel of flour, and twenty-six chicks, which he raised in a box by his bed. But he soon landed a radio job with more substantial rewards.

In 1923, Dr. John R. Brinkley, proprietor of the Brinkley-Jones Hospital in the small town of Milford, Kansas, had applied to the Federal Radio Commission for a license for a hospital radio station. "It was found," reported *Radio Digest* six years later, "that the entertainment and health lectures given over the station for the entertainment of the patients in the hospital were well received by the listening public." Within two years KFKB had increased its output from 1,000 to 5,000 watts, enabling it, particularly at night, to reach several surrounding states. The *Radio Digest* article continued:

The slogan of KFKB, "The Sunshine Station in the Heart of the Nation," was contributed by a little shut-in, a poor crippled girl who said that the friendly attitude of the station and the good cheer brought to the homes of those who were forever crippled made her think that the station was a beacon of sunshine, and since the station is located within 12 miles of the geographical center of the United States, the "heart of the nation" was appropriate.

Unlike its contemporary KWKH, in Shreveport, Louisiana, where, *Radio Digest* reported a few months later, disc shows constituted 85 percent of the output, KFKB played no phonograph records. It accepted only a moderate amount of advertising, which was "carefully scrutinized. Anything broadcast over this station is absolutely reliable and dependable."

Much of this, like much about Brinkley, is hooey. It was a planted story, in effect a KFKB press release that *Radio Digest* simply printed without editorial intervention. By December 1929, when the article appeared, the station was heading for trouble. It may have been true that it took little outside advertising, but only because it was preoccupied with its own, peppering its listeners with ads, and programs that were thinly disguised ads, for Brinkley's dubious remedies and unconventional therapies, especially one for restoring the flagging male sex drive by sur-

JUST real folks, those Old Time entertainers heard regularly over KFKB. From left to right you see: Roy Hall, guitar; Forrest Larkan, piano; Sam McRee, Jr., harp; Elmer Allen, guitar; Rudy McRee, singer; Uncle Bob Larkan, fiddle; Sam McRee, Sr., fiddle; Mildred McRee, banjo and singer.

From *Radio Digest,* December 1929. (Author's collection)

gically implanting slices of goat glands. The American Medical Association, outraged by his claims, and perhaps even more by his vulgarity in promulgating them over the airwaves, charged that he conducted a "medical question box" several times a day and, when listeners wrote in, prescribed his own medicines—which could be bought only at drug stores approved by the Brinkley Pharmaceutical Association. Meanwhile the *Kansas City Star* ran a campaign of anti-Brinkley stories, roundly describing him as a quack and a fraud. Less was made of the fact that the *Star* owned a rival station, WDAF.

By the summer of 1930 Brinkley had lost both his licenses, as a medical practitioner and as a broadcaster. He took himself off to Del Rio, Texas, and built a new station, XER, across the Mexican border in Villa Acuña, beyond the reach of U.S. broadcasting laws. It was the birth of the "border radio" phenomenon that would be so supportive of country music in the following decade. (And twenty years later, of rock 'n' roll. XER's descendant XERF was the original night-time home of the legendary disc jockey Wolfman Jack.)

But until 1930 Brinkley and KFKB were a force in their part of the country. Brinkley was well known enough to run for governor of Kansas in 1930, *after* losing his license, and again two years later, on both occasions securing around 30 percent of the vote. In a 1930 poll held by *Radio Digest*, listeners to KFKB—"Kansas First, Kansas Best"—voted it the most popular station in the United States, by a huge margin. One of its attractions was its large quota of live music, and its leading hillbilly band for several years was Fiddlin' Bob Larkan and His Music Makers. In 1925 the band contributed two morning shows and another in the afternoon, filling two and a half hours of the schedule. The family moved to Milford—and, when Brinkley had to quit Kansas, followed him to XER, though they appear not to have stayed there long.

The constitution of the Music Makers on KFKB is uncertain, though it almost certainly included Larkan's son Forrest on piano, but when the opportunity came for the band to record it was a family group: father and son, with Larkan's daughter Alice and her husband

William Sherbs on guitars. At two sessions in 1928, for OKeh and Vocalion, they cut a dozen issued sides. Half of them are waltzes, mostly played at the fairly brisk tempo customary on hillbilly records at that time, but Larkan's piercing tone invests them with haunting melancholy. Others are boisterous reels that give young Forrest Larkan a chance to romp on the piano keys, while his father, sounding decades older than his fifty-eight or so, chants strange verses over and over: "The higher up the monkey climbs, the higher up the monkey climbs, the higher up the monkey climbs, the greater he shows his dut-dut-duddle-duh-duh-dee-da . . . The women wear no clothes at all, the women wear no clothes at all, the women wear no clothes at all, but they get there just the same. . . ." Ribald rhymes like these were collected in profusion in Larkan's part of the country by the Ozark folklorist Vance Randolph, and maybe these fragments are all that OKeh would okay of longer and racier texts.

Their place in history secured by this curious jumble of decorous dance tunes and elliptical ribaldry, the Music Makers played for a few more years, until Bob Larkan died, from asthma, in 1942.

Playlist
•• *Echoes of the Ozarks Volume Two* (County CD-3507): "The Higher Up the Monkey Climbs," "Kansas City Reel," "Prairie County Waltz," "Saturday Night Waltz"

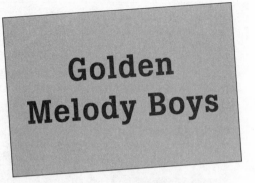

Golden Melody Boys

Dempsy Jones (1891–1963) • Philip Featherstonhaugh (1892–1969)

Iowa in the 1920s: a good place to find corn and Republicans. For country music, not quite so good. Halfway through the decade, in Shenandoah, in the southwest corner of the state, the seedsman Earl May launched KMA, promoting his products to the station's largely rural audience with programs of old-fashioned music. There was even, briefly and obscurely, a May's KMA record label, but no one of lasting interest appeared on it. The only old-time act in '20s Iowa to leave an identifiable bootprint on the welcome mat of history was a duo from Cedar Rapids known as the Golden Melody Boys.

They were Dempsy Jones, who sang and played guitar, banjo, and tiple, and a fluent mandolin player named Philip Featherstonhaugh,

Golden Melody Boys, 1927: Dempsy Jones, Phil Featherstonhaugh. (Courtesy of Big Boy Woods)

GOLDEN MELODY AT WJAM SAT. EVENING

Well - Known Broadcast-ers at Local Station

The Golden Melody boys will appear at station WJAM tomorrow evening from 8 to 8:45. These princely entertainers, composed of Dempsey Jones, banjo, and Philip Featherstonhaugh, mandolin, have gained a high reputation in the city for their clever playing, singing and comedy making.

Dempsey Jones has composed four songs which he expects to publish soon, all of which he will include on Saturday's program. In order to determine which is the most popular, he will appreciate it if radio listeners will express their votes by calling the station phone 1546. The names of these selections are: "Nobody Goin' to Miss Me When I'm Gone," "I Wonder Why Nobody Cares for Me," "Cabin Home," and "Sweet Lady." Almost all those who have heard them on previous occasions generally choose the same piece. Listen in tomorrow and see if your choice is the same as the others.

All the latest popular tunes will be included in their program. "Demps" and "Phil" know how to play as do few local players. Each has strummed his favorite instrument since childhood. Jones has been banjoist and vocal soloist for Clark's orchestra for more than six years. Featherstonhaugh has been instrumental in teaching many local persons the fine art of the mandolin, several of whom have since become moderately famous.

If you've never heard these men "doing their stuff," you'll want to hear them Saturday; if you've heard them before, you'll never what to miss them.

(Author's collection)

or Featherstonehaugh, or Featherstone—no one seems sure which. The *Cedar Rapids Republican*, which ran several stories about them in the '20s, invariably used one of the longer forms of the name (though with several different spellings), and that's how Bill Jones, Dempsy's son, knew him too. On the other hand, World War I records have him down as Featherstone, as do copyright registrations of his compositions.

Iowa acquired hundreds of thousands of new settlers in the latter part of the nineteenth century, so Jones and Featherstonhaugh (to settle for the commonest form) were typical in having come from elsewhere. Featherstonhaugh (and it's pronounced the way it looks, not, as in the lah-di-dah English manner, Fanshawe) was born in Illinois, but by 1900 his parents had moved to Linn County, Iowa. Jones was born in the small community of Fountain Run, Kentucky, later moved to Illinois, and in 1911 to Cedar Rapids; there he worked for Quaker Oats, in construction, and for a newspaper, though his main occupation was as Linn County Recorder, a post he held for twenty-eight years. He also had a spare-time career in baseball, first playing, then managing. Featherstonhaugh, according to Bill Jones, "didn't have much of a profession" outside music: "Phil never worked too much. He got in trouble a couple of times." Like in 1925, when he was run in for transporting liquor in an automobile and fined $300.

The duo start showing up in the local press in late 1925. The *Cedar Rapids Republican* reported on January 8, 1926:

Dempsey [sic] Jones and Phil Featherstoneaugh [sic], the Golden Melody boys, are to present a Pacific coast program at 12:05 a.m. Friday, and every fan in town is expected to stay up and listen to KWCR. The boys will play a strictly harmony program. Four of the selections will be Dempsey's own, and fans are asked to telephone in their opinion of them, that he may know which would better lend itself to publication.

A fuller account appeared in the paper a week later, when Jones solicited a similar radio vote on his compositions over WJAM. Further name checks in the press suggest they were on radio a good deal at this time. In October '26, Jones placed joint third in the hog-calling contest at the Cedar Rapids Free Fair.

In October '27 Demps and Phil, as they were known to their fans, traveled to Chicago and recorded half a dozen numbers for Paramount. Among them were two of Demps's radio-tested compositions, "I Wonder Why Nobody Cares for Me" and "Cabin Home." They returned for further sessions in January and October 1928. The repertoire they trotted out in the studio is a fascinating potpourri of whiffs from the past. "Dad never played anything modern," his son says, and the discs of the Golden Melody Boys bear that out: pretty songs of nostalgia like "Cabin Home" and "When the Golden Rod Is Blooming Once Again" segue into the minstrel argot of "Gonna Have 'Lasses in de Mornin'," while "The Cross Eyed Butcher" is a comic song made up of two venerable jokes and "The Old Tobacco Mill" is a parody of "My Grandfather's Clock," with lifelike sounds of tobacco juice being spat into a can.

But although the material is well-worn, the stylists make something fresh out of it. Mostly Demps plays tiple, an instrument with a small guitar-like body and four pairs of strings, roughly a hybrid of a mandolin and a ukulele, while Phil plays conventional mandolin. The sound they make together has no precise parallel in old-time music, a bubbling sixteen-string polyphony, the tiple's chords unrolling a soft, springy carpet for the mandolin to caper on, most animatedly in the instrumental show-off pieces like "Sabula Blues" and "Freak Medley."

All but one of the Paramount recordings were issued (and the one that was overlooked, "Blushing Bride," survives on a test-pressing), and most of them appeared on the subsidiary Broadway label too, which suggests that these were among the better sellers for this rather hit-and-miss operation. An exception might have been the two-part sketch "Uncle Abner and Elmer at the Rehearsal"—hardly a sketch at all, really, just a couple of songs and a few lines of wooden dialog. After a pretty duet on "Didn't He Ramble," Part II ends with a brass oldie.

"Uncle Abner, what do you think about my execution?"

"Well, from what I've just heered, I'm in favor of it."

Jones's obituary in the Cedar Rapids *Daily Record* mentions that he "made 18 records on a commercial basis," which is exactly right so far as the Paramounts are concerned, but he had evidently forgotten that he had remade a handful of them for Gennett in 1931. Perhaps he wasn't sure whether they were issued, an uncertainty that might well be shared by record collectors, few of whom have ever sighted one.

During the '30s Demps had a family band, Dempsy Jones and the Jones Boys, with his three sons and another kid; Bill played washboard, while his youngest brother dressed as a girl and played jug. They played for lodge events, in hotels, for conventions, and so forth. The largest crowd they ever appeared before, Bill remembers, was 60,000, one Cornhuskers Day. In the TV era they had a show, the Case County Fair, on WMT. "A hillbilly act is what

we did," Bill recalls. "The old man'd call us on and we'd trail on the stage and stand there, look like stupid jerks for a while. My dad was a hell of an entertainer. He could tell stories all night and never repeat. When he died, everything just fell flat."

Featherstonhaugh, meanwhile, had left Cedar Rapids for California, where, according to Bill, he was killed in a gambling joint, an assertion I've been unable to verify. In the years since then, the music of the Golden Melody Boys has almost been forgotten. The few tracks reissued on LP disappeared again when the LPs did, and the only item currently in print is the one that wasn't issued in the Boys' lifetime. But at least one of their songs caught a later ear, and thanks to that discriminating band from Chapel Hill, North Carolina, the Red Clay Ramblers, "Cabin Home" has found its way back into the old-time repertoire.

Walter Coon

(1899–1950)

Histories of early country music will tell you little about Detroit, at least until the 1940s. By then there were enough transplanted Southerners to form a niche audience, first for the bluesy duets of the York Brothers, later for various bluegrass bands whose members had left Kentucky or east Tennessee to work at the Ford plant and other factories. But there was country music in the Motor City before any of that. Kirk Knight, who became

Walter Coon (seated, far right). (Courtesy of Margaret Mackin)

chief announcer at WEXL in the suburb of Royal Oak, Michigan, in 1931, recalled years later that the Depression had curious effects on programming. Unable to afford a record library, the station's owners decided to devote airtime to live hillbilly music. "We had more hillbillies than we had records."

One of those hillbillies was the singer, guitarist, and harmonica player Walter Coon. He called himself "The Arkansas Railsplitter," but he was a fourth-generation Michigander, born in Saginaw. As a young man he worked as a cabinet maker, as a baker, and in an automobile factory in Flint, but when his wife Marie died in 1931 he moved to Detroit, where he worked at the Tip Top Bakery and had a Monday morning show on WEXL, sponsored by the Royal Oak Shopping Guide. He shared airtime with the "radio priest" Fr. Charles Coughlin, pastor of the Shrine of the Little Flower Church in Royal Oak, who was drawing a vast audience with his idiosyncratic brand of socialist oratory. Coon knew him well enough, his daughter Margaret Mackin says, "to go to his office and have a shot and smoke cigars."

Local papers were soon reporting that "Walter Coon of WEXL can pluck a guitar

and sing them thar hill-william songs on the air" . . . "Walter Coon sings ever so appealingly of the honor of the family, little sister, big brother or what have you. Some of those old songs make you want to analyze life, no?" . . . "Walter Coon makes his entrance into the ranks of popular hill-billy tune dispensers with a record of 315 letters in one morn's mail" . . . "Walter Coon split our po' hearts with a song depicting the tragedies of beastly booze . . . dying mother, drunken father, starving child. You know, boo hoo, how it goes, boo hoo. . . ."

The song referred to in the last of those notices was probably "Father's a Drunkard and Mother Is Dead," one of the dozen numbers Coon put on disc during a year-long connection with Gennett Records in 1929–30. The song had been published in 1866, "as sung by Little Effie Parkhurst at the Great Temperance Gatherings in New-York." Also in that vein was "Come Home Father," a. k. a. "Father, Dear Father, Come Home with Me Now," inspired by T. S. Arthur's temperance novel *Ten Nights In A Bar-room*, a best-seller of the mid-nineteenth century.

Another of Coon's Gennett sides was "Fly

Away Birdie to Heaven," written by the vastly prolific Charles K. Harris, who also grew up in Saginaw, some thirty years earlier. Harris's compositions—"There'll Come a Time," "Fallen by the Wayside," "'Mid the Green Fields of Virginia," and many others—litter the repertoires of old-time country singers like golden leaves in fall (also one of his themes). In the words of his publisher, "Others strive for ragtime art, Harris reaches for the Heart."

In a less read-'em-and-weep vein, Coon sang "Fond Affection" and "Creole Girl," the latter a rare hillbilly recording of "The Lakes of Pontchartrain," which much later became embedded in the Irish folk repertory. He tells their stories pleasantly, in a light voice that belies his stocky build, to a plain guitar accompaniment, playing an occasional verse on harmonica.

But at a couple of sessions he offered a different music, romping through medleys of old-time dance tunes with a lineup of harmonica, jew's harp, guitar, and bones. He himself could play all those instruments, but the billing "Walter Coon and The Joy Boys" implies he had some help, and details of a later session give us the names of Walter Hamacker and Louis Bawmbach, who may have been those happy fellows. However they were executed, sides like "Huskin' Bee" are delightful, the harmonica and jew's harp chasing each other round the melodies like Tom and Jerry.

Walter Coon's small discography includes some curious entries, sadly never issued. "On a Tom Thumb Golf Course" would have been inspired by the early '30s craze for minigolf, which led to the construction of tens of thousands of miniature courses and made a fortune for Garnet Carter's Tom Thumb franchise. A National Tom Thumb Open Miniature Golf Tournament was held in 1930 on Lookout Mountain in Chattanooga, Tennessee, with a first prize of $2,000. Coon's song may have been a unique musical document of this fad.

In his radio days, however, he seems to have sung more conventional stuff, such as "Red River Valley" and "Twenty-One Years," which may go some way to explaining why he did not record again. There was evidently talk of it, because one of the clippings about his WEXL days preserved by his daughter mentions that "a certain recording company is negotiating with Walter to put some of his ditties on the revolving discs," adding that "he was a favorite of the phonograph era before he became a radio entertainer." But the only disc he is known to have made after 1930 was a single acetate copy, for use by WEXL, of the cowboy song "Way Out There" coupled with "The Lansing Hotel Fire," a song he wrote about the destruction, in December 1934, of the Kerns Hotel, in which thirty-two people died.

As well as his radio programs, on WMBC in Detroit as well as WEXL, Coon gave performances in stores, beer gardens, and hospitals. The Good Fellows Club of Maybury Sanitarium, thanking him for a "wonderful musical program," commented that "the entertainment was so entirely different from our usual ones that it has been the favorite topic with all the patients for the past two days." At one of those events, in 1940, he met the woman who would become his second wife, Fanny Margaret Wulotz. He carried on working at the Tip Top Bakery, but an accident with a biscuit-cutting machine, in which he lost the tip of an index finger, more or less ended his musical career, and he died a few years later.

Playlist
•• *The Cornshucker's Frolic Vol. 1* (Yazoo 2045): "Huskin' Bee"

Jules Verne Allen

(1883–1945)

Songs about cowboys and cattle trails, once Hollywood and the recording industry got hold of them, were soon puffed up by heated imagination and sweetened orchestration into a hyperbolic and highly self-conscious subgenre of popular music. But for a few years in

Jules Allen

(OTM collection)

contemporaries, he had songs that were not derived from the life and work of a cowboy yet smelled of the smoke of long-gone pioneer fires, such as the early settler song "Little Old Sod Shanty" and the Gold Rush ditty "The Days of Forty-Nine." Of the latter piece William Koon and Carol Collins wrote in *Old Time Music*:

> [It] has a realistically romantic ring of the past which few songs in America have generated. The tale of the last of the just haunts one as the old miner wanders around seeing his youth and his cohorts spent on the founding of the new West. So, although this song is not directly about the cowboy, it still has enough of the remembrances of the range past that the beauty of the ruin is still visible.

There is a literary turn to cowboy song, and you learn without much surprise that many of its makers were at least part-time men of letters: poets like Badger Clark, who wrote "A Border Affair" ("Spanish Is the Lovin' Tongue"), D. J. O'Malley ("When the Work's All Done This Fall"), and Curley Fletcher ("The Strawberry Roan"), or the journalist Will Barnes and the novelist Owen Wister. Allen, however, seems not to have written any of the songs he recorded, relying rather on John A. Lomax's collection *Cowboy Songs and Other Frontier Ballads*, published in 1910, one of the few works of folksong scholarship that can claim to have exercised an influence on folksong itself. Except when the text is too long for a record, as in "The Dying Cowboy" (a.k.a. "Oh, Bury Me Not on the Lone Prairie"), where he slashes Lomax's eighteen stanzas to a manageable seven, Allen is remarkably faithful to the book, and in several songs gives us the Lomax text almost verbatim.

But where did a "cowboy songster" perform when not in a recording studio or a radio station? Newspaper files give us some answers. In the summer of 1930, newly married and living in Taos, New Mexico, Allen was busy on the show circuit, featuring in *Days of '49* in Flagstaff, Arizona, and participating in a large traveling show for the First American organization, also with Native American and Mexican performers, which set out from Albuquerque at the beginning of August for a tour of eastern New Mexico. "The youngsters went wild when Jules sang 'Little Joe the Wrangler,'" wrote the *Albuquerque Journal* when the caravan hit the city, "and he came back at them with a cowboy melody about the hard life of punching cows." Two days later he was

the 1920s it was possible to hear original songs of the West, many of them dating back to the late nineteenth century, in penny-plain versions by men and women who had actually been working ranch hands.

One of the most appealing was the arrestingly named Jules Verne Allen. Born in Waxahachie, Texas, he worked on cattle drives around the turn of the century, and later in rodeos and the Buffalo Bill–type cowboy extravaganzas that were popular in the '10s and '20s. In his forties he began singing on radio stations in Texas and California, and in 1928–29 he recorded twenty-two cowboy songs, blues ballads, and folksongs for Victor, delivering them soberly in a small, weatherbeaten voice to the accompaniment of a clip-clopping guitar and sometimes a fiddle or harmonica.

If Allen's were the only cowboy songs to survive on records, we should still have a fine, representative sampling: trail tales like "Little Joe, the Wrangler," "When the Work's All Done This Fall," and a long text of "Chisholm Trail," and bunkhouse singalongs like "Home on the Range" and "Cowboy's Lament" (a.k.a. "Streets of Laredo"). In common with other cowboy singers, he enjoyed the technical vocabulary of the trade: the story of the feisty horse Zebra Dun is packed with the Spanish-American lingo of saddlery. Also, again like many of his the star of an evening concert, singing half a dozen of his numbers before yielding the stage to "Indian dancers."

In 1933 he followed Lomax's example and published his own collection of songs and stories of the range, titled *Cowboy Lore*. In May the *Albuquerque Journal* trailed it in its column "Around Albuquerque," though reserving the lead for the Yacht Club's impending meeting on Feminism. *Cowboy Lore* is well thought of by aficionados of the Old West and has been reprinted. Allen continued to write, contributing articles on cowboy song to *New Mexico* magazine.

Although a 1930 clipping quoted him as being about to go to California "to make records on a recently signed contract," he seems not to have done so, but his discs went on selling: a handful of them were rereleased in the '30s on the label of the Montgomery Ward mail-order store and altogether sold over fifty thousand copies. He continued to sing on radio, appear on the rodeo circuit, and work as a part-time police officer around El Paso, Texas.

Powder River Jack Lee

(1872/3–1946)

Playlist

•• *Country* (Frémeaux FA 015 2CD): "The Days of Forty-Nine," "The Dying Cowboy" •• *Western Cowboy Ballads & Songs 1925–1939* (Frémeaux FA 034 2CD): "Cowboy's Lament," "The Gal I Left Behind Me," "Jack o' Diamonds," "Little Joe, the Wrangler" •• *Cattle Call: Early Cowboy Music and Its Roots* (Rounder CD 1101): "Little Joe, the Wrangler" •• *When I Was a Cowboy Vol. 1* (Yazoo 2022): "'Long Side the Santa Fe Trail" •• *When I Was a Cowboy Vol. 2* (Yazoo 2023): "The Gal I Left Behind Me" •• *Hard Times Come Again No More Vol. 2* (Yazoo 2037): "Little Old Sod Shanty"

"They told me I'd find you here, Jack Lee," said the tall cowboy. He took a sip of whisky and replaced the glass quietly on the bar. "And they told me you stole my song."

Lee was shorter and stockier, and had to lift his head to meet the other man's gaze. He faced him defiantly. "Took that song, sure 'nough, and put it on a record, which is more than you had the horse sense to do, Gail Gardner. Made somethin' of it. You want to make somethin' of *that*?"

"I don't give a durn about phonograph records," Gardner replied. "Nothin' but playthings for kids and old folks. I care about my song. You took my song and printed it in your damn book and called it your own. 'Words and music by Jack Lee.' Excuse me—'*Powder River* Jack Lee.'" He spat on the floor. The saloon was silent.

"And you kin prove otherwise?" said Lee.

"I could if I cared to," said Gardner, "but you know that song for mine as surely as I know you for a lyin', thievin', half-assed excuse for a cowboy. And we're goin' to settle this thing the way cowboys do. Come outside and have your hide whipped."

. . . or maybe not. Jack Lee probably knew better than to be anywhere in the vicinity when Gail Gardner was around. After all, Gardner *did* write "The Sierry Petes," and Lee *did* change its name to "Tying A Knot In The Devil's Tail," and record it and publish it and put his own name to it, and there are words for behavior like that, unvarnished cowboy terms like "hornswoggling." The singer and historian John I. White, in his 1976 book *Git Along, Little Dogies*, described Lee tactfully as an "itinerant cowboy troubadour and poet" who "suffered from an overactive imagination," but in a letter to me a few years earlier he had been a little more candid: "I realize Jack was making

(OTM collection)

his living the only way he knew how, but I don't mind stating in public that he was careless with the truth . . . the old song rustler."

But White did add, "He was a good singer," and that brings us to the heart of this otherwise slightly disreputable tale. Jack Lee is a performer of enormous character and charm, qual-

ities on plain view in his recording of "Tying A Knot In The Devil's Tail." The song tells of two drunken cowboys, Buster Gigs and Sagebrush Sam, who light out for the "Siree Peaks" (Gardner's "Sierry Petes," the Sierra Prieta range near his home in Prescott, Arizona), where they meet "the Devil himself jest a prancin' down the road"

(OTM collection)

By 1932 they were singing over KFBB in Great Falls, Montana. Later that year they played a charity engagement at New York's Bellevue Hospital, eliciting a piece in *Time* magazine that described Lee as "a leathery, garrulous, honest-injun cowboy from the wild old West. . . . He played a harmonica with his nose. He sang 'Never Tie a Knot in a Billy-Goat's Tail.'" He also gave his opinion of "radio cowboy" artists, a theme to which he often returned. "Just a lotta drugstore cowboy singin'," he said dismissively in a 1937 interview, and in the introduction to his 1938 folio *Cowboy Songs* he rails against yodeling: "I have never known nor met a cowboy in my life who was interested in applying this method of singing to any range songs of the west. If authenticity is to be preserved for posterity, then the present type of mushroom radio singers who yodel will have to be discountenanced. . . ."

From their home in Deer Lodge, Montana, or later Phoenix, Arizona, the Lees kept themselves in the public eye by astute self-promotion. Jack was an admirer of the Western painter Charles M. Russell, dedicated his songbook to him, and campaigned to have a bronze bust of the artist installed in the Montana state historical library in Helena. He dealt the press stories about how he had gone round the world three times with Buffalo Bill, and played for five presidents. FDR had even invited him on to his private train. In 1938 Jack and Kitty performed at the National Folk Festival.

In February 1946 Jack Lee was killed in an automobile accident near Phoenix. Two months later the Helena *Independent Record* reported that "He did not leave very much in worldly goods" and that Kitty was blind—"But friends have rallied to her relief and her future is safely provided for, according to an article in the Phoenix, Ariz., Republic, a copy of which was sent to old friends here. Powder River Jack rode this section of Montana and in Wyoming, in the wild old days, and many old-timers knew and loved him."

and leave him roped, branded, de-horned, and with ten knots tied in his tail. The narrative is as bold and improbable as the landscape in which it is set, and Lee delivers it with no superfluous drama but much enjoyment, in a small, dry, gnarled voice, to the jaunty rhythm of his own and his wife Kitty's guitar. The text follows the original closely. Gardner would later refer dismissively to "a garbled version" put about by "a dude-ranch entertainer," but Lee's alterations are unexceptionable and sometimes better: "I'm sick of the smell of burnin' hair" is brilliantly amended to "I'm getting tired of cowography."

Jack Lee and Kitty Miller met as youngsters in the 1890s. He was a performer on Buffalo Bill's Wild West Show, she a bareback rider on the rival 101 Wild West Show. It isn't clear when they quit the show circuit for music, but they must have had some reputation by 1930 to persuade Victor to record them. As well as "Tying a Knot" they filled a canvas with brawling cattle-trail life in "Powder River, Let 'Er Buck," while "My Love Is a Cowboy," a song The Girls of the Golden West would do a few years later, teased the listener with lines like "He tipped me a wink, as he gaily did go, for he wished me to look at his bucking bronco."

Playlist

•• *Western Cowboy Ballads & Songs 1925–1939* (Frémeaux FA 034 2CD): "Tying a Knot in the Devil's Tail" •• *Cattle Call: Early Cowboy Music and Its Roots* (Rounder CD 1101): "Tying a Knot in the Devil's Tail" •• *When I Was a Cowboy Vol. 1* (Yazoo 2022): "Tying a Knot in the Devil's Tail" •• *When I Was a Cowboy Vol. 2* (Yazoo 2023): "My Love Is a Cowboy"

The Cartwright Brothers

Bernard Cartwright (c. 1897–1955) • Jack Cartwright (1901–??)

Amidst the Stetsoned and chapped company of cowboy singers like Jules Allen or Powder River Jack Lee, Bernard and Jack Cartwright might seem at first sight like a couple of city dudes. The smartly jacketed young men photographed in a 1929 record catalog look as if they have just breezed in from a tea dance. In fact they were Texas small towners, who brought an affecting simplicity to prairie ballads like "Utah Carroll" and "The Dying Ranger."

The Cartwrights grew up in the flatland of West Texas, in the Knox County community of Munday. "By the time I was twelve," Jack recalled, "Burn and I were playing together. Fiddle and guitar, they went together just as sure as bread and butter. First we played the square-dance tunes. Next we began to play music for round dancing—polkas, schottisches, waltzes, and one-steps, and later foxtrots. Burn read and wrote music and could play anything, including the classics. So we commenced to play for our home dances, then for community dances in dance-halls. Jazz and swing arrived, but the people we played for liked our music better."

The owner of the Eiland Drug Store, who was also a Columbia Records dealer, mentioned the brothers to a company salesman, and when a Columbia recording crew next passed through Dallas, in December 1927, the Cartwrights were called for an audition. "So we made 'Kelley Waltz' and 'Honeymoon Waltz,'" said Jack, "and we were off and running." They also recorded a couple of breakdowns, which Columbia passed over. The company had been impressed by the excellent sales of the Leake County Revelers' coupling of "Wednesday Night Waltz" and "Good Night Waltz," which they had recorded earlier that year, and that

probably encouraged them to prefer the Cartwrights' waltzes. They were duly rewarded with sales of over 45,000 copies, the Columbia hillbilly list's best-selling instrumental record of 1928.

When the company called the brothers back to the studio a year later, however, they wanted not dance music but Western songs like "When the Work's All Done This Fall" and "Get Along Little Dogies," probably because they had sold well for other labels, notably Victor, and Columbia didn't have them in their catalog. The brothers sang them as duets, and there, Jack confessed, "we hit a snag. My voice has such a narrow range, we could sing very few pieces together."

Despite fair sales, Columbia dropped them after that second session, but in 1929 the Cartwrights hooked up with Victor. They recorded some more vocal duets like "Pickaninny Lullaby," and another instrumental coupling, but the best performances were solo vocals by Jack. On one, "Texas Ranger," he set aside his guitar and sang with just Bernard's fiddle for accompaniment, a haunting performance.

By then Bernard had moved to Boerne (pronounced, appropriately enough, "Bernie") and Jack to nearby San Antonio. In the mid-'30s, their recording career over (they had made just fifteen issued sides), they played on the San Antonio stations WOAI and KTSA. A surviving program shows them filling half an hour's airtime with ten pieces of "old fashioned music" such as "Chicken Reel" and "Ragtime Annie." Away from the radio studios, much of their work was for commercial sponsors: in a photo from the late '30s they are playing on a makeshift stage, promoting Liberty Mills' Heart's Delight Flour.

Bernard quit playing in 1938 and worked as Boerne's postmaster. Jack carried on, sometimes switching to banjo or bass; he had rescued a bass from the dump at the Kelly Field USAF base and patched it up. In the '40s came the square-dance revival, which he welcomed as "the most regular and easiest playing I had ever done." But by the mid-'50s Bernard had died, Jack had retired, and their records were forgotten, except by collectors. "Texas Ranger" came to the attention of a new generation of old-time music lovers when it was included on the 1966 RCA-Victor LP *Authentic Cowboys and Their Western Folksongs*. In time that too disappeared, but a few of the Cartwrights' sides have been reinstated on CD, and they hold their own among the finest of old-time Western recordings.

	Number	Size	List prc.

CARTER FAMILY—Continued

Little Moses	V-40110	Storms Are on Ocean	20937	
Lulu Wall	V-40126	Sweet Fern	V-40126	
My Clinch Mountain Home	V-40058	Wandering Boy	20877	
No Telephone in Heaven	V-40229	When Roses Bloom	V-40229	
Poor Orphan Child	20877	Wildwood Flower	V-40000	
River of Jordan	21434	Will You Miss Me	21638	
Single Girl, Married Girl	20937			

CARTWRIGHT BROTHERS—Guitars

Cartwright Brothers

Dying Ranger (Vocal)	V-40198	Texas Ranger (Vocal)	V-40198
Pretty Little Doggies (Vocal)	V-40247	Wandering Cowboy (Vocal)	V-40247
San Antonio	V-40147	Zacatecas—March	V-40147

		Number	Size	List prc.
Casey Jones *Willie, the Chimney Sweeper*	Vernon Dalhart *Ernest Rogers*	20502	10	.75
Catfish Medley March *Argentine Rag*	Jimmie Wilson's Catfish String Band *Jimmie Wilson's Catfish String Band*	V-40216	10	.75
Catfish Whiskers *She's Comin' 'Round the Mountain*	Jimmie Wilson's Catfish String Band *Wilson's Catfish String Band*	V-40163	10	.75
Chain Gang Song *Runaway Train*	Vernon Dalhart *Vernon Dalhart*	19684	10	.75
Change In Business All Around *Singing with Guitar and Harmonica* *Gal of Mine Took My Licker From Me*	Carolina Twins *Carolina Twins*	V-40243	10	.75
Charles Giteau *Henry Clay Beattie*	Kelly Harrell *Kelly Harrell*	20797	10	.75
Charley, He's a Good Old Man *with Violin, Guitar, Banjo* *For Seven Long Years I've Been Married*	Harrell *Kelly Harrell*	21069	10	.75
Charlotte Hot Step *Guitar Duet with Harmonica* *Red Rose Rag Guitar Duet*	Fletcher and Foster *Fletcher and Foster*	V-40232	10	.75
Cherokee Rag *Violin, Banjo and Guitar* *On the Banks of the Kaney*	Henry's String Band *Henry's String Band*	V-40195	10	.75
Chewing Gum *with Guitar and Autoharp* *I Ain't Goin' to Work Tomorrow*	The Carter Family *The Carter Family*	21517	10	.75
Chicken *with Piano* *Married Man in Trouble*	Vaughan Happy Two *Vaughan Happy Two*	V-40001	10	.75
Chisholm Trail *with Guitars* *Cowboy's Love Song with Guitars*	Jules Allen (The Singing Cowboy) *Jules Allen (The Singing Cowboy)*	V-40167	10	.75

9

A page from the 1929 Victor catalog of "Old Familiar Tunes and Novelties." (OTM collection)

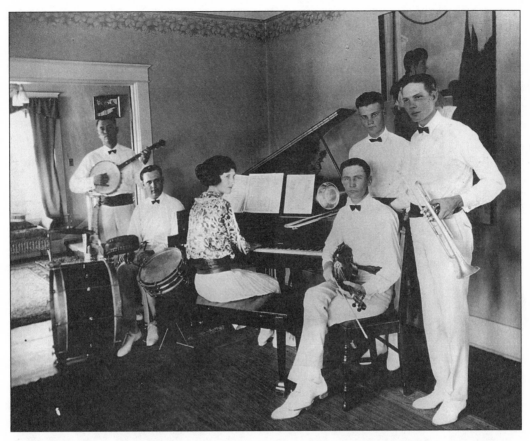

A Cartwright band of the 1930s. Left to right: U. R. Houser, P. G. Barton, Lorena Wilson, Bernard Cartwright, Larry Burton, Clayborne Harvey. (OTM collection)

Playlist
•• *When I Was a Cowboy Vol. 1* (Yazoo 2022): "Texas Ranger," "Utah Carroll" •• *When I Was a Cowboy Vol. 2* (Yazoo 2023): "The Dying Ranger," "Get Along Little Dogies"

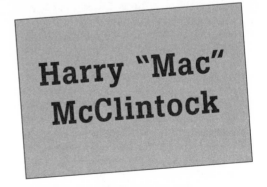

Harry "Mac" McClintock

(1882–1957)

The opening credits of *O Brother, Where Art Thou?* roll over fields of golden grain, to the tune of "The Big Rock Candy Mountains," "where the handouts grow on bushes and you sleep out every night . . . where the boxcars all are empty and the sun shines every day, on the

Harry "Mac" McClintock and radio friends, 1930. (OTM collection)

birds and the bees and the cigarette trees, the lemonade springs where the bluebird sings . . ." It's the anthem of the hobo, the bindlestiff, the tramp, the bum: the itinerant searching not for employment but for idleness, for a "land that's fair and bright . . . where they hung the jerk that invented work." But the man who wrote and sang it was very far from a layabout.

His name was Harry Kirby McClintock, which his friends shortened to "Mac." He was born in Knoxville, Tennessee, but by the age of fourteen he had left home to ride the rails with, as he put it later, "as choice a collection of bums as could be found in North America." His experience of hobo life—snatching free rides on slow-moving freight trains, panhandling for loose change, eating and sleeping in alfresco "hobo jungles"—inspired not only "The Big Rock Candy Mountains" but other pieces like "Hallelujah! I'm a Bum," irreverently set to the tune of the old hymn "Revive Us Again."

The dying light of the nineteenth century and the dawn of the twentieth saw Mac exchanging the road for the sea. As an army mule skinner he journeyed to the Philippines, China, and Africa, where he caught some of the Boer War. In Australia he played his banjo at outback jamborees before taking ship for England in time for the coronation of Edward VII. Back home in the United States he signed on as a railroad switchman. The early years of the century were a boom time for the railroad freight business, and a "boomer" could find work anywhere. Mac was doubly qualified for work opportunities, because by now he had a bag of songs that he could unpack wherever he found an audience. He also joined the newly founded Industrial Workers of the World or "Wobblies," an organization devoted to the socialist ideal of "One Big Union," and "Hallelujah! I'm a Bum" became the IWW's unofficial anthem.

By the early '20s Mac was married and living a more settled life in San Francisco, well placed to profit from another booming industry: radio. In 1925 he began singing and telling stories on station KFRC's Blue Monday Jamboree. Calling himself "Haywire Mac," he assembled a "Haywire Orchestry" of musicians to accompany his songs of hobos and cowboys. In 1928 he landed a contract with Victor Records. His first sides were cowboy favorites like "Get Along, Little Dogies" and "The Old Chisholm Trail," the latter jauntily accompanied by a bunkhouse trio of fiddle, harmonica, and guitar, but his disc of "Hallelujah! I'm a Bum" coupled with "The Bum Song" was the biggest seller. When it was issued in Australia, the record labels carefully explained, lest the titles caused a blush, that "bum" was a slang expression for a tramp or hobo.

"The Big Rock Candy Mountains" soon followed, and it is that original recording of September 1928 that we hear in *O Brother*. In the years since he wrote it, the song had been copyrighted by others, but, thanks to his radio listeners, Mac was able to find some of the postcards on which he had printed the song in 1905, and thus established his claim.

Mac could still be heard on the airwaves as late as the '50s. When he died, the *San Francisco Chronicle* hailed him as a "pioneer radio hillbilly," but he had also worked on screen, big and small, and if someone had told him that forty years later he would be heard in a hit movie, he wouldn't have been at all surprised. After the life of adventure he'd had zigzagging across the globe, being coopted into the crazy world of the Coen Brothers would be just one more twist.

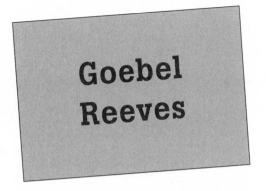

Goebel Reeves

"The Texas Drifter"
(1899–1959)

How do, folkses! This is station H-O-B-O, operating on a vagrancy of from thirty to ninety days, by authority of your local police force. . . ."

The Texas Drifter was off again—or rather on: on some one-room station in some one-horse town, some time in the 1930s, giving out with his crazy patter, reading jokes from men's magazines, reciting his own poems, and singing Western favorites like "Little Joe the Wrangler" and "Railroad Boomer" with his inimitable whooping yodel.

Playlist

•• *When the Sun Goes Down Vol. 6: Poor Man's Heaven* (Bluebird 50958): "Hallelujah! I'm a Bum" •• *Bona Fide Bluegrass & Mountain Music* (BMG Heritage 43600): "The Big Rock Candy Mountains" •• *Western Cowboy Ballads & Songs 1925–1939* (Frémeaux FA 034 2CD): "The Old Chisholm Trail," "Sam Bass" •• *Train 45: Railroad Songs of the Early 1900's* (Rounder CD 1143): "Jerry, Go Ile That Car" •• *Cowboy Songs on Folkways* (Smithsonian/Folkways CD SF 40043): "Utah Carl" •• *When I Was a Cowboy Vol. 1* (Yazoo 2022): "Goodbye, Old Paint," "Sam Bass"

(Author's collection)

In some ways he was a forerunner of Woody Guthrie, his feet always itching to be on the road and his pen itching to write down the stories he heard there. "I have truly seen America first," he began one of his songs, alluding to an advertising slogan of the day:

I have truly seen America first, riding on a
    dirty freight train,
I've been from the 'Frisco Golden Gate to
    the rockbound coast of Maine,
Yes, I've harvested wheat in Kansas, cut ice
    in Montreal,
But the work I done in Texas was the
    worst jobs of them all. . . .
Now there I was way down in Texas, and
    I'd never picked cotton in my life;
The end of those Texas cotton bolls, my
    friend, was sharp as a butcher knife.
I picked that stuff for a week and two days
    and I almost broke my back,
I asked the man for my pay and he said I
    still owed for my sack. . . .

The Texas Drifter knows perhaps better than the poet who first said it that "music has charms to soothe a savage breast." "There's been many a stampede stopped by a cowboy's singing and the lives of thousands of little dogies saved," says this colorful singing wanderer from the lone prairie.

Goebel Reeves in Nashville, c. 1938. (Courtesy of Dave Sichak)

He was the first disc-balladeer of hobo life and a member of the Industrial Workers of the World. But there was also a red-nosed comedian inside the Drifter, who would take over to tell mother-in-law jokes or sing his eye-opening specialty "I Learned about Women from Her," actually his own setting of a poem by Rudyard Kipling:

She taught me the gipsy folks' belay, a kind
    of volcano she were;
She knifed me one night when I wished she
    was white,
And I learned about women from her. . . .

Goebel Leon Reeves really was a Texan, born in Sherman, north of Dallas, not far from the Oklahoma line. He learned his trade by singing on medicine shows, in saloons, anywhere he could find an audience. "Barbershops," he said, "were always good." He claimed that he had appeared in about fifty films, both silent and talkies. An impromptu performance in a New York restaurant led to him being booked for the coast-to-coast radio show presented by crooner Rudy Vallee. The network also sent him to Chicago to sing at the 1933 World's Fair. But sophisticated listeners greeted his tales of dying hobos and condemned prisoners with snickers rather than handkerchiefs, and Reeves soon returned, with relief, to local radio and its rustic audiences.

It was there, unfortunately, that he was probably at his best—unfortunately, because there was no way of capturing his on-air antics. On a station in Birmingham, Alabama, he ran an amateur talent program called "Who's Who in Radio, and if So, Why." In Denver, Colorado, he gave out the station ID as "KFEL—Kan't Find Enough Liquor." In Jackson, Tennessee, his show was so popular that the city made him honorary mayor.

Appropriately for an avid globetrotter—he rambled widely in the Far East and spent two years in Japan—he had a remarkable appeal overseas. Two dozen of his records, a third of his output, were released in the UK during the '30s, and some in Ireland and Australia. It helped that he was cast in a similar mold to Jimmie Rodgers, a guitar-playing yodeler with a hotline to the worlds of hobo and brakeman, ranch house and penitentiary. Reeves admired Rodgers, and occasionally it shows. His two-part song "The Drifter" is an extended version of Rodgers's "I've Ranged, I've Roamed, I've Travelled," while "Miss Jackson, Tennessee" is a blue yodel, but not quite in the Rodgers manner. As a yodeler, Reeves owed nothing to any man. A reporter for *Rural Radio* tried to transcribe it:

"Hy–dle–leedle–odle–ladd–EE–oo–OO–br–br–BR–BR–" and then he breaks off in the upward swing of "br's" to make a noise that sounds too high to have come from a human throat. It is like the rapid picking of a short-stopped banjo string. Once you've heard it, you will never forget it. The Texas Drifter needs no patent or copyright on his trademark because nobody can ever steal that theme song.

At the time the magazine's interview was published, he was singing on WSM in Nashville and touring with Pee Wee King's Golden West Cowboys. "But by the time this reaches print," the writer added, "the roaming urge may have struck, in which case he hops [on] his motorcycle and speeds away."

In fact, not long afterward he more or less gave up music and returned to an earlier pursuit, working as a merchant seaman. During World War II he settled in a suburb of Los Angeles and did voluntary work for the city's Japanese-American community. He carried on writing poetry until his death. Country music had long forgotten him, but he didn't care. In his view, it had already drifted too far from the common people he had spent so many years entertaining.

Playlist
• *Hobo's Lullaby* (Bear Family BCD 15680)
• *Sounds like Jimmie Rodgers* (JSP JSP 7751 4CD) [most of CD3 is by Reeves]
•• *American Yodeling 1911–1946* (Trikont US-0246): "The Yodelin' Teacher"

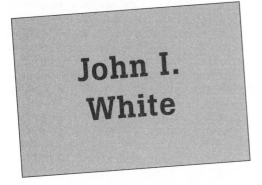

John I. White

(1902–92)

John I. Who? If the reader is puzzled, it's understandable. Although Mr. White is entitled to a small but meaningful paragraph in the annals of country music, his name is likely to be unfamiliar to anyone but a devotee of old-

time music, for the good reason that scarcely any of his records actually carried it. He was often Whitey Johns; occasionally he was Jimmie Price; from time to time he was The Lonesome Cowboy or Lone Star Ranger. It was under the last of those pseudonyms that he made his boldest mark on the page of history.

In the late 1920s and through the '30s, numerous hillbilly recordings, perhaps as many as a couple of thousand titles, were issued outside the United States: in Australia, the UK, Ireland, even India. It would be difficult, at this point, to determine what was the best seller among them—probably something by Jimmie Rodgers or Gene Autry, who had fans in all those territories. But one of the contenders might be a 1930 UK release on the Imperial label, "Eleven More Months and Ten More Days," credited to "Lone Star Ranger (Orchestral Accompaniment)." The song is a humorous novelty about being in jail, sprinkled with ancient jokes (Prisoner: "What time is it?" Warder: "What do you care? You ain't goin' anywhere!"); the "Orchestral Accompaniment" is a quartet of fiddle, clarinet, banjo, and guitar. The number must have caught the British fancy: Imperial issued White's recording again a few years later, it came out a third time on the Rex label, and a rival version by the citybilly duo Fields & Hall also racked up many sales. Half a century later, copies were still turning up in junkshops.

"Eleven More Months" was one of almost a score of recordings that White cut between the summer of 1929 and the spring of 1931. A few of them were cowboy or pioneer songs like "The Little Old Sod Shanty," but mostly they were new hillbilly compositions from the song mills of Tin Pan Alley like "Calamity Jane" or "Farm Relief Song." Back then, American chain stores could unload huge quantities of such records on to the market. Each of White's numbers appeared on anything from four to a dozen labels, or even more: "Eleven More Months" came out on nineteen. (Which was one of the reasons for all those pseudonyms.) If you were to collect every issue of every song in John White's discography, you would amass more than a hundred discs.

Anonymized though he was by the record industry, John White is not a figure of mystery. He lived long enough to correspond with collectors and to write articles, in which he revealed that his recording career was an accident. "Arthur Satherley of the American Record Corporation in New York needed a hillbilly singer," he wrote, "and asked Roy Smeck whether he knew one. Although I was only a

(OTM collection)

casual acquaintance whom Smeck had seen from time to time singing cowboy songs at radio station WOR, he somehow felt that I might qualify."

Smeck was a studio musician, expert on almost anything with strings but specializing in banjo, ukulele, and Hawaiian guitar. He accompanied White on all his recordings, picking banjo or guitar, doubling on harmonica, sometimes tripling on jew's harp, occasionally joined by a studio fiddler. It's likeable, jaunty music, not old-timey as an Uncle Dave Macon would have understood it, but closer to the idiom of Vernon Dalhart. Indeed, several of White's records were deliberate covers of pieces Dalhart had cut for other companies. And that, for White, became a problem.

Though not a Westerner by birth or upbringing—he was born in Washington, D.C.—John White had a genuine love of cowboy songs. Manufactured hillbilly songs like "Pappy's Buried on the Hill," he wrote years afterward, "didn't seem very genuine to

me. I lost interest and bowed out." But before he left the studio arena he did manage to record two bona fide cowboy numbers, "Whoopie- Ti-Yi-Yo (Git Along Little Doggies)" and Curley Fletcher's "Strawberry Roan," and for those he was, at last, credited in his own name. He continued to sing on radio until 1936 before quitting the music business and devoting himself to his job in a map-making company.

In retirement in the '60s and '70s he pursued his lifelong interest in cowboy songs, writing about them in magazines like *American West*. Eventually he produced a book, *Git Along, Little Dogies: Songs and Songmakers of the American West*, published by the University of Illinois Press in 1975. Packed with memoirs of Western poets and songwriters like Owen Wister, Gail Gardner, and Carl T. Sprague, and studies of cowboy anthems like "Home on the Range" and "Zebra Dun," it remains an outstanding work of (in the best sense of the term) amateur scholarship. It's certainly what John

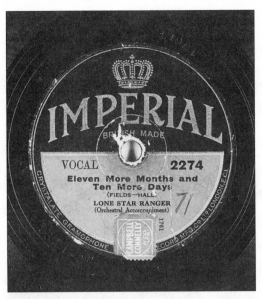

(Author's collection)

White would have wished to be remembered for, rather than his brief fling in the Depression-era record business.

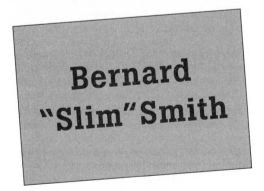

Playlist
•• *Western Cowboy Ballads & Songs 1925–1939* (Frémeaux FA 034 2CD): "Whoopie-Ti-Yi-Yo (Git Along Little Doggies)"

Bernard "Slim" Smith

(1899–1991)

What Bernard Smith really wanted to talk about was—his word—lockism.

I had painstakingly traced him across six decades, from Pope, Mississippi, to Memphis, New York, and finally Atlanta. He was impressed that someone should go to that much trouble, just because of a few obscure records he had made more than half a lifetime ago, but the same impulse that had once produced a fit of songwriting and recording, the urge to jump into something he hadn't done before and make his mark in it, was now pressing him to tell me about his career as an inventor—of a special automobile wax, of unspecified devices for the Georgia Power Company and the Lockheed Aircraft Corporation, but especially of a pick-proof lock. "I'm a hatcher-upper," he said. "You can ask me any kind of question regarding chemicals or mechanical-operated devices, and I won't stutter."

The questions I most wanted to ask, though, were about his 1931 record of the "Bread Line Blues," a wry commentary on the hard times Smith could have seen from his New York apartment window: "All of us good folks in distress, but I'm gonna get somethin' offa my chest . . . vote away those blues, the bread line blues." It's an odd record. Smith hasn't much of a voice, and what he has he handles awkwardly, having trouble fitting the words to the tune. As a writer he is no Woody Guthrie. But he was lucky in his accompanist: between the exchanges of political opinion by the cartoon figures of a "big-mouthed elephant" and a "long-eared mule," Bennie "King" Nawahi cuts loose with capering solos on Hawaiian guitar.

For all that, "Bread Line Blues" gives us an authentic hillbilly observation of the Great Depression. It is one of the few country songs of its day to say things as bald as "we ain't got nothin' but a carload of tax and the doggone load's just breakin' our backs," or "we've gotta do something or we're all gonna croak." And although there were other records by hillbilly singers gazing at the ruin around them, in dismay or resignation or with a sardonic grin, they were mostly by more seasoned performers. Smith lacked that professional touch; he sounds like an average Joe who has fortuitously found himself in front of a recording microphone, and it makes more immediate and believable this communique from the forgotten men of the soup queue and the shanty town.

Not that Smith himself was on the bread line. He had known hard times as a young farmer in Mississippi, losing his corn to drought and his cotton to the boll weevil. So he moved to Memphis, where he sold stock in the Piggly Wiggly store chain and made enough money to buy a new Hudson automobile. When it was stolen, he invented that

Benny Nawahi (front, center) with the Rocky Mountaineers. (OTM collection)

pick-proof lock ("pericentric pin-tumbler mechanism, adoptable to all classifications of lockism"), took his design to New York, got it patented, and in due course became the chief locksmith for the city.

While in Memphis he had become friendly with Bob Miller, piano player on the excursion boat *Idlewild* and an ambitious songwriter and publisher with an office on Beale Street. Miller preceded him to New York, where he quickly established himself on the music scene; over the next twenty-odd years he would compose and publish hundreds of hillbilly numbers. When Smith arrived, they began writing together—but not for long.

I went home on a little vacation, back to Mississippi, and the farmers down there was really talkin' the blues. What they wanted was the farm relief. So I said, "Well, I might be able to write a song, and we'll get it on records for the farmers." Well, I wrote the song, lyric and melody, "The Farm Relief Blues." I had a lead sheet made in Memphis and I sent it to Bob. You know what happened? I got the letter of heartaches, the letter that really hurt me. Bob

says, "Dear Bernard, The song that you sent me—I must tell you, I'm writing one myself." And he told me that his song was already booked for Brunswick. So I said, "Well, I can't lose this thing. I'm gonna go in there with Vernon Dalhart." Bob had his copyright on a "Farm Relief Blues," so I changed mine to the "Farm Relief Song."

Dalhart recorded the "Farm Relief Song" on five labels and it was a sizable hit. Miller's Brunswick disc tanked. "His lyric wasn't quite as exact," Smith reflected. "It didn't fit the farmer exactly." After that things between them were never the same. As Smith put it, "you can just go so far with a friend, and then if you step on his toes you're gonna hurt him."

With a hit song to his name, Smith was able to talk to publishers and record companies. He made a handful of quirky discs in his own name or variants of it: "Bread Line Blues" was credited to Slim Smith, while as Charles B. Smith he sang the endearingly kooky "My Little A-1 Brownie," probably the only hillbilly song about cameras, accompanied by King Nawahi tearing off hot solos on four instruments—Hawaiian guitar, standard guitar, mandolin, and harmonica—and a young clarinet-playing bandleader who added to his income by doing anonymous session work, one Benny Goodman. He knocked around with vaudeville personalities of the day like the banjoist Eddie Peabody, whom he memorably described as "a futuristic artist, and he needed no introductory." He went on radio with Nawahi a couple of times, but the guitarist refused to sign a contract for a long-term engagement on WHN and soon afterward found a better gig in California. "So I quit the music business, heartbroken, and I just put all my time and effort in the lock business."

In the late '40s he moved back south, and after a few years settled in Atlanta. He made a last foray into the music business in 1954, when he got the head of RCA-Victor's Atlanta office interested in a song about the murder of Albert Patterson, a lawyer in Phenix City, Alabama, who was running for state attorney general on an anti-corruption platform. " 'Phenix City Patterson'—oh, it was a clever lyric." This time someone beat *him* to it. But he never gave up songwriting: when I met him in 1978 he had composed what he called "a patriotic song" for Jimmy Carter, and was just waiting for the president to do something to earn it.

Postscript: Around 2004, the Nashville country music journalist Robert K. Oermann played a tape of "Bread Line Blues" to a fellow member of the Music Row Democrats, to illustrate his thesis that the political sentiment of country music isn't invariably right-wing. The song found its way to another MRD, the country songwriter Tim O'Brien, and inspired a rewrite, "Republican Blues," which can be heard on the MRD web site. Bernard Smith, a man of unquenchable technological curiosity, would have been tickled pink.

Playlist
•• *The Columbia Label: Classic Old Time Music* (BACM CD D 057): "My Little A-1 Brownie" •• *Mountain Blues* (JSP JSP 7740 CD): "Bread Line Blues" •• *Hard Times Come Again No More Vol. 1* (Yazoo 2036): "Bread Line Blues"

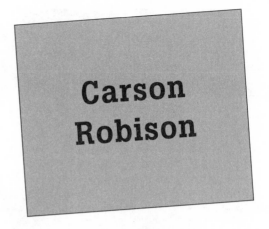

Carson Robison

(1890–1957)

S ongwriter, guitarist, and singer, Carson Robison had all the skills necessary to make a mark in country music, and for many years he exercised them prodigally, but perhaps his greatest achievement was to translate the music for people who had no cultural attachment to it. Almost uniquely among American performers, he found an audience in Europe. Three times in the 1930s he crossed the Atlantic to tour and make records, and after he returned home his fans tuned in to recorded programs beamed from Radio Luxembourg by "Carson Robison and his Oxydol Pioneers." (Oxydol, the band's sponsor, was a leading brand of detergent.) As the writer of a 1938 profile in *Rural Radio* magazine chose to put it, the Pioneers "are in a large measure responsible for the vogue of popular mountain music there. The limehouse [sic] lads still can't get over Carson's rendition of 'She'll Be Coming Round a Jolly 'Ole Hillside.' "

The bandleader of the '30s was already a veteran of the country music business. He had left his native Kansas and a budding radio career in the early '20s to become a session musician in New York. Initially he worked with the singer and ukulele player Wendell Hall, known as "The Red-Headed Music Maker," who had had a huge hit in 1923 with the novelty song "It Ain't Gonna Rain No More." Subsequently Robison played guitar behind hillbilly singers, accompanied Hawaiian-style guitarists like Roy Smeck, and enjoyed a hit of his own with a whistled version of the popular tune "Nola."

For several years he worked closely with Vernon Dalhart, playing guitar and singing tenor harmony on "My Blue Ridge Mountain Home" and scores of other records. He also learned the trick of writing for the country disc market.

Sincerely yours
Carson J Robison

Carson Robison
Recording Artist

(OTM collection)

Whenever the papers carried news of a train crash, bank robbery, or kidnapped child, Robison was only hours behind them with a song about it. Topical compositions had a short, albeit vigorous, shelf life, but his Western-styled pieces like "When It's Springtime in the Rock-

ies" and "Sleepy Rio Grande" became country standards. His records of them with the singer Frank Luther, his partner after an acrimonious breakup with Dalhart in 1928, were six-figure sellers.

Though he occasionally worked with back-

(OTM collection)

CARSON ROBISON
AND
HIS OXYDOL PIONEERS

Bill Mitchell Pearl Mitchell   John Mitchell

Carson Robison

ROBBINS MUSIC CORPORATION
799, Seventh Avenue, New York

English Distributors and Agents:
FRANCIS, DAY & HUNTER, Ltd
138-140, Charing Cross Rd. London. W. C. 2.

(OTM collection)

woods figures like Kelly Harrell or Fiddlin' Powers, Robison had never sounded like a southern mountaineer. By the early '30s, when he created the Buckaroos (renamed the Pioneers when performing outside the United States), with the Mitchell brothers on banjos and guitars and Pearl Pickens as resident cowgirl singer, he was riding a pop-country trail, taking a direction quite different from contemporaries like J. E. Mainer or Bob Wills.

"After a complete study of the songs of mountain, range and plain," wrote the *Rural Radio* reporter,

> he concludes that they're the only American music. It is Carson's contention that they will outlast any Tin Pan Alley product because they are not based on fancy but real fact. They tell real stories, never exaggerating the true sentiments and emotions of the people they discuss.

The claim was a tad disingenuous. The office where Robison wrote songs like "Goin' Back to Texas" or "Home Sweet Home on the Prairie" ("Land of friendship and freedom, where there's never a tear dimmed eye") was spiritually situated on Tin Pan Alley West, and his celebrations of cowboy life, like those of his contemporaries The Sons of the Pioneers, were idealized paintings rather than documentary photographs. To listeners overseas, in particular, Robison's songs evoked an image of trail riders round a campfire that matched their impressions of the West gained from B-movies and Zane Grey novels. The picture was sentimental and inaccurate, but what would you expect? Robison was not a lecturer in American Studies; he was a weaver of dreams.

In his own estimation, he was a good deal more than that. On his missionary trips to Europe and Australasia, when he was safely out of earshot of people who knew better, he talked himself up as a founder of country music. "You will be surprised to learn," he wrote in an article in 1932,

> that previous to 1924 there were no "hill-billy" records. When I first put the idea forward to gramophone companies they could not see it. After some insistence, one of them decided to experiment, and gave me full rein in picking the titles. . . . We were finally inspired to give the natives exactly what they wanted, which, naturally, was something that they knew. . . . After a while we started to worry about the well of original hill-billy songs going dry. The

obvious answer to this was to educate the natives in a new type of song based on the old standards. . . . We still had to make simplicity our primary aim, because the backswoodsmen began to learn the new tunes from the records, and play them on their own crude instruments.

How the backswoodsmen playing their crude instruments on the Grand Ole Opry would have greeted this sweeping claim we can only guess, but the article appeared in *Rhythm*, a British music magazine, so it was unlikely to come to their notice.

In September 1936, perhaps in recognition of their transatlantic appeal, Robison and his group were chosen to represent American folk music in an international radio hookup linking the United States and Europe. Their part of the program, between segments of Native American music and the Fisk Jubilee Singers, was devoted to cowboy songs, and they performed "The Streets of Laredo" and "Roll Out, Cowboys."

Like any old pro, Robison was not fazed by change. When the United States entered World War II he wrote and recorded peppy recruiting songs poking fun at Hitler and Mussolini, and updated Frank Luther's most notorious song to produce " 'Here I Go to Tokio,' Said Barnacle Bill, the Sailor." Later he made albums of square-dance music, and even threw his hat into the rockabilly ring with "Rockin' and Rollin' with Granmaw." But the surprise hit of his later-life career was a slow-talking, gum-chewing, rocking-on-the-porch narration, "Life Gets Tee-jus, Don't It?" In it, wrote the essayist Bob Coltman,

> [he] flatten[ed] the conventional rural nostalgia with the contempt of a man who had been there. The delivery was resigned, cantankerous, sour—and if it seemed at first hearing to be for laughs, there was an echo in it too of "How tedious and tasteless the hours. . . ." "Tee-Jus" was a talking blues; no doubt Robison the transplanted Kansan had been scornfully amused at the wide-eyed New York reception of Woody Guthrie and his talking blues, a balloon, he may have thought, asking to be punctured. But his picture of an Erskine Caldwell homeplace populated by sloth and flies is just a little too carefully drawn, and after laughing, the listener wonders. . . .

Robison died not long afterward, leaving as his memorial a portfolio of several hundred songs and a shelf of innumerable discs. Many of them speak only faintly to us; it's typical of our times, perhaps, that we should like "Left My Gal in the Mountains" less than his mock blues "Woman Down in Memphis." But his output remains a remarkable record of one ingenious writer's experiments with the form and subject-matter of country music over three decades.

Playlist
• *Home, Sweet Home on the Prairie* (Living Era CD AJA 5187)
• *Way Out West in Texas* (Old Homestead OH-4134)
•• *Country Music Pioneers on Edison* (Document DOCD-1102): "Nonsense" •• *Serenade in the Mountains* (JSP JSP 7780 4CD): "The Back Porch, Parts 1 & 2," "Birmingham Jail," "An Evening on the C R Ranche Parts 1 & 2," "Everybody's Goin' but Me," "Left My Gal in the Mountains," "Oklahoma Charley," "Settin' by the Fire," "The Wolf at the Door" •• *Howdy!: 25 Hillbilly All-Time Greats* (Living Era CD AJA 5140): "Goin' to the Barn-Dance Tonight," "In the Cumberland Mountains," "The West Ain't What It Used to Be" •• *The Singing Cowboys in the Movies* (Living Era CD AJA 5338): "There's a Bridle Hangin' on the Wall" •• *Cattle Call: Early Cowboy Music and Its Roots* (Rounder CD 1101): "Carry Me Back to the Lone Prairie"

Frank Luther

(1899–1980)

Imagine the history of popular music as a gigantic map, with the town names replaced by song titles. Find "Barnacle Bill the Sailor"

and "Three Billygoats Gruff." They will be quite far apart, but draw a line connecting them, making sure that it passes through "Home on the Range," "Will the Angels Play Their Harps for Me," and "Popeye the Sailor Man." You are beginning to trace the contours of one of the most remarkable careers in American music, the singing and songwriting life of Francis Luther Crow, professionally known as Frank Luther.

Luther belongs to the almost forgotten company of recording studio journeymen, artists who could turn their voices to anything: today a hillbilly ballad, tomorrow a dance band refrain, next week a set of children's songs—from "Oh Dem Golden Slippers" to "A Gay Caballero" to "The Story of Babar." Suave or cornball, naughty or nice, Luther gave a professionally finished performance of whatever was put in front of him. And much of that was country music, in the era when it had just emerged as a commercial entity and was swiftly being turned, by Luther and his contemporaries Carson Robison, Vernon Dalhart, and Frank Marvin, into an industrial product.

It was through the older and more experienced Robison that Luther got into the country music business. Born in Larkin, Kansas, he grew up in California—he may be the first country artist to be associated with

Frank Luther, Carson Robison, Murray Kellner. (OTM collection)

(OTM collection)

Bakersfield—and studied voice and piano in college. By 1926 he was touring with a male quartet, the De Reszke Singers, and the following year he joined another, The Revelers, a well-known radio and recording act. Then in 1928 he fell in with Robison, who had just called time on the best-selling country duet act of the period by ending his association with Vernon Dalhart. Luther, who could do a perfect imitation of Dalhart's nasal hillbilly manner, was clearly the sidekick Robison was looking for. Their partnership would last almost four years, and their wax works occupy almost thirty packed pages of the discography *Country Music Records*.

Most of their records sold in tens of thousands, some even better: "When It's Springtime in the Rockies," coupled with "Sleepy Rio Grande" on a 1929 Victor disc, shifted almost 150,000 copies, the sort of total only Jimmie Rodgers could be relied on to exceed. Their audience was not only in the United States: Robison & Luther records appeared in Canada, Australia, and, in considerable numbers, in the UK, though their identities were often cloaked by the pseudonym "Bud & Joe Billings."

Robison & Luther were chiefly a record act. Outside the studio, Luther continued to tour with The Revelers, worked with the humorist Will Rogers, and wrote a bunch of songs. One of the most successful was the comedy number "Barnacle Bill the Sailor," salty in both senses, which he or Robison recorded for more than twenty labels. When the duo dissolved in 1932, Luther formed a trio with his wife Zora and Leonard Stokes that was popular on both records and radio. For a spell in 1934 Stokes was replaced by Ray Whitley, who was impressed by Luther's professionalism:

> Frank was a perfectionist who knew exactly what he wanted on each song we recorded. He had the ability to select marvelous songs, musicians, and arrangements—he A&R'd our sessions. . . . [It] gave our records the sound of better orchestration than was typical of most country records at that time.

Then, in the late '30s, Luther found a whole new audience. For a while he had been making records in sets, for themed albums with titles like *Home on the Range* or *American Folk Songs*. (These were the original record albums, consisting of three or four discs, each in a stiff paper sleeve, bound into a book-like folder.) Years earlier he had done some nursery rhyme discs for the kiddie market. Now he combined these strategies to make dozens of albums of old songs for new listeners: fairy tales, stories from *Mother Goose, Raggedy Ann,* and *Winnie the Pooh, T'was the Night before Christmas.* . . . Someone tagged him "the Bing Crosby of the Sandpile Set," but he took the job of entertaining children very seriously, seeing his records as tools of "teaching through entertainment," and persevered with it for more than twenty years.

Given the vast changes in the cultural world of the child between Luther's heyday and the present, it's hardly surprising that his contribution to the music of childhood has largely been forgotten. In country music, too, though his smooth delivery is really not so very different from that of, say, Jimmie Davis, he has for many years been almost totally marginalized, his readily available back catalog no more than a few tracks on compilations. But diligent web searching will reward both the ardent Lutheran and the uncommitted enquirer with spirited renditions of "Hallelujah, I'm a Bum" (a deft imitation of "Mac" McClintock's original) and "How to Make Love," topical pieces of the Depression era like "Eleven Cent Cotton" and "Outlaw John Dillinger," and the six-part medley of cowboy songs that is "Home on the Range." It may not all be country music as we know it, or think we know it, but it was once, and it's time it took its place in the historical record.

Otto Gray & His Oklahoma Cowboys

For most hillbilly bands of the 1920s, fame amounted to being known in their own community and perhaps a few surrounding counties. Thanks to radio, some became household names in several states. Celebrity on a larger scale was more elusive, but a few acts achieved it, thanks to the industry and ingenuity of leaders who understood the power of promotion and the concept of a brand image. By far the most successful of these were Otto Gray's Oklahoma Cowboys.

The band came into being in 1921 when a group of businessmen in the small town of Ripley, Oklahoma, a few miles southeast of Stillwater, created a musical organization to play at dances and other community events. After going out for a time as the Old Time Fiddlers or the Ripley Cowboy Band, they signed up Billy McGinty, a celebrated cowboy, Spanish-American War veteran, and former member of Buffalo Bill's Wild West Circus, and began to spread the name of McGinty's Oklahoma Cowboy Band through broadcasts from KFRU in Bristow.

Late in 1925 the band came to the attention of Otto Gray, a forty-one-year-old entrepreneur from Stillwater, who secured them a couple of weeks' work, early the following year, on the Orpheum theater circuit in Missouri. The booking had a dramatic effect: most of the band resigned and were replaced. Tempting as it may be for a modern reader to interpret this as a managerial coup, the explanation is more mundane. The original members had jobs outside music, and while they didn't mind fitting in an occasional broadcast or high school concert, they were not available for full-time touring. Already they had had to call in deputies: for a gig in Tulsa they had co-opted Leonard Fulwider, a singer and guitarist who was later associated with the area's other well-known stringband, Jack Cawley's Oklahoma Ridge Runners from Stillwater.

So Gray rebuilt the group with personnel who *were* available, such as Dave Cutrell, a mustachioed, buck-toothed singer known as "Pistol Pete." In May 1926 the band recorded in St. Louis for OKeh, but only one side was issued, "Cow Boy's Dream." On the reverse, Cutrell gave a solo rendition of his specialty "Pistol Pete's Midnight Special," namechecking both McGinty and Gray. Over the next three or four years there were further personnel shuffles, as Gray brought in his son Owen, or "Zeb," who sang and played guitar, and his own wife Florence, always billed as "Mrs. Otto Gray" or "'Mommie' Gray," who sang. By 1930 the Oklahoma Cowboys had a relatively settled lineup of Owen and "Mommie" Gray, the Allen brothers, Wade ("Hy") on banjo and Lee ("Zeke") on fiddle, and "Chief" Sanders, regularly described in the band's write-ups as of part Cherokee stock, who played the cello. A later addition was "Rex, the Radio Dog."

Keen to be in the band himself, Gray put in some time practicing on fiddle, until he overheard his men planning how to "keep Otto from playing." After that he concentrated on announcing, rope tricks, and—his chief skill—promotion. So astute was he as a publicist that the Oklahoma Cowboys soon became the most famous Western band in the

Otto Gray & His Oklahoma Cowboys on NBC, probably 1930. (Courtesy of the Washington Irving Trail Museum)

nation. The lines of their tour itineraries snaked all over the Southwest and Midwest, and eastward at least as far as Syracuse, New York, in the North and Danville, Virginia, in the South.

" 'Oh, Bur-r-y me not on the lo-o-o-o-ne prairie'—this, the plaintive song of 'The Dying Cowboy[,]' is familiar to countless radio and record fans from one end of the country to the other," wrote the *Circleville* [Ohio] *Herald* on September 20, 1929, trailing the band's appearance at the Cliftona Theater the next day.

It has, in fact, reached a peak of popularity where it bids fair to become a permanent fixture as one of the true American folk songs. And, beyond a doubt, [the band] . . . have had much to do with bringing this about. Not only "The Song of The Dying Cowboy" but 40 or 50 other characteristic ballads of the western prairies owe much of their popularity to this colorful group of entertainers.

There is nothing "synthetic" about Otto Gray and his inimitable cowhands. They are real westerners. Everyone of these six foot musicians and singers have known what it means to ride creaking leather on the pitching back of a spirited pony—to live for days and weeks on the open range far away from human habitation and companionship. . . .

When their fame began to spread throughout the range country there grew a demand for their services to play and sing for all sorts of "get-togethers" characteristic of the open-hearted West. From this to radio and the stage was but one short step for these long limbed cowmen. And, of course, their guitars and banjos travelled right along as an indispensable part of their equipment.

When the band played the State Theatre in Lima, Ohio, in May 1930, the *Sunday News* devoted almost an entire page to linked ads from the Lima Cadillac Company ("Otto Gray Demands Better Service than Ordinary from an Automobile So He Drives a Cadillac") and the J. W. Rowlands radio store ("You'll Hear Them Better If You Own a Victor Radio"). About this time the Oklahoma Cowboys were broadcasting daily on WLW in Cincinnati, where, Gray claimed, they received "over a thousand letters and hundreds of telephone requests every day." "I am a little girl, eleven years old," wrote a listener from Ohio, "and I don't have any papa and mama anymore, but we have a nice radio in the home, and I do like to hear songs about Mother that 'Mommie' sings." "I am a cripple and I haven't walked for twenty years," wrote another. "I am sixty-four years old, and only in the way, just like the

Otto Gray & His Oklahoma Cowboys read their fan mail, 1930. (Courtesy of the Washington Irving Trail Museum)

song 'Mommie' sang this evening." (Are these testimonials a little too good to be true?)

In August 1930 the Oklahoma Cowboys made their first appearance in the East, on WGY in Schenectady, New York. "Coming here unheralded," wrote the trade paper *Billboard*, "Gray and his cowboy unit proved to be an overnight sensation. . . . Since [then] they have played to RKO Proctor theaters in Schenectady, Albany and Troy to turnaway business."

And so it continued. During 1930–33 the band had programs going out from stations in Syracuse, Rochester, Schenectady, and elsewhere in New York state, as well as from KMOX in St. Louis and WCAU in Philadelphia, and were featured coast-to-coast on the Camel Pleasure Hour. In June 1931 they were the first country band to be featured on the cover of *Billboard*. Around that time ads began to appear in the trade press for a copycat band, Ken Hackley's Oklahoma Cowboys, who billed themselves as "Nationally Known Radio Entertainers" and traveled with a dog that looked

suspiciously like Rex. Gray swiftly put his attorneys on the case.

Several newspapers ran a photo of the Gray band squatting with their instruments in front of "one of the three custom-built limousines in which they travel." *Billboard* reported on this in more detail in May 1932: "Otto Gray's new $20,000 car is wired for sound reproducing and equipped with a radio receiver and transmitter . . . [and] with an observation platform and reclining chairs." Gray and his wife occupied a trailer, towed by one of the cars, "which is akin in design to the coaches of the new style railroad trains," as the *Newark* [Ohio] *Advocate* breathlessly reported in June 1934, "[and] contains an electric refrigerator, a small range and . . . running water [and] berths for three people along with other conventional pieces of furniture."

That the Grays could range across a dozen states in an ancestor of today's luxurious tour buses while the nation was mired in the Depression eloquently confirms a claim made for them in several newspaper articles: "No radio feature in recent years has caught the popular fancy or gripped the imagination like the program offered by these boys from the plains of Oklahoma."

No recordings of these programs are known to survive, and fancy and imagination must be satisfied with the band's studio recordings, of which they made a couple of dozen between 1928 and 1931. Evidentially speaking, these are a few steers short of a herd. There must have been more to their act than these plodding performances of nonsense songs like "Barefoot Boy with Boots On" and "It Can't Be Done," or the quasi-blackface "Tom Cat Blues" and "The Terrible Marriage," with its dialog that might have been lifted from an Emmett Miller routine. A clearer clue to their impact lies in Mrs. Gray's renditions of "mother" songs such as "Your Mother Still Prays for You, Jack" and "Be Home Early Tonight My Dear Boy," plain almost to the point of amateurishness yet rather touching. But fortunately the variety and vitality of the Cowboys' stage show can be resurrected through film. *Billboard* reported on July 4, 1931, that the band "trouped into town yesterday and signed contracts with Film Exchange calling for six talkie shorts." One survives and has been issued on DVD, fourteen minutes of quick-change virtuosity featuring rope tricks, twin fiddling, songs, comedy business, and a routine in which each musician plays one instrument with his left hand and another with his right.

In the hard times of 1934–35 even as popular an act as the Gray band could no longer be assured of profitable touring. They made a final swing through the Midwest and on to New York in early 1936, and then Gray retired to his farm in Stillwater, where, a few years later, he found another outlet for his creativity in breeding miniature cattle. The Oklahoma Cowboys had had a long and remarkable run, but it was time to move over: their old-time cowboy songs would have paled beside the more richly colored repertoire of Gene Autry and The Sons of the Pioneers.

Playlist
• *Early Cowboy Band* (BACM CD D 139)
•• *Serenade in the Mountains* (JSP JSP 7780 4CD): "4000 Years Ago," "Who Stole the Lock" •• *When I Was a Cowboy Vol. 2* (Yazoo 2023): "Cow Boy's Dream" (McGinty's Oklahoma Cowboy Band)

The movie short is on the DVD *Times Ain't Like They Used to Be* (Yazoo 512).

Bridge: Country Music in Transition

As well as its many weightier consequences, the Depression closed a chapter in country music. With its grip tightening on the rural and small-town South, people could no longer afford records, even at the knockdown prices at which stores were trying to rid themselves of their stock. The record companies responded by slashing their pressing orders, discovering that artists who had once sold in six figures were now struggling to make four. (The Carter Family's "Wildwood Flower," released in January 1929, topped 120,000 copies; exactly three years later their "Sunshine in the Shadows" sold 4,329.) Programs of location recording, which had once had the major labels chasing each other round the South, visiting five or six cities a year to record talent, were cut to the bone: there were just three trips in 1931, two in 1932, and in 1933 none at all. One by one, most of the companies went broke or were swallowed by businesses that were not primarily interested in recording—at least, not hillbilly music.

The first sign of recovery came in 1933, when Victor, one of the very few survivors, launched a new label, Bluebird, but the discs were priced at 35 cents, as against 75 cents before the Crash, and at first the recordings were mostly reissues. The following year Brunswick reactivated its Vocalion marque and the British-owned Decca Records entered the business, both with a 35-cent tag but offering mainly new recordings, an initiative that Bluebird swiftly followed. These three labels would dominate hillbilly record making for the rest of the decade and into the '40s.

In the words of a popular hillbilly song, there was a change in business all around— but it went far beyond the shifts of company ownership and the strategies of pricing. The bleak plateau of the early '30s was littered with bones. In particular, the lean years seemed to have starved out the old-time

(Author's collection)

fiddlers and stringbands. The Skillet-Lickers, Fiddlin' John Carson, and Ernest Stoneman made their final bows in 1934; once bankable names like the Carolina Tar Heels, the Leake County Revelers, or the Kessinger Brothers had rung their last tills years before. The country would not see their like again.

What the record buyers and radio listeners of New Deal America now demanded of their country music was that it tell them stories. Instrumental music retired to the back of the stage, where it has remained; now was a time for singers, whether solos, duets, or trios. Veterans like Bradley Kincaid and Mac & Bob were able to carry on for a time, dangling their charm bracelets of ballads and heart songs. Gene Autry, The Sons of the Pioneers, and The Girls of the Golden West extolled the West in tales of sagebrush and saddle, echoed in Canada by Wilf Carter and Hank Snow. Cliff Carlisle and Bill Cox spiced the blue yodel with sex, while Jimmie Davis, once a skilled operator in that line of work himself, remade himself as a genial dispenser of country comfort. The old templates were discarded, as the new voices of the mid-'30s set about giving country music a thorough and, as it would prove, permanent makeover.

(Author's collection)

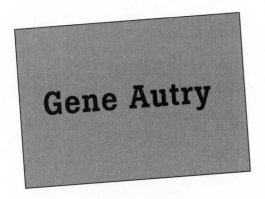

Gene Autry

(1907–98)

For the generation that grew up in the decade after World War II, Gene Autry was likely to be no stranger. They might know him as the star of evocatively titled Westerns like *The Sagebrush Troubadour* and *Blue Canadian Rockies*, or as the hero of gaudily jacketed hardbacks like *Gene Autry and the Golden Ladder Gang* ("In the eerie half-light before sun-up of a desert morning, a lone rider broke his fireless camp and rode carefully out of a concealing tangle of mesquite and catclaw. . . ."). Or maybe as the voice that every Christmas told the story of Rudolph the red-nosed reindeer.

Predictably, those were the Gene Autrys that were remembered when he died. Those, and Autry the businessman, owner of a baseball team, a record label, and a publishing company, entrepreneur of radio, rodeo, and real estate. The tale of the Texas-born, Oklahoma-raised ranch boy who makes millions out of a talent for singing to a guitar and swinging a six-gun is one of those quintessential farmhouse-to-penthouse stories that we love because they reassure us that the American dream works, that anybody can become anything.

Yet few of his obituarists gave much space to Autry's music. "After making several popular records in New York, he received a Hollywood offer," ran one notice, and with that the reader was transported to the Republic lot. Yet by then Autry had made scores of recordings for at least half a dozen companies, had had radio exposure on the WLS National Barn Dance and National Farm & Home Hour and on other stations, and had logged hundreds of personal appearances throughout the Midwest. With hits like "Silver-Haired Daddy of Mine" (1931) or "The Yellow Rose of Texas" (1933)—both duets with fellow ex-railroader Jimmy Long, his recording partner for several

years—he was finding himself as a western singer. But much of his work up to that point had been in a radically different style.

The young Gene Autry was an out-and-out Jimmie Rodgers fan. Actually, that's tactful. He was a song rustler who repeatedly raided the Rodgers ranch for rowdy blues ideas about high-steppin' mamas and do-right daddies, framing them, as Rodgers did, with a guitar and a yodel. Often he just covered Rodgers's hits, so adeptly that a casual listener might mistake him for the original. A less skillful guitarist than his model, he soon came to rely on accompanists to season the plain fare of his performances, and many of his early sides have tangy solos and fills by Roy Smeck, on Hawaiian guitar or banjo, or Frankie Marvin, on steel and standard guitars, harmonica, and, occasionally, vocal effects, such as the cluckings and crowings on "Stay Away from My Chicken House."

Blue yodelers in New York City, October 1931: Gene Autry (seated) with (left to right) Wilbur Ball, Jimmy Long, and Cliff Carlisle. (Author's collection)

BACK FROM HOLLYWOOD
Gene Autry
THE ORIGINAL
OKLAHOMA YODELING COWBOY

ECORDS

ADIO

TAGE

CREEN

Now Making a
PERSONAL APPEARANCE TOUR
of the Country

WITH HIS OWN SHOW
THE GREATEST OF ITS
KIND IN THE COUNTRY
•

STARRING IN
MASCOT'S SERIAL

(Author's collection)

(Author's collection)

Rodgers died in 1933, and Autry respectfully doffed his hat in obituary songs like "When Jimmie Rodgers Said Goodbye," but he had already begun to pack up his blues, perhaps to distance himself from the other Rodgers copyists who had come along in his wake, more likely because he saw a greater future in songs of the range. The Autry of the later '30s and '40s would devote himself to the purple prairies of the Western movie and the purple poesy of the Western song.

Only a blue yodel fanatic would regret the move. Songs like "The Last Round-Up," "Take Me Back to My Boots and Saddle," and "Back in the Saddle Again" elicited something new from Autry, an acutely balanced blend of virility and sentiment. Like The Sons of the Pioneers, he discovered a seemingly inexhaustible lode of songs that were simultaneously romantic and chaste.

At the start of the '40s he was probably the most profitable country singer in the United States, and not only there: his records were issued by the dozen in Australia, in the UK, and in Ireland, where he and his horse Champion had toured to great acclaim in 1939. Jimmie Davis ritually covered his songs for a rival label. Meanwhile his movies, of which he had been making several a year since 1935, generally partnered with the comedian and multi-instrumentalist Smiley Burnette, created a contingent of fans who voted him the top Western star five years running. Features like *South of the Border* and *Melody Ranch* also won him, in 1941, the National Parent-Teachers Film Award for "wholesome entertainment for children." (Evidently the jailbirds, loose women, and other roisterers of his early work had been forgotten, or he forgiven for them.) By 1940 he had a network radio show and in 1950 he successfully moved into television. In 1941 he bought a 2000-acre ranch near Berwyn, Oklahoma, and soon afterward the town changed its name—to Gene Autry, Oklahoma. Several staffers worked full-time dealing with his correspondence, and in 1948 the postmaster general formally presented him with his twelve-millionth fan letter.

Then in 1960 he gave it all up. It was good timing: the spirit of the coming decade, with its aggressive music and revisionist Westerns, would not be welcoming to a middle-aged horse-opera star with a preference for sunny jogalong songs.

Playlist
• *That Silver Haired Daddy of Mine* (Bear Family BCD 15944 9CD) [a definitive collection of everything Autry recorded in 1929–33, with lengthy notes and discography]
• *Blues Singer 1929–1931* (Columbia/Legacy CK 64987) [excellent selection from Autry's Blue Yodel Period]
• *The Singing Cowboy* (Living Era CD AJS 279 2CD) [spans eighteen years of Autry's work, but most tracks come from the mid-'30s onward and are lush Western movie music]
•• *Memories of Jimmie Rodgers* (Bear Family BCD 15938): "The Death of Jimmie Rodgers," "The Life of Jimmie Rodgers," "Memories of Jimmie Rodgers," "When Jimmie Rodgers Said Good Bye" •• *Western Cowboy Ballads & Songs 1925–1939* (Frémeaux FA 034 2CD): "Back in the Saddle Again," "The Life of Jimmie Rodgers," "Panhandle Pete," "Way Out West in Texas" •• *The Singing Cowboys in the Movies* (Living Era CD AJA 5338): "Dust," "Ridin' Down the Canyon" •• *Down in the Basement* (Old Hat CD-1004): "Atlanta Bound"

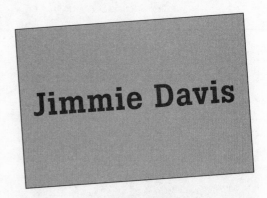

Jimmie Davis

(1899–2000)

A country singer whose career spanned eight decades and a notable figure in southern politics who was twice governor of Louisiana, Jimmie Davis will not be forgotten by musical or political historians. But perhaps his strongest claim for immortality is "You Are My Sunshine," a song that has grown too big to be contained by country music and has become a popular standard. A few years ago it featured in a UK advertising campaign, and in novelty gift shops you can buy a plastic sunflower that

will sing it to you. When Bob Dylan became a DJ on XM Radio in 2006, it was the second song he played. Behind the story of "You Are My Sunshine" lies another, stranger tale, but it was only one of many in Davis's curious career.

James Houston Davis was born poor in rural Louisiana, but he made it to college, where he sang in a quartet. A little later he had a radio program on KWKH in Shreveport, one of the South's most powerful stations. From 1928 onward his popularity on air was translated on to records: at first sentimental and cowboy songs, then raunchy blues like "She's a Hum Dum Dinger from Dingersville" or "Bear Cat Mama from Horner's Corners," all of them decorated, following the example of Jimmie Rodgers, with mellifluous yodeling. He didn't just sing blues but had blues musicians play with him and even, most unusually in that period, record with him. Davis's collaboration with the African-American slide guitarists Ed Schaffer and Oscar Woods on "Sewing Machine Blues" is in both senses one of the bluest items in the hillbilly record library. In another of their joint productions, the hymn pastiche "Down at the Old Country Church," Schaffer joins Davis in the singing. That wasn't just unusual: it was unprecedented.

Fascinating though Davis's blues songs are, not least for their strange conceits and comic exaggeration, and remarkable though it is to hear a future lawmaker sing "you ought to see that cock and pussy" (in a song ostensibly about quarrelsome animals), there is more to his work than transgressive storytelling. In a voice as blithe as a mountain stream he dispensed heart songs, tales of the rails like "Doggone That Train," and a gorgeous tribute to his home state, "Where the Old Red River Flows."

After four years with Victor, Davis switched in 1934 to the new Decca label, where his first recording was the wheedling love song "Nobody's Darlin' but Mine." It was a crossover hit before the phrase was coined, covered by Bing Crosby, and soon Davis put the blues behind him, but it was not the last he would hear of them. When he ran for governor in 1943, his opponent Jimmy Morrison tried to embarass him by holding public rallies and playing his smutty old records like "Red Nightgown Blues." All it did was give the listeners something to smile at and shake a leg to. "If you're gonna *dance*," said Morrison in disgust, "go ahead and elect the son of a bitch."

Davis had already entered public life as Shreveport's Commissioner for Public Safety, which enabled him to put his steel guitarist, Charlie Mitchell, and other members of his band on the city's payroll. "I always picked good men for the band," he told the *Port Arthur News* in 1942, "and they make good policemen." According to musicians who knew him then, Davis used his position as police chief to build his song folio: if a musician was hauled in on a charge, Davis would quietly bury the case in exchange for the rights to some songs. Even without a charge sheet to their name, hard-up writers would often sign away a half-share in a song for a timely cash offer. Consequently the catalog of songs solely or jointly credited to Davis includes many to which his claim is more legal than authorial. Floyd Tillman, who saw half of the revenue from his composition "It Makes No Difference Now" go into Davis's pocket, told me dismissively, "Jimmie Davis never wrote a song in his life."

But when it came to "You Are My Sunshine," Davis always insisted that it was his bright idea. When country music scholars produced evidence that other artists had recorded the song before he did, he fabricated even earlier sessions when, he said, he had recorded it but had not been satisfied with his performance, so had held it back. The real story seems to be that he bought it, for $35, from a musician who needed money for his wife's hospital bills.

In the late '30s and '40s Davis was a country star of almost the same magnitude as Gene

Jimmie Davis, Bill Teichman, Floyd Tillman. (Bear Family Records)

Autry, often recording the same songs, such as "Sweethearts or Strangers" or "I Hung My Head and Cried," with similar accompaniment. Like Autry, too, he got in on the Western movie business, appearing in titles like *Strictly in the Groove* and *Shotgun Guard*. After his first term as governor he quit the dance halls but continued to sing on radio and make records, gradually moving into gospel music. He still sang at election meetings, but the last time he ran for office, in 1972, it did not seem to work so well, and he abandoned both public performing and politics to concentrate on his immense publishing business.

In his later years, with no political prestige at stake, he was not embarrassed to reminisce about his disreputable early recordings, but he was wary of questions about authorship, and some other topics elicited an odd reaction. Talking to him once about the singer Buddy Jones, whom he not only gave a job on the police force but introduced to Decca, I casually asked about Buddy's lesser-known brother Buster, who played steel guitar with him. Davis stiffened and snapped, "Where did you get that name?" If there was a story there, it did not look as if Davis was going to tell it. A politician through and through, he knew when to keep his mouth shut.

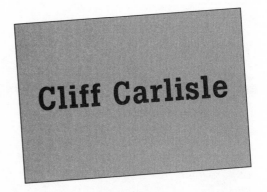

Cliff Carlisle

(1904–83)

A blues with a yodel. It may not sound like much now, but in the 1920s a lot of careers were carved out of that curious amalgam. Jimmie Rodgers started it, and after him came a seemingly endless procession. Many would live and die as disciples, obscure figures such as Howard Keesee and Jess Hillard, and be remembered only by historians. But some used the legacy of the Singing Brakeman as a ticket to ride in other directions. Gene Autry, for one. Jimmie Davis, for another. Or Cliff Carlisle.

Raised in the countryside outside Louisville, Kentucky, Carlisle was attracted in equal measure to blues and Hawaiian music. As he would say later, "My music is a cross between hillbilly and blues—even Hawaiian music has a sort of blues to it." Teamed with the singer and guitarist Wilbur Ball, he went on the vaudeville tent show circuit where many would-be country entertainers learned their trade in the '20s. "I think Wilbur and I were the first yodeling or blue yodeling duet," he wrote years later to the Australian researcher John Edwards. "At least that is what people say." Actually the Tennessee duo of Fleming & Townsend preceded them by about a year in putting harmonized yodeling on disc, but Carlisle and Ball were probably the first recording artists to duet on a *blue* yodel.

Carlisle opened his recording log in 1930, with a session for Gennett. It consisted largely of Rodgers covers like "Desert Blues" and "Memphis Yodel," but Carlisle had a distinctive touch on the Dobro resonator steel guitar, and when he yodeled he sometimes exchanged Rodgers's manner for a sort of high-pitched scat-singing closer to the style of the comic singer Cliff Edwards, alias "Ukulele Ike." At this point Carlisle was also making a name on the Louisville stations WHAS and WLAP, where he and Ball went under the billing of the

Cliff Carlisle (right) and Wilbur Ball, c. 1931. (OTM collection)

Lullaby Larkers, and his career took off. Rodgers must have heard about him, because when he recorded in Louisville in June 1931 he had Carlisle back him on "When the Cactus Is in Bloom" and "Looking for a New Mama." They also did some shows together.

A few months after that session Cliff was in New York, extending his own recording portfolio, and recalled Jimmie singing a number about a rooster: "What makes a Shanghai crow at the break of day? To let the Dominicker hen know the head man's on his way. . . ." As he

Cliff Carlisle in later life. (OTM collection)

told the story years later, "Ralph Peer wouldn't let him record that. It was kind of a risqué tune at that time. Just a little off-color, see. But I remembered that in my head. I got the first verse out of it and then I wrote the rest of the song. I knew it would be all right because Jimmie was a good friend. And I knew Ralph wouldn't let him cut it."

By 1932 Carlisle was working solo, but in the years that followed he was often partnered by his younger brother Bill, who was also a whiz with a blues and a yodel. On one of their records they even staged a fight over who would do what. "Hold it, buddy," says Cliff indignantly as Bill starts to yodel. "This is *my* 'Mouse's Ear Blues,' and *I'll* do the yodeling." It isn't the only unusual feature. "Mouse's Ear Blues" is, probably uniquely in the corpus of recorded hillbilly music, a song about defloration. "My little mama, she's got a mouse's ear, but she gonna lose it when I shift my gear."

By the mid-'30s, when he was working on WBT in Charlotte, North Carolina, and recording for Bluebird and Decca, Cliff was making a fair bid to corner the hillbilly disc market in sniggery songs about roosters and ashcans (as you might guess, there was an occasional *double entendre* loitering in this vicinity) and humorously violent tales of marital discord like "Hen Pecked Man," "Pay Day Fight," or "A

Wild Cat Woman and a Tom Cat Man," where Cliff's boisterous flights of fancy are powered by the twin engines of his Dobro and Bill's inventive flat-picked guitar. But he interspersed these rounders' boasts with pretty love songs, now and then a ballad like "Black Jack David," and a carriage-load of evocative train and hobo songs such as "Pan-American Man." He also worked with singer-guitarists Fred Kirby and Claude Boone and made some fairly excruciating records with his preteen son Tommy. By the end of the decade he had been on four record labels and made almost 200 sides.

His last '30s session, made with Bill and mandolinist Shannon Grayson, is a detailed cross-section of country music just prior to World War II. There are covers of recent hits like "Wabash Cannon Ball" and "Sparkling Blue Eyes," blues, original heart songs, gospel, and more: "Footprints in the Snow" layered between "The Unclouded Day" and "Sally Let Your Bangs Hang Down." With that sort of skill in occupying all the bases of the country market, it was hardly surprising that Cliff and Bill weathered the war years and subsequent changes in country music quite successfully. Their family group, The Carlisles, with various sons and daughters, was popular on the Grand Ole Opry and had hits in the '50s with "Too Old to Cut the Mustard" and "No Help Wanted." Bill was the more outgoing performer, though, and the group was his more than his brother's.

In the mid-'50s Cliff retired to a quiet life of painting, fishing, and church work, interrupting it only to make a couple of not very memorable albums for small labels. "Sometimes I feel like I'd like to go back in the business," he told an interviewer in 1970, "but at my age and with the health problem I have, I don't think it's worth it." He changed his mind, though. Soon afterward he was reunited with Wilbur Ball, and over the next few years they occasionally played for college audiences or at folk festivals.

(OTM collection)

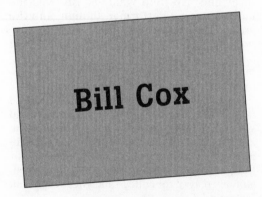

Bill Cox

(1897–1968)

"William Jennings 'Billy' Cox," wrote Ken Davidson in 1967, "is one of those unfortunate songwriters who should be financially comfortable, but because of his lack of honest advice is now almost destitute." Davidson, a longtime fan of old-time music, was then living in Charleston, West Virginia, and had been recording the area's musicians, such as Clark Kessinger, for his Kanawha label. He knew that Cox, a contemporary of Kessinger and a

significant figure in old-time music's recording history, had once been active in Charleston, but it wasn't until Kessinger mentioned it that he discovered Cox was still there—surviving on social security, although he had written one of the biggest country hits of the 1940s.

A Charlestonian by birth, Cox began playing guitar and harmonica and writing songs in his teens and eventually became quite well known in his home town. When WOBU came on the air in 1927 he auditioned with a Vernon Dalhart number, "I'm Doin' the Best I Can," and a harmonica piece and was taken on. He quickly became one of the Charleston station's star performers, but his light was sometimes fitful. According to Robert Fredericks, son of the station's owner Walter Fredericks, "Bill was a reprobate from the word go. To get him to perform, the first thing you would have to do would be to sober him up." Because he was unreliable about showing up for his radio slots, Walter Fredericks suggested that he make records, which could be played in his absence. Cox duly hitched up with Gennett, who recorded him enthusiastically. Two productive sessions in 1929, another two in 1930, and a fifth in 1931 generated forty-four sides, many of them issued under pseudonyms: Luke Baldwin, Charley Blake, Clyde Ashley. Cox told Davidson he'd heard people saying, "That Luke Baldwin's a better singer than Bill Cox."

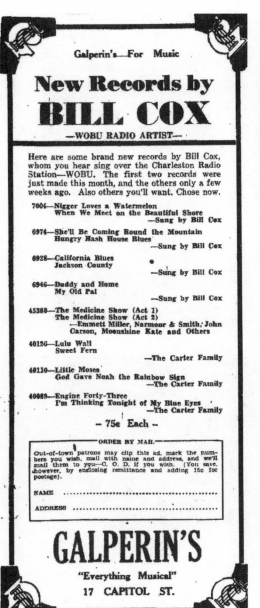

Music store ad, Charleston, West Virginia, November 1929. (Author's collection)

(OTM collection)

1940 it ran to 150 titles. He remade many of his earlier songs, fortified his position as a composer of satirical or salacious blues, and became a celebrant of the New Deal in numbers like "N. R. A. Blues" and, following the 1936 election, "Franklin Roosevelt's Back Again."

By then he had teamed up with the singer and guitarist Cliff Hobbs, who would partner him on all his subsequent records. In 1937 they introduced a song Cox had written, based on letters from an uncle who had joined the army, shipped out to the Philippines, and married an island girl. At the time "Filipino Baby" didn't make much impact, but a few years later Cox had the disconcerting experience of hearing it sung to him by a guest artist on WOBU's successor WCHS, Cowboy Copas. Asked where he had heard it, Copas replied that he'd learned it from a record. Cox put him wise about its authorship, but evidently Copas didn't advertise that fact as much as the composer would have wished, because some time later Cox told him tartly, "It wouldn't give you the lockjaw to mention my name when you sing that song."

The subsequent history of "Filipino Baby" would rob not only Cox's pride but his pocket. In 1944 Copas recorded the song for King. It was a huge hit and helped to put King on the map of the postwar disc business, but all the writer saw of the publishing royalties was $500. By then he had quit music and returned to one of the two day jobs he had held on to since his teens, working in the boiler room of Charleston's Ruffner Hotel. The other job was at the Kelly Axe Factory, but he must not have

Like his near-contemporary on Gennett, Cliff Carlisle, Cox was a deep-dyed Jimmie Rodgers fan and played the Rodgers card on several of his discs, such as "My Old Pal" and "Daddy and Home," but he soon persuaded Gennett to accept some of his own material, such as "Alimony Woman" and the predictive comedy numbers "In 1992" and "When the Women Get in Power." Also like Carlisle, in the early '30s he quit Gennett for ARC, where he briskly extended his recording log, until by

Bill Cox in front of his house, 1966. (OTM collection)

cared for it much, since he wrote a song about it and was fired. (This may be the story behind the unissued Gennett recording "The Old Axe Shop.") He did see some income from another of his compositions, "Sparkling Brown Eyes," which was recorded by Tex Ritter and others, and possibly from "Sally Let Your Bangs Hang Down" when it was riotously reenacted by the Maddox Brothers & Rose, but he never went back to performing in public.

In the '60s Cox's New Deal songs came to the attention of the New Lost City Ramblers, who recorded "Franklin Roosevelt's Back Again" and "The Democratic Donkey (Is in His Stall Again)," and Cox began to acquire a reputation as a political songwriter who could stand unabashed a step or two behind Woody Guthrie. By then he had put his old repertoire on a high shelf and was writing mainly religious songs, but Davidson persuaded him to look back over his career, and in 1967 Cox made his comeback with an album containing many of his most characteristic songs. Unfortunately it came too late to mend his fortune.

Playlist
• *The Dixie Songbird* (Tri-Agle-Far 705) [his 1967 Kanawha album]
•• *Mountain Blues* (JSP JSP 7740 4CD): "Georgia Brown Blues," "Got the Drunken Blues," "Kansas City Blues," "Long Chain Charlie Blues," "N. R. A. Blues," "Oozlin Daddy Blues" •• *Sounds Like Jimmie Rodgers* (JSP JSP 7751 4CD): "A High Silk Hat and a Gold Top Walking Cane," "Jackson County," "Lay My Head beneath the Rose," "My Rough and Rowdy Ways," "When We Meet on the Beautiful Shore," "Where the Red, Red Roses Grow" •• *My Rough and Rowdy Ways Vol. 2* (Yazoo 2040): "My Rough and Rowdy Ways"

Mac & Bob

Robert A. Gardner (1897–1978) • Lester McFarland (1902–84)

One of the toughest threads in the fabric of country music is the Victorian parlor ballad, the sentimental song that captivated our grandparents or great-grandparents. Stories of separated lovers and neglected sires, of homeless orphans and consumptive children, fill the songbooks of early country artists, none more prolifically than those of the two men who called themselves Mac & Bob.

Lester McFarland and Robert Gardner met in 1915 as teenaged students at the Kentucky School for the Blind in Louisville. Mac, from Gray, Kentucky, was already proficient on several instruments, and taught Bob to play guitar. In 1922 they took up music full-time, Mac playing mandolin and singing the tenor harmony to Bob's lead. Based in Knoxville, near Bob's birthplace in Oliver Springs, Tennessee, they began performing at schoolhouses, county fairs, and other such events. By 1925 they had graduated to the Keith vaudeville circuit and were broadcasting regularly on station WNOX. A local agent for Brunswick Records tipped the company off about the popularity of the new act, and in October 1926 the duo was called to New York to make records.

"When the Roses Bloom Again," their second release, was hugely successful, selling in six figures. Brunswick recalled them in December, again the following May, and at regular intervals for the next five years, amassing a catalog of nearly 200 recordings. Many of them were issued over and over again: "Three Leaves of Shamrock," their version of the song Charlie Poole called "Leaving Dear Old Ireland," appeared on thirteen labels.

To scan Mac & Bob's discography is to step back into a world where life and love are fragile blooms, and tears are quick to fall. "Are You Tired of Me, Darling?," "The Blind Child's Prayer," "I'll Be All Smiles Tonight," "The Letter

OLD
Southern Tunes

Lester
McFarland
and Robert A. Gardner

Vocalion Records
ELECTRICALLY RECORDED
PLAY ON ALL PHONOGRAPHS

(OTM collection)

That Came Too Late" . . . it is hard to read the titles without a sniff. Interweaving these songs of inconstancy and ill-fortune are reassuring old-time sacred numbers like "The Old Rugged Cross" and "Rock of Ages." The gravity is occasionally lightened by a comic song, and now and then by a somewhat stiff-collared blues.

Whatever the material, the duo's plaintive harmony, anticipating duets like the Blue Sky Boys but with more schooled diction and less southern accent, floats upon a rippling stream of mandolin, with occasional splashes of harmonica or fiddle, these too played by Mac, who never allowed his blindness to interfere with making music. When recording the gospel song "Hold Fast to the Right," he later recalled, he read the words and music of the verse in Braille, then played and sang the chorus from memory.

Familiar songs from yesteryear, presented simply and without an obtrusively "hillbilly" character, turned out to appeal not only to American record buyers but overseas ones as well, in Australia, South Africa, Ireland, and especially in the UK, where a Mac & Bob fan could build a collection of more than two dozen records, including several songs never issued in the United States. Only a chance hearing, though, would have alerted this hypothetical admirer to one of the act's British issues, since "Many Happy Returns of the Day" on the Mayfair label was credited, bizarrely, to the Florida Waltz Orchestra.

In 1931 Mac & Bob moved to Chicago, and for some years had a radio slot on the WLS National Barn Dance, where they were listened to attentively by the young Bill Monroe. Evidently the partners then took a break from each other's company, for in 1935 Bob was working in San Diego with Ernie Newton (in later years a well-known session bass player in Nashville) and Mac in Pittsburgh with the Virginian singer Blaine Smith. But the duo reunited to sing over KMA in Shenandoah, Iowa, an important country music station in those days, before returning to WLS in 1939. There they remained until 1950, when Bob retired from music to devote his life to religious work. After a few years as a solo, Mac too left the station, to join the staff of the Chicago State Hospital.

Mac & Bob were reunited in 1964 for the fortieth anniversary of the National Barn Dance. Some years later a Chicago admirer, Dave Wylie, reissued some of their old records on his Birch label, adding a few new recordings sung by the almost septuagenarian Mac. But apart from a couple of tracks on compilations, Mac and Bob died without seeing any others of their once so popular recordings reinstated on LP, and it would take a further two decades before they received the tribute of a CD. As they sang on one of their records, "When I'm gone, you'll soon forget."

Playlist

• *Songs for Country Home Folks Vol. 1* (BACM CD D 067)
• *Songs for Country Home Folks Vol. 2* (BACM CD D 116)
• *Mac & Bob* (Old Homestead OH-4158)

(OTM collection)

Bradley Kincaid

(1895–1991)

Today his name means little to the fans of stringband music or blue yodels, but there was a time when Bradley Kincaid was one of the superstars of country music. When his clear, quiet voice came over the airwaves from WSM's Grand Ole Opry or WLS's National Barn Dance, hundreds of thousands of listeners shushed the kids, bent closer to their radios, and slipped into a world of folklore and fable.

There was a space in country music in those days between the raucous cackling of an Uncle Dave Macon and the crooner's sexiness of a Jimmie Rodgers: room for ballads like "Barbara Allen" and the tragic love songs of "The Fatal Wedding" and "The Little Rosewood Casket." Kincaid, singing blithely to his little "houn' dog" guitar, filled that space, and in doing so won the hearts of a nation. In the years between the two world wars he was not only one of radio's biggest names, outranking in listeners' polls even celebrities like Al Jolson, but sold hundreds of thousands of songbooks and records.

Yet he was more than just an efficient supplier of mail-order nostalgia. When he sang to the audience of Chicago's WLS he was addressing not only the "old" Americans who had been around since settler days but the European newcomers who populated the

(OTM collection)

It all began in Chicago in 1926. Churchgoing, earnestly bespectacled, the young man from Garrard County in the Cumberland Mountains of Kentucky had enrolled in the YMCA College; he was newly married and determined to make something of himself. If he was headed anywhere as a singer, it was in the direction of classical music, and his only public performing was with a YMCA quartet. But a chance invitation to appear on the National Barn Dance and sing a ballad or two rewrote his plans.

"After I'd been singing there for three or four weeks," he told his biographer Loyal Jones, "here was this basket full of fan mail. A big laundry basket about the size of a desk." In his five years on WLS he received a third of a million letters. As well as his singing he presided over a radio club for teenagers, the Twelve and Twenty Club, and worked as a station announcer, giving the farmers in his audience information on markets, weather, and other agricultural topics. His first song folio, *My Favorite Mountain Ballads and Old-Time Songs*, ran through six large printings in sixteen months. The station sent him out for personal appearances and he was a hit there too. "After holding many audiences past the customary half-hour allotted to him to perform," remembered a WLS staffer, "he would meet his admirers back stage or outside the theaters, cheerfully shaking hands and signing autographs until the next show. Bradley was approachable and the people loved him. He was like a next door neighbor whose welcome never wore out."

In later years he was equally popular on stations elsewhere. A fan in Wisconsin wrote to him in 1934:

After you left WLS we have not been able to follow your programs, until recently I picked up your cheery voice from WLW [Cincinnati] . . . it is a real treat to sit back and enjoy those beautiful, sad, sweet numbers. . . . Radio means so much to us rural people as we cannot afford expensive concerts or shows, thus radio brings entertainment to fill our long winter nights.

By the summer of 1935 he had moved on to WBZ in Boston. In his time in New England he toured with the young Grandpa Jones, who remembered how Kincaid held audiences spellbound. But, as Jones also recalled, "Bradley's songs, you've got to really listen to them because they're slow and tell a story." On the ever noisier stage of country music in the

farmlands of the Midwest. For these new Americans, Kincaid seemed like an ancestral voice, a storyteller transmitting in his songs the oral literature of the past, fair maidens and wooing frogs and all. Because many of his stories were drawn, if one traced them back far enough, from the great stock of European folktales, they were familiar and reassuring to the Norwegian farming family cast adrift in the vast prairies of Minnesota or Wisconsin. Amid the brash modernism of jazz and the Charleston, Kincaid represented other times, other values. It was music like his that a listener from Racine, Wisconsin, commended in a letter to the WLS magazine *Stand By*:

The guitar, harmonica, yodeling and sweet, old-time ballads are more clean and wholesome than the modern day jazz. If more people kept their radio dials set at 870 kilocycles [the WLS frequency], the world would be much better for it, I can tell you.

'40s, now stacked with drumkits and steel guitars and populated by charismatic figures like Bob Wills and Hank Williams, one unassertive man with a little guitar and a bag of ballads was all too likely to be drowned out. In 1950 he retired to run a radio station and music store in Springfield, Ohio.

For years he steadfastly refused to make a performing comeback, but in 1974 he changed his mind and appeared at Renfro Valley's Traditional Music Festival, and was received so well that he made a habit of it. "His fingers were stiff," wrote Reuben Powell, a Springfield old-time music enthusiast, in a letter to me, "but his voice is just as good as it ever was, and he remembers every song he ever used in his act." He also responded to the demands of his fans for LPs of the old songs and in 1963, in a four-day stint for the small Texas label Bluebonnet, recorded 162 of them. What an old pro.

(Author's collection)

Playlist
• *Old Time Songs & Hymns* (Old Homestead OH-4014) ['60s recordings]
•• *Memories of Jimmie Rodgers* (Bear Family BCD 15938): "The Death of Jimmie Rodgers" (two versions), "Jimmie Rodgers' Life," "The Life of Jimmie Rodgers," "Mrs. Jimmie Rodgers' Lament"

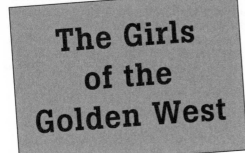

The Girls of the Golden West

Millie Good (1913–93) • Dolly Good (1915–67)

Early in 1933, WLS put a new act on the roster of the National Barn Dance: a yodeling, guitar-playing, harmony-singing cowgirl act called The Girls of the Golden West. Later

that year, in its annual *Family Album*, the station provided its listeners with a photograph of the duo, appropriately garbed in leather waistcoats, fringed skirts, and knotted neckerchiefs. "You may be glad to know," added the caption writer, "the name of the town near where they were born—Muleshoe, Texas."

Already the legend was being woven. Actually Mildred Goad and her sister Dorothy were born in southern Illinois and spent their teenage years in the city of East St. Louis. They found they could sing in harmony, Dolly learned to play guitar, and they began to make a name on local radio, first changing their surname to Good, because it was easier to understand, then becoming The Girls of the Golden West. Not long after they moved to Chicago and WLS they secured a deal with Victor's Bluebird label, and with the combined promotion of radio and records they became the first nationally successful sister act in country music.

The records solidified the myth of Muleshoe. The Girls' first recording was "Started Out from Texas," and their next session produced a "Round-Up Time in Texas" and a "Home, Sweet Home in Texas." They acquired the

Millie (left) and Dolly with fellow WLS artist Red Foley. (Author's collection)

accoutrements of the showbiz cowboy: hats, elaborately decorated boots, studded belts, guns. ("They were real guns," Millie recalled, "but they didn't have any bullets in them.") The WLS publicity people put it about that the Girls made their own outfits, which they did.

Country music in the '30s was a very different business from country music in the '20s. In the first place, it was much more *of* a business: radio celebrity and the resulting tours and personal appearances gave artists a potential audience in the millions. Then, thanks in part to Hollywood's long love affair with the West, there was a vogue for Western music. WLS's vast audience, concentrated in the midwestern states of Illinois, Wisconsin, Iowa, and Missouri, had few personal connections with the Old West; many of them, indeed, were only first-generation Americans. Yet as they plowed and sowed and reaped a new existence for themselves on the limitless prairies, they found it easy to respond to songs and stories about life on the frontier.

The Girls' choice of Western music, then, was well judged. Another good move was

something they had no choice about: being women. The '30s were the first era of female stars in country music, and there was no better place to launch a quest for stardom than WLS. When Millie and Dolly arrived the station already had the Three Little Maids (the Overstake Sisters), Linda Parker, and Lulu Belle (of Lulu Belle & Scotty), and later they would add Patsy Montana. Patsy became hugely popular and her records probably outsold the Girls', but they had the advantage of expert stringband accompaniments by the Prairie Ramblers. The Girls' discs were much simpler, just sweet, limpid harmony duets with a guitar to keep time. In that softness of approach they might be seen as female counterparts of the Delmore Brothers, though with one big difference: the Girls had virtually nothing to do with the blues.

After almost five years at WLS, when, Millie remembered, "we were never out of a job," the sisters moved to another prominent station, WLW in Cincinnati. Initially they were sponsored by Pinex Cough Syrup and had a show with Red Foley; later they were on the Boone County Jamboree, the ancestor of the Midwestern Hayride. They took a break for four years while Millie devoted herself to her family, but in 1946 they reunited and remained on WLW until 1949, by which time there was a new generation of country women such as Rose Maddox and Molly O'Day. Songs like Millie and Dolly's, redolent of shacks, hitching rails, and prairie sunsets, faded out of the country music picture and were replaced by more lurid scenes of car wrecks and urban nightlife. But The Girls of the Golden West are not without their musical legacy. More than half of their records were issued in Australia, where they were listened to with attention by the cowgirl singers Shirley Thoms and June Holms.

In the '50s and '60s Millie and Dolly devoted themselves to their families. (Dolly's husband was Tex Atchison, fiddler with the Prairie Ramblers, while Millie had married Bill McCluskey, who managed WLS road shows.) They broke from domestic cover just once, to make some albums for the Bluebonnet label in Texas. Thirty years on from their debut, they still made the West sound golden.

Playlist
•• *O Brothers! Family Harmony in Old-Time Music & Bluegrass* (Living Era CD AJA 5467): "Roll Along Prairie Moon" •• *The Ultimate Yodelling Collection* (Pulse PLS CD 630): "I Want to Be a Real Cowboy Girl" •• *Cattle Call: Early Cowboy Music and Its Roots* (Rounder CD 1101): "My Love Is a Rider (Bucking Bronco)" •• *American Yodeling 1911–1946* (Trikont US-0246): "Will There Be Any Yodelers in Heaven?" •• *Flowers in the Wildwood: Women in Early Country Music 1923–1939* (Trikont US-0310): "Round-Up Time in Texas" •• *Times Ain't Like They Used to Be Vol. 6* (Yazoo 2064): "Whoopee-Ti-Yi-Yo Git Along Little Doggies"

(Bear Family Records)

Wilf Carter

(Montana Slim)

(1904–96)

They built them to last, the Western singers. Gene Autry was ninety when he died, Roy Rogers eighty-six, Hank Snow eighty-five. Wilf Carter almost made it to ninety-two. There must be something beneficent to both spirit and body about singing of sunsets over the Rockies, campfires on the high sierras, cool water, and tumbling tumbleweeds.

None of those themes came to Carter as a birthright, since he was born in Nova Scotia, but as a young man he took to the cowboy's trade and rode the borderline between ranch work and entertainment in shows like the Calgary Stampede. In spare moments he would pick guitar and sing for his colleagues, a hobby that grew into a secondary career on radio.

In December 1933, waiting in Montreal for a voyage on a cruise liner, he auditioned for Victor. His first record coupled a yodel song, "My Swiss Moonlight Lullaby," with a true-crime narrative, "The Capture of Albert Johnson," and listeners at the time would have been entitled to wonder if Carter was edging his horse toward the hitching post that had been used for the last time, only a few months before, by Jimmie Rodgers. But the yodeling on "Lullaby" had a fresh Alpine tang quite unlike Rodgers's, and it reconnected the hillbilly yodel song with its primary source, the Swiss (or *soi-disant* Swiss) yodeling troupes who brought their own kind of mountain music to America's vaudeville theaters in the early years of the twentieth century.

At least, that's one way of interpreting the evidence. The conscientious historian will note that there are also yodel-like techniques in Hawaiian singing, and indeed yodel-mocking effects in Hawaiian guitar playing—and Hawaiian musicians similarly infiltrated American show business on the vaudeville circuit, in the same period as the warblers from the Alps. The interlacing of the yodel into American vernacular music has been a complex process, and we may never entirely figure out the pattern.

Carter, at least, declared his source, with lyrics about "Swiss mountain chalets" and the like, and although it might have been a throw-back, it proved successful enough to recall him to the studios many times over the next few years, cutting songs like "I Miss My Swiss" and "My Little Swiss Miss and Me," along with more conventional hillbilly subjects such as "The Roundup in the Fall," "Take Me Back to Old Montana," and "Cowboy Lullaby."

Soon Victor gave him the fake ID of Montana Slim to help his records catch on south of the Canadian border. Within a couple of years of his debut recording, he had a network radio show in New York and was a disc star not only in North America but in the UK (where his Regal-Zonophone 78s can still be found), and even more in Australia, where he molded the style of fellow guitar yodelers like Tex Morton and Slim Dusty. Frank Ifield, whose early career was in Australian country music before his '60s pop hit "I Remember You," made his debut on disc with a Carter song, "There's a Love Knot in My Lariat."

Except for a break in the '40s when he was injured in a car accident and retired to his Calgary ranch to raise beef cattle and a family, Carter was always a presence on the Canadian country scene. Though he didn't tour so much in his middle and later years, he could be relied on to show up on the summer rodeo circuit. Meanwhile he and Victor retained the affection of his rural fans with regular new albums, more than a score of them. Though they might be a little more lavishly produced than his early recordings with just a guitar, they seldom pulled Carter far from the narrative terrain he had made his own, a peaceful land of prairies and valleys, cowboys on the trail, and aged mothers at home in log cabins. It was a dream country, but he was faithful to its memory longer than anyone in country music, and was rewarded for his fidelity by being voted, when he was eighty, into the Canadian Music Hall of Fame.

Hank Snow

(1914–99)

Hank Snow sang country music so naturally that it was always a jolt to remember that it was, strictly speaking, foreign to him. The music was born in the American South and West, but Snow was a Canadian, born in Liverpool, Nova Scotia. "America—I just loved the sound of it," he said, thinking back. "I would go to any movie if it showed anything of America." Perhaps it seemed like an escape route to a boy whose stepfather treated him "like a dog. I still carry scars across my body from his beatings." And before long he did

(Bear Family Records)

where," two of his other hits, "I'm Movin' On" was his own composition. He had further success in the '50s and '60s with numbers like "Rhumba Boogie," "I Don't Hurt Anymore," and "Yellow Roses." By the end of his career it was estimated that he had sold 70 million records and had more than forty Top Ten country hits.

Although by the mid-'60s Snow's heyday as a hit-maker seemed to be more or less over, he continued to tour widely and to rack up steady international sales of his many albums. By 1987, when he was dropped from RCA's roster after a unique unbroken association of fifty years, he had recorded over a hundred of them. Some were conceptually designed to present sections of his vast repertoire, such as railroad, hobo, and cowboy songs, or his personal collection of Canadian country music. He also recorded tributes to predecessors like The Carter Family and, of course, Jimmie Rodgers. Together with Tubb, he was among the founders of the Jimmie Rodgers Memorial Day, held annually in the singer's hometown of Meridian, Mississippi.

By the '70s Snow had come to be recognized in the business as one of country music's founding father figures. It was a role he occupied with composure rather than exuberance: warm and communicative enough on stage, off it he was taciturn and a little chilly. Aspects of Snow can surely be detected in Henry Gibson's portrayal of country star Haven Hamilton in Robert Altman's film *Nashville*: the dignity that borders on self-importance, the improbable coiffure.

Once absorbed into the Grand Ole Opry cast, Snow never left it. For traditionally minded fans his few minutes on the show each week sometimes seemed like an oasis of unreconstructed country singing—and of picking, for he was a fine guitarist who could hold his own, as he demonstrated on several records, with a virtuoso like Chet Atkins. Even his dress sense belonged to an older school. Long after most country artists had deserted them, Snow strode out weekly in costumes florid with cactuses, aglint with sequins.

Ever mindful of his miserable childhood, Snow quietly did a great deal of work for the cause of abused children. He also made a point of playing for U.S. troops in Vietnam. He secured U.S. citizenship in 1958 and was elected to the Nashville Songwriters Hall of Fame in 1978 and the Country Music Hall of Fame in 1979. It took a while, but the man from the far North was at last fully accepted by the music he had always loved.

escape, running away to sea and working on fishing trawlers.

A two-week stint unloading salt from a freighter gave him the money he needed, six dollars, to buy his first guitar by mail order. While still in his teens he had his own radio show on CHNS in Halifax, and he was twenty-two when he made his first record, "Lonesome Blue Yodel," for the Montreal branch of RCA Victor. It was immediately apparent from his singing, yodeling, and guitar playing that he was deeply imbued with the spirit of Jimmie Rodgers, who had died three years earlier. Even his nicknames—first "The Yodeling Ranger," then "The Singing Ranger"—recalled phrases from Rodgers's songs.

Over the next dozen years or so, he made almost a hundred recordings for the Canadian market. They sold well, especially "The Blue Velvet Band," but were seldom issued in the United States. He made several fruitless attempts to build his reputation outside Canada, finally securing a toehold in the American country music business on the Big D Jamboree, the Saturday night barn dance program on KRLD in Dallas.

One of his backers was Ernest Tubb—like Snow, a Rodgers devotee—and it was at Tubb's prompting too that he was offered a spot on the Grand Ole Opry. Snow's place on the most venerable of country shows was assured by the success of "I'm Movin' On," which topped the country chart for almost half of 1950 and became his most famous number. Country DJs would later vote it their all-time favorite record.

Like the railroad anthem "Golden Rocket" and the tongue-twisting "I've Been Every-

Playlist
- *The Singing Ranger* (Bear Family BCD 15426 4CD)
- *The Singing Ranger Vol. 2* (Bear Family BCD 15476 4CD)
- *The Thesaurus Transcriptions* (Bear Family BCD 15488 5CD) [1950–56]
- *The Yodeling Ranger* (Bear Family BCD 15587 5CD) [1936–47]
- *The Singing Ranger* (Living Era CD AJA 5476)

•• *Sounds like Jimmie Rodgers* (JSP JSP 7751 4CD): "The Hobo's Last Ride," "Polka Dot Blues," "Wandering On" •• *The Ultimate Yodelling Collection* (Pulse PLS CD 630): "Lonesome Blue Yodel," "Yodeling Back to You" •• *Mystery Train: Classic Railroad Songs, Volume 2* (Rounder CD 1129): "Waiting for a Train"

The most economical battery operated radio ever built! Long-life Philco Battery Block gives you almost double the power at one-third the cost... eliminates cumbersome, expensive wet batteries and undependable wind chargers. New low-drain tubes cut current drain two-thirds... combine with new High-Output Speaker to give you unequalled tone and performance at the price.

Philco offers these 1940 Anniversary Farm Radios in a big selection of beautiful cabinet styles...all at *new low prices.* See them at your nearest dealer's—or mail coupon.

Liberal Trade-In Allowance for your Old Radio or Phonograph. Free Trial. Long Time to Pay. Mail Coupon for Full Details.

From *Southern Agriculturist,* November 1939. (Author's collection)

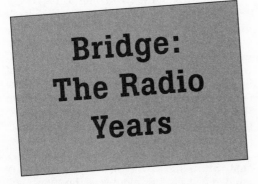

Bridge: The Radio Years

The mid-1930s to the mid-'50s, the two decades approximately bounded by the repeal of Prohibition and the arrival of rock 'n' roll, were the Golden Age of hillbilly radio. Country musicians had been toting their fiddles and guitars into radio stations almost since the invention of the medium, and many of those already discussed were wafted over the airwaves during the '20s. But as the nation emerged from the darkness of the Depression, the "On Air" light of the radio studio signaled a new path for the hillbilly artist. Every daybreak, lunchtime, and early evening, the rural radio network would deliver to its audience of farmers and small-towners a sustaining menu of crop reports, cookery advice, comedy—and country music.

Powerful 50,000-watt stations such as WLS in Chicago, WBT in Charlotte, North Carolina, WSB in Atlanta, KWKH in Shreveport, Louisiana, and WLW in Cincinnati joined Nashville's WSM in disseminating country music coast to coast and northward into Canada. Others, almost as far-reaching, included KMA in Shenandoah, Iowa, and WHO in Des Moines, KVOO in Tulsa, Oklahoma, KMOX in St. Louis, WBAP in Fort Worth, WFAA and KRLD in Dallas, WMC and WREC in Memphis, WNOX in Knoxville, WCKY in Covington, Kentucky, WHAS in Louisville, WWVA in Wheeling, West Virginia, and WWNC in Asheville, North Carolina. These were augmented by the even stronger signals of stations in south Texas that dodged U.S. government regulations by siting their transmitters across the border in Mexico, whence they deluged the whole of North America and far beyond with country music programs sponsored by the manufacturers of hair dyes, laxatives, and cures for impotence.

Artists associated with these stations became household names, and the relationships their listeners began to form with them by tuning in to their programs were enriched by stories, interviews, and biographical tidbits in radio-oriented magazines such as WLS's

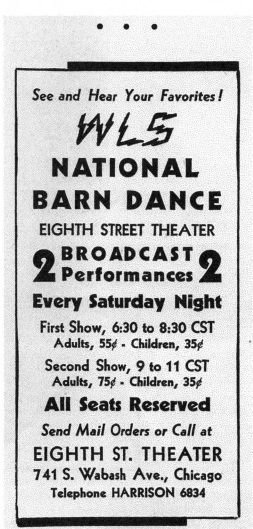

See and Hear Your Favorites!

WLS
NATIONAL
BARN DANCE

EIGHTH STREET THEATER

2 BROADCAST 2
Performances

Every Saturday Night

First Show, 6:30 to 8:30 CST
Adults, 55¢ - Children, 35¢

Second Show, 9 to 11 CST
Adults, 75¢ - Children, 35¢

All Seats Reserved

Send Mail Orders or Call at

EIGHTH ST. THEATER
741 S. Wabash Ave., Chicago
Telephone HARRISON 6834

(Author's collection)

(Author's collection)

Hillbilly and the Kids." This emblematic radio artist, Steele reports, has become

the core of an industry which rings the cash registers of radio and entertainment to the tune of $25,000,000 a year. . . . [Last year] radio presented him in something close to 5,000 different programs. . . . He has been comin' 'round the mountain in droves for eleven years now until the question of where to find his successors is getting to be a problem. In spite of the depletion of his replacement ranks, the number of hillbillies employed in radio in 1934 [sic] is so large that if all of them were laid end to end—they would be in the position they were most accustomed to before the lure of easy radio money brought them out of their cow pastures.

Clearly delighted with this incisive pen-picture of the indigenous Southerner, Steele elaborates on it: "The lazy lout of the mountains has been transformed into a potent factor in big business. . . . The hillbilly at home is lucky if he has a pair of personal overalls . . . he generally is the despair of his mammy and the goal of many a pappy's swiftly impelled boot-toe. . . ." The piece concludes, as such com-

Stand By, Rural Radio, and *The Mountain Broadcast and Prairie Recorder.* Mail from listeners was an index of an artist's appeal, and popular acts routinely received it by the sackfull. Many stations responded by sending out picture postcards of their talent. Some offered an illustrated annual every year. It was a radio culture whose power and pervasiveness we today can barely imagine.

It was also a spectacle that made other inhabitants of the radio world blink. In January 1936 the weekly magazine *Radio Guide* published a piece by WLS newscaster Harry Steele entitled "The Inside Story of the Hillbilly Business," with the lead-in: "Your Contributions to It Every Year Help to Pile up a Fabulous Fortune for Mr. and Mrs. Ezra K.

mentaries from outside the culture regularly did, with a fine fanfare of condescension:

. . . there will be no let-up in the spread of the enterprise so long as generation succeeds generation to keep alive the informal music which pulls out all the stops on that most important of all the great organs—the human heart.

Gee, thanks, Mr. Steele. By a pleasant irony, a year or two later, Steele, now in the employ of a radio advertising company, was despatched to Texas to work on station XERA—as the on-air announcer for The Carter Family.

(OTM collection)

Lulu Belle & Scotty

Scotty Wiseman (1909–81) • Lulu Belle Wiseman (1913–99)

A surefire way to amuse politically sophisti-cated friends is to play them country songs inspired by the anti-Communist fervor of the 1950s, like Red River Dave's "The Red Deck of Cards" or, better yet, Lulu Belle & Scotty's "I'm No Communist," where the duo harmonize on the perky chorus: "I like this pri-vate ownership, I want to be left alone, let the Government run its business, and let me run my own." Catch that snappy banjo, too!

To be fair to Lulu Belle & Scotty, this is by no means characteristic of their work, which leans more toward the Victorian sentimental-ity of Scotty's heart songs like "Have I Told You Lately That I Love You," or "Remember Me" ("when candle-lights are gleaming . . . remem-ber me at the close of a long, long day"), later popularized by the Bailes Brothers and, for another generation, by Willie Nelson on the album *Red-Headed Stranger*. They also had an affection for rube comedy material like the moonshiner's anthem "Mountain Dew," Scotty's rearrangement of an older song by Bascom Lamar Lunsford.

The story of this amiable duet begins in Chicago in the early '30s. Both Myrtle Eleanor Cooper and Scott Wiseman were North Car-olinian twentysomethings enjoying a profitable exile on WLS's National Barn Dance. Founded in 1924, a decade later this weekly show was not only the most popular music program on WLS but the Midwest's leading showcase for country talent, furnishing county fairs and other events with a roster of acts like Red Foley, the Prairie Ramblers, and The Girls of the Golden West.

Country music entrepreneur John Lair gave Myrtle her stage name and first paired her with Foley, but she soon teamed up, musically and romantically, with banjo songster Scott. Ini-tially their marriage was kept secret from the WLS audience. The station, Lulu Belle recalled, was "afraid it would take away from our appeal. So we didn't announce it until later, until our first baby was on the way. Then, when I was about five or six months along, we started singing a little song called 'Somebody's Coming to Our House,' and the next day the presents started arriving." Scotty proudly announced the birth of their daughter Linda

(OTM collection)

or stripe design with a large sash around the waist, old-fashioned pantalettes hanging over the tops of high-topped shoes. . . . [Scotty] dresses very modestly in blue corduroy trousers with suspenders and a gray-checked shirt with open neck.

The duo's affectionate on-stage rapport and likable old-fashioned music endeared them to a generation of WLS listeners. Some of them were so impressed by Scotty's songs about his home state that they made trips there. "Just returned from our vacation to Scotty's Land of the Sky," wrote the Hubers of Evansville, Indiana, to *Stand By*. "We can easily understand now why he sings so many beautiful songs about Carolina and Old Smoky Mountains." Another Hoosier opined that "a Barn Dance without Lulu Belle would be like spring and summer without flowers and trees," while a listener from Cudahy, Wisconsin, enthused: "We like Lulu Belle and Scotty and Patsy [Montana] so well that we have purchased records of them and can hear them whenever we want to. However, nothing can take the place of the National Barn Dance."

Lou over the air and the couple were rewarded with "closets of baby clothes." In February 1936 listener Leone Neises of Raub, North Dakota, wrote to *Stand By*:

Last Saturday the louder Scotty sang, the louder the wind whistled around our cabin, as if it, as well as we, were shouting congratulations to Scotty and Lulu Belle. . . . *No*, a thousand times *no*, don't put your swell old time programs on the shelf to make room for jazz!

In the magazine's May 9 issue, columnist Jack Holden reported:

Lulu Belle has appeared on 1546 barn dance programs. During each broadcast she chews 12 sticks of gum. Each stick measures three inches in length; 1,872 sticks of gum or a total of 459 feet three inches [*sic*: Holden's math is a little off] of "wax." If this were stretched out as only Lulu Belle can do it, the wad of gum would reach from here to the Wrigley building.

Less eccentric detail was provided a few months later for a reader who wanted to know how Lulu Belle & Scotty dressed for their appearances on the National Barn Dance.

Lulu Belle . . . looks just about as you would imagine—hair in braids with a big red hair ribbon, a red-figured gingham dress of plaid

Lulu Belle & Scotty's WLS fame not only secured them a recording contract (ultimately several) but, in due course, opportunities to appear in movies—rustic musicals with titles like *Hi, Neighbor*—and on TV. They cut some sides for Vogue, who brightened the mid-'40s with their line of lusciously colored picture discs. Even after they retired in 1958 and returned home to North Carolina, they were regularly persuaded back into recording studios, where they cut albums for Starday and Old Homestead. Scotty diversified into selling real estate and farming, while Lulu Belle stood as a Democratic candidate for the North Carolina state legislature and, although canvassing an electorate of traditionally Republican sympathies, won a seat for two terms of office. Their last performance together was at the Nashville Fan Fair in 1979.

Playlist
• *Have I Told You Lately & Snickers* (Old Homestead OH-4010)
•• *The North Carolina Banjo Collection* (Rounder CD 0439/40): "Sugar Babe" •• *Flowers in the Wildwood: Women in Early Country Music 1923-1939* (Trikont US-0310): "Wish I Was a Single Girl Again"

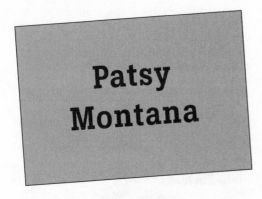

Patsy Montana

(1914–96)

One of the most frequently cited statistics in country music history is that Patsy Montana was the first female singer to make a record that sold a million. The record was "I Wanna Be a Cowboy's Sweetheart," and seventy years later it is as much a part of the musical mythology of the Old West as Gene Autry's "Back in the Saddle Again" or The Sons of the Pioneers' "Tumbling Tumbleweeds." In fact there is no hard evidence that it did reach the magic total, and the scrupulous historian should probably conclude that it did not. Let's just say that "Sweetheart" was a very big hit and leave it at that.

She was born Ruby Blevins in Hot Springs, Arkansas, and went to school in Hope. Always fond of singing, and with some skill on the violin, she edged into country music in her teens, winning a talent contest while visiting relatives in California. That led to an engagement with the singer Stuart Hamblen, whose daily radio show had a spot for Ruth & Lorraine, The Montana Cowgirls. Ruby joined them to make a trio, and soon afterward Hamblen gave her the stage name she would use for the rest of her career. During another family visit, to Arkansas, she sang on KWKH in Shreveport, Louisiana, where she met the local star Jimmie Davis, and in November 1932 she recorded with him, singing harmony, yodeling, and playing fiddle. Victor seized the opportunity to get her singing on her own, yielding her first record, "When the Flowers of Montana Were Blooming" and "I Love My Daddy Too."

The following year she took a trip to Chicago for the World's Fair and dropped into the offices of WLS. "When I was home on vacation," she told me, "I had heard the Girls of the Golden West over WLS and wrote them my first fan letter. I admired their Western singing and harmony. Their manager answered my letter and asked me to come by WLS and see

him. I did drop by WLS, but it was to see my mother's favorite announcer, Hal O'Halloran." Program manager George C. Biggar suggested that she audition for the Prairie Ramblers, four musicians from Kentucky who were building a name on the station but needed a girl singer. As Patsy would say in later years, "I never went home." For the next decade she was one of the brightest stars of WLS's roster, alongside Lulu Belle & Scotty, Red Foley, and Arkie, "The Arkansas Woodchopper."

At first her records were issued as by the "Prairie Ramblers with Patsy Montana," but after her huge hit in 1935 she took primary billing on her dozens of discs, many with "Cowgirl" or "Montana" in the title and almost all with her adept yodeling—though this was not to every listener's taste. "Patsy," begged Mrs. Irene Warren of Cairo, Missouri, in a December 1935 letter to *Stand By*, "don't ruin your sweet voice yodeling." She also headlined thousands of broadcasts and personal appearances.

One of WLS's most popular shows, of which Patsy and the Ramblers were cast members, was Smile-a-While, aired at 5:30 every weekday morning. Like much of the station's programming, it combined entertainment with information, offering a Farm Bulletin Board and a weather report covering fifteen states. A *Stand By* article of March 1937 reported:

A French Canadian trapper writes from the deep snow of Northern Ontario, telling of the cheer the program brings to his lonely cabin. . . . The letters pour in, hundreds, thousands of them from folks in every walk of life—farmers, trappers, truck drivers, housewives, shut-ins, policemen, ranchers, bakers, night watchmen—from Alaska to Mississippi and Texas, and from Maine to the [Panama] Canal Zone.

This is an aspect of country music's history that is too seldom acknowledged, since it left few aural documents to posterity. Even more widely and vividly than records, rural radio put the voices of Patsy Montana and her colleagues in the homes and hearts of millions.

In 1940 Patsy left the Prairie Ramblers to work as a solo on the West Coast. After World War II she endeavored to maintain a career without compromising her belief in old-time music, but increasingly found herself acting out the musical policies of more progressive producers. By the '50s she had given up recording and more or less retired to family life—she had been married since 1934 to Paul Rose, whom she met in Chicago when he was

Patsy Montana with the Prairie Ramblers: left to right, Jack Taylor, Tex Atchison, Ken Houchins, Chick Hurt. (OTM collection)

working as an assistant to Mac & Bob—but she later returned to the business in a duo with her daughter Judy Rose.

In the '70s she was recognized as one of country music's foremothers, made her debut on the Grand Ole Opry and the Renfro Valley Barn Dance, and was received with great affection when she made the first of several visits to the UK in 1971. Four years later, in a letter to me, she reported that she had played her first folk festival (and loved it) and was booked to talk at a UCLA forum on women in

(OTM collection)

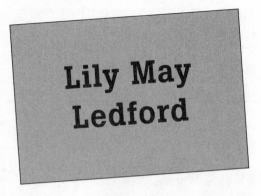

Lily May Ledford

(1917–85)

In the summer of 1936, they were building a new road alongside the Red River in Powell County, Kentucky. Among the crew, wielding pick and shovel, was a tall nineteen-year-old girl. A week later, her boots and overalls swapped for hightop shoes and a calico dress, Lily May Ledford was in Chicago, singing and picking banjo for a WLS radio microphone on the stage of the National Barn Dance. "Three cheers for Lily May, the fiddlin'est gal from the mountains of old Kentucky," wrote Leota Hinkle of Bloomington, Indiana, to *Stand By*. "Her banjo playing and singing takes you back to her mountain home. I think she has a nice personality and above all is natural. Naturalness is what we want in radio entertainment."

It was a country girl's dream: from rags to radio, farmwork to stagework. In later years Lily May would remember just how long a journey it was. "A huge poor family we were, and the only way to survive in those wild, beautiful hills of Eastern Kentucky was through the combined efforts of each and every child and adult—ginseng digging, corn plowing and hoeing, berry picking, woodcutting, hauling, trapping, fishing, hunting, pickling, hog slaughtering, soap making, quilting. . . ."

The confessed "laziest one in the family," the ten-year-old Lily May would hide behind a rock, trying to play tunes on her father's banjo or an old fiddle. On a neighbor's radio she listened to The Carter Family, Jimmie Rodgers, and the Skillet-Lickers. By her late teens she had won several fiddle contests, and had a band with her sister Rosie and brother Cayen, the Red River Ramblers.

In 1935 she auditioned for the National Barn Dance and joined the cast as a solo, but her Svengali, the WLS music librarian and talent manager John Lair, had other ideas. A fellow

country music. "I've often wanted to get into the college circuit," she wrote, "but didn't think I was 'folksy' enough but the students seem to go for my yodeling. So at last . . . I have my gimmick."

Over the next dozen years or so she was a regular at Western musical gatherings. She made albums for Birch, Old Homestead, and Flying Fish, her '30s and '40s recordings began to be reissued, and she had an appreciative letter from Ronald and Nancy Reagan. In 1987 she was inducted into the National Cowgirl Hall of Fame, an award she had more than earned with her happy, uncomplicated, evocative songs of sunsets, saddles, and life "out west of the Great Divide."

Playlist
• *The Original Cowboy's Sweetheart* (Living Era CD AJA 5516)
•• *Western Cowboy Ballads & Songs 1925–1939* (Frémeaux FA 034 2CD): "I'm an Old Cowhand" •• *Cattle Call: Early Cowboy Music and Its Roots* (Rounder CD 1101): "I Wanna Be a Cowboy's Sweetheart" •• *Flowers in the Wildwood: Women in Early Country Music 1923–1939* (Trikont US-0310): "My Poncho Pony"

Lily May Ledford, with banjo, and a 1940s line-up of the Coon Creek Girls: Opal Ambergy (bass), Irene Ambergy (guitar), and Bertha Ambergy (fiddle). (Author's collection)

Kentuckian, in 1937 he returned south to found the Renfro Valley Barn Dance, broadcast on WLW in Cincinnati or on WCKY, in nearby Covington, Kentucky. Among its charter members were the Coon Creek Girls: Lily May, Rosie on guitar, Violet Koehler on mandolin, and Daisy Lange on bass. Lily May switched back and forth from banjo to fiddle, though her most popular numbers were banjo songs such as "Pretty Polly" and "Banjo Pickin' Girl." Networked by CBS, the Renfro Valley Barn Dance made its cast members into national stars, but in 1939 the Coon Creek Girls had the extra thrill of being invited to the White House to play for President Roosevelt and his English guests, King George VI and Queen Elizabeth.

Throughout their career the group affected an old-fashioned Victorian look. "Oh, yes, Mr. Lair preached to me all the time about staying that way," Lily May recalled. " 'Stay the mountain girl that you are,' he would say. 'Don't start getting permanent waves. Don't overdo the makeup. And don't lose your mountain brogue. It will get you a million dollars.' "

" 'Course," she would add with a laugh, "it didn't get me a million dollars."

But it did help to earn her a long career in country music. With a shift of personnel (Violet and Daisy left and were replaced by Lily May and Rosie's younger sister Susie), the Coon Creek Girls played on the Renfro Valley Barn Dance and Old Dominion Barn Dance for twenty years. They were reunited in 1968 for the Newport Folk Festival and a County album, and in the '70s and '80s, encouraged by Mike Seeger, Lily May performed as a solo. The group's name lives on in a bluegrass band called the New Coon Creek Girls, while Lily May's son J. P. Pennington led the pop-country band Exile, which had a string of hits in the '80s.

But her chief legacy is that as a banjo-picking, band-leading woman, she inspired many other women to think the unthinkable and contemplate a frontline career in country music.

The "Lily May" cartoon strip ran in *Stand By* in October–November 1936. (Author's collection)

(Author's collection)

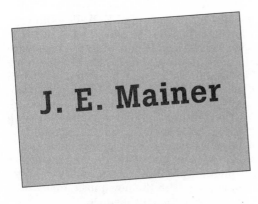

J. E. Mainer

(1898–1971)

Music hath charms, the playwright tells us, to soothe a savage breast, but what can it do for the irritable bowel or the spastic colon? This was not an idle question in the Depression. Southerners whose health had been impaired by inadequate diet constituted a ready-made market for remedy peddlers. The best way to reach that audience was advertising on radio, and one of the most effective forms of advertising was sponsoring programs of hillbilly music.

In 1933 James and Hubert Fincher, a father and son from California, opened an office in Charlotte, North Carolina, to promote in the Southeast their product Crazy Water Crystals: a mineral compound, sourced from springs in Mineral Wells, Texas, which—how to put this?—laid the gentle hand of regularity upon the fevered brow of an errant metabolism. "Hillbilly music was used from the beginning," recalled Hubert Fincher, "because of its great popularity, wide acceptance, and the availability of talent." Within months their programs were being aired on more than a dozen stations in Georgia and the Carolinas. In 1934 they bought time on WBT in Charlotte for a Crazy Water Crystals Barn Dance, featuring Dick Hartman's Tennessee Ramblers, the Monroe Brothers, and the Jenkins String Band, with Snuffy Jenkins on banjo. Over the next few years many more acts would join the Barn Dance, among them the Dixon Brothers and J. E. Mainer's Crazy Mountaineers.

Joseph Emmett Mainer and his brother Wade, nine years younger, had grown up in the hill country near Asheville, North Carolina, where J. E. absorbed fiddle music from his father and other local players. The brothers began playing together in 1923, now living in Concord, outside Charlotte. Mainer's Mountaineers came into being about 1932, swelled to a quartet by a pair of singing guitarists, "Daddy" John Love and Zeke Morris. Soon after they were taken on by Crazy Water Crystals, they drew the attention of Bluebird Records, and their first session in 1935 immediately produced a massive hit,

(OTM collection)

"Maple on the Hill." (Bluebird's sales figures have not been retrieved, but a reissue several years later on Montgomery Ward sold over 29,000 copies, making it the store label's second biggest hillbilly seller, after The Carter Family's coupling of "Picture on the Wall" and "Will You Miss Me When I'm Gone?") Like many of the group's numbers, "Maple on the Hill" was delivered as a plaintive vocal duet by Wade and Zeke, but Mainer's Mountaineers were exceptional in that they could turn themselves into about five different bands, also rendering wild fiddle-led breakdowns, blue yodels in the style of Jimmie Rodgers sung by John Love, rustic comedy, or gospel quartet numbers such as "Lights in the Valley."

They met Bluebird's demand for recordable material by ransacking the hillbilly catalogs of the pre-Depression years. In June 1936, facing their third session in ten months, they went back to 1927 and the Georgia Yellow Hammers for "The Old and Faded Picture" and "Johnson's Old Grey Mule," and to Blind Alfred Reed for "Why Do You Bob Your Hair, Girls?" A year later they took several leaves from The Carter Family's songbook before borrowing Oscar Ford's version of "Kiss Me Cindy," and in 1938 they tipped their hats gratefully to Charlie Poole ("If I Lose, Let Me Lose") and Clarence Greene ("Back to Johnson City").

During the course of these sessions the band increasingly favored vocal duets, at first by Wade and Zeke, later by their successors Leonard Stokes and George Morris, who so thoroughly dominated the sound of the band that at the 1938 session credited to Mainer's Mountaineers they were the only participants. Playing mandolin and guitar and singing numbers like "I Once Loved a Young Man," they sound very much like their contemporaries the Blue Sky Boys, and in doing so they give us a pointer to what is historically important about Mainer's Mountaineers. The band united two strains of hillbilly music: the Appalachian stringband formation of fiddle, banjo, and guitar, with its careful balance of instrumental parts, and the "brother duet" tradition of close harmony singing. Those were two crucial elements of what would be bluegrass, and it would only need Bill Monroe and Earl Scruggs to develop the roles of mandolin and banjo.

Until World War II Mainer's Mountaineers were enormously popular, not only in the Southeast, where they pulled listeners' letters by the thousand with their broadcasts on WBT and, later, WPTF in Raleigh, North Carolina, but elsewhere in the nation, thanks to the enormous reach of their broadcasts from the border station XERF. Wade Mainer—whom Bluebird had also been recording with Zeke Morris separately, so that there were Mainer–Morris duets under the Mainer's Mountaineers rubric *and* in their own names—broke away and formed his own band, bringing in Homer Sherrill or Steve Ledford on fiddle, and had a hit in 1939 with "Sparkling Blue Eyes." J. E. riposted by making Mountaineers of Snuffy Jenkins and singer-guitarist Clyde Moody, later a member of Bill Monroe's Blue Grass Boys: two more connections with the new music that would take shape in the mid-'40s.

For years J. E. led his band round the small-town schoolhouse circuit, putting on musical shows and—impervious to the shifting currents of racial etiquette—supplementing them with blackface playlets like "Sambo Suing Liza for a Divorce." In the '50s he did some recording for King, he played into the tape recorder of Alan Lomax when the folklorist went in pursuit of southern music in 1959–60, and in 1963 he made an album for Arhoolie, which led to an appearance at a folk music festival in Berkeley. Later he ran a mail order business from his home in Concord, sending out erratically typed flyers about his own records and tapes. He had plenty to sell, because he had done a deal with another colorful country music figure, Uncle Jim O'Neal of Rural Rhythm Records, whereby J. E. and his friends made an album whenever the whim took them. The series got as far as Volume 16. J. E. never retired.

Playlist

• *Run Mountain* (Arhoolie CD 456) [1963 recordings]
• *J. E. Mainer's Mountaineers 1935–1939* (BACM CD D 122)
•• *When the Sun Goes Down Vol. 10: East Virginia Blues* (Bluebird 60085): "The Longest Train" •• *Mountain Gospel* (JSP JSP 7755 4CD): "In a Little Village Churchyard," "Just over in the Gloryland," "Lights in the Valley," "This World Is Not My Home" •• *O Brothers! Family Harmony in Old-Time Music & Bluegrass* (Living Era CD AJA 5467): "Maple on the Hill" •• *Good for What Ails You: Music of the Medicine Shows 1926–1937* (Old Hat CD-1005 2CD): "Kiss Me Cindy" •• *Bluegrass Bonanza* (Proper PROPERBOX 29 4CD): "Run Mountain" •• *Southern Journey Vol. 1: Voices from the South* (Rounder CD 1701): "Three Nights Drunk" •• *Southern Journey Vol. 5: Bad Man Ballads* (Rounder CD 1705): "Columbus Stockade" •• *American Yodeling 1911–1946* (Trikont US-0246): "Yodeling Mountaineer"

work on a steel-bodied National had the sharp tang of older music. In particular it was reminiscent of Darby & Tarlton, one of the leading country acts of the previous decade. It was, in fact, Jimmie Tarlton who had inspired Howard to take up steel guitar.

The three men met in a North Carolina cotton mill, work the Dixons had followed, on and off, since their childhood in Darlington, South Carolina. The long hours, low pay, and choking, lung-destroying air of the textile mills inspired some of Dorsey Dixon's most telling compositions. "Weaver's Life," set to the melody of the old sacred song "Life Is Like a Mountain Railroad" ("Weaver's life is like an engine, coming round the mountain steep . . ."), Dorsey Dixon gave to Tarlton, who recorded it, as "The Weaver's Blues," in 1932. In the same year Dorsey wrote "Weave Room Blues" ("Working in a weave room, fighting for my life . . ."), but this he held on to, and when he and Howard opened their own recording account in 1936, it was the first song they cut.

A year later they recorded another of Dorsey's songs, an admonition against drinking and driving called "I Didn't Hear Anybody Pray." "When the '36 Fords came out with a V-8 engine," Dorsey's son, the Reverend Dorsey M. Dixon Jr., told Dorothy Horstman, "[they] began to kill people all over the nation. The

The Dixon Brothers

Dorsey Dixon (1897–1968)• Howard Dixon (1903–61)

When Dorsey and Howard Dixon began playing together seriously in the mid-1930s, their sound was already old-fashioned. The popular male duets of the day either played mandolin and guitar, like the Monroe Brothers and the Blue Sky Boys, or opted for a pair of standard guitars, like the Callahan Brothers. The Dixons' raw blend of Dorsey's agitated picking on standard guitar and Howard's slide

(Author's collection)

wreck took place at the Triangle Filling Station in Rockingham, North Carolina. Dad went down and seen the wreck, seen the whiskey, blood and glass on the floor of the car. He knew some of the people in the crash." In 1942, retitled "Wreck on the Highway," the song was a hit for Roy Acuff, though it took Dorsey several years to establish his copyright and begin to earn royalties.

In the middle and late '30s the Dixons were well known in the Southeast through their broadcasts on WBT in Charlotte, North Carolina, and WPTF in Raleigh. Bluebird Records capitalized on their name, recording more than sixty numbers in less than three years. As well as the mixture of topical compositions and old favorites that he shared with his brother, Dorsey recorded gospel songs with his wife Beatrice, while Howard teamed up with singer-guitarist Frank Gerald under the billing of The Rambling Duet. Although Howard was a fine singer as well as an incisive steel guitar player—listen to his solo vocal on "Dark Eyes" or "Greenback Dollar," despondent but resolute—the dominant flavor in the brothers' music was Dorsey's quavery, pungently accented singing, which lends fervor to his sacred songs and numbers like "Down with the Old Canoe," a moral lesson on human arrogance drawn from the *Titanic* disaster. Perhaps it was that godly aspect of the Dixons' music that earned them bookings like their concert in October 1935 at Elmira Graded School, "sponsored by the West Burlington Missionary society of the M. E. church." "The performers," said the *Burlington Daily Times-News*, "have an excellent program including black face comedian and string music."

Neither their personal appearances nor their recording and radio work earned the Dixons enough to release them from the bondage of the cotton mills. Their last recordings were in 1938, and by the '40s they had more or less retired from public performance. Both of them had maintained links with their friend Wade Mainer, Howard playing with him for a while and Dorsey co-writing some songs with him. Howard died after suffering a heart attack at work at the Aleo Mill in East Rockingham, North Carolina, while Dorsey left the same mill only when his sight began to fail him. After record collectors tracked him down at his home in East Rockingham, he had a brief later-life career in the '60s, recording for Testament and for the Archive of Folksong at the Library of Congress, and appearing twice at the Newport Folk Festival.

Playlist
- *How Can a Broke Man Be Happy?* (Acrobat ACMCD 4022)
- *Dixon Brothers—Volume 1 (1936)* (Document DOCD-8046)
- *Dixon Brothers—Volume 2 (1937)* (Document DOCD-8047)
- *Dixon Brothers—Volume 3 (1937–1938)* (Document DOCD-8048)
- *Dixon Brothers—Volume 4 (1938)* (Document DOCD-8049) [includes tracks by Howard Dixon with Frank Gerald, and by the Dixie Reelers, a spin-off group from J. E. Mainer's Mountaineers]
- *Weave Room Blues* (Old Homestead OH-4151)
- *Spinning Room Blues* (Old Homestead OH-4164)
- *Babies in the Mill* (HMG 2502) [Dorsey Dixon's Testament album, recorded in 1962]

The Callahan Brothers

Walter "Joe" Callahan (1910–71) • Homer "Bill" Callahan (1912–2002)

Brother duet," to a lover of old-time music, instantly prompts names like the Delmore Brothers or the Blue Sky Boys, who led the way in gentling down the country vocal manner to fit the intimate setting of rural radio. But behind those leaders files a troop of lesser-known siblings: the Dixon Brothers, the Shelton Brothers, the Morris brothers, and many more. Several of those acts have connections with North Carolina, either by birth or through working on country-friendly radio stations like WBT in Charlotte, WWNC in Asheville, or WPTF in Raleigh. One such duo is the Callahan

Perfect was one of the ARC group of labels. The same couplings, with the same catalog numbers, would appear on Melotone, and sometimes on the chain-store labels Oriole (exclusive to McCrory's stores), Romeo (S. H. Kress), or Banner (W. T. Grant). This release sheet is from around April 1937. (Author's collection)

Brothers, Walter and Homer, who grew up in Madison County, North Carolina.

They were barely into their teens when they began playing together, Walter on guitar, Homer on almost anything. In 1933, their duet yodeling at an Asheville festival caught the ear of W. R. Calaway, a recording scout for ARC, and early the following year they made their first records. "She's My Curly Headed Baby" was a solid hit, but their numerous ARC discs all seem to have sold respectably, and some were noticed by other artists; "Little Poplar Log House on the Hill" was later recorded by The Carter Family.

The Callahans were not averse to borrowing ideas themselves. No detective work is required to explain their fondness for blues and yodeling, but it's interesting that in that respect, and particularly in the duet yodeling, they also seem to have cocked an ear to Fleming & Townsend, the duo from west Tennessee who had some success in the early '30s, partly with risqué material. The Callahans followed them down that alley too, and their discography is littered with titles like "She's Killing Me," "Somebody's Been Using That Thing"

MONOGRAM PICTURES Presents JIMMY WAKELY in "SPRINGTIME IN TEXAS" with DENNIS MOORE, LEE "LASSES" WHITE and the CALLAHAN BROTHERS & Their Blue Ridge Mountain Folks.   Printed in U.S.A.

(OTM collection)

(borrowed from the portfolio of hokum blues artists Tampa Red & Georgia Tom), or "She Came Rollin' down the Mountain," which was too saucy to be released and came to light only when a test pressing found its way on to an LP in the '70s.

Having put in a year at WWNC, the Callahans moved in 1935 to WHAS in Louisville, Kentucky, and in 1937 to WWVA in Wheeling, West Virginia, two more key locations in the rural radio landscape of the period. Walter then returned home and Homer continued as a solo, working with John Lair's Renfro Valley Barn Dance troupe. The brothers reconnected in 1939, then went west, ending up at KRLD in Dallas, where they would remain for the rest of their professional career.

With a roster including Molly O'Day & Lynn Davis and the fiddlers Georgia Slim Rutland and Howdy Forrester, KRLD was becoming a major player in hillbilly radio, a position they solidified when they instituted a Saturday night variety show, the Big D Jamboree. Homer and Walter, now renamed Bill and Joe, respectively, contributed their warm, buffed harmony to the program, but something more: they had embraced the fashion for country-with-comedy, and Bill in particular was an accomplished funny man. The brothers were also heard beyond the reach of KRLD, thanks to the many transcription discs they cut for the Sellers company in Fort Worth, which were played on the border radio stations.

Talented, personable, and amusing, the Callahans were well qualified to move into cowboy movies, and did so in features like *Springtime in Texas* (1945), starring Jimmy Wakely, with whom they worked for a while afterward. Bill also did a good deal of session work on bass in the late '40s, and later added another role when he managed the singer Lefty Frizzell. Such versatility was useful, because the brothers' musical style, despite the contemporary decoration it received on their later records (they carried on making them until 1951), was falling from favor. By the end of the '50s Joe was back in Asheville while Bill was working for a Dallas auto parts company. Joe (Walter) died at sixty-one, but Bill (Homer) survived him by more than thirty years, day-jobbing as a photographer but keeping a toe on the country music stage almost up to the time of his death.

Playlist
• *Callahan Brothers* (Old Homestead OH-4031)
•• *Tennessee Saturday Night: The Rural Route to Rock 'n' Roll* (Jasmine JASMCD 3519): "Rattle Snake Daddy" •• *Mountain Blues* (JSP JSP 7740 4CD): "Brown's Ferry Blues No. 2," "Rattle Snake Daddy" •• *American Yodeling 1911–1946* (Trikont US-0246): "Gonna Quit My Rowdy Ways"

Claude Casey

(1912–99)

Claude Casey was a singer, yodeler, guitarist, bandleader, and songwriter, but above all he was a radio artist. One of the most popular acts in the Carolinas during the 1930s and '40s was The Briarhoppers, a gang of singers, pickers, and funsters on Charlotte's WBT. Many passed through its ranks, but the core members were Roy "Whitey" Grant and Arval Hogan, who specialized in old-time heart and gospel songs, Fiddlin' Hank Warren, singer-guitarists Fred Kirby and Don White, and Casey, who wrote much of the group's new material and was a featured yodeler.

Born in Enoree, South Carolina, Casey grew up in Virginia. In his early twenties he appeared on the Major Bowes Amateur Hour, a nationally popular show from the Fox Theater in Brooklyn, broadcast by WMCA, that plucked amateur musicians from nonentity and turned them into media stars. (An interesting idea—perhaps it could work today.) He won a place on one of the show's touring units, singing in overalls and a red bandanna under the sobriquet of "The Carolina Hobo." After

Now on tour — **TWO OF THE NATION'S TOP ENTERTAINERS**

CLAUDE CASEY *and* FRED KIRBY

Direct From

WBT **CAROLINA HAYRIDE** • **CBS** **CAROLINA CALLING**

Presenting

The BRIARHOPPERS

AN OUTSTANDING 30 MINUTE STAGE SHOW

• • •

RCA VICTOR — SONORA AND SUPER DISC RECORDING ARTISTS

CLAUDE CASEY'S **FRED KIRBY'S**

RCA VICTOR RECORDS

"Look in the Looking Glass"
"Days Are Long, Nights Are Lonely"
"Journey's End"
"I Wish I Had Kissed You Goodbye"
"Two Little Girls With Golden Curls"
"My Little Tootsie"
"I Wish I'd Never Met You"
"Family Reunion In Heaven"

SUPER DISC RECORDS

"Juke Box Gal"
"Carolina Waltz"
"It's Hard To Lose These Lonesome Blues"
"Living In Dreams"

Appeared in Republic Picture

"Swing Your Partner"

SONORA RECORDS

"Atomic Power"
"Honey Be My Honey Bee"
"I've Been A Fool Too Often"
"My War Torn Heart"
"The Wreck of The Old 97"
"Deep In The Bottom of The Sea"
"Boogie Woogie Farmer"
"My Little Boy Blue"
"Casey Jones"
"It's The Beginning of The End"

"That's How Much I Love You"
"After All These Years"
"Downright Lonely, Downright Blue"
"I Can't Tell That Lie to My Heart"

SUPER DISC RECORDS

"God Made This Country"
"The Almighty Dollar"
"I Thank My Lucky Star"
"A Greater Power"

(OTM collection)

a spell with Fats Sanders' Country Cousins—featuring Effie, the Hillbilly Strip Dancer—he returned south, formed his own band, the Pine State Playboys, and made several dozen recordings for RCA Victor.

One of their sessions, in a Charlotte hotel, was held during a heat wave. Casey remembered tubs of ice being brought in and placed in front of electric fans, so that the band could cool down between takes. When the fans were turned off and the microphone on, they stripped to their underwear before launching into numbers like "Down with Gin."

Casey's records sold well enough, but it was as a broadcasting Briarhopper that he won a kind of stardom. "Whenever you say 'Claude Casey' around WBT," wrote a fanzine in 1946, "you'll see a lot of people with that look on their faces that means 'there's a good guy.' But to the boys and girls in WBT's mail room, the name of Claude Casey only means a lot of work. Claude has averaged well over 75 cards and letters a week, and on several occasions has been known to crown the mailbags with over 250 responses from a single song on a 15-minute program." A song, maybe, like "Journey's End," or "Days Are Long, Nights Are Lonely," or "Send Me the Pillow You Dream On"—just some of the compositions Casey came up with in his Briarhopper days.

Casey had looks as well as musical talent, and it wasn't long before Hollywood gave him parts in musical features aimed at what *Variety* magazine called "hix in the stix"—*Swing Your Partner* with Dale Evans, *Square Dance Jubilee*, *Forty-Acre Feud*, and others. He joined the Screen Actors Guild and continued to appear in films into the '70s.

The Briarhoppers broke up in the '50s, and in 1961 Casey founded radio station WJES in Johnston, South Carolina, running it with his wife and one of his sons and taking his turn as a disc jockey. He liked to finish his show in traditional rural radio style: "Now it's time to take a little trip down to my wife's husband's mortgaged home and see if the neighbors have been good to us and throwed anything over the backyard fence. If the Good Lord's willing and the boss is not mad, see you tomorrow along about the same time."

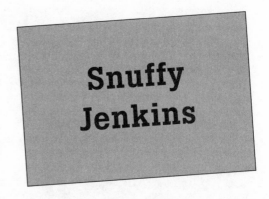

Snuffy Jenkins

(1908–90)

Earl Scruggs has not talked a great deal about the banjoists who came before him, and it's easy to assume, though he has never made such a claim himself, that he more or less invented the three-finger roll that lies at the heart of bluegrass banjo picking. In fact he had predecessors going back to the 1920s, in the very part of North Carolina where he was raised.

We don't know much about forgotten figures like Rex Brooks and Smith Hammett. We have a little more information about blind Mack Woolbright, a Cleveland County neighbor of Scruggs whose playing of the G chord in "Home

The W. O. W. String Band, with Snuffy Jenkins (back row, center), was one of the family of bands sponsored on North Carolina stations in the 1930s by Crazy Water Crystals. (Author's collection)

Playlist

•• *Doughboys, Playboys and Cowboys* (Proper PROPERBOX 6 4CD): "Pine State Honky Tonk"

Sweet Home" so thrilled the younger man, and we can even relive that experience when Woolbright quotes the tune in his wonderful 1927 disc of the comic song "The Man Who Wrote Home Sweet Home Never Was a Married Man." But, thanks to his long and active life in music, we know quite a lot about DeWitt "Snuffy" Jenkins, a man of whom Don Reno, another bluegrass pioneer, said: "He was the first one who ever put it together. He had perfected, as far as I'm concerned, a three-finger roll."

Jenkins, who was born, like Scruggs, in Harris, North Carolina, started playing music semi-professionally in the mid-'30s, when he and some of his relatives and friends, under the name of the Jenkins String Band, joined the Crazy Water Crystals Barn Dance on WBT. He went on to play with J. E. Mainer's Mountaineers and then, on WIS in Columbia, South Carolina, with the singer and announcer Byron Parker, "The Old Hired Hand," an enormously popular figure with southeastern radio listeners.

"We'd play a lot of these little old schoolhouses down there," he remembered, "for fifteen and twenty-five cents admission. And five of us made a living like that." It's been calculated that the WIS Hired Hands traveled nearly half a million miles, taking their music to hundreds of thousands of listeners all over the Carolinas, Georgia, Virginia, and Tennessee. "One time we were playing," Jenkins recalled, "and all of a sudden it seemed like we couldn't breathe. Then we realized that no air could get in because the windows were full of people."

Through his radio and personal appearances, Jenkins's fluent three-finger picking fell on the ears of younger experimenters like Scruggs and Reno. "I don't claim to have taught either one anything," he said in later years, "but I was about the first to go on the air with this type of playing." "When I heard Snuffy," Reno said, "I could see that he had unwound something and straightened it out to the point where it did have a flowing melody to it and not a bunch of jerks and stops."

The younger men received most of the credit for banjo innovation because they were in high-profile bands with recording contracts and wide radio exposure. Jenkins had a quieter life in local radio and later TV, playing with longtime friends like fiddler Homer "Pappy" Sherrill and diversifying as a guitarist and washboard player. He made few records, and it wasn't until the early '60s that he began to be recognized in bluegrass circles, when he recorded some banjo instrumentals for the influential Folkways album *American Banjo Tunes and Songs in Scruggs Style*.

In the '60s and '70s he and Sherrill made some colorful albums for Folk Lyric and Rounder which painted in the backdrop to bluegrass, especially its origins in the extrovert music of '30s radio and touring shows. Amid boisterous vocal numbers, stringband reels, and talking blues, Jenkins picks tunes like "Spanish Fandango" and "Twinkle, Twinkle, Little Star," displaying the melodic fluency that so impressed Don Reno.

Playlist

• *Pioneer of the Bluegrass Banjo* (Arhoolie CD 9027) [1962 recordings]
• *Byron Parker & His Mountaineers* (Old Homestead OH-4169) ['40s recordings]
•• *Classic Bluegrass from Smithsonian Folkways* (Smithsonian/Folkways SFW CD 40092): "Cumberland Gap" •• *Close to Home: Old Time Music from Mike Seeger's Collection* (Smithsonian/Folkways SF CD 40097): "Going to Lay Down My Old Guitar" (with Ira Dimmery)

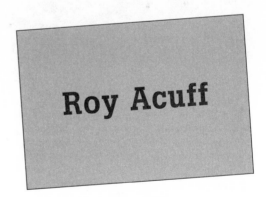

Roy Acuff

(1903–92)

Roy Acuff never intended to be a musician. Growing up in Maynardville, Tennessee, he learned a little about fiddling from his father, but his first career bid was in baseball. Sidelined by sunstroke, he put in some more work on the fiddle and on his singing. He built a reputation first on medicine shows, then on WNOX in Knoxville, whose Midday Merry-Go-Round was a training ground for many country artists.

Roy Acuff & the Smoky Mountain Boys, 1942/43. (OTM collection)

In 1936 he made his first recordings with his Crazy Tennesseans, introducing two of the mainstays of his career, "Wabash Cannonball"—though it was sung in this first version by one of his bandsmen, "Dynamite" Hatcher—and the haunting sacred song "Great Speckled Bird" ("my inheritance to me is like a speckled bird": Jeremiah 12:9). Unlike many earlier country artists, Acuff sang not with the dispassionate voice of balladry but with the fervor of personal testimony that he had absorbed in church. His affecting sincerity brought him fame throughout the Southeast, and in 1938 he joined the Grand Ole Opry, country music's radio gateway to the nation. Soon he was its leading figure.

Which may explain why one of his records was issued somewhat covertly. At the end of the session that produced "Wabash Cannon-

ball" and "Great Speckled Bird"—and another popular record, "Freight Train Blues," also sung by Hatcher—the band cut loose on a wild hoedown tune equipped with lyrics that had nothing to do with railroads or religion: "I wish I was a milk cow, down on my Lulu's farm, I'd never kick when Lulu come to polish up my horn . . ." Unlike some other examples of hillbilly *double entendre*, "When Lulu's Gone" was at least issued, coupled with the less exuberant but equally suggestive "Doin' It the Old Fashioned Way"—but as by the Bang Boys.

In the '40s, his band renamed the Smoky Mountain Boys, Acuff became a nationwide star through jukebox hits like "Wreck on the Highway," "Fire Ball Mail," and "Pins and Needles (In My Heart)," and by mid-decade he was touring cross-country and into Canada. Meanwhile movies such as *Grand Ole Opry* (1940), *Hi, Neighbor* (1943), *O My Darling Clementine* (1944), *Sing Neighbor Sing* (1945), *Cowboy Canteen* (1945), *Night Train to Memphis* (1946), and *Smoky Mountain Melody* (1948) brought his shy smile to music lovers beyond the reach of the Opry's traveling tent shows. He was also a favorite radio artist with U.S. troops overseas. In November 1942 fellow hillbilly musician William Ralph Cross wrote from Hawaii to *The Mountain Broadcast and Prairie Recorder*, "Most all the soldiers [here]

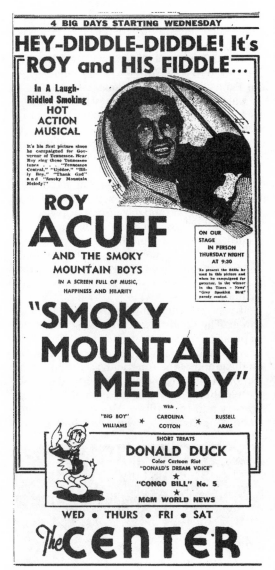

like Roy Acuff and his Smoky Mountain Boys. More power to you, Roy, you are liked as far as you are heard."

Such was his fame in his native state that in the '40s he was twice the Republican nominee for governor. "I know I can be elected . . . if I want to," Acuff told the press in November 1943, "because there's not a man in the state who has any more friends than I have and friends mean a lot more than a political machine. . . . I've sung and fiddled and shaken hands up and down every pig track and county road in Tennessee." But, he concluded, "the idea of being governor doesn't excite me much," mainly because it would have meant a substantial loss of income—in 1943 he earned more than $200,000—and in July 1944 he withdrew his name from the ballot. In 1948 he did run for office, taking his band on the campaign trail like Louisiana's Jimmie Davis and Texas's "Pappy" O'Daniel before him, but was defeated.

In 1944 he and the songwriter Fred Rose formed the publishing company Acuff-Rose. By the early '50s it was Nashville's biggest publishing house, its stock including not only Rose's huge output but the songs of Hank Williams. Yet new style setters like Williams and Webb Pierce, with their franker approach to postwar problems, made Acuff's style seem old-fashioned, and he lost his hold on the country record market. Nevertheless, fans routinely traveled hundreds of miles to the Opry to hear him sing "Wabash Cannonball" once more, accompanied by long-serving sidemen like banjo and dobro player Pete Kirby, alias Bashful Brother Oswald, and fiddler Howdy Forrester. In 1962 he was elected to the Country Music Hall of Fame.

Acuff was suspicious of long-haired rock musicians who expressed an interest in country music, and it amazed Nashville when he participated in the Nitty Gritty Dirt Band's 1972 triple album *Will the Circle Be Unbroken?* But it was a momentous cultural exchange and a template for other meetings of the old and the new.

As a stalwart of the Opry for more than three decades he encouraged the development of the Opryland theme park, and, having presided over its opening in 1974, spent the rest of his days living in the middle of the complex. His dressing room was a place of pilgrimage for musicians and fans, aware that he was one of the last carriers of country music's simpler yet still potent heritage.

Playlist
• *Hear the Mighty Rush of Engine* (Jasmine JASMCD 3547)
• *The King of Country Music* (Living Era CD AJA 5244)
• *King of Country Music* (Proper PROPERBOX 70 4CD)
•• *The Iron Horse: Vintage Railroad Songs 1926–1952* (Buzzola BZCD 008): "Devil's Train," "Life's Railway to Heaven" •• *Country* (Frémeaux FA 015 2CD): "Fire Ball Mail," "Wreck on the Highway" •• *Country Music 1940–1948* (Frémeaux FA 173 2CD): "Jole Blond" •• *Steel Rails: Classic Railroad Songs, Volume 1* (Rounder CD 1128): "Wabash Cannon Ball" •• *Raw Fiddle* (Rounder Select 1160): "When Lulu's Gone"

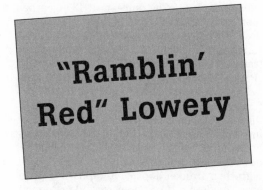

"Ramblin' Red" Lowery

(1905–73)

For a man whose brief musical career was spent almost entirely in Tennessee, "Ramblin' Red" Lowery has a curious celebrity beyond its borders, at least among record collectors. Around 1935 the British label Panachord, in one of its irregular flirtations with the American hillbilly catalogs to which it had rights through its parent company Decca, issued in quick succession two discs by him. It seems an odd decision, since Lowery was hardly well known even in American hillbilly circles, and Panachord usually chose more prominent figures like Goebel Reeves or Mac & Bob, but the explanation lies in the music, most obviously in the song titled "Ramblin' Red's Memphis Yodel": Lowery was cut from the Jimmie Rodgers pattern, and Rodgers had been popular with British record buyers for years. The Panachord discs, however, made no discernible impact on the British public, and today they rank among the rarest of hillbilly recordings.

With no clue to his provenance other than the word "Memphis" (if indeed it was a clue), following Lowery's trail decades later was something of a challenge. The key that unlocked his story was a piece of paperwork from the files of W. R. Calaway, sometime recording manager for the Brunswick Record Corporation, in which an artist signed over his rights to fifteen songs so that a New York publisher could produce a songbook. The contract identified the artist "known as 'Ramblin' Red' Lowery" as one Earl L. Winchester of Erin, Tennessee.

That was his birthname, but soon afterward his mother, Cora Daphne Burns Winchester, remarried, and Earl was raised by Will Lowery, an Erin barrel-maker. From his early teens he was a rambler. "A lot of the history about him I couldn't tell you," said a cousin, "because he was here, yonder, and everywhere. That was why he picked up that name 'Ramblin' Red.'" (The "Red" came from his hair.) At some point

he made his way to Memphis, and by 1933 he had joined the hillbilly roster of WREC. The owner of a local music store put him in touch with Calaway, and in January 1934 Lowery journeyed to New York to cut seventeen sides for Brunswick's Vocalion label.

Calaway was presumably interested in him as a Rodgers disciple, since Rodgers's death a few months earlier seemed to have left room in the market for new blue yodelers, and he duly commissioned four "Memphis Yodel" songs, but Lowery also had original, if still rather Rodgers-like, material such as "Mother, Pal and Sweetheart" and "Lonesome Weary Blues," which Calaway recorded and then promptly passed on to the better-known Callahan Brothers, who recorded them too. (Another of Lowery's compositions, "Take Me Back to Tennessee," believed to have been his signature piece, was later put on disc by the fiddler and singer Arthur Smith.)

It was a terrible time to begin a recording career. The country was struggling out of the Depression and in a year or two sales would begin to pick up, but 1934 marks a nosedive on the graph of the American record industry. Although his songbook was published in 1935, with a photograph of the confidently smiling Lowery and the billing "Famous Radio and Recording Artist," fewer than half of the

(OTM collection)

Vocalion sides had been issued and only a couple of them were at all widely circulated. By 1940 Lowery was back in Erin, chicken farming and running, unsuccessfully, for sheriff. After that he fades into the Tennessee landscape, and the last we hear of him is in Lenoir City, near Knoxville, where his wife had family, and where he died.

A familiar tale, then, of missed chances and unfortunate timing—but was "Ramblin' Red" really that unlucky? Dexter Gray, who played harmonica with him for a year or two on WREC, remembered him as "a big, rough-lookin' fellow" but "with a good personality," and that may have come across on radio, but his records are rather plain, the songs delivered without a great deal of expression, the guitar playing functional rather than exciting. Gray thought "he sounded a lot like Ernest Tubb," which is near the mark, but he doesn't have the Texan's warmth, nor that of their shared model, Jimmie Rodgers. He could write couplets that Rodgers might not have been ashamed to put his name to—

> Standing on the railroad, looking up at the moon,
> Hopin' and prayin' I'll be travelin' pretty soon. . . .
>
> I've rambled this wide world over, Lord,
> I've been most everywhere –
> You're the only gal I ever found was really on the square.

—but when he sings them you don't hear Rodgers's wry, imperturbable geniality.

What "Ramblin' Red" Lowery represents for us is the journeyman country singer, standing at the microphone in the studio of WREC, enjoying his fifteen or thirty minutes of fame every Friday, sponsored by the Buchanan Seed Company—or indeed in any studio, any day, for any sponsor. This, more than records, was how Depression America heard country music. It may not have been the best country music—it was rather like watching a competent B-movie, played by stock-company actors rather than stars—but it was there every week, at a familiar spot on your radio dial, and in those hard times you took what you could get and were thankful.

Playlist
•• *Sounds like Jimmie Rodgers* (JSP JSP 7751 4CD): "Bum on the Bum," "Ramblin' Red's Memphis Yodel No. 1"

The Delmore Brothers

Alton Delmore (1908–64) • Rabon Delmore (1916–52)

The sound of the Delmore Brothers—a sly blues or a wistful train song, told to the rhythm of mellow guitars—echoed through country music across three decades. As boys they played alongside the Skillet-Lickers, as men they sat shoulder to shoulder with Merle Travis and Grandpa Jones.

Not many could boast a track record like that. Of the thousands of artists who made records in the 1920s and '30s, remarkably few kept up with the changing sounds of the postwar years, let alone adapted to them and became even more successful. Bill Monroe; the Blue Sky Boys, though you could hardly say they adapted; Bill Carlisle, but he restyled himself so much you could hardly recognize him. The Delmores' special talent was to devise an approach to the blues which they could retune to the shifting signals of public taste.

The key song of their early career was "Brown's Ferry Blues," a succinct catalog of Depression images and men's-room jokes: "Hard luck papa standing in the rain, if the world was corn he couldn't buy grain. . . . Two old maids playing in the sand, each one wishin' that the other 'n' was a man. . . . Hard luck papa can't do his stuff, the trouble with him, he's been too rough. . . . Lawd, lawd, got them Brown's Ferry Blues." Their guitars—Alton

(OTM collection)

For a magazine whose editorial office was in downtown Nashville, a stone's throw away from WSM, *Rural Radio* was either surprisingly deaf to Opry gossip or tactfully concerned to ignore it. Within a few months of the article appearing, the Delmores were sacked from the show. Their problems with alcohol were well known—"the people here, they treat me fine: they give me beer, they give me wine," they sang disingenuously in "The Nashville Blues"—and Rabon's unreliability in particular made it impossible for WSM's management to keep them on.

After that they switched restlessly from one radio station to another. In March 1939 *Rural Radio* reported them on WSBZ, Greenville, South Carolina, but in May the magazine replied to an enquirer, "We are unable to tell you where the Delmore Brothers are at present." On the same page, ominously enough, there appeared this response to another reader: "The boys that you heard and thought were the Delmore Brothers are the Andrew[s] Brothers, newcomers to WSM."

By the mid-'40s, however, the Delmores were on WLW in Cincinnati, in time to be on hand at the birth of the city's most famous record label, and the rebirth of their own career. Through the '40s and into the '50s, on King records like "Hillbilly Boogie" and "Mobile Train Boogie," with their pounding string bass, sock-rhythm guitars, and rippling lead picking by session musicians like Zeke Turner, the Delmores offered another take on the blues. The easygoing swing of their earlier music was exchanged for a more aggressive beat that now seems like rock 'n' roll a few bars early. At the same time they recycled their close-harmony elegies to life on the road and the rails. Their biggest postwar hit, however, straddled both categories. "Blues Stay Away from Me" was built on a rock-solid riff that circulated through the music of the period, blues and country, like a raging virus, but the feather-light vocal harmony and the wailing harmonicas of Wayne Raney and Lonnie Glosson invested it with melancholy.

So the brothers became record and radio stars not once but twice, yet with all their problems and differences they might as well have titled their hit song "Success Stay Away from Me." In any case, Rabon died while still a young man. Close-harmony singing depends on real, personal, living-in-each-other's-pocket closeness, which is why brothers do it so well, and with Rabon gone, Alton was only half an

playing rhythm on a standard model, Rabon picking lead on a four-string tenor guitar—jinked and twirled round the merry tune.

It was a huge hit, one of the best-selling hillbilly discs of the '30s. The brothers, who had already joined the cast of the Grand Ole Opry, made dozens more discs, and went on the road accompanying Uncle Dave Macon, and later the fiddler Arthur Smith. In 1938, five years after the release of "Brown's Ferry Blues," *Rural Radio* ran a story about the song and the men who made it.

Alton and Rabon were born on an Alabama farm, and lived there during the early part of their lives. Home was the farm and cotton gin operated by their father five miles from Athens, on the Brown's Ferry Road. The boys found that of all the songs they sang, the light, comedy songs were most popular. Alton sat down and wrote the Brown's Ferry Blues, using the road for the title, and thinking all the time that it was so obscure and unknown that it would never attract any attention. When Alton and Rabon appeared at an old-time fiddlers' contest, and entered competition, they would almost always win first prize with this appealing song. They formed a minstrel show, and played about the country. Everywhere they went, the Brown's Ferry Blues was the song everyone asked to hear.

City School Auditorium
CULLMAN, ALA.
Saturday August 9th

— 2 BIG SHOWS —
Matinee 3:00 P. M. — Night 8:00 P. M.

Radio Broadcast Direct
From The Stage Over
WAPI 3:00 to 3:30

North Alabama Radio
Stars Jamboree
AMATEUR CONTEST

50 RADIO STARS — IN PERSON 50
Featuring
ARTHUR SMITH & HIS DIXIE LINERS
● ●
DELMORE BROTHERS (Alton & Rabon)
(Grand Ole Opry — Decca and Bluebird Records)
● ●
ZEKE THE HAYSEED and His Happy
Valley Jamboree
● ●
Hog Calling — Guitar — Banjo — Quartet
Yodelers & Fiddlers Contest
● ●
A SHOW YOU'LL NEVER FORGET
Souvenirs for the Kiddies
Admission 20c & 35c

(Author's collection)

Playlist
• *Freight Train Boogie* (Ace CDCHD 455) [King recordings]
• *Fifty Miles to Travel* (Ace CDCHD 1074) [King recordings]
• *Sand Mountain Blues* (County CCS-110) [King recordings]
• *Brown's Ferry Blues* (County CCS-CD-116) [Bluebird recordings]
• *Blues Stay Away from Me 1931–1951* (Frémeaux FA 5057 2CD)
•• *When the Sun Goes Down Vol. 10: East Virginia Blues* (Bluebird 60085): "Brown's Ferry Blues" •• *Country Boogie 1939–1947* (Frémeaux FA 160 2CD): "Down Home Boogie," "Mobile Boogie" •• *Country Music 1940–1948* (Frémeaux FA 173 2CD): "She Left Me Standing on the Mountain" •• *Guitare Country 1926–1950* (Frémeaux FA 5007 2CD): "This Train" •• *Hillbilly Blues* (Living Era CD AJA 5361): "Peach Tree Street Boogie" •• *O Brothers! Family Harmony in Old-Time Music & Bluegrass* (Living Era CD AJA 5467): "Blue Railroad Train," "Goin' Back to the Blue Ridge Mountains," "The Weary Lonesome Blues" •• *Mystery Train: Classic Railroad Songs, Volume 2* (Rounder CD 1129): "Red Ball To Natchez" •• *American Yodeling 1911–1946* (Trikont US-0246): "Lonesome Yodel Blues"

act. He carried on for a few years as a solo, but spent more time writing magazine stories, which the magazines rejected. He left an unfinished but fascinating autobiography, *Truth Is Stranger than Publicity*.

Lonnie
Glosson

(1908–2001)

By the dawn of the twenty-first century, country musicians who had recorded as long ago as the early 1930s were a diminishing band. The harmonica player Lonnie Glosson, then in his nineties, had first been heard on

(OTM collection)

I know you've always wondered what makes it sound so much different to the ordinary harp, and we're going to send you, absolutely free of any extra charge, our play-by-ear instructions that will show you and tell you exactly how to play the harmonica and how to choke it, how to make the train whistle, how to make it actually talk.

And friends, this entire deal only costs three dollars and ninety-eight cents.

Glosson was born and grew up in rural Arkansas, where he learned harmonica from his mother and hillbilly songs from the many amateur musicians around. After some teenage years rambling round the country playing for change in barbershops, he settled in St. Louis and made his radio debut, about 1925 or '26, on KMOX. By 1930 he had moved on up to the WLS National Barn Dance in Chicago, and he later put in time on the Renfro Valley Barn Dance, the Grand Ole Opry, and WCKY in Covington, Kentucky, across the Ohio river from Cincinnati.

Anyone in Cincinnati in the late '40s was likely to hook up with King Records, the city's premier label for country music and blues. Along with the thirteen-years-younger Raney, Glosson worked for a while with the Delmore Brothers. He also had a hand in writing Raney's King record of "Why Don't You Haul Off and Love Me," which vied for top spot on the country chart during 1949 with Hank Williams's "Lovesick Blues."

When rock 'n' roll began to crowd the airwaves in the later '50s, Glosson and Raney went different ways, Raney to found his Rimrock label and build a recording studio in Concord, Arkansas, Glosson to a seemingly endless itinerary of personal appearances, mostly in schools. As well as his harmonica specialties of fox chases, train impressions, and "I Want My Mama," where he imitates a child crying "I want my mama . . . I want some water . . . ," he would sing country and gospel songs with guitar. "I still play the tunes I learned when I was growing up in Arkansas," he said in a 1981 interview.

That interview appeared in *Bluegrass Unlimited*—an odd publication, on the face of it, to feature a musician who had never been part of bluegrass, but it turned out that many older festival-goers remembered him fondly from his broadcasts, so he embarked on a new career playing for them. Soon Raney came out of retirement to join him, and for a few years the two veterans gave bluegrass festival audiences an authentic taste of old-time rural radio.

wax in 1932, though few copies of Broadway 8333, "The Fox Chase" and "Fast Train Blues," escaped onto the market. In any case, records were never as important to Glosson as radio. It's impossible to calculate how many hours on air he logged in a career extending across seven decades. His show with fellow harmonica player Wayne Raney, which ran from about 1947 until past the mid-'50s, was sent out on transcriptions to more than 200 stations in the United States and Canada.

Sponsored by the Kraft Company, manufacturer of harmonicas, the show's job was to sell the instrument to listeners, with a carrot of a free instruction book. Raney claimed they shifted more than 5 million harmonicas with their friendly person-to-person approach, which they recreated, years afterward, for a TV documentary:

A great big happy howdy to you, neighbors. We're going to be demonstrating the talking harmonica, and we want you to get a pencil and a piece of paper ready, because we're going to tell you how that you too can have the talking harmonica just exactly like the ones your old friends Lonnie Glosson and Wayne Raney plays.

Playlist
• • *Black & White Hillbilly Music* (Trikont US-0226); "Lonnie's Fox Chase" • • *The Roots of Rap* (Yazoo 2018): "Arkansas Hard Luck Blues"

Grandpa Jones

(1913–98)

The comic "grandpappy," shuffling on stage in flannel shirt and braces, perhaps with one or two of his front teeth blacked out, is a staple of southern humor. For over sixty years Grandpa Jones preserved that well-loved routine, first on radio, then on television for the millions who watched the long-running country comedy show *Hee Haw*. "Hey, Grandpa," cast members would chorus, "what's for supper?" and Jones would reply with a litany of white soul food: cornbread and country ham, butter beans and blueberry cobbler.

Musically, too, he played spokesman for the bib-overall-wearing class, retailing with enormous relish and racing banjo rhythms stories of moonshine, hound dogs, and hot biscuits. The combination of banjo playing and rustic narratives placed Jones squarely in the tradition of earlier country performers like Uncle Dave Macon, whose place on the Opry he more or less took over and filled for fifty-two years.

Born in Niagara, Kentucky, one of ten children of a tobacco farmer, Louis Marshall Jones grew up with music: his father fiddled, his mother sang and played concertina. When he was sixteen he won a talent contest on WJW in Akron, Ohio, singing and yodeling a Jimmie Rodgers number, and it launched him into radio, where he took the billing of "The Young Singer of Old Songs."

In 1935 he and his accomplice "Bashful Harmonica Joe" Troyan were invited to join the singer Bradley Kincaid, then hugely popular on both radio and records. Claiming that Jones's on-air manner during their early morning shows was crotchety, Kincaid jestingly labeled him "Grandpa." Jones went with the joke, donning a battered felt hat and peering through little round spectacles.

All this time he had been playing guitar, but during a spell on the Midnight Jamboree on WWVA in Wheeling, West Virginia, in 1937–38, he encountered the banjo-playing Cousin Emmy. "I thought that was the finest thing I ever heard, that thumb string lick she did," he said later, "and I kept after her and finally got her to show me how she did that." It would be a few more years, though, before he permanently exchanged the guitar for the banjo.

During World War II he spent some time in Germany, playing for U.S. troops with his Munich Mountaineers. He returned to reclaim his spot on WLW's Boone County Jamboree. Like his fellow WLW performers Merle Travis and the Delmore Brothers, he hooked up with King Records; in fact it was Jones and Travis who launched King, with an obscure 1943 disc credited to the Shepherd Brothers.

As well as scoring radio and jukebox hits with his King discs of "It's Raining Here This Morning," "Eight More Miles to Louisville," "Old Rattler," and "Mountain Dew," Jones joined the Delmores and Travis to record old-fashioned gospel quartet numbers as the Brown's Ferry Four. (The name was taken, rather incongruously, from the Delmores' mildly off-color hit "Brown's Ferry Blues.") Their albums stayed in print for decades. Years later Jones would recreate this sober, elegant music with Buck Owens and Roy Clark in the Hee Haw Gospel Quartet.

Grandpa Jones first walked out on to the stage of the Grand Ole Opry in 1946, accompanied by his fiddle-playing wife Ramona Riggins Jones, whom he had met back in WLW days when she was playing with Sunshine Sue & The Rock Creek Rangers. They continued to record for King—when he quit the label in 1956, he had logged almost 120 sides—but subsequent spells with Victor and Decca were not markedly successful. In the '60s and '70s he did a bunch of albums for Monument, and later a few for CMH, including *Grandpa Jones Family Album*, where he and Ramona were joined by several of their children who had taken up music.

Grandpa and Ramona Jones in Richmond, Virginia. (OTM collection)

By the '70s Grandpa Jones was a fixture on *Hee Haw*, but so far as the Opry was concerned he was one of the show's very few old-timey survivors, along with his great friend and fishing buddy Stringbean. Round about this time he received a long-distance compliment: the cast of the album *Korean Grand Ole Opry*—"*Stateside!*" (Cho Hun Records), featuring acts like Joe Ching Joe, Kimchi Chet Atkins, and Numb Nuts, is headed by Rice Paddy Granpa Jones.

In 1978 he was inducted into the Country

Music Hall of Fame and in 1984, with the assistance of country music historian Charles Wolfe, he produced his autobiography, *Everybody's Grandpa*. Thanks to his sharp memory and superb personal archive, it's one of the most detailed accounts we have of a country performer's professional life. He continued to appear on the Opry until a few weeks before his death.

Playlist
• *Steppin' Out Kind* (Ace CDCHD 1098) [King recordings]
• *An American Original* (CMH 9044)
• *28 Greatest Hits* (King 5012) [King recordings]
•• *Country Music 1940–1948* (Frémeaux FA 173 2CD): "Eight More Miles to Louisville" •• *Bluegrass Bonanza* (Proper PROPERBOX 29 4CD): "It's Raining Here This Morning," "Mountain Dew," "Old Rattler," "Uncle Eph's Got the Coon"

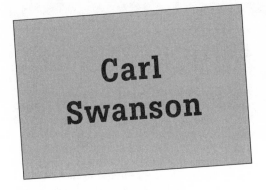

Carl Swanson

(1908–??)

Carl Swanson is one of a small company: the men and women, working in the profoundly American idiom of hillbilly music, who were not native North Americans. Indeed, "small" may sell him short: a poll of experts elicited only two other claimants, the singer Christine Endeback, the "Little Swiss Miss" of WLS, actually born in the Netherlands, and Raney Van Vink, who in the late 1920s played guitar on some records with the Spartanburg, South Carolina, accordionist Homer Christopher, and was born in Belgium. You might, if you searched among the myriad radio bands of

the '30s and '40s, be able to extend the list with an Italian-American or two. But for now, Carl Swanson can fairly be described as a rare bird.

He was born in Norway and crossed the Atlantic in 1926. A mandolin player since childhood, he reminded himself of home by playing old airs from Norway and Sweden. Then one day he caught the sound of singing and guitar playing from a room nearby. It was his first contact with country music.

In 1932 he auditioned for the Major Bowes Amateur Hour, teaming up with a couple of guitarists to sing "Empty Saddles in the Old Corral." "They had this hook," he remembered, "and if they didn't like you, they just came out and pulled you off," but the audience approved of the youngster with the odd accent and he won second prize. Among the radio listeners that night was a singer and guitarist originally from Cullman, Alabama, named Jake Watts. A few days later he called up and suggested they work together. He had heard of a vacancy for a hillbilly act on a station upstate, but he needed a second instrument and someone to sing a high harmony part.

They rehearsed by busking in Manhattan taverns, and a Swedish girl got them a booking for their first proper public appearance, at a Finnish dance hall in Harlem. In 1934, billing themselves "Jake & Carl, The Original Nightherders," they auditioned for WTIC in Hartford, Connecticut, and won a slot, besting the duet act of Jimmy & Dick, later popular on WEEI in Boston. By 1935 they had moved to WTAM in Cleveland, Ohio, where they shared airtime with Bradley Kincaid, and over the next three years to stations in Schenectady and Rochester, New York.

Meanwhile the music publisher and songwriter Bob Miller trained them on records of Mac & Bob and secured them recording sessions with ARC in 1937 and Bluebird in 1939. Most of the songs they cut were Miller's, like his parody "What Would You Give (In Exchange for Your Mother-in-Law)," "When the White Azaleas Start Blooming," and, amusingly given Swanson's background, "Hill Billy Boy from the Mountains." They also received an offer from Decca, but Watts thought they should stay with Bluebird. As it turned out, Bluebird never called them back, although someone there told Swanson that as a mandolin player he was second only to the famous Dave Apollon.

They also published a song folio, notable for its outrageous reconstruction of Swanson's personal history. "[He] hails," the publisher's hack reported, "from the Black Hills of North Dakota . . . and comes from a sturdy stock of Swedish Pioneers, that settled in the North

Carl Swanson outside his store with Kitty Wells and Johnny & Jack. (OTM collection)

West. . . . He worked in the wheat fields of the great North West and the potato fields of Canada . . . was a real cowpuncher at a ranch in Butte, Montana . . . and soon won fame at a Rodeo in Cheyenne, Wyoming. During the long lonesome evenings of the great Roundups, Carl sang to the stars, the little doggies and the hardened cowpunchers. Even the little prairie dogs seemed even more docile at the softness of Carl's soft voice." Not a word of this is true.

Jake & Carl separated in 1940 or '41. Watts briefly partnered Don Sullivan in the Ozark Boys and was involved with hillbilly music until the '50s, but his career was cut short by blindness. Swanson, however, followed a winding and eventful trail through the music business of the '40s and '50s. He wrote songs for other artists, such as the wartime composition "The K. P. Blues," recorded by Wilf Carter. (K. P. meant Kitchen Police, an unloved chore in the armed services.) He treated the world to the lugubrious homily "Marijuana, the Devil's Flower." There were records with his Swedish-born wife Berget as "Jane & Carl, The Sunshine Pals." But he was best known as the disc jockey "Mr. Sunshine" on WRUN, Utica–Rome, a popular station in the Central New York area, owned by Dick Clark's father. He also ran a record store in Utica, celebrating its opening day by giving away a hundred copies of a Sun record by a young singer he liked, Elvis Presley.

One of his triumphs as a disc jockey, he liked to recall, was to spot, while on vacation in Europe, the French song "Le Trois Cloches" by Les Compagnons de la Chanson, and bring the disc back to play on his two daily shows. Thanks to his plugging, the industry took notice and an English translation, "The Three Bells," was a hit for the country group The Browns.

By the end of the '50s, Swanson was a little frustrated. His act with his wife had been put on permanent hold while she raised their four daughters, so he began to develop a business of supplying promotional gifts for banks and other companies. Then in 1977, his enthusiasm for music refreshed, he put out an album of mandolin tunes, *Mandolino-Texas Country*. Disc jockey response was so favorable that he decided to move to Nashville, settling in the suburb of Hendersonville. The album got some airplay, and he was invited to appear on Ernest Tubb's Record Shop's Midnight Jamboree, where he had the enormous satisfaction of playing "San Antonio Rose" and "The Tennessee Waltz" with Roy Acuff and the Smoky Mountain Boys: a reward for his long, loyal love affair with the music he first heard, all those years before, as a Norwegian boy in a New York apartment.

Bridge: Western Swing and Honkytonk

Around the middle point of the 1930s and the deepest of the Depression, a new music came swaggering out of the Southwest, brash and full of itself and spoiling for a fight. It was country, but not as The Carter Family knew it. There were fiddles and guitars, but the fiddles swerved through the tunes like drunken drivers, with little respect for the melody, and the guitars were hooked up to AMPLIFIERS, or rather AMpliFIerS—the equipment was erratic in those days—and on top of that brouhaha were instruments seldom heard in this context, clarinets and saxophones, bleating and blaring and generally making a whoopee alien to the Calvinists of Clinch Mountain.

We call it Western Swing, but no one did at the time. For the musicians it was what you played for people who wanted to have a good time, and there was no need to give it a name. The record companies, committed to the filing system of "mountaineer's song" and "descriptive novelty" and so forth, labeled it "hot dance," the same description they used for, say, Clarence Williams' Washboard Band, whom we'd now call a jazz group. Fair enough: a kind of hillbilly jazz is what much of it was, its key players ardent fans of Benny Goodman and Count Basie, Cab Calloway and Fats Waller. The fiddlers cocked their ears to Joe Venuti and Stuff Smith and the singers to Bing Crosby and Jack Teagarden, but the steel guitarists listened only to their inner jazzmen, for no one had developed a style on their instrument in earlier jazz, unless you counted the Hawaiian hot men like Sol Hoopii, and so they made it up as they went along.

Mesmerizing in the dance hall, hot dance music was no less exciting when it issued from a radio in a farm parlor, and for several years bands like Bob Wills' Texas Playboys and the Light Crust Doughboys, sponsored alike by flour companies, radiated throughout Texas and Oklahoma. But as the winds stripped the prairies, many of their listeners deserted their dried-up farms to go west. Many more followed when the United States entered the war and created thousands of jobs in the munitions factories and shipyards of southern California. With them went the bands, stuffing their ranks with extra musicians, turning themselves into Western equivalents of the Tommy Dorsey or Glenn Miller orchestras, as they played virtually round the clock in the vast ballrooms of suburban Los Angeles. This is when the term "Western Swing" begins to appear, attached first to the stage-filling sweeping-strings ensemble of Spade Cooley.

Back in the Southwest, the musicians who had stayed behind played in smaller groups, elaborating an elegant chamber version of Western Swing—still excellent music for radio set or nightclub, but also adeptly doubling as the typical accompaniment for a new breed of vocalists dispensing worldly wisdom and tales of all too human frailty. The honkytonk singers put fresh colors on country music's palette: the chill blue of loss, the dull grey of loneliness, the fiery red of illicit passion. In their songs of slipping around and walking the floor, men like Ernest Tubb, Floyd Tillman, and Rex Griffin prepared the ground and planted the seeds for the harvest soon to be reaped by Hank Williams.

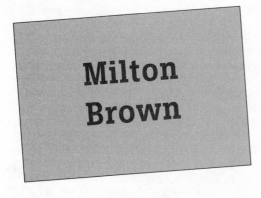

Milton Brown

(1903–36)

Bob Wills called Milton Brown "the greatest singer for Western bands that ever was." Having made a reputation and a fortune out of the music, Wills could afford to be generous, at least about Brown's singing. Would he have been so quick to praise him as a bandleader?

In the mid-1930s, when both men were rising fast on the southwestern music scene, it seemed to many people that Brown and his Brownies might have more potential than Wills' Texas Playboys. Even men who worked for Wills

thought well of their rival. "Milton had a fine band—oh, gosh, man, great," said Playboy guitarist Eldon Shamblin. "If he hadn't got killed, he'd probably really have been somethin' else."

Brown was involved in a car wreck, on the way home from a nightclub, on an April night in 1936, and died in the hospital five days later. At the time Wills's recording career was just getting under way, but Brown already had two dozen discs on the market and had recently returned from a mammoth session in New Orleans where the Brownies cut forty-nine sides in three days. What's more, the Brownies were widely considered a hotter and more cohesive band than the Playboys. If anyone had been taking bets on Western Swing's first star, the smart money might well have been on Milton Brown.

He grew up in Stephenville, Texas, and, from his mid-teens, in Fort Worth. In his twenties he worked as a cigar salesman. Cheery and outgoing, he began singing around Fort Worth, and in 1930 joined W. Lee O'Daniel's Light Crust Doughboys. His two-year stay in the band was commemorated by a 1932 disc of "Sunbonnet Sue" and "Nancy Jane," credited to the Fort Worth Doughboys, the lineup consist-

The Fort Worth Doughboys, c. 1932: Sleepy Johnson, Bob Wills, Milton Brown, W. Lee O'Daniel. (Author's collection)

The Musical Brownies, c. 1936. Left to right: Wanna Coffman, Cecil Brower, Bob Dunn, Cliff Bruner, Milton Brown, Ocie Stockard, Derwood Brown. (Author's collection)

ing of Brown, Wills, and guitarists Derwood Brown (Milton's younger brother) and "Sleepy" Johnson.

Wills broke away from the sponsor the following year, but Brown had already left to form the first Brownies with Derwood on guitar, fiddler Cecil Brower, pianist Fred "Papa" Calhoun, banjoist Ocie Stockard, and Wanna Coffman on bass. By 1935, when he started recording for Decca, he had added the restlessly inventive Bob Dunn, first wizard of the amplified steel guitar, and in 1936 the young Cliff Bruner was hired as a second fiddler.

In an avalanche of records, the Brownies established themselves as the leading hot dance band in Texas. Brown's warm voice could take on with equal success a Bing Crosby–styled pop number like "Avalon," a Cab Calloway shout song like "Chinatown My Chinatown," the sentimental waltz "My Precious Sonny Boy," and a raunchy "Texas Hambone Blues." Meanwhile the Brownies created instant swing with their two hot fiddlers, the amazing Dunn, and a just-won't-quit rhythm section. What it must have been like to hear them over the air from WBAP in Fort Worth, or out at the Crystal Springs dance pavilion! If Wills had been listening in, he might have quaked in his boots.

Someone who *was* listening in was the young Johnny Bond. "When I was still in High School in Marietta, Oklahoma, 100 miles North of Fort Worth," he recalled in a letter to the writer, "I used to miss my lunch hour just to sit by a radio to tune in Milton Brown."

But Milton's death changed the course of Western Swing history. Derwood held the

band together for a while and they made a few more records, but the spark had gone. For the time being—though he would meet some challenges when he moved to the West Coast—Bob Wills could hog the swing highway, confident that no one was likely to run him off the road.

Playlist

• *Western Swing Chronicles Vol. 1—Milton Brown and His Musical Brownies* (Origin OJL-1000)
• *Milton Brown & His Musical Brownies* (Proper PROPERBOX 59 4CD)
• *The Complete Recordings of the Father of Western Swing 1932–1937* (Texas Rose TXRCD 1 5CD)
•• *When the Sun Goes Down Vol. 1: Walk Right In* (Bluebird 63986): "Garbage Man Blues" •• *Country* (Frémeaux FA 015 2CD): "The Hesitation Blues" •• *Western Swing: Texas 1928–1944* (Frémeaux FA 032 2CD): "I'll Be Glad When You're Dead You Rascal You," "Louise Louise Blues," "Talking about You" •• *Hillbilly Blues 1928–1946* (Frémeaux FA 065 2CD): "Somebody's Been Using That Thing," "Texas Hambone Blues" •• *Country Boogie 1939–1947* (Frémeaux FA 160 2CD): "Taking Off" •• *Western Swing: Hot Hillbilly Jazz & Blues* (Living Era CD AJA 5214): "Chinatown My Chinatown," "Yes Sir!" •• *Doughboys, Playboys and Cowboys* (Proper PROPERBOX 6 4CD): "Bring It On Down to My House Honey," "Brownie's Stomp," "Confessin' (That I Love You)," "Down by the O-H-I-O," "The Eyes of Texas," "My Galveston Gal," "Nancy Jane" (Fort Worth Doughboys), "Oh You Pretty Woman!," "Sunbonnet Sue" (Fort Worth Doughboys), "Who's Sorry Now," "The Yellow Rose of Texas"

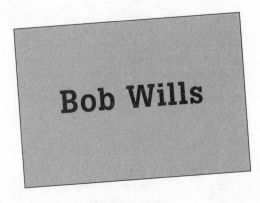

Bob Wills

(1905–75)

If Milton Brown's music was cheerful, Bob Wills's was jubilant. As delivered by his singer Tommy Duncan, a Cowtown Crosby, even the blues was bathed in sunlight. No music from the 1930s is so determined to weather the Depression with head held high, its optimistic smile broadened by youthful high spirits and Texan expansiveness. Consider Wills's best-known number: the words tell a wistful tale of lost love, but when the band addresses it, "New San Antonio Rose" is all buoyancy, a flower not drooping but bright with color.

Wills and his Texas Playboys had been on the road for some six years before they achieved the suave ensemble work of 1940's "Rose" and established themselves as the premier big band in Western music. "Big" is the keyword. There were plenty of Texas groups with seven or eight musicians playing hot dance music, but the Playboys in their glory days were a double-figured aggregation, an *orchestra*, with the moxie to go up against major league big bands like Tommy Dorsey's or Benny Goodman's, play the same venues and pull bigger crowds, without compromising the country dance character of their music. It might sometimes be corn, but, aside from a few clunkers of the "Waltz You Saved for Me" stripe, it was at least hot corn.

The Wills pot was continuously on the boil during the '40s, when the Playboys were based in California, first playing on Foreman Phillips's dance halls round Los Angeles, later at clubs and auditoriums up and down the coast, as well

BOB WILLS AND HIS TEXAS PLAYBOYS go to town!

Theater lobby card for *Rhythm Round-Up* (1945). (Author's collection)

The Texas Playboys at the Trianon Ballroom, Oklahoma City, c. 1950. Left to right: Eldon Shamblin, Everett Stover, Bob White, Tiny Moore, Carl Gadel (driver), Jimmy Widener, Bob Wills, Billy Jack Wills, Johnny Gimble, unknown, Keith Coleman, Luke Wills, Mancel Tierney, Herb Remington, "Poppa" John Wills. (Author's collection)

as making movies, and cutting transcriptions for the Tiffany organization. Those relaxed, happy recordings showcase some of Wills's finest lineups, with men like the bluesy electric guitarist Lester "Junior" Barnard, electric mandolinist Tiny Moore, and hot fiddler Joe Holley. When they play out-and-out jazz—tunes like "Crazy Rhythm" or "Take the 'A' Train"—they can match any of their contemporaries. But among those finished performances are wonderfully impromptu tracks like "Frankie Jean," where Duncan and Barnard remember an old record by the blues singer Memphis Minnie.

The vein of blues runs deep in Western Swing. Eldon Shamblin, who had two long spells as guitarist in the Playboys, observed: "You take these old blues which so many of these songs are made up of—tunes that Bob done like "Corrine Corrina"—and you throw a good rhythm section behind those things, and

a vocal, and, man, you got all kinds of inspiration." The Playboys' first recording, "Osage Stomp" in 1935, was learned from the Memphis Jug Band, and 1936's "Swing Blues #1" took some of its lyrics from Blind Lemon Jefferson. The chart for the swing instrumental "Big Beaver" was based on Wills's recollection of a tune he heard in his rural Texas youth, which "[the] colored people always sang as they was goin' to the cottonfield." "Bob liked colored people real well," said Shamblin. "He liked their singing and he liked everything they done."

Wills and his legacy have considerable admirers: Merle Haggard, Willie Nelson, Waylon Jennings—broad-shouldered friends, who sometimes edge facts out of the way. Haggard titled his album of Wills songs *A Tribute to the Best Damn Fiddle Player in the World*. He should have known better. Beside fiddlers like

Louis Tierney, Joe Holley, or Jesse Ashlock—and that's looking no farther than the Playboys—Wills was merely average: competent with a hoedown, ready enough with the broad gestures of the blues, but with no great facility as an improviser, none of the racy virtuosity of a Cliff Bruner or a J. R. Chatwell. Haggard is surely enough of a musician to recognize that, and even if he weren't, he has had men in his organization who knew the score, ex-Playboys like Shamblin or fiddler Johnny Gimble. Call Bob Wills the best damn *bandleader*, if you like. As his brother Johnnie Lee said, "He had some kind of something that when he walked on the bandstand he got more attention than the band. It was a different band, nearly, when he walked up."

Some of that was due to apprehension. Wills expected every man on the stand to keep his eyes on him, ready to take a solo at a wave of the hand or a sideways glance. "He might give you a chorus on anything," remembered Shamblin. "Even a waltz! . . . He'd just say, 'Get it.' . . . We never wrote out solos for nobody. We wrote out the ensemble stuff, and the choruses was every man for himself. Nothing cut and dried, because the old man didn't like it that way."

"After the war," Shamblin recalled sadly, "you never did have the big band like we had before." There were exceptions—in Oklahoma City, around 1950, it went up to thirteen—but mostly Wills headed an eight- or nine-piece group, which inevitably lacked the oomph, the sheer wide-screen blare of the great days. As the rooms became smaller, the audiences older, the tempos slower, and the leader's drinking more of a problem, it was past reputation rather than present achievement that kept the Texas Playboys in business. Wills finally shut up shop in 1964, but artistically his shelves had been empty for years.

There is a more poignant ending to the story. In December 1973, Haggard gathered former Playboys like Shamblin, Gimble, and steel guitarist Leon McAuliffe to join their old boss in a "Homecoming" session. For a while Wills was able to play his part, then he had a stroke, from which he never regained consciousness. The musicians completed the album imagining him still among them, still fiddling and singing as of old, still unleashing his famous holler, "aaa-haa!"

Playlist
• *San Antonio Rose* (Bear Family BCD 15933 11CD+DVD) [complete recordings, 1932–47]
• *Legends of Country Music* (Columbia 93858 4CD)
• *Rare California Airshots 1945–1946* (Country Routes RFD CD 24) [dim but atmospheric]
• *The King of Western Swing* (Living Era CD AJA 55250)
• *Boot Heel Drag* (Mercury 170 206 2CD) [complete MGM recordings]
• *Take Me Back to Tulsa* (Proper PROPER-BOX 32 4CD) [1932–50 recordings]
• *Anthology 1935–73* (Rhino 70744 2CD) [spans his entire recording career]
At the time of writing, most of the CDs that once documented the '40s Tiffany transcriptions had been deleted, but if you find any of that material on Rhino, Kaleidoscope, or Edsel, grab it.

The Light Crust Doughboys

Seventy years ago, Texans by the thousand would turn on their radios every weekday at 12.30 P.M. for a program of music and fun by the Light Crust Doughboys, sponsored, as the band's announcer, Parker Willson, would unfailingly mention, "by the Burrus Mill & Elevator Company of Fort Worth, millers of Light Crust flour." The program was carried by the major stations in Fort Worth, Dallas, Houston, and San Antonio. After Bob Wills there was no more popular swing band in the Lone Star State.

They made almost as many records as Wills, too, yet by comparison with him or the much less prolific Milton Brown, the Doughboys have been ungenerously treated by West-

The Light Crust Doughboys, February 1934. Left to right: (standing) Ramon DeArman, Leon Huff, W. Lee O'Daniel, Clifford Gross, Herman Arnspiger; (seated) Leon McAuliffe, Sleepy Johnson. (OTM collection)

ern Swing's reissuers and historians. You might say they were too versatile for their own good. Fiddlers Cecil Brower and Kenneth "Abner" Pitts, lead guitarist Muryel "Zeke" Campbell, and pianist John "Knocky" Parker were hot players by instinct, and on numbers like "Blue Guitars" or "Knocky Knocky" they found an authentic hillbilly jazz groove, but between those performances they recorded a great deal of lightweight novelty material.

And why not? After all, one of their biggest hits was "Pussy, Pussy, Pussy," a novelty song ostensibly about a shrill-voiced woman (played by banjoist Marvin "Smokey" Montgomery) standing on her porch calling for her cat (played by guitarist and bassist Ramon DeArman). When it was let loose on the market in 1939 it sold in carloads, especially to jukebox suppliers. Actually "Pussy" had some hot playing, but there was less room for finger-busting solos in such Doughboy charts as "We Must Have Beer" or "Horsie, Keep Your Tail Up!"

Incidentally, the flipside of "Pussy" featured Knocky Parker playing "Gin Mill Blues." Jazz pianist Joe Sullivan was no doubt bemused to

earn more money from this recording of his composition than he did from his own. Speaking of earnings, the "Pussy" kitty received an unexpected donation in 1996 when the record was used on the soundtrack of the Demi Moore movie *Striptease*.

In later years Montgomery, who was credited with composing "Pussy," would play down the rowdy side of the Doughboys' repertoire. We let Bob Wills play the honkytonks and dance halls, he would say, and we concentrated on our radio shows, with a spot every day for an old hymn. Knocky Parker, however, remembered his Doughboy days rather differently, with regular gigs playing for dances in what he wryly called "sub-standard places."

There was another respect in which the Doughboys differed from the Wills and Brown outfits, and indeed most of the other Western Swing bands: they didn't give a lead role to an electric steel guitar. During their heyday in the middle and late '30s, in fact, they seldom hired a steel player at all, which you might think would have left them seeming just a little old-hat and out of touch.

Left to right: Muryel Campbell, Cecil Brower, Jim Boyd, Parker Willson, Kenneth Pitts, Ramon DeArman, Marvin Montgomery, John "Knocky" Parker. The back of this 1938/39 postcard noted that the Light Crust Doughboys could be heard at 12:30 pm, Monday through Friday, over WBAP (Ft Worth), WFAA (Dallas), KPRC (Houston), WOAI (San Antonio), KARK (Little Rock, Arkansas), and KELD (El Dorado, Arkansas). (Author's collection)

By Western Swing standards the Doughboys were an unusually settled organization—once they *did* settle down. The original lineup of 1932 included both Wills and Brown, but within three years each had left to pursue his own bandleading career, and the band's nominal leader, the businessman W. Lee O'Daniel, had fallen out with Burrus Mill. He went off to form another band, his Hillbilly Boys, taking the Doughboys' popular lead singer Leon Huff and leaving them with a couple of hot fiddlers, Cliff Gross and Kenneth Pitts, and not much else. O'Daniel later ran for the Texas governorship, using his band as a campaigning tool, and is the direct inspiration for the "Pappy O'Daniel" character in *O Brother, Where Art Thou?*

Fortunately the pool of musicians in the Dallas–Fort Worth area was seldom understocked, and the Doughboys quickly recruited Montgomery, who had arrived in town from Iowa with experience in vaudeville and medicine shows, singer/guitarist Dick Reinhart, and bassist Bert Dodson. Subsequent Doughboys lineups embraced Brower, Campbell, Parker, DeArman, and singer/guitarist Jim Boyd, brother of bandleader Bill.

They remained a popular radio and record act through the war years. *The Mountain Broadcast and Prairie Recorder* reported in November 1942 that the band had a new daily morning show on WBAP, Fort Worth, and other stations of the Texas Quality Network, but now as Parker Willson & The Coffee Grinders, because they were sponsored by the Duncan Coffee Company. In peacetime, with Burrus Mill renewing their support, a new Doughboys lineup was created, with Montgomery still occupying the banjo chair, and they continued to play, mostly around north Texas, for decades. On record they were less active: there were some sessions in the '50s for King, and a commemorative album or two in the '70s. In the '80s, after a few years' break, the band re-formed with Montgomery and bassist Art Greenhaw as co-leaders. In 1995 they were named official musical ambassadors for Texas, and they subsequently received several Grammy nominations, including one in 2000 for a gospel collaboration with James Blackwood and The Jordanaires. Montgomery died that year, last of the original flour power band.

Playlist

• *Guitar Jump 1947–48* (BACM CD D 094)
•• *Western Swing: Texas 1928–1944* (Frémeaux FA 032 2CD): "Blue Guitars," "Just Once Too Often," "Pussy, Pussy, Pussy" •• *Western Cowboy Ballads & Songs 1925–1939* (Frémeaux FA 034 2CD): "Oh! Suzannah!" •• *Nite Spot Blues* (Krazy Kat KK CD 20): "Bugle Call Rag," "Sluefoot on the Levee," "Tea for Two" •• *Western Swing: Hot Hillbilly Jazz & Blues* (Living Era CD AJA 5214): "Blue Guitars," "Knocky Knocky," "Mama Won't Let Me" •• *Doughboys, Playboys and Cowboys* (Proper PROPERBOX 6 4CD): "Blue Guitars," "Good Gracious Gracie," "Just Once Too Often," "Let's Make Believe We're Sweethearts," "Mean Mean Mama (From Mena)," "Pussy, Pussy, Pussy"

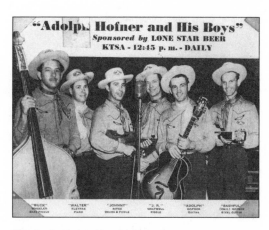

(Kevin Coffey collection)

Adolph Hofner

(1916–2000)

Shiner. Schulenberg. New Braunfels. You hardly expect to hear country music in towns with names like these. Lying on either side of old Highway 90 (now I-10) between Houston and San Antonio, these are strongholds of polka music. More than a century has passed since their foreparents left Bohemia, Moravia, or Czechoslovakia for the baking flatlands of south Texas, yet here people still play waltzes and polkas and sing in the Old World tongues.

But there is a country music connection, for all that. Between Shiner and the interstate lies the small town of Moulton, birthplace of a man who would weave a new pattern with the strands of polka music and Western Swing.

Adolph Hofner was born into a Czech-German family and grew up speaking Czech.

The first music he remembered hearing was by local Czech orchestras such as the Baca family band, and discs of Al Jolson or Hawaiian groups. By the time they were in their teens, he and his brother Emil, two years younger, were playing Hawaiian music themselves, Emil on steel, Adolph on standard guitar. The family had moved to San Antonio in '26, and The Hawaiian Serenaders, as the brothers called themselves, managed to pick up forty or fifty cents a night playing in the city's clubs. "We didn't know but ten, fifteen, maybe twenty songs, you know," Adolph told me. "So we played them over and over."

They were still teenagers when the hot sun of Western Swing rose in the southwestern sky. Adolph, whose ambition was to become a singer, was particularly taken with Milton Brown & His Brownies. "Now that's what sold me on Western music," he remembered. "Because *they had a band*." He didn't think Bob Wills's first records sounded as smooth as Brown's, and he didn't care much for Tommy Duncan's singing, but he loved Brown's. "I even changed my style of singing to try to sound like Milton."

He joined Jimmie Revard's Oklahoma Playboys as a singer and rhythm guitarist and made his recording debut with them in October 1936. He would continue to show up for Revard's sessions, Emil alongside him, for the next four years, but in 1938 he was offered his own contract with Bluebird Records and cut a couple of dozen sides. Also in '38 he sang on some Bluebird discs with Tom Dickey's Show Boys, one of them a cover version of Jimmie Davis's hit "It Makes No Difference Now," which Bluebird's distributors placed in almost every jukebox in south Texas. Eli Oberstein, Bluebird's recording manager, was convinced that Adolph could succeed as a mainstream country-pop singer. "He was going to make another Bing Crosby out of me," Hofner remembered with a grin.

He had kept his day job as a mechanic, and it wasn't until 1939 that he formed a full-time band. "I got a royalty check of $101 and bought a PA. After Leming [a few miles south of San Antonio] there's a barbecue place with a tree in front. That's where we played our first job, on May 13, 1939." Bookings came more profusely after his regional hit with the South American waltz song "Maria Elena." (Revived by a guitar group, Los Indios Tabajaros, the tune was an international best seller in the '60s.) In 1941 he signed with OKeh, who promoted him as the "husky, he-man leader of one of the West's outstanding string bands" and featured him as guest reviewer of their August releases of "country dance and folk song" (as they then labeled their country product). In the war years, billed as Dolph Hofner & His San Antonians, he worked for the promoter Foreman Phillips's chain of dance halls around Los Angeles, playing for huge crowds of workers from the shipyards and munitions factories. He was now in the same league, as well as on the same label, as Spade Cooley and Bob Wills, but although he recorded some strong sellers like "Alamo Rag," "Cotton-Eyed Joe," and "Jessie Polka," his contract was not renewed and he returned home to San Antonio.

Adolph had never broken his bonds with the music of his youth. In the middle of their sessions of country and swing tunes he and Emil would occasionally sing a Czech waltz or polka, and throughout the late '40s and '50s, when there was something of a polka craze, they played a lot of that music, and recorded it, too, for their new label Imperial—tunes like "Blue Bonnet Polka," "Alamo Schottische," and the ever-popular "Shiner Song," better known to many of Hofner's Czech-American listeners as "Farewell to Prague."

Around 1950 Adolph won the sponsorship of Pearl Beer, and for the next thirty-odd years his Pearl Wranglers were a fixture on the San Antonio music scene, broadcasting on KTSA and putting out singles on the Sarg label which cumulatively amount to a glossary of Texas music: waltzes and hoedowns, regional standards and rockabilly—everything from "Milk Cow Blues" to the "Dude Ranch Schottische." The Sarg connection also gave Adolph the opportunity to promote a teenaged Doug Sahm. Meanwhile the Pearl Wranglers served their polka-country-swing mix at the Farmer's Daughter dance hall, where they were filmed in the mid-'80s for the British Channel 4 series

The A to Z of C&W. Adolph continued to play until incapacitated by a stroke in 1993.

Playlist
• *South Texas Swing* (Arhoolie/Folklyric CD 7029)
•• *Country* (Frémeaux FA 015 2CD): "Alamo Rag" •• *Western Swing: Texas 1928–1944* (Frémeaux FA 032 2CD): "Brown Eyed Sweet" •• *Hillbilly Blues 1928–1946* (Frémeaux FA 065 2CD): "I'll Keep My Old Guitar" •• *Doughboys, Playboys and Cowboys* (Proper PROPERBOX 6 4CD): "Better Quit It Now," "Cotton Eyed Joe," "I'll Keep My Old Guitar"

Cliff Bruner

(1915–2000)

The Western Swing players of the 1930s were the young guns of country music, and few were younger, or sharper-shooting, than Cliff Bruner. When he joined Milton Brown's Brownies in the summer of 1935 he was just a few months past his twentieth birthday—"a little bitty skinny thing," as his pal Leo Raley described him—but already he was building a reputation for inventive, unpredictable fiddle-playing.

How he came by that skill is something of a mystery. Other swing fiddlers of his generation, such as J. R. Chatwell or Buddy Ray, listened to records and broadcasts by jazz violinists like Joe Venuti or Stuff Smith. Cliff must have been aware of that kind of playing, but coming from a family of poor folks, often on the move in search of work, he didn't have the means or the leisure to spend hours listening to the radio or records.

Left to right: Leo Raley, Hezzie Bryant, Dickie McBride, A. B. Carroll (announcer), Cliff Bruner, Randall Raley, Moon Mullican, Joe Thames. (OTM collection)

By his mid-teens he was on the road as a semi-professional musician, playing for small-town farmers in south Texas, even working with Raley and other young hopefuls on a trav-eling medicine show. Yet despite this rustic apprenticeship he was able to add a vivacious swing accent to the Brownies' already excit-ing ensemble, and the almost fifty sides he

At Jack Dempsey's Broadway Bar & Cocktail Lounge, Broadway near 49th, New York City, c. 1944. Left to right: Link Davis, Moon Mullican, Harris Dodd, Cliff Bruner. (Author's collection)

recorded with the group at a three-day session in March 1936 are among the glories of early Western Swing.

The history of this music would assuredly have been very different had Milton Brown continued to vie with his then Oklahoma-based rival Bob Wills, but Brown's early death broke up the Brownies and dispersed his musical legacy. Bruner, for his part, moved to the Texas Gulf Coast, securing a radio show on Beaumont's KFDM and maintaining a relationship with Brown's record label, Decca. At his first session for them in February 1937 he led a lineup of his Texas Wanderers that included Leo Raley on amplified mandolin, former Brownie Fred "Papa" Calhoun on piano, and Dickie McBride as primary singer. Recordings like "Milk Cow Blues," "Shine," and "Oh You Pretty Woman" were attractive and seem to have sold well, but there was better to come—and hits, too, with the first recordings of Floyd Tillman's "It Makes No Difference Now" and Ted Daffan's "Truck Driver's Blues."

As Wills' Texas Playboys gradually created a big-band sound, some of the Texas groups opted for more of a "chamber jazz" approach, with fiddle, steel guitar, and piano taking their solos in turn over an understated rhythm. Bruner's September 1938 sides, featuring him with Raley, pianist and singer Moon Mullican, and the incomparable Bob Dunn, another former Brownie, on amplified steel guitar, are virtuoso examples of small-group hot music. Dunn's solo on "When You're Smiling" is imaginative jazz improvisation of the first order.

When I first reissued that recording in the '70s, on the compilation *Beer Parlor Jive*, the LP somehow made its way to a record store in Houston and came to Bruner's notice. He wrote to say how pleased he was, and mentioned that at the age of sixty, though his day job was selling insurance, he was still playing a couple of times a week, and still leading a group called the Texas Wanderers ("the most versatile band in Houston," said his business card).

Not long afterward he retired—from insurance—and made himself more available for musical work. Over the next decade or so he cut a few albums, including one with a long-time fan, the Texas swing fiddler and Nashville studio musician Johnny Gimble. His earlier recordings continued to trickle out on LP and CD, culminating in 1997 in Bear Family's boxed set, which emphasized in the clearest possible terms what former colleagues had long been saying about Cliff Bruner to anyone who would listen: that he was one of a handful of musicians who defined the original sound of Western Swing in all its zingy, unpredictable verve.

It was gratifying, too, that such a tribute appeared while its subject was still around to enjoy it. Bruner played less in his later years but was honored by Texas musical organizations, participated in Western Swing reunions, and appeared in a film or two. As one of the Western Swing enthusiasts whom Cliff and his wife Ruth hospitably entertained, I remember how much he liked to recall those wild early years of the music—and how diffident he was about claiming his rightful place in that story.

Playlist

• *Cliff Bruner and His Texas Wanderers* (Bear Family BCD 15932 5CD) [includes all Bruner's Decca sides from the '30s and '40s and his later recordings for the Houston label Ayo and other marques; co-produced and superbly annotated by Western Swing historian Kevin Coffey]
•• *Western Swing: Texas 1928–1944* (Frémeaux FA 032 2CD): "Draft Board Blues," "Milk Cow Blues," "Truck Driver's Blues" •• *Country Boogie 1939–1947* (Frémeaux FA 160 2CD): "Too Wet to Plow" •• *Western Swing and Country Jazz* (JSP JSP 7742 4CD): "Bring It On Home to Grandma," "I Wish I Could Shimmy like My Sister Kate," "Old Joe Turner Blues" •• *Western Swing: Hot Hillbilly Jazz & Blues* (Living Era CD AJA 5214): "I Wish I Could Shimmy like My Sister Kate," "When You're Smiling" •• *Doughboys, Playboys and Cowboys* (Proper PROPERBOX 6 4CD): "Corrine Corrina," "Draft Board Blues," "Kangaroo Blues," "One Sweet Letter from You," "San Antonio Rose," "That's What I Like about the South," "Truck Driver's Blues"

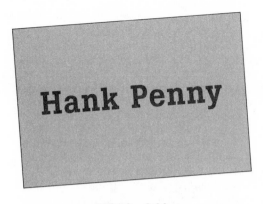

Hank Penny

(1918–92)

Thinking about Hank Penny, one is irresistibly reminded of the career of a near contemporary, the jazz clarinetist Artie Shaw. Both led successful bands in the Swing Era. Both were witty and articulate men. And both left a line of ex-wives on Alimony Alley.

Of course, Penny's swing was a different concoction from Shaw's. Though not from Texas—he was born in Birmingham, Alabama—he was an early fan of the Texas swing bands of the 1930s, especially Milton Brown's, and by 1937 he was singing and playing rhythm guitar in a swing combo of his own, the Radio Cowboys, on the WSB Atlanta show Crossroads Follies. Between 1938 and

(Author's collection)

1941 different lineups of this group recorded some fifty sides for the Vocalion and OKeh labels.

By 1944 Penny was MCing the Boone County Jamboree on WLW in Cincinnati, and was among the first hillbilly signings to King Records. But where it was happening for Western Swing was California, and soon Penny moved out there to do session work. Within a couple of years he was living in Los Angeles and heading his California Cowhands at the Venice Ballroom, the Riverside Rancho, the Painted Post, and other dance venues. He would later join Spade Cooley, the "King of Western Swing," as a comedian, and diversify into club ownership, creating the Palomino in North Hollywood.

Penny's entry in *The Encyclopedia of Country Music* devotes twenty-odd lines to his prewar bands and merely notes that he later "began recording for the King label." This is topsy-turvy. Although Penny's own evaluation of his late '30s lineup was enthusiastic—"We swung like a garden gate, we were a real heavyweight group"—he was unsatisfied with their recordings, and it's true they lack the vigor or character of the King sides, which feature up to a dozen musicians, among them steel guitarists of the caliber of Noel Boggs, Herb Remington, and Speedy West, playing a kind of big-band Western Swing not much less powerful than Cooley's. Their more than seventy recordings for King included hits like "Steel Guitar Stomp," "Steel Guitar Polka," "Won't You Ride in My Little Red Wagon," and "Bloodshot Eyes." The last two, Penny's own compositions, have often been recorded by other artists; "Bloodshot Eyes" was a huge success for the rhythm and blues singer Wynonie Harris. Tracks from the last two King dates in 1949–50 like "Jersey Bounce," "Tuxedo Junction," and the extraordinary "Hillbilly Bebop" are classics of the period.

The relationship between Penny and King's boss Syd Nathan—two men with clear, but different, ideas about how things should be done—was turbulent.

Syd was a gruff, overbearing type of individual who learned to whisper in a sawmill. . . . He always wanted to be involved in everything that was taking place. I vividly remember one session where he kept coming into the studio from the control booth, telling my people how he thought the tune should be played. Finally, I cornered Syd and told him to keep out of the studio. . . . After the session

I was so mad that I just threw my guitar in the case and stormed out of the studio. Later Syd came up to me and said, "Damn, Hank, I just love it when you get mad."

Nathan commemorated the occasion by titling one of the troublesome tunes "Penny Blows His Top."

It was not the first time the impulsive and quick-tempered Penny had tangled with an employer. The previous year, 1945, while playing at the Venice Ballroom, he had fallen out with the promoter Foreman Phillips.

[He] couldn't tolerate the free spirit of our music and he told me that I had to fire Noel Boggs, [guitarist] Jimmy Wyble, and [fiddler] Harold Hensley because they were, in effect, too good. They wouldn't stick to the melody, and Phillips hated instrumental breaks of any kind. . . . We told him we could not accept his decision, and walked out.

Between 1950 and 1952 Penny was signed to RCA Victor, producing entertaining sides

Playlist
• *The Standard Transcriptions* (Bloodshot 806)
• *Hollywood Western Swing: The Best of Hank Penny 1944–1947* (Krazy Kat KK CD 25) [King recordings]
• *Hillbilly Be-Bop: The King Anthology 1944–1950* (Westside WESA 914) [King recordings]
•• *Hillbilly Honeymoon* (Acrobat ACMCD 4015): "White Shotguns" •• *Sunshine State Swing: Western Swing on Los Angeles Radio 1944–1949* (Country Routes RFD CD 22): "Still Water Runs the Deepest," "We Met Too Late" •• *Solid South: Western Swing on Los Angeles Radio in the 1950s* (Country Routes RFD CD 25): "Big-Footed Sam," "Farewell Blues/I'm Moving On," "Flamin' Mamie," "Ship of Broken Dreams," "Tater Pie," "Taxes, Taxes," "Waiting Just for You," "Won't You Ride in My Little Red Wagon/Steel Guitar Rag" •• *Western Swing: Texas 1928–1944* (Frémeaux FA 032 2CD): "Chill Tonic" •• *Guitare Country 1926–1950* (Frémeaux FA 5007 2CD): "Hillbilly Jump" •• *Doughboys, Playboys and Cowboys* (Proper PROPER-BOX 6 4CD): "Cowboy's Swing," "Mississippi Muddle," "Steel Guitar Stomp," "Tobacco State Swing," "Wildcat Mama"

like "Taxes, Taxes," and in 1954–57 he was on Decca, with featured singer Sue Thompson, one of the five women who married him. But probably the best representation of Penny-style Western Swing was on some radio transcriptions he recorded for Standard in 1951, among them the immortal title "Progressive Country Music for a Hollywood Flapper."

Penny spent much of the '60s in Las Vegas, doing more stand-up comedy than singing, and was subsequently a DJ and occasional movie actor. He was pleased by the revival of interest in Western Swing in the '70s and talked about it volubly and informatively to researchers, but his plan to get another band together was never realized.

Bob Skyles & His Skyrockets

If you throw the name of Bob Skyles & His Skyrockets into a discussion between fans of old-time music, stand well back. Something about this amiable bunch of Texas plainsmen brews a storm in that normally placid teacup. There is a record collector in Florida who loves the band so much that he has created a decorative web site for them, with old photographs and sound samples. But a well-known producer of country reissues, when approached to put out an album, listened to a few minutes of a sample tape, muttered something unprintable, and binned it.

Why? Pictures tell part of the story. The Skyrockets may have had a fiddle and a guitar or two, but their front line bulged with accordions, clarinets, even trumpets and trombones. Clearly this is no old-time string-band, but then, neither were most of the groups around Texas in the 1930s. The Skyrockets' problem is that they were not really a Western Swing band either. Instead of steel

Bob Skyles & His Skyrockets, 1936: Sanford, Bob, Clifford, and Doc Kendrick. (Kevin Coffey collection)

Bob Skyles & His Skyrockets, Tokio Club, Hobbs, New Mexico, 1938. Left to right: Sanford Kendrick, Dave Hughs, Clifford Kendrick, Bob Kendrick, Max Bennett, Frank Wilhelm. (Kevin Coffey collection)

guitars and swing fiddles they boasted ocarinas and cowbells. Their trademark was the bazooka, a sort of bass kazoo that sounds like someone mooing down a length of lead pipe.

The word to reach for here is "novelty." The Skyrockets were Texas's answer to the Hoosier Hot Shots, a Midwestern novelty band of the period that played Tin Pan Alley hillbilly numbers and deliberately cornball Dixieland jazz featuring washboards and motor horns, a kind of Three Stooges of country music. They were enormously popular on both radio and records, and in the annals of musical anarchy they occupy the chapter immediately before Spike Jones. Sharing the in-joke, the Skyrockets even made a record called "We're Not the Hoosier Hot Shots."

The bazooka, too, had a contemporary cultural reference. Middle America was already familiar with its whoopee-cushion effects, thanks to its use by the radio personality Bob Burns. Bob Skyles duly namechecked him, and his home town of Van Buren, Arkansas, on the band's first recording, "The Arkansas Bazooka Swing."

The Skyrockets originated in Brady, Texas, as a family band, led by guitarist "Doc" Kendrick and featuring his sons Clifford, Sanford, and, in particular, Bob, who played fiddle and clarinet and sang. In the mid-'30s they moved far down into southwest Texas to Pecos, where they broadcast on the local radio station and quickly came to the attention of Bluebird Records, which regularly visited Texas to record the hot new sounds of the Western Swing bands.

Persuaded to change their name to the snappier Skyles, the ex-Kendricks initiated a series of discs embodying what the Western Swing researcher and Skylesologist Kevin Coffey has well called "one of the oddest repertoires and approaches in prewar country music." Occasionally they tackled existing numbers, antiques like "Rubber Dolly" or "The Old Grey Goose," but mostly they devised their own material, strange little comic songs about "Rodeo Ann," "Hot Tamale Pete," and women built like great big fiddles, set to a sock-guitar shuffle rhythm with outbreaks of noise on slide-whistles, tubas, musical saws, anything they could lay their hands on that sounded . . . different.

"We thought all that stuff was terrible," drummer Cliff Kendrick told the Scots writer Duncan MacLean, another fan, who interviewed him for his book *Lone Star Swing*.

"Corny as hell. The record company, they wanted a comedy band, see, like the Hoosier Hot Shots. We hated it. But we went along with it—fooled around, played that stupid whoopie-whistle. Bob came up with all those dumb songs—we never played them in the clubs, you know; we played straight dance stuff, and jazz, then. But hell, who were we to complain? Those records sold well, earned us a bit of money. And that's what it was all about."

After a few years with Bluebird the band's star began to wane. They switched to Decca, made some much duller sides, then disappeared into California and broke up. Bob and Cliff died in the late '90s, but Sanford Kendrick lived long enough to see the Skyrockets' unique contribution to American music acknowledged, at last, on CD.

Playlist
- *Bob Skyles and His Skyrockets 1937–1940* (Krazy Kat KK CD 29)
- *Doughboys, Playboys and Cowboys* (Proper PROPERBOX 6): "Hot Tamale Pete"

The Swift Jewel Cowboys

Texas oil has given a smooth run to many careers in country music, but the kind that greased the wheels of the Swift Jewel Cowboys never gushed darkly out of Texas sand or Gulf seabed. The Cowboys ran on salad oil. Jewel Oil and Shortening gave them their homely name. They played at grocery stores and opened supermarkets. A Jewel packet-top was a free ticket to their show. Country music in cahoots with country business: one of the founding principles of the country music business.

The idea for the Swift Jewel Cowboys came to Frank Collins, manager of Swift's refinery in Houston, Texas, one spring day in 1933: he would create a hillbilly band to promote the company's products through broadcasts and personal appearances. The following year Collins and his invention were transferred to the Swift office in Memphis, and the SJC made their first broadcast, on WMC, on November 4, 1934. Within a couple of years their programs were going out on stations in Memphis, Little Rock, and Nashville, and for eight months in 1938 the CBS network aired them to over eighty affiliates. Meanwhile they were known throughout the Mid-South for their personal appearances, playing what their posters called "Old Time Entertainment including Tunes and Songs of Yesterday." Their records, when they finally made some in the summer of 1939, told a rather different story. They were hot hillbilly jazz—a kind of Western

Swing, except that they weren't operating in the West.

That wasn't the only difference. At first glance, fiddler "Jose Cortes" (Alfredo Casares), accordionist Kokomo Crocker, guitarist Slim Hall, and bassman Curly Noland look like a conventional core group, and the addition of reeds player Lefty Ingram and cornetist Pee Wee Wamble seems to ally them with contemporaries like Bob Wills. But there was no steel guitar, and the difference that made was crucial. The horns play a more upfront role than in the Texas Playboys, blending with fiddle and accordion, and on a few tunes harmonica, to create a sound unlike any in, or on the edge of, '30s country music. At times the color and texture of their arrangements are almost Ellingtonian. As Lefty Ingram explained it to me,

About the boys playing swing and light classics—Pee Wee and I had been brought up in that style of music long before the cowboy

The Swift Jewel Cowboys in the studios of WREC, Memphis, 1936/37. Left to right: Kokomo Crocker, "Jose Cortes," Wiley "Flash" Walker, Jim Sanders (MC), Lefty Ingram, Slim Hall, Curly Noland. (Author's collection)

(Author's collection)

career, and by using some of that class of music caused many people to listen to us that did not care for cowboy music.

The harmonica was played by Jimmy Riddle, then a young man, his long association with Roy Acuff still in the future. He wasn't a full-time Swift Jewel Cowboy but, since he could play several instruments, he often deputized for members when they took time off. He later played in a band directly descended from the SJC, the Crustene Ranch Gang, who were very hot around Houston during World War II; a fellow member was the mandolinist Tiny Moore. Another musician who had a spell in the SJC was the fiddler and singer Wiley Walker, who later formed a popular duet with Gene Sullivan and had the original hit recording of "Blue Eyes Crying in the Rain."

In addition to their indoor gigs in high schools or Safeway stores, the SJC were a draw at rodeos, horse shows, and state fairs, because as well as their musical skills they could also claim to be the "Only Mounted Cowboy Band in America," offering "Two Hours of Thrills and Spills" with their "Educated Horses." "I suppose I am responsible for [that] brainstorm," wrote Lefty Ingram.

All the boys, being of, or with, farm or ranch background, could pick and rope. The boys, at our own expense, bought nine or ten head of bronks. Only two had ever been saddled or handled in any way. We intended to live up to our *name*—so with the loss of a lot of skin

and eating lots of Tennessee soil, we broke and trained seven of the ten to do poses, trick ride, etc. . . . This all led to our booking with rodeos. We played a short musical program, did a few horse stunts and each of us rode a steer out of the bucking chute.

"Don't Fail to See the Famous Desert Scene, the Roman Races, Trick and Fancy Roping and Riding," bellowed their posters and flyers. Often an afternoon like that in the open air would be followed by an evening dance, perhaps on Main Street, perhaps in the American Legion Hall, where the SJC would "open the faucet on syncopation."

According to a press release of 1939 or 1940, the band's log for the year showed 765 engagements: more than 200 school dates, another couple of hundred outdoor events, seventy vaudeville shows, fifty-three dances, and miscellaneous appearances at fairs, trade days, hospital benefits, and other functions.

The rodeo connection is important in country music—artists like George Strait or Red Steagall made their name on that circuit—and the SJC should probably be credited as pioneers. But after only a few years they had to hang up their spurs, as the band was whittled down by military call-up, and by the time the war was over the members were scattered and country music was changing. Pee Wee Wamble, the last survivor, was still playing Dixieland jazz in Memphis in the '90s, but when he died in 2002 the Swift Jewel Cowboys were all gone.

Playlist

•• *Western Swing and Country Jazz* (JSP JSP 7742 4CD): "Bug Scuffle," "Chuck Wagon Swing," "Coney Island Washboard," "Dill Pickle Rag," "Fan It," "Little Willie Green (From New Orleans)," "Memphis Blues," "Memphis Oomph," "My Untrue Cowgirl," "Raggin' the Rails," "Rose Room (in Sunny Roseland)," "Swingin' at the Circle S," "Willie the Weeper," "You Gotta Ho-De-Ho (to Get Along with Me)" •• *Western Swing: Hot Hillbilly Jazz & Blues* (Living Era CD AJA 5214): "Bug Scuffle" •• *Hillbilly Blues* (Living Era CD AJA 5361): "Fan It" •• *Doughboys, Playboys and Cowboys* (Proper PROPERBOX 6 4CD): "My Untrue Cowgirl"

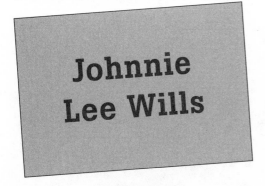

Johnnie Lee Wills

(1912–84)

Working in the same business as a more famous brother is not calculated to flatter the ego. But if you don't mind spending much of your time in his shadow, you may get to enjoy a little of the sun. That, at least, was the experience of Johnnie Lee Wills.

In his twenties he filled the role of tenor banjoist in his brother Bob's Texas Playboys. Tenor banjo is not a particularly demanding instrument, and an untalented or lazy man might have been content just to strum rhythm and have fun. But Johnnie Lee was unwilling to be a passenger, even on the fast-rolling gravy train that was Bob Wills's band, and when Bob suggested he form a group of his own, he took it on.

"Bob was getting his band bigger," he recalled, "and wasn't needing a banjo player, . . . and there was some other boys

there that we knew was good musicians. So he wanted to see what I thought of starting a little band, and I could play the places that he was missing."

So in 1940 Johnnie Lee put together a six-piece group featuring fiddler Cotton Thompson, pianist Millard Kelso, and electric guitarist Lester "Junior" Barnard, a musician way ahead of his time, as he demonstrated the following year when the band made their first recordings, as Johnny Lee Wills & His Boys, for Decca. Barnard was a natural blues player, as he proves in the elegant bent-note phrases he scatters throughout "Devil's Blues" and "Milk Cow Blues," while in the faster "Too Long" his solo explodes from the ensemble like a fat man leaping through a plate-glass window.

As so often, it was the unplanned song that took off. "When we got to 'Milk Cow Blues' this guy [the recording director, Dave Kapp] said, 'No, haven't you got another one?' and we just kept on that it was the best tune we had. He finally let us do it, but it was the last record he released [from the session]." (Actually it was the fourth of five releases.)

"Milk Cow Blues" was a jukebox smash, and something more. Most histories call it a remake of the song recorded in 1934 by the blues singer and guitarist Kokomo Arnold, but the Wills text has only a few lines in common with Arnold's and the melody is different. In fact it is this "Milk Cow Blues"—for which the credit should really go to Cotton Thompson, who sang on the record—rather than the blues original that has passed into southern tradition. It is surely the version Elvis Presley had in his mind when he recorded it one fateful day in Memphis, some thirteen years later.

During World War II Johnnie Lee looked after the Texas Playboys while Bob was in uniform. Afterward Bob stayed in California and Johnnie Lee held on to the Playboys' old gig in Tulsa, Oklahoma, broadcasting on KVOO and playing for dances at Cain's Ballroom. Photographs from the '40s and '50s often show him with a fiddle. "It was easier to hold than a banjo," he would say, chuckling. "I never was considered a fiddler. I could play lead with two other fiddles with me [to] play the harmony."

In 1949 he signed with Bullet, a newish independent label in Nashville, and immediately had a hit with "a crazy tune—back then they wanted crazy tunes—called 'Rag Mop,'" a bouncy medium-fast blues with Cooleyesque fiddle section work and a nonsense vocal. It

Johnny [*sic*] Lee Wills & His Boys, 1941: Junior Barnard, Luther Jay Wills, Harley Huggins, Johnnie Lee Wills, Cotton Thompson, Millard Kelso, Joe Holley. (OTM collection)

Johnnie Lee Wills at Cain's, Tulsa, Oklahoma, possibly late 1950s. (OTM collection)

would have been bigger, but the number was covered by better-known pop acts such as the Ames Brothers and the Jimmy Dorsey Orchestra, and the Wills record was sidelined. Johnnie Lee did have a regional hit in 1962, during the Twist craze, with a tune called "Blub Twist," featuring tenor saxophonist Glenn "Blub" Rhees. "I never did get any money out of it," Johnnie Lee remembered, "but it done good. Helped me across country as far as booking dances, raising my price a little."

He quit the business in 1964 and built a big Western-wear store in Tulsa, but the revival of interest in Western Swing during the '70s reseated him in the bandleading saddle. Several good veteran musicians had not been invited, or did not want, to play with the Original Texas Playboys unit that had been reassembled by Leon McAuliffe, so Johnnie Lee was able to form an excellent band of his own, which recorded *Reunion* (Flying Fish, 1978) and other albums.

Playlist

• *The Band's a-Rockin'* (Krazy Kat KK CD 18) [good collection of the Decca and Bullet material]
•• *Hillbilly Blues 1928–1946* (Frémeaux FA 065 2CD): "Milk Cow Blues" •• *Country Boogie 1939–1947* (Frémeaux FA 160 2CD): "Square Dance Boogie" •• *Country Music 1940–1948* (Frémeaux FA 173 2CD): "Lazy John" •• *Tennessee Saturday Night: The Rural Route to Rock 'n' Roll* (Jasmine JASMCD 3519): "Rag Mop" •• *Hillbilly Blues* (Living Era CD AJA 5361): "Milk Cow Blues"

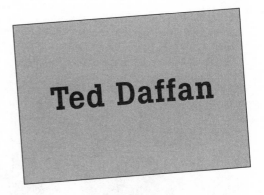

Ted Daffan

(1912–96)

Not everyone who makes it in country music starts out planning to. Take Ted Daffan. One day he would write and record one of the most famous of all honkytonk songs, but in the summer of 1932, a nineteen-year-old Houston high school graduate, all he was thinking about was the Hawaiian-style music he had seen a local boy play on steel guitar. He decided he was going to teach himself to play it too, with his fifty-cent instruction book and his five-dollar pawnshop guitar.

Within about a year he was playing with a Hawaiian group on Houston's KTRH. Not long afterward he joined Leon Selph's Blue Ridge Playboys, and then the Bar-X Cowboys. At that point he exchanged his acoustic steel for one of the new amplified models, a Volutone. He was listening keenly to the hot steelmen like Bob Dunn, who played with Milton Brown, and Bob Wills's Leon McAuliffe, but he didn't try to match their jazz inflections: "I stuck mostly to straight lead."

He was also trying his hand at song lyrics. By 1939–40 he was making records, first with Shelly Lee Alley, then with the Bar-X Cowboys, and, as he told Nick Tosches in 1975,

I knew that I had to write original songs . . . they weren't interested in hearing an unknown do some songs somebody else had already hit with. So I was searching frantically for a commercial idea. After dances we'd stop at these little roadside cafes for hamburgers or chili, and I noticed the truck drivers always stopping in these cafes, and it occurred to me that if someone wrote them a song, they would play it, even if it wasn't very good. And so I wrote the song "Truck Driver's Blues," 'em they loved it. In fact, I've had hundreds of 'em ask me, *tell* me that I must have been a truck driver. Of course, I never had.

TED DAFFAN

Ted is twenty-eight years old and has been a professional musician for the past eight years. During that time, he wrote songs as a hobby. It never occurred to him that they might be commercial, but about two and a half years ago a recording company used one of his songs and it was a big hit. On the strength of this, Ted received a contract to record his own songs with his own band and he has turned out one good song after the other. One of his latest and best "Worried Mind" is featured in this folio.

Ted Daffan's Texans, c. 1941. Left to right: Buddy Buller, Ralph C. Smith, Daffan, Chuck Keeshan, Harry Sorensen, Elmer B. Christian. (OTM collection)

He tried the song out on Decca's Dave Kapp, who didn't think much of it—until he heard how popular it was at dances, whereupon he told several of his contracted artists to try recording it. Cliff Bruner got there first, and had a hit. But not having the chance to record his own number was no setback for Daffan. Columbia's Art Satherley, impressed by the success of what may be the first country trucking song, signed him up and was immediately rewarded with solid sales for Daffan's compositions "Worried Mind" and "I'm a Fool to Care." As Daffan recalls in Dorothy Horstman's *Sing Your Heart Out, Country Boy*, he wrote "Fool to Care" with the Ink Spots in mind, and the bridge ("I know I should laugh/And call it a day . . .") was designed to be spoken by the group's bassman, Bill Kenny, but the Ink Spots' label wasn't interested. Songs like these, however, were mere *hors d'oeuvres* to the main dish that was to arrive on the turntable in 1943, the twin-peaked landmark in country music that was OKeh 6706, coupling "No Letter Today" and "Born to Lose."

"Where did 'Born to Lose' come from?" Tosches asked, doubtless echoing a thousand previous enquirers. "That one has to remain my secret," Daffan replied. Tosches persisted. "I heard that it came from an expression during a card game." Daffan was unmoved. "I can neither confirm nor deny it."

There are a few sidelights on Daffan's million-seller. It was cut in February 1942, but war business took over Columbia's pressing plants and it was more than a year before they could get around to manufacturing the record. And although Daffan usually delivered his own songs, sometimes in duet with guitarist Chuck Keeshan, "Born to Lose" was sung by the fiddler Leonard Seago, and "No Letter Today" by Seago and Keeshan. Daffan does at least play the steel on them. The drummer, of all people, was the novelty bandleader Spike Jones.

Ted Daffan autographed this photograph for Leo Raley. (OTM collection)

Daffan made a good living in California in the mid-'40s but by the end of the decade his sales were dropping and he returned with relief to Texas ("I hated touring"). He ran his own Daffan label for some fifteen years, generating a few regional hits such as his own composition "Tangled Mind," and he lived long enough to see "Born to Lose" take its place among the sacred texts of country music.

Playlist
• *Born to Lose* (Jasmine JASMCD 3547)
•• *Western Swing: Texas 1928–1944* (Frémeaux FA 032 2CD): "Blue Steel Blues"
•• *Country Music 1940–1948* (Frémeaux FA 173 2CD): "Born to Lose" •• *Howdy!: 25 Hillbilly All-Time Greats* (Living Era CD AJA 5140): "Born to Lose" •• *Doughboys, Playboys and Cowboys* (Proper PROPERBOX 6 4CD): "Blue Steel Blues"

(1918–85)

Way out on the plains of west Texas lies the town of Big Spring. Unlike Lubbock, a hundred miles north, the home of Buddy Holly, it is not a place of musical pilgrimage, but it has a certain cachet for lovers of Western Swing. Here, more than fifty years ago, a local bandleader built a dance hall that would become a frontier outpost, a last resort of old-fashioned Bob Wills–styled music. There it stands on a bare lot, the Stampede—"Home," as it says in big letters above the double door, "of Hoyle Nix and His West Texas Cowboys."

(Author's collection)

From his boyhood Nix loved Bob Wills, getting up at night to listen to his broadcasts on a car radio. "He's the finest that I'll ever get to hear," he told Joe Specht in a 1977 interview for *Old Time Music*.

"Did your band more or less copy his songs?" asked Specht.

"We done them as close as we could," replied Nix.

"I didn't mean *copy*," said Specht, perhaps feeling he had been tactless, but Nix was not offended. "We tried to do them as close to the way he done them," he repeated, adding, "because he done them right."

Hoyle Nix was born into a musical family: his father played fiddle, his mother guitar, his younger brother Ben mandolin. "There was fiddle players plumb back to my great-great-grandfathers, on both sides." He played his first tune when he was six.

West Texas in the '40s was farming country, but in the immediate aftermath of World War II the farm business was depressed. "So I started my own band," Nix remembered. "And after that, why, we went to eating better, you know." He played his first gig in a local honky-tonk in 1946. Soon the West Texas Cowboys were well known—in West Texas. In 1949 they recorded for Star Talent, having a regional hit with their first release, "Big Ball's in Cowtown." The style was pure Wills, down to the trademark holler, "Yeaah, come here, mama, the hogs has got me!"

Nix recorded further singles in the '50s and '60s, some with a lineup of Wills alumni like guitarist Eldon Shamblin, pianist Millard Kelso, and fiddler Louis Tierney. The records exist in a time warp: they are almost all Western Swing favorites from the Wills and Milton Brown songbooks like "My Mary," "Ida Red," and "I Don't Love'a Nobody." You hardly hear rock 'n' roll knocking at the door, but it was.

"We had some trouble, you betcha. I'd get one of the boys in the band that didn't do much singing. I'd let him sing that type of songs. We'd fix up about four songs that we could do, and that's as far as we went."

Nix built the Stampede in 1954, pulling in 1,100 customers on the opening night. He sometimes booked other acts, but the hall was usually his on a Saturday. Most other nights the band played in surrounding towns like Midland, San Angelo, Abilene, Sweetwater, and Snyder. In later years Nix often met women who had danced their first dance to his music when they were teenagers. "That's the kind of people that keeps me in business."

Being a West Texas Cowboy was hard

Hoyle Nix's Stampede, Big Spring, Texas, 1977.
(OTM collection)

work. Typically they played for four hours,
with one intermission of ten or fifteen minutes; if it was a rodeo dance, no intermission.

"Can someone in the band slide off the
stage every now and then?" Specht asked.

"He better not," rejoined Nix. "He won't get
to slide back on if he does."

The playing came at the end of a day's work
on the farm, plus the drive to the gig, which
might be anything up to 150 miles. "It's not an
easy life," commented Nix. "But it's not a bad
life, either."

And it enabled him to meet his hero. "I met
Bob in 1952, at the American Legion Hall in Colorado City, and we became very good friends.
The first time we booked him at the Stampede,
we sat down and had a long talk. We was raised
just about alike, on a farm. My dream was to get
to play with him, and that came true. That was
the biggest thrill of my life."

Nix's band was the last that Wills ever
appeared with, in 1973. Nix was also present
at Wills's final recording session, for the album
. . . For the Last Time. "He came in there in
his wheelchair and he was in real good spirits.
He couldn't do much hollering, but he did the
best he could. Then that night he had that massive stroke. And the next day I done all his hollering."

Not long afterward Hoyle made an album
of his own, *Hoyle Nix & His West Texas Cowboys,* assisted by his sons Larry and Jody and
his brother Ben. It opened with—what else?—
"San Antonio Rose."

"Do you have any more goals in life?"
Specht asked at the close of the interview.

"Well," said Nix, "I'd like to play for thirty
more years, if I could."

He was spared for just eight. Jody took over
the band, and, as far as we know, they play at
the Stampede still.

> **Playlist**
> •• *Wanderers Swing: Texas Dance Hall
> Music* (Krazy Kat KK CD 11): "Choose the
> One You Want" •• *Playboy Boogie* (Krazy
> Kat KK CD 21): "I'm All Alone," "You're
> Throwing Life Away," "May You Never Break
> a Heart Like You Broke Mine"

Rex Griffin

(1912–58)

Today, few but old-timers and record collectors recognize the name of Rex Griffin.
But spend a little time listening to his songs
and reading about his life, and it will quickly
dawn on you that here was one of those artists
who erect a fresh signpost on the country
music highway, one that points down an
untrodden road to a new destination.

Griffin stands midway between Jimmie
Rodgers and Hank Williams, between the self-
mockery of the blue yodel and the self-
revelation of honkytonk music. It was his
version of "Lovesick Blues," rather than the
earlier recording by the blackface comedian
Emmett Miller, that inspired Williams's, while
his own composition "The Last Letter"—"a
suicide note set to music," as the historian
Kevin Coffey calls it—is an early example, perhaps the earliest, of the personal, confessional
country song.

He was born Alsie Griffin, the son of a fiddler and farmer, near Gadsden, Alabama. He
made his radio debut while still in his teens,
and through the '30s and '40s he was seldom

(Bear Family Records)

without a slot on air somewhere: Chattanooga, Birmingham, Atlanta, New Orleans, Memphis, Dallas, Chicago, Miami. In 1935 he cut his first sides, with jaunty accompaniments on banjo and guitar, reminiscent of some of Jimmie Rodgers's work. His next session revealed more of his character, as he dropped the banjoist and concentrated on guitar-accompanied yodel songs such as "I'm Just Passing Through" and "The Walkin' Blues," and in 1937 he came up with one of the quintessential jukebox discs of the era, "Over the River" coupled with "The Last Letter."

Griffin recorded three dozen sides for Decca between 1935 and 1939 and must have been a rewarding disc property, but the rich melancholy of his voice, so perfectly tuned to the small tragedies of loss and regret that were his most typical compositions, appealed to fellow artists as well as the public. Ernest Tubb admired him so much that he wrote him a fan letter, and during the '50s Tubb was his most practical supporter, commissioning as many songs from him as he could afford to buy.

By then Griffin's star was fading. He had no radio slot, and after a session for King in 1946,

no more recording opportunities either. His younger brother Buddy, a good singer and guitarist, cut some of his compositions for small Texas labels, but few were issued. Rex's last writing success was with "Just Call Me Lonesome," a 1955 hit for Eddy Arnold and Red Foley. Diabetes and drinking had slowed him down for some time, but it was something else that finally got him. While in New Orleans in the summer of 1957, he went for a medical checkup. An X-ray indicated tuberculosis. Characteristically chipper, he wrote to Buddy, "I guess you know one of my pictures won me a free vacation, with all expenses paid for about a year." The "vacation" lasted until his death.

Some years later Jack Greene revived "The Last Letter" and Ernest Tubb cut a whole album of Griffin's compositions. In 1970 he was remembered by his profession when he was elected to the National Songwriters Association's Hall of Fame. But it took almost another three decades before his legacy was revealed in all its wealth and variety by a lavish boxed set.

Playlist
• *The Last Letter* (Bear Family BCD 15911 3CD)
•• *The Ultimate Yodelling Collection* (Pulse PLS CD 630): "The Last Love Call Yodel," "Lovesick Blues" •• *American Yodeling 1911–1946* (Trikont US-0246): "You Got to Go to Work"

Buddy Jones

(1906–55)

What do you think of when you hear the phrase "white blues singer"? A rail-thin, hard-faced mountaineer like Roscoe Holcomb,

Jimmie Davis and His Gang KWKH—1130 kc.

Charlie Mitchell
Cliff Bruner
Herschel Woodal
Buddy Jones
Tex Swain
Sincerely JIMMIE DAVIS
Jerry Bozeman
Ruth Macheca

(OTM collection)

perhaps. Jimmie Rodgers in his railroad gear, nostalgic for the iron road. Or maybe just some Blue John Doe, grimly toting the sack of tough living, lean times, hard traveling.

Buddy Jones sang the blues, but he wasn't that sort of blues singer. He did have a spell of impermanence, though. Born in North Carolina, he lost his father, grew up in foster homes, and drifted round the country before being reunited with his mother in his late teens, in Port Arthur, Texas. Buddy, his brother Buster, and his step-father Joe began playing their guitars and banjos at parties. Leaving home after a family disagreement, the Jones boys worked with traveling tent shows and wound up in Shreve-port, where they played in saloons and on radio. They also met Jimmie Davis, then an offi-cer of the city's court and a radio singer spe-cializing in Rodgers-style blue yodels.

In 1934 Davis, who had been a successful recording artist for several years (and at one session had called Jones in to accompany him), talked the new Decca label into recruiting him-self and Buddy for their hillbilly catalog. Buddy also married, quit working in joints, and, using Davis's connections, joined the Shreveport Police Department. For the rest of his life he would be known to fellow citizens as a genial, plump-faced traffic officer. But for record buyers his name promised something a little less upright. Between 1935 and 1941 he made several dozen recordings whose titles were

studded with words like "honkytonk," "jail," "doghouse," or "hangover." Low-life songs.

Most of them were blues, and there Jones took over a role his friend Davis had once played. As a young man Davis had sung about bearcat mamas and gals in red nightgowns, but as he climbed the political ladder he couldn't go on singing that stuff. Jones, on the other hand, could get away with it. One of his best-known numbers was called "She's Sellin' What She Used to Give Away." It wasn't about stock market trading. A couple of others were talking blues in the style of Chris Bouchillon, but way raunchier; "Huntin' Blues," a narrative of a night-time escapade with a pliant girl-friend, has all the zest of Davis at his most indecorous. But generally Buddy's blues were the wry, humorous reflections of a man who'd been around, seen a lot, and wasn't likely to be surprised by much. You catch the tone from titles like "I Can't Be Bothered" or "I'll Get Mine Bye and Bye." From time to time, too, as in "Settle Down Blues" and "Sailing Blues," he sounds as if he has been listening closely to the popular black bluesmen of the '30s.

He was generally backed by musicians on Davis's payroll or from the Texas swing bands Decca was recording, like fiddler Cliff Bruner, electric mandolinist Leo Raley, or steel guitarist Bob Dunn, though usually it was Buster Jones who played steel with him, in a hot, jazzy manner similar to Dunn's. Moon Mullican played clipped

Cover of 1940 catalog. (Author's collection)

blues phrases at the piano. It was the sound of Western Swing, a kind of prototype honkytonk, a starter before the main course that would come from Ernest Tubb and Floyd Tillman.

In his forties Jones began to scale down his musical activities. One of his last gigs was in 1955, on a bill with Elvis Presley. "Buddy sang 'Little Red Wagon,'" recalled a fellow policeman. "The audience went wild." He died the following year. Driving to work after a heavy lunch, he had a heart attack and crashed into a tree.

Playlist
• *Police Officer & Honky Tonk Singer* (BACM CD D 014)
•• *Western Swing: Texas 1928–1944* (Frémeaux FA 032 2CD): "Settle Down Blues" •• *Hillbilly Blues 1928–1946* (Frémeaux FA 065 2CD): "Mean Old Lonesome Blues" •• *Country Music 1940–1948* (Frémeaux FA 173 2CD): "Red Wagon" •• *Sounds like Jimmie Rodgers* (JSP JSP 7751 4CD): "Dear Old Sunny South by the Sea," "Mean Old Lonesome Blues," "Shreveport County Jail Blues," "The Women ('Bout to Make a Wreck Out of Me)" •• *Hillbilly Blues* (Living Era CD AJA 5361): "Settle Down Blues" •• *Doughboys, Playboys and Cowboys* (Proper PROPERBOX 6 4CD): "Mean Old Lonesome Blues," "Rockin' Rollin' Mama," "Streamlined Mama," "The Women ('Bout to Make a Wreck Out of Me)"

(OTM collection)

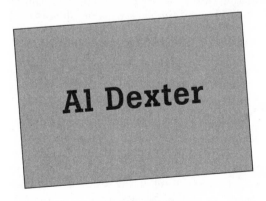

Al Dexter

(1902–84)

It's 1942. Jukebokes in civilian bars and military canteens alike ring with the new nationwide hit: "Lay that pistol down, babe,

lay that pistol down." A curious refrain for a nation that has just gone to war.

The song, "Pistol Packin' Mama," belonged to Al Dexter, an amiable forty-year-old Texas honkytonk singer and guitarist who had been making discs for the southwestern tavern trade since 1936. "Honky Tonk Blues" and "New Jelly Roll Blues" had been moderate regional hits, but he'd never had anything as hot as "Pistol." He sold an alleged million copies of his own recording in six months, and it was later covered by two of the leading pop acts of the day, Bing Crosby and the Andrews Sisters.

"Al Dexter's music," wrote Nick Tosches in 1976, prefacing his interview of the singer in *Old Time Music*, "was an alembic in which bubbled the forces of old-timey blues, Western Swing, honkytonk, and outright pop. As such it was an incipient form of modern country music."

He was born Albert Poindexter in Jacksonville, Texas, worked as a handyman, and owned a bar or two. His '30s recordings were with a trio, the stylish electric guitarist Bobby Symons, rhythm guitarist Luke Owens, and bass player Jack True, who also recorded on their own as the Nite Owls. His debut release, "Honky Tonk Blues," may be the first country song to use the term "honkytonk." "I never heard it before," said Dexter.

HERE SHE COMES!

That Pistol Packin' Mama!

A DEAD-AIM DAME....SHE'S QUICK
ON THE DRAW....in a picture
riddled with rhythm, romance
and riotous hilarity!

Pistol Packin' Mama

BASED ON THE SONG BY AL DEXTER

RUTH
TERRY
ROBERT
LIVINGSTON
WALLY. VERNON • JACK LARUE
WREN TALBOT and THE KING COLE TRIO

Shown at
1:00-3:20-5:40
8:00-10:20

PLUS! ADVENTURE-LADEN MYSTERY!

"ADVENTURE IN IRAQ"
with JOHN LODER • RUTH FORD • PAUL CAVANAUGH

WELLER STARTS • TODAY!

(Author's collection)

Later in the '30s he led an otherwise all-black band in Longview, Texas. "We did everything. At that time, you could play all night if you wanted to. Dance too. And they sold beer all night."

The idea of "Pistol Packin' Mama" came from a barroom conversation with a girl whose boyfriend's wife came after her with a gun. As Dexter recounted it, "I said, 'I told you to leave that married man alone. That woman's gonna kill you 'bout that man.' She said, 'Yeah, but Dex, I love that little cross-eyed man.' So I got the idea, 'Lay that pistol down, babe.'

"Somebody up at Columbia [Records] wanted to drop me one time. [Producer] Art Satherley told him, 'Someday that boy'll make a record that'll knock your hat off.' And sure enough I did."

Wartime America heard one shot of "Pistol" and surrendered to it. The newspapers of 1943 and '44 are flecked with stories about its irresistible appeal. In October '43 the New York Yankees celebrated their championship victory over the St. Louis Cardinals with a dressing-room singsong, seguing from the "Beer Barrel Polka" into "Pistol Packin' Mama," "which they adopted a few weeks ago as their marching chorus." In March '44 a wire story from U. P. reported that "a detachment of Marines entertained a group of natives on Kwajalein Atoll in the Marshalls by singing 'Pistol Packin' Mama.' The natives . . . countered with 'Rock of Ages.' " Columnist Erskine Johnson ran this story in October '43:

> Al Dexter, the obscure hill billy singer who wrote the current song hit, "Pistol Packin' Mama," is set to collect close to $250,000 in royalties and for its sale to Republic studio. He explains the hit: "It's just a case of a fellow dreaming for 14 years and nothing happens. Then one night he has a nightmare and it makes him a fortune." Success has not changed Dexter. Like all singers, he still calls his guitar a "starvation box."

Three months later Republic's movie based on the song was in theaters and doing excellent business.

Dexter never repeated the success of "Pistol Packin' Mama," but he continued to justify Satherley's faith for several years. (He didn't do so well repaying his wife's: in 1948 she sued for divorce, charging him with "associating with strange women.") In 1946 "Guitar Polka" topped *Billboard*'s list of "Most Played Juke Box Folk Records" for fifteen weeks running and ended up as the year's "second most played folk recording," giving Dexter the edge over Bob Wills as the year's "top folk song recording artist." But records like "Guitar Polka" couldn't compete with the rootsier sounds of rock 'n' roll, any more than Dexter could write in the new idiom. "I just can't figure out where the beat goes," he complained. He quit the business in the '60s and went into real estate, but he had some good copyrights to bring in money, like "Too Late to Worry," and as late as the '70s he was getting sizable checks for "Pistol" 's use in a TV commercial.

Floyd Tillman

(1914–2003)

Floyd Tillman had a big, cheerful egg of a face. It was the face of a simple, honest man, and it was something of a shock to see it grinning at you over the shoulder of somebody else's wife. At least, that was how it seemed to the country fans of 1949, when Tillman went where few country singers had gone before— into the shadowy world of the low-rent rendezvous, the illicit assignation, the motel on the edge of town.

Its subject was that most commonplace of sins, adultery, but some say "Slippin' Around" was the first country song to boldly wear the scarlet letter. Not that the singer is happy in his backstreet love: Tillman delivers the song like a man confessing a moral flaw, no trace of triumph in his voice, not a hint of the seducer's pride. Even so, the record scared the pants off a lot of radio station programmers, and to make the song palatable to the sponsors of the

Lucky Strike Hit Parade Tillman had to bowdlerize the key lines "Though you're all tied up with someone else, and I'm all tied up too" to the anodyne "I guess I had it coming, there's nothing I can do."

Tillman's warm Texas tone, like Ernest Tubb's but lighter and smoother, had already been pleasing jukebox patrons in the Southwest for a decade, and nightclubbers for even longer. As a teenager in San Antonio he played guitar and sang with Adolph Hofner. By the end of the '30s he was working out of Houston with Leon Selph's Blue Ridge Playboys, and in March 1939 he made his recording debut singing with the band. Over the next few years he also recorded with the Village Boys, another Houston combo, and in his own name, and he had considerable success with numbers like "They Took the Stars Out of Heaven" and "Each Night at Nine," but it wasn't until after World War II that he turned a regional reputation into a national one, recording for Columbia hits like "I Love You So Much It Hurts," "Slippin' Around" (though that was bigger for Jimmy Wakely and Margaret Whiting on Capitol), and "This Cold War with You."

Almost everything he recorded Tillman wrote himself, but he let what proved to be his most successful copyright get away—for a time. "Jimmie Davis wanted it. He offered me $200 for it, but I held out for $300. I bought it back twenty-eight years later." There was still plenty of life in it, because the song was "It Makes No Difference Now," one of country music's incontestable standards.

"I was sitting in my car in a drive-in having a cold one waiting for a phone call," Tillman reminisced to Dorothy Horstman. "It never came. 'Oh, well,' I said, 'it makes no difference now.' The first verse flowed out in my mind as if I were hearing it on the radio. I borrowed a pencil from the car hop and wrote it on the back of an envelope." The number was an instant hit with the public but Tillman's producer was concentrating on recording uptempo numbers for the jukebox market and turned it down. Cliff Bruner promptly got hold of it and recorded it for Decca and in less than three months it had been covered by Davis (also for Decca), Adolph Hofner (Bluebird), and the Light Crust Doughboys (Vocalion)— and then a year later by the Sons of the Acadians, for Decca yet again but this time in Cajun French.

Like many of his honkytonk confrères, Tillman would probably have gone down under the tidal wave of rock 'n' roll, but he got out early. "It was a daily rat-race," he said, "and

Floyd Tillman and his band, KTHT, Houston, Texas, 1940s. Left to right: Darrell Raley, Floyd Tillman, Lew Frisbee, Sam Baker, Leo Raley, Marge Tillman. (OTM collection)

I got tired of it." By the '60s he was, commercially speaking, a yesterday's man, but he was not forgotten: in 1970 his peers voted him into the Songwriters Hall of Fame, and the doors of the Country Music Hall of Fame opened in 1984. That award was presented to him by Willie Nelson, who later wrote, in the notes to a reissue album, "I am maybe the world's biggest Floyd Tillman fan." One of Tillman's last projects was an album of duets with Nelson and other admirers like Merle Haggard, George Jones, and Dolly Parton, but he did not live to see it out.

Playlist
• *I Love You So Much It Hurts* (Bear Family BCD 16415 6CD) [spans 1936–61]

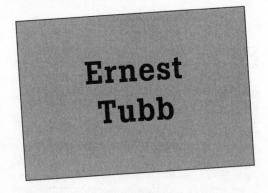

Ernest Tubb

(1914–84)

One line of a song gave you most of what there was to know about Ernest Tubb. He was not a naturally gifted singer, but he told his stories directly and, whatever their subject, reassuringly. Things may look bad, his voice implied, but they'll get better. It had

Ernest Tubb with a Jimmie Rodgers guitar.
(Bear Family Records)

a power to console that people responded to immediately. "I could listen to him for hours," wrote a fan. "His voice never grates on the nerves like some voices but has a restful quality."

He sang, says his biographer Ronnie Pugh, "with an audible smile. You didn't have to see him: something in that warm, drawling baritone told you he was happy."

Not because he had had it easy. He grew up in small-town Texas, never dirt-poor but never flush with money. His teens were shadowed by the Depression, and his nineteenth year by the death of his idol, Jimmie Rodgers, whose every record he had bought and treasured. "I thought my world had come to an end," he would recall. "I worshiped him so much that for a time I was convinced that I wouldn't live past age 35 either." He had heard other country music, like the cowboy songs of Jules Allen, or "Mac" McClintock's buoyant hobo anthem "The Big Rock Candy Mountains." But the hickory-smoked voice of the Blue Yodeler wove a spell upon the young Tubb from which he never quite escaped, nor wished to.

He had always liked singing, and by the age of twenty he had his own radio show in San Antonio. On an impulse he approached Carrie Rodgers, Jimmie's wife, who also lived in the city, and asked for her opinion of his work. She liked it well enough to write letters of recommendation to potential employers. One was to Jimmie's old label, Victor, and in 1936 Tubb made his first disc, a pair of tribute songs to Rodgers, written by Rodgers' sister-in-law and collaborator Elsie McWilliams. He accompanied himself on one of the singer's guitars, lent

by Carrie. It was sincerely meant, but many artists were following in Rodgers's footsteps, and even with his widow's support Tubb might have had little future as a disciple. Then his life's route was interrupted with a "Detour" sign. An operation on his tonsils left him unable to yodel, and singing Rodgers's songs without yodeling was like serving chili without crackers.

Undeterred, he furthered his radio career with songs of his own and his friends. By 1941 he was on Fort Worth's KGKO, singing a new song he'd written called "Walking the Floor over You." His Decca recording got on to every jukebox in the Southwest, followed, over the next few years, by numbers like "Tomorrow Never Comes" or the wartime chart-toppers "Soldier's Last Letter" and "Rainbow at Midnight."

Listening to these now, you're struck by their economy. Over a quiet rhythm guitar and bass Tubb tells his plain man's tales, interspersed by melodic phrases from an electric guitarist. That's all. Later he would add fiddle and steel guitar, and later still he would ride with large posses of studio musicians, but the nucleus of his performance was always that matter-of-fact drawl and its burden of hard times and good times, love and loss.

In 1942 Tubb moved into movies, as the singing lead in *Fighting Buckaroo* and *Riding West*. The following year, now established as one of the nation's best-selling hillbilly recording artists, he was added to the roster of the Grand Ole Opry. "From the reports that have been coming in from correspondents from coast to coast," enthused Floy Case in *The Mountain Broadcast and Prairie Recorder*, "this tall, slender Texas lad with the dark wavy hair and twinkling blue eyes is singing his way into the hearts of the people everywhere." In 1947 he opened a record shop in Nashville, and the following year WSM began broadcasting the Midnight Jamboree from there, after the Opry had gone off the air. Both store and show became Nashville institutions. For decades, the country music lover's Nashville itinerary included a visit to Ernest Tubb's Record Shop on Lower Broadway. Guest appearances on the Midnight Jamboree helped to turn young wannabes like Carl Smith, Loretta Lynn, and George Hamilton IV into stars.

Meanwhile, ET did a lot of phoning home. He had to, in order to talk to his family, because he was constantly on tour, playing as many as 200 dates a year. It got so that he couldn't sleep in a regular bedroom: he had to be in a bus, feeling the road slip away beneath him, before he could slip away too. And when, in 1982, emphysema forced him to quit, he didn't last very much longer. Perhaps, after all those years of smiling at crowds from nightclub bandstands before launching into "Waltz across Texas," there was no other tune he cared to dance to.

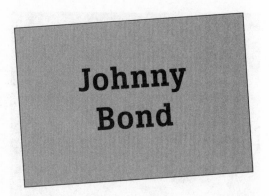

(1915–78)

Johnny Bond was captivated as a boy by the magic of Jimmie Rodgers. A teenager in rural Oklahoma, he heard the records of "America's Blue Yodeler," and that was it: a die cast, a pathway marked out, a life determined.

He began playing guitar in high school, and by his early twenties he was singing on radio in Oklahoma City. With two new friends, Jimmy Wakely and Scotty Harrell, he formed a trio called The Bell Boys (because they were sponsored by the Bell Clothing Company) and began to make a name, singing popular songs of the day and Western numbers in the style of The Sons of the Pioneers. But after a couple of years Bond and Wakely decided that for a

Playlist
- *Let's Say Goodbye Like We Said Hello* (Bear Family BCD 15498 5CD) [1947–53]
- *Yellow Rose of Texas* (Bear Family BCD 15688 5CD)
- *Walking the Floor over You* (Bear Family BCD 15853 5CD) [1937–46]
- *Early Hits of the Texas Troubadour* (Living Era CD AJA 5322)
- •• *When the Sun Goes Down Vol. 10: East Virginia Blues* (Bluebird 60085): "The T.B. Is Whipping Me" •• *Country* (Frémeaux FA 015 2CD): "I Ain't Honky Tonkin' Anymore" •• *Hillbilly Blues 1928–1946* (Frémeaux FA 065 2CD): "Fort Worth Jail," "Mean Mama Blues" •• *Country Music 1940–1948* (Frémeaux FA 173 2CD): "There's Gonna Be Some Changes Made around Here" •• *Sounds like Jimmie Rodgers* (JSP JSP 7751 4CD): "The Last Thoughts of Jimmie Rodgers," "Married Man Blues," "Mean Old Bed Bug Blues," "My Mother Is Lonely," "The Passing of Jimmie Rodgers," "The Right Train to Heaven," "Since That Black Cat Crossed My Path," "The T.B. Is Whipping Me" •• *Howdy!: 25 Hillbilly All-Time Greats* (Living Era CD AJA 5140): "Walking the Floor over You" •• *The Ultimate Yodelling Collection* (Pulse PLS CD 630): "Married Man Blues," "Mean Old Bed Bug Blues"

(OTM collection)

future in Western music you had to go west, and in 1940 they set out for Hollywood. Harrell didn't want to go with them, and his place was taken by Dick Reinhart, a talented musician who had recently moved to Oklahoma City. Reinhart was a few years older than Bond and Wakely and had a good deal of experience in the business: he had made his first record back in 1929 and had sung and played guitar or bass in a succession of Western Swing bands, including the Light Crust Doughboys and, most recently, the Hi-Flyers and the Universal Cowboys.

Their break came when Gene Autry needed a new backing group for his nationally networked radio show, Melody Ranch. With the help of the singer Johnny Marvin, whom they had met back in Oklahoma City and whose brother Frankie was a close associate of Autry, the team of Bond, Wakely, and Reinhart secured the job. Shortly afterward they also landed a recording deal with Decca, under the name of Jimmy Wakely & His Rough Riders. A year later Bond began a parallel recording career for Columbia as Johnny Bond & His Red River Valley Boys, while Reinhart led his Lone Star Boys on OKeh. The three lineups had a good deal in common, delivering Western numbers arranged for a vocal trio with small-band accompaniments featuring L.A. studio regulars like fiddler Carl Cotner and accordionist Paul Sells (both heard on Autry's discs of the time), with Wakely, Bond, and Reinhart sharing the guitar and bass roles. The trio also appeared in several Western movies below headliners like Autry, Roy Rogers, and Tex Ritter.

It was during the '40s that Bond revealed himself to be a top-class songwriter, whether in the Western idiom of his classic "Cimarron," which he first recorded with the Jimmy Wakely Trio in 1940, or all-purpose country songs like "Those Gone and Left Me Blues," "I Wonder Where You Are Tonight," well known in the recording by Bill Monroe but also a '70s hit for Johnny Rodriguez, and "Tomorrow Never Comes," a 1944 hit for Ernest Tubb. "Do not search for a great song among mine," he said later, "because you will not find it. . . . Instead seek only a simple, touching thought combined with a simple melody." Such humility fails to do justice to compositions like "Set 'Em Up, Joe," with its audacious rhyming—"I'm goin' home, pack my trousseau, gonna live just like Robinson Crusoe"—and its dry wit: "I wanna try and forget my woes, with something aged in wood, and while we're on the subject, Joe, I sure hope my credit's good." His was an ideal delivery for such sentiments, downbeat and quietly amused, yet he could also put across a love song like " 'Til the End of the World" with grace and feeling.

In the '50s Bond was a regular on radio and TV shows like Hollywood Barn Dance and Town Hall Party, expanding his range from singing to scriptwriting, comedy, and MCing. His recording career was less spectacular than his ex-partner's—Wakely was extremely successful as a solo, both on records and in movies—but he had some hits, backed in typical West Coast swing style by musicians like Merle Travis and steel guitarists Joaquin Murphey or Noel Boggs.

Bond's career, like so many in the Western music business, nosedived in the rock 'n' roll era, though he made a comeback in the '60s with the novelty song "10 Little Bottles," and into the '70s could still elicit a warm reception at events like the annual Fourth of July festival in Kerrville, Texas. In later life he turned writer, composing an autobiography, *Reflections*, and a short book on the recordings of Jimmie Rodgers, and recalling old buddies in biographies of Gene Autry (which, because of its candor, was never published) and of Tex Ritter.

> **Playlist**
> • *The Heart and Soul of the West* (Jasmine JASMCD 3512)
> • *I Like My Chicken Fryin' Size* (Jasmine JASMCD 3541)
> • *Johnny Bond & His Red River Valley Boys* (Living Era CD AJA 5360)
> •• *Country Music 1940–1948* (Frémeaux FA 173 2CD): "Draftee Blues"

Red River Dave McEnery

(1914–2002)

Red River Dave McEnery spent his long life with one foot in country music and the other in tabloid journalism. Tirelessly chronicling the passing show of world news, from headline stories to curious column fillers, he accumulated a portfolio that spanned "The Ballad of Patty Hearst" and "The Night That Ronald Reagan Rode with Santa Claus."

Some of his compositions faded as fast as the newsprint that inspired them, like "The Clinging Lovers of Kenya," about a couple who—shall we say—could not be extricated from their embrace, or "The Ballad of Sandra West," a Texas woman who wrote in her will that she wanted to be buried in her Ferrari. But in "Amelia Earhart's Last Flight," the story of the pioneering flier who vanished over the Pacific in 1937, Red River Dave planted a sturdy tree in the memorial garden of country music's tragedy songs. And, like any good journalist, he was not just versatile, he was quick. In 1946, for a publicity stunt, he wrote fifty-two songs in twelve hours—while handcuffed to a piano.

His early days as an entertainer were spent on the rodeo circuit as a rope-twirler, but during the '30s he became known on radio for his cowboy songs and yodeling. (His professional name came from one of those songs, "Red River Valley.") At the New York World's Fair in 1939 he participated in an experimental television broadcast, which may have been the first to feature a country singer. Around that time he met the prolific songwriter and publisher Bob Miller, then riding high on the success of his wartime composition "There's

Red River Dave, with Bill Benner (fiddle) and Roy Horton (bass), at the RCA Exhibit, New York World's Fair, 1939. (OTM collection)

a Star Spangled Banner Waving Somewhere," recorded by another singer and yodeler, Elton Britt. Dave, whose own writing career had begun conventionally enough with pieces like "The Stars over Laredo," immediately saw where the songwriting action was and wrote "I'd Like to Give My Dog to Uncle Sam."

In the early postwar years he was widely heard on the Mexican border radio stations, and, more legitimately, on WOAI in his home town of San Antonio, Texas, where he teamed up with the Texas Top Hands, a polka-swing band led by accordionist/pianist Walter Kleypas. "This Pair of Juke-box Favorites Spell Box Office $$$$$," proclaimed their full-page ad in the 1946–47 *Billboard Encyclopedia of Music.* "A great combination on Radio, Records, Stage and Screen." Tall and good-looking, Dave fit the mold of a Hollywood singing cowboy, and soon his resumé was swelled with credits for *Swing in the Saddle* (1948), *Echo Ranch* (1949), and a bunch of short features.

A few years on, he brought off a skilful left-and-right by taking Wink Martindale's hit song "Deck of Cards" and hauling it into the Red-baiting atmosphere of the McCarthy era. In Dave's "The Red Deck of Cards," an American serviceman freed from a Korean prison tells how his captors used playing cards to teach the tenets of Communism: "They told us that the ace meant that there is the one God: the State. And the deuce meant that there were two great leaders: Lenin and Stalin. . . ."

Red River Dave's politics were more sophisticated than that might imply. Another of his compositions was "The Ballad of Emmett Till," based on a notorious news story of the '50s about a young black man in Mississippi who was accused of disrespecting a white woman and died at the hands of lynchers.

For much of the '60s and '70s Red River Dave was a familiar figure around the publishers' offices and musicians' hangouts of Nashville. He was hard to miss, because with his long white hair, mustache, and beard he looked strikingly like the well-known photograph of Buffalo Bill. He also held a "church" for musicians in a room in the Hall of Fame motel, where he preached and did rope tricks. On a stack of small-label 45s he carried on logging his responses to the big stories of the day: "The Ballad of Billy Graham," "The Ballad of Marilyn Monroe," "The Ballad of Three-Mile Island," "The Flight of Apollo Eleven" . . . There was a song about the mass suicide of evangelist Jim Jones and his followers in Jonestown, Guyana, and another about the Iranian hostage crisis.

No one has commemorated him yet with a "Ballad of Red River Dave," but they should. As country music historian Charles Wolfe rightly said, "A catalog of Red River Dave's event songs reflects nearly every aspect of modern American history."

Playlist
• *The Yodelling Cowboy Sings "Amelia Earhart's Last Flight" and Other Country, Story and Western Songs* (Jasmine JASMCD 3559)

Leo Soileau

(1904–80)

Until the 1960s there was probably no genre of American music as conservative as Cajun. The community it sprang from and served was virtually confined to southwest Louisiana and a small portion of southeast Texas. Take a map of Louisiana and run your finger due west from Baton Rouge, roughly between the old highways 90 and 190. Along that strip and each side of it, in towns like Ville Platte, Mamou, Opelousas, Basile, Eunice, Rayne, and Lake Charles, lies the heartland of Cajun music. Job opportunities during World War II extended it into southeast Texas, from the border city of Port Arthur up to Houston.

Around the midpoint of the last century, Cajun Louisiana was predominantly rural, agricultural, Catholic, and—most important of all, so far as the music was concerned—French-speaking. People listened to music that rang with reminders of their shared past, waltzes and two-steps that had changed only slowly in the 200 years since the original Acadians,

Leo Soileau's Three Aces, c. 1935. (OTM collection)

French settlers in Nova Scotia, were driven out and found their way round the coast of America to the Louisiana bayous. Saturday-night dances retained much of the flavor described by Alcée Fortier in 1890:

> Having heard that every Saturday evening there was a ball in the prairie, I requested one of my friends to take me to see one. We arrived at 8 o'clock, but already the ball had begun. In the yard were vehicles of all sorts, but three-mule carts were most numerous. The ball room was a large hall with galleries all around it. When we entered it was crowded with persons dancing to the music of three fiddles. I was astonished to see that nothing was asked for entrance, but I was told that any white person decently dressed could come in. The man giving the entertainment derived his profits from the sale of refreshments. . . . The break-up would only take place at 4 or 5 o'clock in the morning. . . . My friend told me that when the dance was over the musicians would rise, and going out in the yard would fire several pistol shots in the air, crying out at the same time: *le bal est fini.*

Leo Soileau grew up in the culture of the Saturday-night *bal*, but a generation later. By then Cajuns had adopted the accordion—not the "stomach Steinway," the chromatic piano accordion, which was hardly known in Louisiana in those days, but the diatonic button accordion, a smaller instrument, easy to carry (if not always to play), but with the limitation that it offers the musician only a few keys to operate in. Huge quantities of them had been imported into the Southwest from Germany, initially to serve the needs of the new settlers from that country. It was an accordion player who made the first recording of Cajun music, Joseph Falcon of Rayne, in April 1928.

Falcon's disc caused a stir in southern Louisiana, partly because it gave the region's music a new status, but also because other musicians felt that Columbia Records might have chosen a superior representative. Local businessmen began to talk up their favorite musicians to agents of rival record companies. Frank Deadline, a jewelry store owner in Opelousas, got in touch with Victor and promoted the Basile duo of Mayuse (correctly Maius) Lafleur and Leo Soileau. Their October 1928 sides were not only the first to present Cajun fiddling but the first to demonstrate the classic Cajun combination of accordion, fiddle, and voice in its tense magnificence. Lafleur's accordion playing is almost painfully exciting, pressing upon the beat, in emotional accord with his plaintive singing, while Soileau's fiddle twines round the two like an ardent lover.

LOOK Who's Coming To The
LIGHTHOUSE!
4000 16TH STREET—ORANGE HIGHWAY
ONE NIGHT ONLY
MONDAY, NOV. 20TH
LEO SOILEAU
AND ITS
MUSIC FRANCAISE
Radio's Outstanding
FRENCH BAND
You've heard them on the radio and recordings. Now hear them in person, playing and singing the favorite French Tunes.
"JOLIE BLANC"
"Comsi Comsa"   "Ma Petite Cherie"
And Other Popular French Numbers
DON'T FORGET
Next Monday—Admission $1 Per Person
─────────•─────────
DANCE SATURDAY, NOV. 18th
WELDON DEAVER   EARL REBERT
And Their
6 MUSICAL ACES 6

Leo Soileau in Port Arthur, Texas, 1944. (Author's collection)

Lafleur never heard his recordings, for he was shot in a brawl nine days later. Soileau found another partner in the accordionist Moise Robin from Arnaudville, and during 1929 they made a dozen fine records for Paramount, Victor, and Vocalion, among them Soileau's mesmerizing "Easy Rider Blues." Soileau also teamed with a cousin, Alius Soileau, from Eunice, playing two fiddles with no other accompaniment. These, along with the breathtaking duets of Denus McGee and Ernest Fruge, bring us as close as we are ever likely to get to the fiddle music heard by Alcée Fortier.

The record companies dated the Cajuns faithfully for another year and then stopped calling. The music would not be heard on disc again for almost four years. By then the accordion had fallen from fashion and the favored sound was of fiddles and guitars, a Cajun match for the hillbilly stringband music of Arthur Smith or Mainer's Mountaineers. This suited Soileau very well. Never wholly committed to the old French repertoire, he was happy to mix it with hillbilly and popular songs, with their more varied tunes and chord progressions, and around 1934 he put together a band to play them. The Four Aces, with guitarists Floyd Shreve and Dewey

Landry and drummer Tony Gonzales, represented the new sound of Cajun club music, and not everybody was ready for it. At their first session for Decca, in Chicago in 1935, the engineer objected that the drums were blasting the cutting needle out of its groove. The problem was solved by stacking pillows round the kit to absorb some of the reverberation. "Well," said the engineer, "I'm learning something."

Over the next couple of years Soileau's Aces and their successors, the Rhythm Boys, recorded more than sixty titles, providing Decca's Cajun list with French waltzes and breakdowns while establishing themselves in the hillbilly catalog with Cajun-style covers of contemporary country hits that Soileau learned from records, such as "I Only Want a Buddy" or "Little Darling Pal of Mine." And more: they exchanged the Red River Valley for Tin Pan Alley, shopping for songs like "I Get the Blues When It Rains," "My Wild Irish Rose," and "Painting the Clouds with Sunshine." No Southern band of the time was more eclectic.

Through the late '30s and into the '40s Soileau led a modernizing movement that drew Cajun music closer to contemporary idioms like Western Swing. He added steel guitar, piano, and string bass, and embraced amplification. During the war years and for a while afterward he had constant work along the Cajun corridor, both on radio and at clubs like the Silver Star in Lake Charles, the Showboat in Orange, Texas, and the Lighthouse in Port Arthur. Unfortunately we have no idea how his music sounded at this point. Cajun music began to be recorded again in the mid-'40s, and after Harry Choates's success with "Jole Blon" it enjoyed a brief vogue, but Soileau didn't figure in that. He retired in 1953: good timing, because the accordion was about to seize the stage again and edge the fiddle into the wings. After a few years working in a Lake Charles oil refinery he moved to Ville Platte, where he spent the rest of his life.

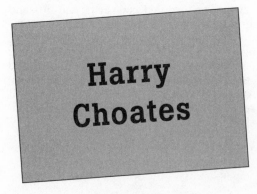

Harry Choates

(1922–51)

Cajun music, as we have seen, had every
reason to be little known. Yet it *is* known
in the larger world, and one of the reasons for
that is the short, turbulent, and musically rev-
olutionary life of the singer and fiddler Harry
Choates.

If you know any Cajun song it's likely to be
"Jole Blon"—"Pretty Blonde." A love song in
fast waltz time, it had been around for years
before Choates recorded it in 1946, but his
lean, bluesy version took off like a rocket in
the Southwest. Originally issued on the Houston label Gold Star, it was licensed to the
larger Modern label in Los Angeles and by January 1947 had risen to fourth place in the
national country chart, where it would be
chased by cover versions by artists as prominent as Roy Acuff and Jimmie Davis. What was
already a standard became an anthem, and
sixty years later "Jole Blon" is to Cajun music
what "When the Saints Go Marching In" is to
traditional New Orleans jazz.

Choates was born in deep Cajun country,
probably in Rayne, Louisiana, a town that
proudly bills itself "the frog capital of the
world," but grew up in Port Arthur, Texas. Fascinated by the honkytonk and Cajun bands he
heard in bars, he took up the fiddle, and before
he was out of his teens he had played with
well-known Cajun bandleaders like Leo
Soileau and Papa Cairo.

In 1940 he made his first recordings, playing fiddle and electric guitar with another popular band of the day, Happy Fats LeBlanc's
Rayne-Bo Ramblers. Formerly a purely Cajun
band, the Ramblers were by then playing Western Swing–influenced honkytonk music, the
songs in English as often as French. Choates
too would make his living in both camps,
switching effortlessly from old Cajun tunes
like "Allons a Lafayette" and "Pauvre Hobo" to
swing numbers such as "Old Cow Blues," a
cover of Johnnie Lee Wills's "Milk Cow Blues,"
or "I've Quit My Cattin' Around."

Harry Choates band, possibly at the Hollywood
Club, Rayne, Louisiana, possibly December
1946. Left to right: Julius "Papa Cairo" Lam-
perez, Choates, Joe Manuel, Eddie Pursley,
unknown. (Kevin Coffey collection)

Harry Choates band, Corpus Christi, Texas, fall 1947. Left to right: Red Fabacher, Pee Wee Lyons, Johnnie Mae Manuel, Choates, Amos Comeaux, Curly Maples. (Kevin Coffey collection)

After the success of "Jole Blon" Choates was a big draw on the Gulf Coast club circuit. He so impressed a couple of Grand Ole Opry stars that they advised him to try his fortune in Nashville, but he was not a man with long-term career goals. "He never looked for what could happen tomorrow," his banjo-player Pee Wee Broussard told researcher Kevin Coffey. "He lived for today."

It was typical that while under contract to Gold Star he should moonlight for another label, Cajun Classics. On one of the sides, "Yes, I Love You," he plays electric guitar, revealing a swing-jazz capability that could have paid his bills on its own. Typically, though, his records show him as a Cajun Bob Wills, interspersing his singing and fiddling with cries of "eh, ha ha!"

His lifestyle was erratic. "I drank when I was on the bandstand," remembered guitarist Red Fabacher, "but he drank all day long." His unreliability was legendary. Musicians as good as Link Davis and steel guitar pioneer Bob Dunn played for him, but he seldom kept a group

together for long. By 1950 he didn't even have a full-time band, and his records, made with pick-up groups or studio musicians, were frequently sloppy, though a session for Allied in the spring of 1951 produced some fine performances.

They would be his last musical testament. In July 1951, while working in Austin with the Western Swing bandleader Jesse James, he was arrested for failing to pay child support to his separated wife Helen. Drying out in jail, he became confused and ill. Friends who visited him also noticed head injuries, perhaps self-inflicted but possibly, as many afterward believed, the result of a beating by a prison guard. He died on July 17, apparently—no inquest report has survived—from cirrhosis. He was twenty-eight and broke. It took a radio appeal to collect the money to send his body home to Port Arthur.

It gives you some idea of how popular he was that after his death several record companies ransacked their shelves for unissued material and rushed out releases. For years afterward his recordings, reissued on 45s and LPs, continued to sell in Louisiana and Texas.

Playlist
- *The Fiddle King of Cajun Swing* (Arhoolie CD 380)
- *Devil in the Bayou* (Bear Family BCD 16355 2CD)
- *Five-Time Loser* (Krazy Kat KK CD 22)
- •• *Cajun Hot Sauce* (Ace CDCHD 591): "Allons a Lafayette," "Basile Waltz" •• *Macy's Texas Hillbilly: The Best of Macy's Hillbilly Recordings* (Acrobat ACRCD 125): "Cat'n Around," "Korea Here We Come" •• *Cajun Honky Tonk* (Arhoolie CD 427): "Jolie Blon's Gone," "Valse de Lake Charles" •• *J'Ai Eté au Bal Vol. 1* (Arhoolie CD 331): "Jole Blon" [the original recording] •• *Cat'n Around* (Krazy Kat KK CD 07): "Cat'n Around," "Harry's Blues"

Molly O'Day

(1923–87)

Scene: Columbia Records' talent department, Christmas 1946. There's a buzz in the air. They've been listening to some new demos and they think they've got something. A female Hank Williams, no less.

You can see why. Two of the songs Molly O'Day had recorded at her debut session were written by Williams, "Six More Miles" and "When God Comes and Gathers His Jewels," and her backing band of fiddle, dobro, rhythm guitars, and bass had the same blue-edged melancholy as Hank's Drifting Cowboys. But there was an even closer parallel, and it was one with implications for the twenty-three-year-old Kentucky mountain girl. What she really sounded like was a female Roy Acuff.

It wasn't just that she picked songs from Acuff's folio too, and sang, as he did, with heart-wrenching simplicity and emotion. Like that pillar of the Opry, she disapproved of honkytonk music and the world it belonged to. Not for her the low lights of the barroom, but the candles of the little country church or the flickering signal lamps of the trains bringing home the coffins of casualties of war. The closest she came to earthly passion was a wistful lost-love lament like "Too Late—Too Late." What she did best was tell moral tales, the stories of "The Tramp on the Street" (her first record, learned from Williams, and an immediate hit), "The Black Sheep Returned to the Fold," and "The Drunken Driver." A lay preacher in a gingham dress, she admonished her listeners, "Don't Forget the Family Prayer," "Don't Sell Daddy Any More Whiskey."

She had come a long way from her beginnings in show business. As Lois LaVerne Williamson from McVeigh, Kentucky, the banjo-playing younger sister of fiddler Cecil "Skeets" Williamson, she started out on WCHS in Charleston, West Virginia, at sixteen. Soon afterward, brother and sister joined singer-guitarist Lynn Davis in the Forty-Niners, and not long after that Lois LaVerne became Mrs. Lynn Davis, professionally known as Dixie

Molly O'Day and Lynn Davis. (OTM collection)

A choice of attractions in Kingsport, Tennessee, February 1946. (Author's collection)

Lee—"one of the best girl entertainers ever in these parts and star of the show," wrote Constance Keith for *The Mountain Broadcast and Prairie Recorder* in March 1942, having heard the band on WBRC in Birmingham, Alabama. "Dixie Lee is 'all-around handy man,' playing guitar, singing in both duet and trio. . . . She also features swell solos with lots of plain and fancy yodeling. The big feature of the week is when Dixie Lee plays her five-string banjo."

Four years later, now Molly O'Day, she had left the yodeling behind, and the banjo came out only occasionally, as on the old murder song "Poor Ellen Smith." But she still had her husband and brother alongside her in the Cumberland Mountain Folks, as well as Mac Wiseman, a great bluegrass singer in waiting, presently picking the stand-up bass. She also had the backing of Columbia producer Art Satherley, who had heard her sing "Tramp on the Street" on the radio and immediately signed her. Satherley set his colleague, the songwriter Fred Rose, the task of finding material for her, and one of the sources he tapped was Hank Williams—who came up, as well as the two songs already mentioned, with "I Don't Care If Tomorrow Never Comes" and "Singing Waterfall," and later "On the Evening Train."

With her tear-stained voice and apple-cheeked girl-next-door looks, Molly O'Day might have been country music's biggest heart-throb, even sex symbol, if she had only been more flexible, more worldly. But she was immovably uninterested in a big-time, big-city career, and when public taste began to shift

from songs of weeping mothers and snow-covered graves, she retired, with relief and her partner, to a life of evangelical work. Into the space she might have filled stepped raunchier women like Rose Maddox and Wilma Lee Cooper.

She left behind her five years of consistently fine records. Her belief in her songs was as uncomplicated as her faith. Bluegrass pioneer Carl Story remembered her singing on the radio with tears running down her cheeks at the sadness of her stories.

In the '60s she cut a couple of albums of sacred songs for small labels, and later she and Davis hosted a radio gospel program in Huntington, West Virginia, where they now lived. But apart from an occasional church event she never performed in public again.

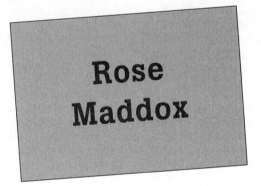

Rose Maddox

(1925–98)

Some time in the 1980s, while she was in England for a series of club dates, Rose Maddox was interviewed on a BBC radio program. Making conversation afterward, the producer asked her if she had met The Judds, then much in the news.

"No," snapped Rose. "Nor do I wish to."

Like many country artists of her generation, Rose was not easily impressed by much latter-

Maddox Brothers & Rose: Cal, Cliff, Rose, Don, Fred. (OTM collection)

day country music. She came up in the honky-tonk era of wailing steel guitars and voices that could knock over beer bottles, and she had little regard for musicians who had not served that kind of apprenticeship.

Her family history reads like a chapter from *The Grapes of Wrath* or a Woody Guthrie lyric. Originally from Boaz, Alabama, the Maddoxes moved west in the Depression, arriving finally in California. Her five brothers, Cal, Cliff, Don, Fred, and Henry, all played instruments, and while she was still in her early teens Rose found herself singing with the family band on small radio stations in northern California cities such as Modesto, Stockton, and Sacramento. "Among their accomplishments," according to an article in the *Modesto Bee* in February 1940, "the trio [then Fred, Cal, and Rose] numbers winning the Centennial Hillbilly contest at Sacramento's Roarin' Camp, and an engagement at Treasure island. All three live with their parents and contribute to the maintenance of the family home."

In 1941 one of the Maddoxes wrote to the fanzine *The Mountain Broadcast and Prairie Recorder*:

We have only been in radio three years but already had daily programs on 31 different stations on the west coast. We receive mail from 15 states and Canada. . . . We play and sing folk songs and ballads. Fred slaps the "dog house" [bass] and MC's the show, Cal plays guitar and harmonica, Rose sings and yodels, and Ken [Cliff?], or "Don Juan the Lavender Cowboy with Two Hairs on His Chest" furnishes the clownin' and all of us are fairly good singers.

By the mid-'40s they were being billed as "America's Most Colorful Hillbilly Band." In the words of Tennessee Ernie Ford, "their costumes made Liberace look like a plucked chicken!"

The '40s music of the Maddox Brothers & Rose, as captured by the lively West Coast indie label Four Star, is exhilarating stuff. On numbers like "Whoa, Sailor" and "Philadelphia Lawyer" the musicians jump into their solos with youthful exuberance, while Rose's voice rises above the knockabout ensemble, sassy and brassy as a cockatoo. In the background, brother Cal bursts into manic laughter. Even conventional heartache songs like "I Couldn't Believe It Was True," "Tramp on the Street," or "Eight Thirty Blues" are put across with vehemence and rhythmic drive. It makes a lot of the country music that followed it seem awfully serious. And dull.

As well as their large stack of regular discs, the group left further documentation of their music on radio airchecks (off-air recordings) that have survived and been issued on CD, thanks to Chris Strachwitz of Arhoolie Records, who as a teenager was an enthusiastic listener to the Maddoxes' broadcasts over KTRB in Modesto.

Rose, "the Sweetheart of Hillbilly Swing," went on to become a leading figure in country music in the '50s and early '60s, with hit records like "Sing a Little Song of Heartache," "We're the Talk of the Town," and "Loose Talk," the latter two duets with Buck Owens. She also cut a collectable album titled *Bluegrass*, with assistance from Bill Monroe and Reno & Smiley. But in some ways the most interesting parts of her career were its beginning and end. By the late '60s she was regarded as something of a throwback, not least because she had remained loyal to the extravagant Western dress style of her youth, a fashion very much *out* of fashion until Emmylou Harris resuscitated it. But she continued to work, and occasionally record, and her early-'80s albums with bluegrass mandolinist Vern Williams's band are full of pep. When she visited Europe, however, many of her bookings were on the rockabilly circuit, where she was fondly remembered for the wild side of her early material.

She found a kindred spirit in Merle Haggard, and he and his Strangers backed her on her 1984 album *Queen of the West*. A decade later Haggard joined her again on what would prove to be her last album, *$35 and a Dream*, duetting with her on his composition "Dusty Memories." We also hear a parting word from Johnny Cash. When she first guested on his show, he recalls, "She was probably the most fascinating, exciting performer I'd ever seen in my life. A total performer."

Playlist

Maddox Brothers & Rose:
- *The Maddox Brothers & Rose* (Arhoolie CD 391)
- *The Maddox Brothers & Rose—Vol. 2* (Arhoolie CD 437)
- *On the Air* (Arhoolie CD 447) [1940–49 airchecks]
- *Live on the Radio* (Arhoolie CD 467) [1953 airchecks]
- *Maddox Brothers & Rose* (Bear Family BCD 15850 4CD) [Columbia recordings, 1952–58]
- *Gonna Shake This Shack Tonight –Ugly and Slouchy* (Bear Family BCD 16796)

Rose Maddox:
- *The One Rose: The Capitol Years* (Bear Family BCD 15743 4CD) [Capitol recordings, 1959–65]
- *Rose of the West Coast Country* (Arhoolie CD 314) [1980s recordings]
- *$35 and a Dream* (Arhoolie CD 428) [1990s recordings]
- *Beautiful Bouquet* (Arhoolie CD 9058) [1982 recording with Vern Williams Band]

Bibliography

This is not a comprehensive bibliography of early country music. It is selective and personal, gathering books and articles that I have found valuable as sources of information and ideas; which is not to say that there are not numerous other books and articles, some by authors included here, that readers may investigate with profit and enjoyment. The editions cited are the ones I used, but more recent editions have been published of some titles.

Ahrens, Pat. "The Role of the Crazy Water Crystals Company in Promoting Hillbilly Music." *JEMF Quarterly* VI: 3, no. 19 (Autumn 1970): 107–9.

Alden, Ray. "Music from Round Peak." *Old Time Music* 19 (Winter 1975/76): 8–16.

Allen, Frederick Lewis. *Only Yesterday: An Informal History of the Nineteen-Twenties*. New York: Harper and Brothers, 1931.

Atkins, John, ed. *The Carter Family* (Old Time Music Booklet 1). London: Old Time Music, 1973.

Barnouw, Erik. *A Tower in Babel: A History of Broadcasting in the United States: Volume 1—To 1933*. New York: Oxford University Press, 1966.

Biggar, George C. "The Early Days of WLS & The National Barn Dance." *Old Time Music* 1 (Summer 1971): 11–13.

Bufwack, Mary A., and Robert K. Oermann. *Finding Her Voice: The Saga of Women in Country Music*. New York: Crown, 1993.

Cauthen, Joyce H. *With Fiddle and Well-Rosined Bow: Old-Time Fiddling in Alabama*. Tuscaloosa: University of Alabama Press, 1989.

Chlouber, Carla. "Otto Gray and His Oklahoma Cowboys: The Country's First Commercial Western Band." *The Chronicles of Oklahoma* LXXV: 4 (Winter 1997–98): 356–83.

Coffey, Kevin. Notes to *Bob Skyles and His Skyrockets* (Krazy Kat KK CD 29, 2002).

———. Notes to *Otto Gray's Oklahoma Cowboys: Early Cowboy Band* (BACM CD D 139, 2006).

———. Notes to *Clayton McMichen: The Legendary Fiddler Vol. 2* (BACM CD D 142, 2006).

Cohen, John, and Mike Seeger, eds. *The New Lost City Ramblers Song Book*. New York: Oak Publications, 1964.

Cohen, Norm. "Walter 'Kid' Smith." *JEMF Quarterly* IX: 3, no. 31 (Autumn 1973): 128–32.

———. "Fiddlin' John Carson: An Appreciation and a Discography." *JEMF Quarterly* X: 4, no. 36 (Winter 1974): 138–50.

———. "Henry Whitter: His Life and Music." *JEMF Quarterly* XI: 2, no. 38 (Summer 1975): 57–66.

———. "Clayton McMichen: His Life and Music." *JEMF Quarterly* XI: 3, no. 39 (Autumn 1975): 117–24.

————. "Riley Puckett: 'King of the Hillbillies.'" *JEMF Quarterly* XII, no. 44 (Winter 1976): 175–83.

Coltman, Bob. "Look Out! Here He Comes . . . Fiddlin' John Carson: One of a Kind, & Twice as Feisty." *Old Time Music* 9 (Summer 1973): 16–21.

————. Review of *Ernest V. Stoneman and the Blue Ridge Cornshuckers* (Rounder 1008). *Old Time Music* 20 (Spring 1976): 45.

————. "Across the Chasm: How the Depression Changed Country Music." *Old Time Music* 23 (Winter 1976/77): 6–12.

————. "Carson Robison: First of the Rural Professionals." *Old Time Music* 29 (Summer 1978): 5–13, 27.

————. "'Sweethearts of the Hills': Women in Early Country Music." *JEMF Quarterly* XIV, no. 52 (Winter 1978): 161–80.

Comber, Chris. "Patsy Montana: The Cowboys' Sweetheart." *Old Time Music* 4 (Spring 1972): 10–11.

Daigle, Pierre V. *Tears, Love and Laughter: The Story of the Acadians.* Church Point, LA: Acadian Publishing Enterprise, 1972.

Daniel, Wayne W. *Pickin' on Peachtree: A History of Country Music in Atlanta, Georgia.* Urbana: University of Illinois Press, 1990.

Delmore, Alton, with Charles K. Wolfe. *Truth Is Stranger than Publicity: Alton Delmore's Autobiography.* Nashville: Country Music Foundation Press, 1977.

Evans, David. "Black Musicians Remember Jimmie Rodgers." *Old Time Music* 7 (Winter 1972/73): 12–14.

Gentry, Linnell. *A History and Encyclopedia of Country, Western and Gospel Music.* 2nd ed. Nashville: Clairmont, 1969.

Ginell, Cary. *Milton Brown and the Founding of Western Swing.* Urbana: University of Illinois Press, 1994.

Green, Archie. "Hillbilly Music: Source and Symbol." *Journal of American Folklore* 78, no. 309 (July–September 1965): 204–28.

Green, Douglas B. *Country Roots: The Origins of Country Music.* New York: Hawthorn, 1976.

Griffis, Ken. "I Remember Johnny Bond." *JEMF Quarterly* XIV, no. 51 (Autumn 1978): 110–12.

————. "Hank Penny: The Original 'Outlaw'?" *JEMF Quarterly* XVII, no. 65/66 (Spring/Summer 1982): 5–9.

Haden, Walter Darrell. "Vernon Dalhart: Commercial Country Music's First International Star." *JEMF Quarterly* XI: 2, no. 38 (Summer 1975): 95–103; XI: 3, no. 39 (Autumn 1975): 129–36.

Hoeptner, Fred, "Goebel Reeves: The Texas Drifter." *Old Time Music* 18 (Autumn 1975): 10–13.

————, and Bob Pinson. "Clayton McMichen Talking." *Old Time Music* 1 (Summer 1971): 8–10; 2 (Autumn 1971): 13–15; 3 (Winter 1971/72): 14–15, 19; 4 (Spring 1972): 19–20, 30.

Horstman, Dorothy. *Sing Your Heart Out, Country Boy.* 2nd ed. Nashville: Country Music Foundation Press, 1986.

Huber, Patrick. "A Hillbilly Barnum: Fiddlin' John Carson and the Modern Origins of His Old-Time Music in Atlanta." *Atlanta History* 46, no. 1 (2004): 25–53.

Humphrey, Mark. "Playboy Days: Eldon Shamblin Talking to Mark Humphrey." *Old Time Music* 23 (Winter 1976/77): 15–22; 24 (Spring 1977): 17–20; 25 (Summer 1977): 25–27.

Jones, Louis M. "Grandpa," with Charles K. Wolfe. *Everybody's Grandpa: Fifty Years behind the Mike.* Knoxville: University of Tennessee Press, 1984.

Jones, Loyal. "The Minstrel of the Appalachians: Bascom Lamar Lunsford At 91." *JEMF Quarterly* IX: 1, no. 29 (Spring 1973): 2–8.

————. "Who Is Bradley Kincaid?" *JEMF Quarterly* XII, no. 43 (Autumn 1976): 122–37.

————. "Buell Kazee." *JEMF Quarterly* XIV, no. 50 (Summer 1978): 57–67.

———. *Radio's "Kentucky Mountain Boy" Bradley Kincaid*. Berea, KY: Appalachian Center, 1980.

———. *Minstrel of the Appalachians: The Story of Bascom Lamar Lunsford*. Boone, NC: Appalachian Consortium Press, 1984.

Kazee, Buell. "Buell Kazee Talking." [Interview with Joe Bussard, Wilson Reeves, and Leon Kagrise.] *Old Time Music* 6 (Autumn 1972): 6–10.

Kerr, Janet. "Lonnie Austin/Norman Woodlieff." *Old Time Music* 17 (Summer 1975): 7–10.

Kienzle, Rich. "Hank Penny." *Old Time Music* 28 (Spring 1978): 5–16.

Kingsbury, Paul, ed. *The Encyclopedia of Country Music*. New York: Oxford University Press, 1998.

Koon, William, and Carol Collins. "Jules Verne Allen: 'The Original Singing Cowboy.'" *Old Time Music* 10 (Autumn 1973): 17–18, 23.

Landress, Dixie. "I Remember Bud Landress." *Old Time Music* 30 (Autumn 1978): 16–17.

LaRose, Joe. "An Interview with Lowe Stokes." *Old Time Music* 39 (Spring 1984): 6–9.

Layne, Bert. "A Skillet-Licker's Memoirs." [Interview with Margaret Riddle.] *Old Time Music* 14 (Autumn 1974): 5–9; 15 (Winter 1974/75): 22–24.

Leadbitter, Mike. "Harry Choates, Cajun Fiddle Ace." *Old Time Music* 6 (Autumn 1972): 20–22.

Lee, R. Alton. *The Bizarre Careers of John R. Brinkley*. Lexington: University Press of Kentucky, 2002.

Lornell, Kip. *Virginia's Blues, Country, and Gospel Records 1902–1943: An Annotated Discography*. Lexington: University Press of Kentucky, 1989.

McLean, Duncan. *Lone Star Swing*. London: Jonathan Cape, 1997.

McNeil, W. K. "Dr. Smith's Champion Horse-Hair Pullers: An Ozark String Band." *JEMF Quarterly* XXI, no. 77/78 (Fall/Winter 1985): 120–26.

———. Notes to *Somewhere in Arkansas: Early Commercial Country Music Recordings from Arkansas: 1928–1932* [boxed 3CD set]. Center for Arkansas and Regional Studies, 1997.

McRill, Leslie A. "Music in Oklahoma by the Billy McGinty Cowboy Band." *The Chronicles of Oklahoma* XXXVIII: 1 (Spring 1960): 66–74.

Malone, Bill C. *Southern Music, American Music*. Lexington: University Press of Kentucky, 1979.

———. *Country Music, U.S.A.* Rev. ed. Austin: University of Texas Press for the American Folklore Society, 1985.

———. *Don't Get Above Your Raisin': Country Music and the Southern Working Class*. Urbana: University of Illinois Press, 2002.

———, and Judith McCulloh, eds. *Stars of Country Music: Uncle Dave Macon to Johnny Rodriguez*. Urbana: University of Illinois Press, 1975.

Marcus, Greil. *Invisible Republic: Bob Dylan's Basement Tapes*. New York: Henry Holt, 1997.

Morgan, John P., and Thomas C. Tulloss. "The Jake Walk Blues." *Old Time Music* 28 (Spring 1978): 17–24.

Nelson, Donald Lee. "The Life of Alfred G. Karnes." *JEMF Quarterly* VIII: 1, no. 25 (Spring 1972): 31–36.

———. "The Lawson Family Murder." *JEMF Quarterly* IX: 4, no. 32 (Winter 1973): 170–73.

———. "Earl Johnson—Professional Musician." *JEMF Quarterly* X: 4, no. 36 (Winter 1974): 169–75.

Nesbitt, Eddie. "A History of the *Mountain Broadcast and Prairie Recorder*." *JEMF Quarterly* XVII, no. 65/66 (Spring/Summer 1982): 23–30.

Palmer, Jack. *Vernon Dalhart: First Star of Country Music*. Denver, CO: Mainspring Press, 2005.

Paris, Mike. "The Dixons of South Carolina." *Old Time Music* 10 (Autumn 1973): 13–16.

————, and Chris Comber. *Jimmie the Kid: The Life of Jimmie Rodgers*. London: Eddison Press, 1977.

Parker, Ray. "G. B. Grayson: A Short Life of Trouble." *Old Time Music* 35 (Winter 1980–Spring 1981): 10–14.

Pinson, Bob. "The Musical Brownies." *Old Time Music* 1 (Summer 1971): 14–16.

Porterfield, Nolan. *Jimmie Rodgers: The Life and Times of America's Blue Yodeler*. Urbana: University of Illinois Press, 1979.

Porterfield, Nolan. *Exploring Roots Music: Twenty Years of the* JEMF Quarterly. Lanham, MD: Scarecrow Press, 2003.

Pugh, Ronnie. *Ernest Tubb: The Texas Troubadour*. Durham, NC: Duke University Press, 1996.

Rattray, Bill, with Jack Cartwright. "The Cartwright Brothers' Story." *Old Time Music* 9 (Summer 1973): 10–14.

Rodgers, Mrs Jimmie. *My Husband Jimmie Rodgers*. Reprinted with a new introduction and chronology by Nolan Porterfield. Nashville: Country Music Foundation Press, 1975.

Rorrer, Kinney. *Rambling Blues: The Life and Songs of Charlie Poole* (Old Time Music Booklet 3). London: Old Time Music, 1982.

Rounder Collective, The. "The Life of Blind Alfred Reed." *JEMF Quarterly* VII: 3, no. 23 (Autumn 1971): 113–15.

————. "Conversation with Clark Kessinger." *Old Time Music* 3 (Winter 1971/72): 4–8.

Russell, Tony. *Blacks, Whites and Blues*. London: Studio Vista, 1970. Reprinted in Oliver, Paul, and others. *Yonder Come the Blues*. Cambridge: Cambridge University Press, 2001.

————. "Kelly Harrell & The Virginia Ramblers." *Old Time Music* 2 (Autumn 1971): 8–11.

————. "Good Old Times Makin' Music: The Preston Young Story." *Old Time Music* 7 (Winter 1972/73): 4–7.

————. "H. M. Barnes' Blue Ridge Ramblers." *Old Time Music* 17 (Summer 1975): 11.

————. "Alias Walter Smith." *Old Time Music* 17 (Summer 1975): 12–17.

————. Notes to *Ernest V. Stoneman and the Blue Ridge Cornshuckers* (Rounder 1008, 1975).

————. "Pep-Stepping with the Mings." *Old Time Music* 20 (Spring 1976): 11–16.

————. "Doc Bailey: Talent Scout, Winona." *Old Time Music* 20 (Spring 1976): 22–23, 25.

————. "The Leake County Revelers: Waltz Kings of the Old South." *Old Time Music* 20 (Spring 1976): 26–35.

————. "Mississippi Directory of Recorded Artists, 1927–36." *Old Time Music* 20 (Spring 1976): 36–42.

————. "Buell Kazee, 1900–76." *Old Time Music* 21 (Summer 1976): 17–18.

————. "Leo Soileau." *Old Time Music* 27 (Winter 1977/78): 5–9.

————. "Chuck Wagon Swing: The Story of the Swift Jewel Cowboys." *Old Time Music* 32 (Spring 1979): 5–15.

————. "Asa Martin: A Memoir." *Old Time Music* 33 (Summer 1979–Spring 1980): 4–7.

————. "The Allen Brothers' Record Sales." *Old Time Music* 44 (Winter 1987/88): 10.

————. *Country Music Records: A Discography, 1921–1942*. New York: Oxford University Press, 2004.

————, and Charles K. Wolfe. "Ramblin' Red Lowery." *Old Time Music* 42 (Winter 1985/86): 15–17.

Savoy, Ann Allen. *Cajun Music: A Reflection of a People*. Eunice, LA: Bluebird Press, 1984.

Seeger, Mike. "Hutch: Sherman Lawson Interview." *Old Time Music* 11 (Winter 1973/74): 78.

Shelton, Robert, and Burt Goldblatt. *The Country Music Story*. New York: Bobbs-Merrill, 1966.

Shirley, Glenn. "Daddy of the Cowboy Bands." *Oklahoma Today* 9 (Fall 1959): 6–7, 29.

Spaeth, Sigmund. *A History of Popular Music in America*. New York: Random House, 1948; London: Phoenix House, 1960.

Specht, Joe W. "An Interview with Hoyle Nix, The West Texas Cowboy." *Old Time Music* 34 (Summer–Autumn 1980): 7–11; 35 (Winter 1980–Spring 1981): 15–18; 36 (Summer 1981): 10–11.

Spielman, Earl V. "An Interview with Eck Robertson." *JEMF Quarterly* VIII: 4, no. 28 (Winter 1972): 179–87.

Stambler, Irwin, and Grelun Landon. *The Encyclopedia of Folk, Country and Western Music.* 2nd ed. New York: St. Martin's Press, 1983.

Strachwitz, Chris. "Mainer's Mountaineers." *American Folk Music Occasional* 1 (1964): 49–60.

Taylor, Jay. "Montana Slim: Canada's Legendary Wilf Carter." *JEMF Quarterly* XIII, no. 47 (Autumn 1977): 118-21.

Tosches, Nick. "Al Dexter." *Old Time Music* 22 (Autumn 1976): 4–8.

———. "Ted Daffan." *Old Time Music* 30 (Autumn 1978): 6–8.

Townsend, Charles R. *San Antonio Rose: The Life and Music of Bob Wills.* Urbana: University of Illinois Press, 1976.

Tribe, Ivan M. "Bill & Joe Callahan: A Great Brother Duet." *Old Time Music* 16 (Spring 1975): 15–18.

———. *Mountaineer Jamboree: Country Music in West Virginia.* Lexington: University Press of Kentucky, 1984.

Van der Merwe, Peter. *Origins of the Popular Style.* Oxford: Oxford University Press, 1989.

Vaughn, Gerald F. "Ray Whitley's Tribute to Frank Luther." *JEMF Quarterly* XIII, no. 45 (Summer 1977): 17–20.

Walsh, Jim. "Favorite Pioneer Recording Artists: Vernon Dalhart." *JEMF Quarterly* XVIII, no. 67/68 (Fall/Winter 1982): 131–45. [Reprinted from *Hobbies*, May–December 1960.]

White, John I. "The Lonesome Cowboy in the Studio." *Old Time Music* 11 (Winter 1973/74): 19–21.

———. *Git Along, Little Dogies: Songs and Songmakers of the American West.* Urbana: University of Illinois Press, 1976.

Wiggins, Gene. "Not Very Aristocratic." *Old Time Music* 26 (Autumn 1977): 5–9.

———. *Fiddlin' Georgia Crazy: Fiddlin' John Carson, His Real World, and the World of His Songs.* Urbana: University of Illinois Press, 1987.

———, with Tony Russell. "Hell Broke Loose in Gordon County, Georgia." *Old Time Music* 25 (Summer 1977): 9–21.

Wolfe, Charles K. "Ralph Peer at Work: The Victor 1927 Bristol Sessions." *Old Time Music* 5 (Summer 1972): 10–15.

———. "Man of Constant Sorrow: Richard Burnett's Story." *Old Time Music* 9 (Summer 1973): 6–9; 10 (Autumn 1973): 5–11.

———. "The Discovery of Jimmie Rodgers: A Further Note." *Old Time Music* 9 (Summer 1973): 24.

———. "Early Country Music in Knoxville: The Brunswick Sessions and the End of an Era." *Old Time Music* 12 (Spring 1974): 19–31.

———. "Making Western Swing: An Interview with Johnnie Lee Wills." *Old Time Music* 15 (Winter 1974/75): 11–21.

———. *The Grand Ole Opry: The Early Years, 1925–35* (Old Time Music Booklet 2). London: Old Time Music, 1975.

———. "Sam McGee." *Old Time Music* 18 (Autumn 1975): 7, 13.

———. *Tennessee Strings: The Story of Country Music in Tennessee.* Knoxville: University of Tennessee Press, 1977.

———. "The Legend of John Dilleshaw." *Old Time Music* 36 (Summer 1981): 12–16.

———. *Kentucky Country: Folk and Country Music of Kentucky.* Lexington: University Press of Kentucky, 1982.

———. "Fiddlin' Powers and His Family." *Old Time Music* 42 (Winter 1985/86): 7–10.

———. "Lee Allen's Radio Days and Other Salty Dog Chronicles." *Old Time Music* 44 (Winter 1987/88): 9–11.

———. "A Lighter Shade of Blue: White Country Blues." In *Nothing But the Blues*, ed. Lawrence Cohn, 233–63. New York: Abbeville Press, 1993.

———. *The Devil's Box: Masters of Southern Fiddling*. Nashville: Country Music Foundation Press and Vanderbilt University Press, 1997.

———. *Classic Country*. New York: Routledge Press, 2001.

———, and Ted Olson, eds. *The Bristol Sessions: Writings about the Big Bang of Country Music*. Jefferson, NC: McFarland, 2005.

———, and Tony Russell. "Two Cow Girls on the Lone Prairie: The True Story of the Girls of the Golden West." *Old Time Music* 43 (Winter 1986/87): 6–13.

Young, Henry. *"Haywire Mac" and the "Big Rock Candy Mountain"*. Unknown place of publication: Stillhouse Hollow Publishers, 1985.